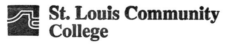

The
Religion
of
Socrates

The
Religion
of
Socrates

———

Mark L. McPherran

The Pennsylvania State University Press
University Park, Pennsylvania

Mark L. McPherran is Professor of Philosophy at the University of Maine at Farmington.

This publication has been supported by the National Endowment for the Humanities, a federal agency which supports the study of such fields as history, philosophy, literature, and languages.

Library of Congress Cataloging-in-Publication Data

McPherran, Mark L., 1949–
    The religion of Socrates / Mark L. McPherran.

        p.   cm.
    Includes bibliographical references and index.
    ISBN 0-271-01581-0
    1. Socrates—Religion.   2. Greece—Religion.   I. Title.
B318.R45M38   1996
292'.0092—dc20   95-45059
                                                         CIP

It is the policy of The Pennsylvania State University Press to use acid-free paper for the first printing of all clothbound books. Publications on uncoated stock satisfy the minimum requirements of American National Standard for Information Sciences—Permanence of Paper for Printed Library Materials, ANSI Z39.48-1992.

For Caitlin and Ian

Through the love I felt for Alcibiades I experienced a kind of Bacchic inspiration. When the Bacchants are filled with the god's power they draw milk and honey from wells which do not even yield water to others. I have no learning to teach anyone and help him in that way, but I thought that through just being with him my love for him might make him better.

—Socrates, in Aeschines' *Alcibiades* (fr. 11; H. Dittmar)

Contents

Acknowledgments

Throughout the long gestation of this book I have been helped by innumerable friends and colleagues. Foremost among them are Thomas Brickhouse, Nicholas Smith, and Gregory Vlastos. Vlastos's 1983 NEH Seminar on Socrates was in many ways a turning point in my career, and it was there—prodded both by Vlastos and the memory of a long-lost, very dear friend—that this project first began to take shape. My subsequent correspondence with Vlastos, his tough—but always collegial—criticisms, his support of my career, and his many important contributions to the study of Socrates have put me profoundly in his debt. Of the many good things his seminar brought me, one of the best was the friendship that soon developed with Brickhouse and Smith, who at that time were in the early stages of the work that eventually resulted in their *Socrates on Trial* (Oxford and Princeton, 1989). My book owes a great deal to our discussions together, to their work, and to their insightful comments on my own work, much of which is found here. Additional valuable responses to the manuscript as a whole came from Hugh Benson and Nicholas Smith; numerous other individuals contributed helpful comments on various sections, in particular Julia Annas, Mary Whitlock Blundell, Linda Britt, John Bussanich, Charles Chiasson, Jonathan Cohen, Eve Browning Cole, Owen Goldin, Daniel Gunn, David Halperin, Wesley McNair, Mitchell Miller, Ronald Polansky, Glenn Rawson, Jennifer Reid, George Rudebusch, Roslyn Weiss, and past anonymous referees. I am also grateful to the National Endowment for the Humanities for awarding me a Travel to Collections Grant (1988) and a Fellowship (1989–90); to Penn State Press and its supportive director, Sandy Thatcher; and to the University of Maine at Farmington for a sabbatical leave in the fall of 1992. Finally, I am indebted to Dale Cooke for his preparation of the indexes.

Still, none of this work would have come into being without the support, love, and patience of my parents; my wife, Susan; my daughter, Caitlin; and my son, Ian. To them, and to the nameless others whose influence runs throughout this book, my thanks and my love.

Various portions of this book are revisions of previously published journal articles. I thank the editors and publishers of the following journals for their assistance and (where needed) their permission to use those materials.

A revised excerpt from "Kahn on the Pre-Middle Platonic Dialogues," *Oxford Studies in Ancient Philosophy* 8 (1990), 211–236, forms part of Chapter 1.2.

A revision of "Socratic Piety in the Euthyphro," *Journal of the History of Philosophy* 23 (1985), 283–309; reprinted in *Essays on the Philosophy of Socrates*, ed. H. Benson (Oxford: Oxford University Press, 1992), 220–241, appears herein as Chapter 2.2.

A revision of "Socratic Reason and Socratic Revelation," *Journal of the History of Philosophy* 29 (1991), 345–374, appears herein as Chapter 4.1.

A revision of "Socrates and the Duty to Philosophize," *Southern Journal of Philosophy* 24 (1986), 541–560, appears herein as Chapter 4.2.

A revision of "Socrates on the Immortality of the Soul," *Journal of the History of Philosophy* 32 (1994), 1–22, appears herein as Chapter 5.1.

A revision of "Socrates on Teleological and Moral Theology," *Ancient Philosophy* 14 (1994), 245–66, appears herein as Chapter 5.2.

A revised excerpt from "Commentary on Morgan" (invited comments on M. Morgan's "Philosophy in Plato's *Sophist*"), *Proceedings of the Boston Area Colloquium in Ancient Philosophy* 9 (1993), 112–129, forms part of Chapter 5.3.

1
Introduction

1.1 Preliminaries and Puzzles

It is now usually acknowledged that there was some sort of religious dimension to Socrates, if only of the critical, threatening kind: Whatever it was about him that made it plausible to try and execute him on a charge of impiety. Of course, he had become a celebrity of the popular imagination with a reputation for argumentative confrontation and subtle intellectual nonconformism well before his famous day in court.[1] Thanks, then, to those many years of provocation—and the genuine philosophical genius underlying his popular portrait—the added drama of Socrates' martyrdom furnished his era with the ideal peg on which to hang an entire literary enterprise,[2] one of the most important examples of which being Plato's dramatic and imaginative *Apology*. Here, faced with a brash young accuser determined to convict him of undermining the traditional religious views of Athens's youth, Socrates speaks in his own defense with force,

---

1. Within the space of three years, for example, Socrates was the subject of three comedies—Ameipsias's *Konnos* and Aristophanes' *Clouds* in 423 B.C., and Eupolis's *Flatterers* in 421B.C.

2. As Aristotle testifies (*Poet.* 1447b11). On this "Socratic Literature" (Σωκρατικοὶ λόγοι), and on the "Socratic Movement" (i.e., the philosophical activity of those who saw themselves as the heirs to Socratic thought), see, e.g., W.K.C. Guthrie (6) 10–13, 165–187; M. Montuori (2); and P. Vander Waerdt (3). On the origins of the Socratic dialogue, see D. Clay.

subtlety, and command that remain if not unequaled then at least unsur
passed.

These very dramatic qualities that have ensured its survival, however
have also left the *Apology*—and the Socrates it portrays—perennial defen
dants in the scholar's docket. For lurking behind the bold front Plato
credits to his master, modern commentators often discern another Socra·
tes, one more ironic, arrogant, and devious, possibly one also more con·
fused and self-destructive. *This* Socrates first mocks the Sophists by par-
odying forensic rhetoric (17a–18a), then later sidesteps the charge of
having failed to acknowledge the gods of Athens by slickly entrapping his
prosecutor with a subtle *ad hominem* diversion (26e–28a). This reading of
the *Apology* finds Socrates a destructive critic of established religion and,
apparently, guilty as charged.[3]

Despite the appeal this interpretation may have for readers who wish to
emphasize Plato's wily and complex literary strategies (and, perhaps, the
hostility to religious superstition they detect in his teacher), it is now commonly held that the *Apology*—in concert with the *Euthyphro* and other
early Platonic works—portrays a Socrates who was not only a rational
philosopher of the first rank, but a profoundly religious figure as well, a
Socrates who believed in gods vastly superior to ourselves in power and
wisdom and shared many other traditional religious commitments of this
sort with his fellow citizens.[4] However, it also seems fairly clear that Socrates was no small-town polytheist who insulated his religious beliefs from
his philosophical convictions. Rather, he understood his religious commitments to be integral to his philosophical mission of moral examination and

3. See, e.g., R. E. Allen (2), 5–7, and A. E. Taylor (4), 8–9.
4. I assume the generally recognized division of Plato's dialogues into early, middle, and
late periods. The early dialogues are *Apology, Charmides, Crito, Euthyphro, Hippias Minor,
Laches,* and *Protagoras* (with *Euthydemus, Gorgias, Ion, Hippias Major, Lysis, Menexenus,*
and *Meno* serving as 'transitional dialogues'; see n. 46). Since the Socrates of book 1 of the
Republic has the distinctive traits of the Socrates of the early dialogues (in contrast to the
Socrates of books 2 through 10), I treat it as an early dialogue as well. I also employ the
common interpretive strategy that takes the early dialogues to represent Plato's attempts at
philosophizing *more Socratico* using fictional re-creations of his teacher, thereby exhibiting
the methods and views of the historical Socrates (with the *Apology* our most reliable source).
For a classic defense of this approach, see G. Vlastos (12), now revised and included in his
(14), 45–106. I follow Vlastos (14), 99–106, in granting Xenophon the status of a confirmatory source (subject to close interpretive scrutiny, however, given Xenophon's overly apologetic tendencies, especially on religious issues). I place the *Phaedo* among the middle-period
dialogues, but I do make passing reference to what might be traces of the historical Socrates
in it. Finally, and despite the potential richness of *Alcibiades I* as a source for Socrates' view
of the soul, I generally avoid it because of its questionable authenticity.

rectification, and in turn, used the rationally derived convictions underlying that mission to reshape the religious conventions of his time. As a result, Socrates made important contributions to the rational reformation of Greek religion, contributions that incited and informed the hugely influential theology of his brilliant pupil and "biographer" Plato. That, in any case, is my thesis. In what follows I intend to demonstrate its plausibility.

Although for most of our intellectual history the general postulate of a religious Socrates has been something of a commonplace, it has had its critics, ancient and modern. The ancient critics seemed to discern in Socrates the marks of an atheistic nature philosopher and the amoral argumentative twistings of a professional teacher of rhetoric, not a religious Socrates, but an impious critic of the gods and religious institutions of Athens (cf. *Ap.* 18a–19d). In the *Apology,* Socrates eloquently and vehemently denies these charges, and those denials—I contend—are reinforced by the portraits of the other early dialogues. These fictional re-creations of Socrates are, among other things, so engaging and lifelike that, when taken in tandem with the corroborating testimony of other Socratic apologists (primarily Xenophon), they acquit him posthumously of the allegations of atheism.[5] Indeed, on a straightforward reading of those accounts, Socrates appears to be in many ways the most pious Greek of his day. Having won that debate, however, these ancient defenders also inadvertently prepared the way for the subsequent heroization of Socrates by many of the early Christian apologists and church fathers.[6]

Plato's and Xenophon's emphatic portraits of Socratic piety made it inevitable that Christians would compare Socrates' "human wisdom" with the divine wisdom of Christ, his unjust prosecution as an atheist with theirs,[7] Socrates' proposed penalty at his trial of thirty minae with Judas's thirty pieces of silver, Socrates in his cell with Christ in the Garden of

5. The theistic Stoics, for example, claimed to be following in Socrates' footsteps and assigned the origins of their main proof of God's existence to him. Cf. Sextus Empiricus *Ad. Math.* 9.88–104, esp. 9.101; J. DeFilippo and P. Mitsis; A. A. Long; and Chapter 5.2 herein. Sextus also finds it natural to group Socrates with Pythagoras and Plato as a leading theist of the ancient world (*Ad. Math.* 9.64).

6. And many Muslim thinkers as well; see I. Alon, who writes, "Next to Aristotle and Plato, . . . Socrates . . . [is] the most mentioned Greek philosopher in Arabic literature" (12); cf. McPherran (7).

7. In the first centuries of Christianity Christians were liable for prosecution as "atheists" in the same way a theistic Socrates could be thought atheistic: by "not recognizing the gods of the state" but "new [unlicensed] divinities" instead (Athenagoras *Presb. Chris.* 4).

Gethsemane, and the former's execution by hemlock with the latter's crucifixion. For many, that comparison revealed Socrates to be a proto-Christian and prophet of Christ, a valuable link between the virtues of intellectual paganism and the revealed truths of Christianity.[8] Hence, the tradition of an unjustly persecuted, religious Socrates became an inspirational fixture and a subject of idealizing literature for thinkers up to and including Petrarch, Ficino, and Erasmus.[9]

Saint Socrates, however, began to unravel with the onset of the Italian Renaissance. First, scholars began to appreciate fully the interpretive difficulties of using accounts by authors as different as Aristophanes and Plato. This weakened previous confidence in the received conception of Socrates and thus gave to those battling for intellectual liberty and religious tolerance new license to follow their interpretive imaginations in a manner favorable to their own political and religious sympathies. Thus some rejected or modified the "myth" of Socrates as a pious and unjustly condemned servant of God, developing in its stead the picture of a freethinking Socrates, a subverter of traditional and civic religion.[10] In tandem with this development, the increasingly philosophical—as opposed to theological—interests of succeeding generations of scholars led to a greater focus on Socrates' contributions to the triumph of rational, scientific culture, to the neglect of the traditional, religious elements in his thinking.[11] Thus began a process of secular canonization that even now in some quarters portrays Socrates as a figure straight out of the Enlightenment. This is the Socrates

8. Justinus the Martyr appears to have been the first to make the parallel (see Justin I *Apol.* V, 3–4, II *Apol.* X, 4–8) and was followed in his admiration by Clement, Origen, Lactantius, and St. Augustine (Clem. *Strom.* I, XIV 63, 3; V, XIV 99, 3; I, XIX 92, 3; *Prot.* VI, 71, 1 ff.; Orig. *Adv. Cels.* III 66, 67; IV 89; VII 56; August. *De vera relig.* c. 39, n. 72; II, 1; *Confess.* I, II; *De consensu evangelist.* I, 12, 18). Not all the church fathers were so impressed, however. Tertullian, for one, accused Socrates of being an immoralist (*Apology* 39, 12) whose attention to a "familiar voice" (Socrates' *daimonion*) shows him to be in the service of a demonic power (*Apol.* 46; *On the Soul* 1, 2–6). There was a similar reaction in the Islamic world. Many thinkers saw important parallels between Socrates and Muhammad, but others, for example, al-Ghazâlî, saw Socrates as a nonbeliever (Alon, 11, 34–35, 41–100).

9. Cf. Petrarch *Familiar. rer.* I, 9; *rer.* VIII, 4; *Seniles* XI, 14; D. Erasmus *Colloquia* Ulmae 1712; *Convivium Religiosum* 175; and his letter to John Colet. See Montuori (2), 6–12. For Ficino, see P. J. FitzPatrick, 165. The temptation to compare and contrast the secular philosopher with Christ, often to the detriment of both, still proves irresistible; see, e.g., F. Davar, Th. Deman (1), W. Kaufmann, A. Toynbee, and R. M. Wenley.

10. E.g., Marechal and Voltaire; see also Montuori (2), 12–25.

11. The popular 1749 biography of Socrates by J. G. Cooper is in this line. In it Cooper uses Socrates' fate to show how false religion can undermine true morality and rational understanding.

to whom I and many others in philosophy were introduced in graduate school: a consummate intellectualist, wholly taken up in agonistic argument, whose "paradoxical" view that "virtue is *knowledge*" (e.g., *Pr.* 349e–350d, 360d; *Mem.* 3.9.5) grounds a moral theory that takes discursive rationality as life's only trustworthy guide.

Thus, instead of a reasonably accurate—or at least, reasonably balanced—assessment of Socrates and his views, one biased reading has been joined by another. Where some saw Socrates as a fifth-century John the Baptist, today others see the antithesis, a philosophical figure inextricably tied to our own contemporary self-conceptions, cultural values, and educational practices.[12] This has given to popular and scholarly culture a Socrates who is not so much a man of his own time as a paradigm of the modern "rationally examined life," and "an early apostle of the liberal ideals of sincerity and self-realization."[13]

This version of Socrates—as opposed to what I contend is the more accurate, more puzzling, and more interesting version—has him pursuing the fundamental questions of morality and value by essentially one method alone: the "elenctic" examination of belief-consistency by the interrogation of an interlocutor.[14] According to the standard "secular" portrait, this

12. As J. Burnet (7), 236, observes: "The most diverse philosophies have sought to father themselves upon him, and each new account of him tends to reflect the fashions and prejudices of the hour. At one time he is an enlightened deist, at another a radical atheist." For further and more detailed discussion of Socratic historiography, see Montuori (2) and FitzPatrick. My account of Socrates, however, differs substantially from Montuori's own attempt to get beyond the many conflicting images of Socrates presented by the literary tradition.

13. M. Nussbaum (1), 44; also see her note 5.

14. The general pattern of an *elenchos* is roughly this: (1) some interlocutor advances thesis *p*; (2) prodded by Socrates, the interlocutor admits that he holds propositions *q* and *r*; (3) through the assistance of Socrates, the interlocutor concedes that *q* and *r* entail not-*p*; (4) whereupon Socrates claims that *p* has been refuted or that the interlocutor is ignorant about *p* (or where *p* is a premise in the argument, that the interlocutor's belief-set is inconsistent); see, e.g., *Eu.* 7a–8b and *G.* 475a–d. There is significant controversy over the issue of whether the *elenchos*—besides showing the inconsistency of an interlocutor's beliefs—also plays a "constructive" role in Socrates' philosophizing by warranting some of his beliefs. Recent expressions of opposition to this—the "anti-constructive" position—include H. Benson (3), (4), (5); and M. C. Stokes (1), 1–35, 440–43. I assume throughout that the more plausible position is the "constructive" one; namely, that Socrates lived an "examined life" by using the *elenchos* to *inter alia* deliberate on courses of action, exhort others to virtue, test the adequacy of virtue-definitions, and secure good inductive grounds for holding true those moral propositions whose negations are constantly defeated under elenctic examination. T. Brickhouse and N. Smith (4), chap. 1, (6), (9), and (12), provide an extensive defense and exposition; see also R. Kraut (1); C.D.C. Reeve, 52–53, 64–166, 176–179; R. Robinson (2); Vlastos (19), chap. 1; and P. Woodruff (1).

dialogical belief-testing procedure rigorously obeys the canons of logic and constitutes Socrates' primary method of philosophical investigation, moral decision-making, and pedagogy. When Socrates claims that "the unexamined life is not worth living" (Ap. 38a5–6), he is thus to be understood as advising everyone to spend part of each day elenctically examining themselves and others in accordance with the rational principles of proper philosophical discourse.[15] For this Socrates, extrarational religious experiences do not themselves contribute to the practice of philosophy, but rather, are the very sorts of things that demand our philosophical scrutiny. Hence, it is not surprising that advocates of this portrait have sometimes understood Socrates to have been a kind of atheist or agnostic, construing his positive references to divine beings and "signs" as instances of his infamous alleged irony.[16] He may talk as though he hears a "divine voice" (Ap. 31d1), but really—goes this line of thinking—this is but a façon de parler: For by such phrases he is simply referring surreptitiously in the language of "the many" to the "divine" inner promptings of his utterly secular, completely human powers of ratiocination.[17] Once again, on this reading the Socrates of the Apology stands guilty as charged.[18]

In my judgment, this portrait of Socrates is the result of slighting and misinterpreting the evidence of our texts (not to mention the cultural forces at work on Socrates from birth). Proponents of this sort of view must at least account for the compelling evidence that Socrates was genuinely religious in the primary sense, a sense recognized both then and now; namely, possessing an intellectual, heartfelt commitment to the view that there exist divine, otherworldly beings of intelligence and power (i.e., gods). Moreover, we have many good reasons for holding that Socrates

15. Cf. Brickhouse and Smith (8), chap. 1, (6), and Vlastos (16) on Socrates' use of the elenchos. Why think, though, that Socrates would allow all human beings to engage in philosophy? First, notice that although we never see Socrates engaged in the elenctic examination of women, he does foresee the possibility of interrogating both men and women in the afterlife (Ap. 41c). We also see testimony that he holds virtue and the means to it—the practice of philosophy—to be free of class and gender distinctions, open even to slaves, foreigners, and young and old alike (Ap. 30a; Meno 85c, 73b–c; Xen. Symp. 2.10; and Chapter 4.2. herein). Cf. K. Seeskin, 110–112; Vlastos (5), 19–21; and P. Ward-Scaltsas.

16. For discussions of Socratic irony, see S. Kierkegaard and, most recent, Vlastos (14), chap. 1. For a critique of Vlastos's account, see Brickhouse and Smith (9).

17. Nussbaum (2), 234.

18. For the most recent example of this line of interpretation, see L. Versenyi (1), (2). Also note, in particular, the attempts of Nussbaum (2), 234–235, and A. Nehamas (2), 305–306, to explain away Socrates' trust in various forms of divination. Vlastos (14), chap. 6, and (12) also finds Socrates guilty of disbelieving in the gods of the Athenian state, but allows that he was nonetheless religious in some sense.

sincerely believed himself to have a unique, *divinely* ordained mission to do philosophy. The key text for this is his bold announcement, "To do this [philosophizing] has been commanded of me . . . by the god through oracles and through dreams and by every other means in which a divinity has ever commanded anyone to do anything" (*Ap.* 33c4–7; cf. 30a).[19]

Given the apparent seriousness with which Socrates took his philosophical mission we also have no reason to doubt his claim to have as his constant guide in matters great and small the promptings of a supernatural voice, the *daimonion* (see, e.g., *Ap.* 40a2–c3, 31c4–d6). The Socratic texts of Plato and Xenophon are filled with such direct and undisguised religious references. To remove them from our texts would be to gut them; it would be "surgery that kills the patient."[20] And to reread them all as sly tongue-in-cheek verbal pandering or as simply allegorical in intent would be to employ a principle of interpretation that, once loosed upon the texts, would know no end, rendering every Socratic utterance fatally indeterminate. So as I see it, the recent scholarly record—the attempt by our generation, like all others, to come to terms with this most influential, strange, and troublesome of philosophers—needs still to devote further serious and detailed attention to the religious dimension of Socrates. For by focusing as tightly as we have on his undeniable contributions to the methods and positions of mainstream contemporary philosophy, we have not yet fully understood and appreciated his unique and groundbreaking contributions to Western religious thought.

It is, then, the fundamental presupposition of this book that we must take seriously the textual evidence for the religious side of Socrates. The extensive and philosophically integrated use of religious language ascribed to Socrates in Plato's early dialogues and elsewhere, I am convinced, make a religious Socrates our best historical bet. That is, the literary figure intended by Plato and other Socratic writers—and so, I shall argue, the actual person as well—should be seen as very much a man of his own time as far as the supernatural is concerned.[21] However, he was also a sensitive critic and rational reformer of both the religious tradition he inherited and the new theological and cultic incursions he encountered as they swept

---

19. Translations from the Greek here and in what follows are by Vlastos, or T. West and G. West, or myself unless otherwise noted.

20. Vlastos (14), 158.

21. Again, for a defense of the view that Plato's early dialogues may serve as a source for the views of the historical Socrates, see Vlastos (12) and esp. (14), chaps. 2 and 3; I discuss this further.

through fifth-century Athens.[22] It is therefore another of my tasks in this book to spell out the methods and results of this Socratic reformation.

Among other things, I discuss in some detail how the Socratic philosophical mission is connected to a theology constituted (in part) by the claims that (1) there are gods (or, possibly, multiple aspects of one god), that (2) we get all, and nothing but, good things from these gods, including information revealed through such extrarational sources as divinely given dreams, that (3) these gods are perfectly wise and moral, and thus, contrary to "the lies of the poets" (e.g., Homer), (4) they have no enmities and are perfectly just, that (5) we cannot improve their nature, that (6) they love pious acts (which by virtue of being pious are also just), and that (7) acts of piety involve our giving service (ὑπηρετική/*huperetikê;* along the lines of servants to masters) to the gods, aiding them in their projects. One of the more interesting implications of this Socratic view—aside from its blanket rejection of divine immorality and conflict—is its modification of the typical propitiatory and apotropaic motivations central to traditional Greek religion. Socrates' religious conceptions, we shall see, severely undercut the requirements and efficacy of conventional cult ritual, and insisted instead on the much more challenging religious obligation of serving the gods' wish to promulgate human happiness by engaging in the sort of philosophical investigation that improves human souls.

If this account is reasonably accurate, however, then Socratic philosophy harbors a troublesome puzzle. For given that Socrates was not only a rationalistic philosopher, but a religiously oriented reformer of Greek religion as well, there appear to be two quite different epistemological orientations implicit in these two aspects of the one man. Again, in his purely intellectualist guise, Socrates informs us (in word and deed) that we must be persuaded only of that proposition best supported by our *reasoning* (λογιζομέῳ [*Cr.* 46b3–6]), and against the backdrop of most contemporary versions of Socrates it is natural to take this as meaning "secular ratiocination," where Socrates' only methods of argumentation and belief-testing are the *elenchos* and *epagogê* (inductive analogy; see, e.g., *Met.* 1078b27–29, *Top.* 105a13).[23] But in those Platonic dialogues commonly thought to be evidential of the views of the historical Socrates, the *elen-*

---

22. These incursions include the demythologizing influence of the nature philosophers (e.g., Anaxagoras), the agnosticism and atheism of Sophists such as Protagoras and Prodicus, new religious imports such as the cult of Asclepius (introduced into Athens c. 420), and the influence of sects such as Pythagoreanism and Orphism.

23. This is Vlastos's view of things; see Vlastos (14), chap. 6, and (8).

chos generally results in a failure to arrive at any reliable moral knowledge claims. Socrates himself constantly confirms these results by proclaiming that he is entirely ignorant of philosophical knowledge of the virtues and is simply "aware of being wise in nothing, great or small" (*Ap.* 21b2–5).[24] This attitude of rationalistic skepticism is—again—in striking contrast with the religious confidence underlying Socrates' conviction seen above that he must philosophize even at the cost of his life in obedience to a command given by the god(s) through oracles, dreams, and divinations, and at apparent odds with his frequent reliance upon the guidance provided by his *daimonion.* Socrates never explains how or why he can be certain that he is not the victim of religious hallucinations, and at first glance we may see little rational justification for his religiously based claims. Moreover, his acceptance and use of extrarational material seems to fly in the face of his philosophical grilling, and repudiation, of the religiously based claims of others. In the *Euthyphro,* for example, Socrates is not at all content with Euthyphro's explanation that he is acting in accord with the demands of piety when he prosecutes his own father for murder (3e–4e). It is also clear that Socrates would not have been appeased in the slightest if Euthyphro had followed Socrates' own lead by claiming to know "à la Socrates" that the prosecution of his father was piously sanctioned by virtue of a divine command issued through a nocturnal vision or daemonic sign.

We are left, then, with an even starker version of our puzzle: Socrates seems both a theist and an agnostic; he both accepts and rejects religiously derived convictions. To defuse this apparent paradox—and thus reconcile the rationalistic, skeptical, and religious tendencies exemplified by our texts—later chapters of this book examine how extrarational sources of belief and the other elements of Socratic theology contribute to Socratic moral decision-making and the Socratic mission as a whole. There we will see that Socrates is among the first in practice, if not in explicit theorizing, to treat discursive reason as a support for—rather than an obstacle to—extrarational revelation.[25] Indeed, Socrates seems to have grounded reliance on his *daimonion* on both inductive and deductive considerations.

24. For other Socratic professions of ignorance, see, e.g., *Ap.* 20c1–3, 21d2–7, 23b2–4; *Charm.* 165b4–c2; *Eu.* 5a7–c5, 15c12, 15e5–16a4; *La.* 186b8–c5; *Ly.* 212a4–7; *HMa.* 286c8–e2; *G.* 509a4–7; *M.* 71a1–7; and *R.* 337e4–5. On this profession, see, e.g., Vlastos (13), and Brickhouse and Smith (8), chap. 2.1.

25. This description is itself somewhat anachronistic, however. For as I show in Chapters 2 and 4.1, the common contemporary distinction between the secular and the sacred was drawn rather differently by Socrates.

There are many other such puzzles and solutions yet to come. These will help to constitute the succeeding chapters of this book, as I attempt to provide an interpretive overview and analysis of Socrates' religious commitments in light of his ethical theory and the religious outlook of fifth-century Athens. Among other things, it is my intent to preserve the Socratic insistence on the value of rational elenctic philosophy while also fully acknowledging how this commitment is crucially shaped by—and, reciprocally, also shapes—Socrates' conception of himself as a divinely guided servant of the gods.

In a study of this kind, the relative importance of its subject and the related motivations of the author and audience are usually taken for granted. Nevertheless (and given the intellectual currents of our time), perhaps it is worthwhile to make a bit of a case for my topic. First, in the last few years Socratic scholarship has been experiencing a period of intense activity scarcely paralleled in its long history.[26] Attempts such as this to establish and map out the centrality of Socrates' religious orientation provide a useful and timely correction to the scholarly record and thus a useful correction to our understanding of ancient history (and so ultimately, perhaps, of ourselves). Socrates also still serves as a paradigm of the intellectual (even the religious) life for both the humanities and popular culture: he is gravely quoted in college catalogs, appears in movies and elsewhere as a stereotype of confused professorial wisdom, and makes cameo appearances before undergraduates in a wide variety of intellectual history courses (where they learn to identify him as the author of the notoriously obnoxious "Socratic method"). It is important to study Socratic philosophy, then, in order to reflect productively on our own vision of what the life of the mind is supposed to look like. And since, as I will show, Socrates' philosophical and religious views are part of one seamless whole, it is thus equally important to uncover and examine the religious strands of his thought.

Last, and without trying in the least to argue directly for this thesis here, I want to assert baldly that there are many truths about morality and the human condition to be gleaned from a study of Socrates' thought, and so

---

26. E.g., two books devoted entirely to the *Apology* have appeared in the last few years: Brickhouse and Smith (12), and Reeve. There exist also Vlastos's major studies, Vlastos (14) and (19); Brickhouse and Smith (8); and collections such as Benson (1), Boudouris, and Gower and Stokes. Note too that the large, well-attended Second International Conference on Greek Philosophy held on Samos in 1990 (from which the Boudouris collection derives) was entirely devoted to the discussion of Socratic philosophy.

to neglect its religious dimension is to neglect useful truths. Although the general topic of religion is fraught with intellectual difficulties and cannot but excite each reader's own sense of its nature, virtues, and vices (and its painful history), to disregard it is to disregard oneself: our relations with others and our own inner worlds of experience are inevitably shaped by (and shape) our own religious attitudes and the historical religious forces behind them. Moreover, and without meaning to define it, religion is in its essence simply part of the common human response to the uncharted territories of life (trying to comprehend their mysteries and terrors, trying to express gratitude for their joys), and in that broad sense we are all of us religious and surrounded by coreligionists.[27] Philosophy, science, poetry, and art are all expressions of the more generous side of this cognitive and emotional response. By paying close attention to the attempt of one of humanity's preeminent thinkers to come to terms with the unknown dimensions of existence (and the limits of the known as traditional Greek religion defined them), we may better learn how to conduct our own similar struggles with greater sensitivity and intelligence.

Despite all the preceding hard-sell, however, the Socrates portrayed below will not make friends with every reader. One prominent scholar of ancient philosophy has, for example, expressed the sentiment that if he ever came to regard my account of Socrates as historically accurate, his previous respect for the man—founded as it is on his admiration for Socrates' contributions to secular, rational inquiry—would plummet. Even those who accept the idea that despite Socrates' resistance to many of the key ingredients of Greek religion he retained much of that religious outlook, may deem my portrait of Socrates unpalatable. For here some may find several key aspects of Socratic religious practice—especially his reliance on the divine guidance of his *daimonion*—at odds with rational theology, indeed, as threatening us with the intellectual legacy of a superstitious, religious-crank-Socrates.

To these reactions the response is obvious: sincere students of ancient philosophy must be prepared to discover (or rediscover) disconcerting truths, discoveries that may well run counter to their own heartfelt, rationally backed, long-standing convictions about Socrates (as well as those concerning philosophy, religion, Greek culture, and the nature of textual interpretation).[28] I confess myself that several of the elements of Socratic

27. G. Murray, 19–23, provides a sensitive discussion of this.
28. When the central topic of a study concerns an ancient religion it seems particularly

religion adumbrated in these pages are in conflict with my own philosophical and theological inclinations. Nonetheless, I do not think my portrait forces on us a superstitious Socrates of the worst sort, or even just a disagreeable zealot. For, I shall argue, we are not faced here with a simple choice between a Socrates who puts a higher trust in impulsive, subjective suggestions than reflective reason and another who instead entrusts his fortunes to the fortress of secular ratiocination. Rather, the Socrates of my account is not just religiously, but completely rationally (and morally) inclined: a man whose theologizing is grounded in discursive reason and who is willing to listen, reconsider, and argue for as long as his interlocutor has breath. It also just so happens that this Socrates has frequently been subjected to unique experiences that he has finally come to regard as divinely given admonitions, and for this view he has what he takes to be reflective, logically adequate reasons. Moreover, the Socrates I portray here insists that the extrarational must be submitted to the court of secular ratiocination whenever possible.

Of course, to feel perfectly comfortable with the Socrates of this interpretation we would have to believe that he really did have a private line to the gods, and given the nature of the evidence required to establish *that,* this particular belief will find few firm adherents. Nonetheless, taking the time and place of his philosophical mission into account, and the important conceptual shifts he helped to initiate and achieve, our high regard for Socrates should only be enriched—not diminished—by the discovery that much of his thought remained vitally tied to the religious traditions of his own time. In fact, I count it as a virtue of my study that the Socrates that emerges from it is something of a puzzle to both his age and ours, strangely rational to his contemporaries, strangely religious to us.

1.2 Presuppositions

Given the nature and aims of this study, I must put my methodological cards on the table by addressing briefly the "Socratic Problem": the problem, that is, of ascribing any views beyond the most general and obvious

---

important to remember that often "the scholar [of religion] fails to permit the alien 'world of meaning' to retain its integrity," because the scholar's ultimate values are directly threatened (J. S. Helfer, 3).

sort to the historical Socrates.[29] Socrates never wrote anything—at least, there are no documents that can reasonably be attributed to him[30]—and thus we must rely on the testimony of others when we attempt to identify the philosophical claims (or just "the sayings of") the real individual Athenian named "Socrates." But the testimony of others in this case is fraught with difficulty. Our different sources say different things, sometimes seemingly contradictory things, about the man; and our authors also probably had various motives for importing a good deal of fiction into their accounts. In particular, and most worrying of all for a study of this sort, is that many of these documents belong to a genre of intentionally apologetic—and thus probably biased—Socratic literature.[31] The preeminent representatives of this are, of course, the works of Plato: but Plato turned out to be one of the most dazzling of literary stylists, the foremost exponent of the dialogue form (D.L. 2.123), and a great philosopher in his own right with a distinctive, innovative philosophical agenda. Hence, and for other reasons internal to each of Plato's texts, there is little doubt that the Socrates of many of his dialogues is a good deal more fiction than fact.

No doubt while he was alive Plato was able to help his readers keep the fictional threads of the dialogues separate from the genuinely biographical and doctrinal ones. Remembering his own criticism of the written word—that texts themselves cannot answer questions on behalf of their authors (*Phdr.* 274c ff.)—Plato could have, for example, informed his puzzled contemporary readers whether or not and to what extent the Socrates of the *Euthyphro* (as opposed, say, to the Socrates of *Republic* Book VII) resembled his old teacher in method and belief. Succeeding generations, however, have had no live Plato and no unimpeachable Rosetta stone to guide their historical inferences and interpretations. Instead, we find ourselves with a disputed number of Plato's dialogues featuring a Socrates that—for reasons of consistency alone—is unlikely to be uttering in every dialogue questions asked and views held by the actual person. And although we

29. For a good summarizing discussion and anthology of important articles on the issue, see A. Patzer. See also Brickhouse and Smith (12), chap. 1; A. H. Chroust (1) and (2); C. J. de Vogel (2); E. A. Havelock (1); A. R. Lacey; W. D. Ross (3); and Vlastos (12) and (14), chaps. 2 and 3.

30. Excepting—if *Phaedo* 60c–61b is to be believed—a hymn to Apollo and some versifications of Aesop's fables (none of which are extant); cf. Diogenes Laertius 2.42 (hereafter "D.L.").

31. For example, besides the two *Apologies* by Plato and Xenophon, we know of those composed by Lysias, Theodectes, Demetrius of Phaleron, Theon of Antioch, Plutarch, and Libanius; see A.-H. Chroust (1), 50.

also possess the testimony of two other contemporaries who seem to have been well acquainted with Socrates (Aristophanes and Xenophon), and that of one who (arguably) heard some accurate reminiscences concerning the life and views of Socrates (Aristotle), using these sources to reconstruct the thought of the historical Socrates is fraught with difficulties that still plague Socratic scholarship.[32]

I cannot here specify in detail these basic problems of interpretation or justify fully my interpretive presuppositions and method. I can only spell out the common scholarly stance I shall be adopting; one that has been argued for elsewhere, one that is additionally warranted by what I and many others deem to be fruitful results. Naturally, criteria of fruitfulness are notoriously idiosyncratic. Where some of us, for example, count an interpretation of some argumentative passage as fruitful because it yields an argument worthy of the talent we find exemplified by the Socrates of Plato's early dialogues, others will see instead a failure to preserve Socrates' deliberate use of fallacy. Be that as it may, it is my hope that readers who are unsympathetic to my approach will nonetheless share in my conviction that even if (unbeknownst to us all) it leads us away from rather than toward an accurate understanding of the historical Socrates, my results at least still contribute to one sort of useful understanding of the ancient, transdialogical *literary figure* of Socrates. And it is that figure, after all, not the man himself, who has exercised his power on so many subsequent generations of thinkers.

The "common scholarly stance" I adopt here is essentially the developmentalist solution to the Socratic Problem as found in Gregory Vlastos's *Socrates, Ironist and Moral Philosopher*.[33] On this account, first of all, the primarily nondialogical *Apology* is assumed to capture the tone and substance of what Socrates actually said in the courtroom, and is thus able to serve as rough historical touchstone.[34] The rest of Plato's early works are

32. I follow most contemporary scholars by regarding these four authors as the only potentially reliable sources of Socratic *logoi* (although I refer to the fragments of Aeschines and others from time to time).

33. This approach began with Aristotle (arguably), was revived by F. Schleiermacher, and is that adhered to by figures such as N. Gulley, Guthrie (6), H. Maier, P. Natorp, J. E. Raven, R. Robinson (2), C. Ritter, and W. D. Ross (3). For recent defenses of this interpretive method that add to Vlastos's arguments, see Brickhouse and Smith (12), chap. 1; D. Graham (1); and McPherran (1) and (3). For recent criticism, see J. Beversluis (3); D. Nails (1) and (2); Nehamas (3); and C. Kahn (3) and (8).

34. Burnet (3), 143–146; Brickhouse and Smith (12), 9; cf. Vlastos (14), 49–50 n. 15, who holds that the *Apology* "may be credited with the same historical veracity as the speeches in Thucydides" (see Thuc. 1.22.1). Note, however, the recent criticism of this view and the traditional early dating of the *Apology* by E. de Strycker and and S. R. Slings, 1–21.

then understood to be *imaginative re-creations*—and so not necessarily *reproductions*—in dialogue form of the methods and doctrines of the historical Socrates.[35] The scenes depicted in the early dialogues (but not the *Apology*) are indeed primarily fictional: but contrary to some critics' occasional imputations, *not always necessarily and entirely* fictional.[36] Rather, as Vlastos has it, we proceed on the reasonable assumption that the early dialogues are the product of a Plato who, in the initial stages of his philosophical career, was a convinced Socratic and so philosophized after the manner of his teacher, pursuing (and publicizing) through his writing the Socratic insights he had made his own (an assumption justified by the independent testimony of Aristotle [and Xenophon to some extent] to the doctrines and methods of the historical Socrates). Thus, in this view the early dialogues *exhibit* Socratic doctrine and method without necessarily or always involving the conscious attempt to reproduce an exact copy of them. This position in no way *excludes* the influence of Plato's artistic craftsmanship and independent philosophical intentions, and so does not hold that literally all the claims and positions in a text are ones Socrates (or Plato) was himself committed to.[37] A dialogue may appear to end in perplexity, but given this interpretation of their composition, that surface perplexity need not mean to a developmentalist that Plato himself had no view on the issue at hand or that Plato had no position—and has exemplified no position—on what the view of the historical Socrates had

35. E.g., Vlastos (5), 1, and (12), 100–101; cf. T. Irwin (5), 195. Note also Vlastos's 1957 remark (5), 3, that "here . . . I speak of *recreation*, not reportage."

36. One such critic, Kahn, follows in the footsteps of earlier skeptics, such as J. Joël, O. Gigon, Chroust (3), and A. Momigliano (1); see, e.g., Kahn (4), n. 53, and (5), n. 5. These scholars hold *inter alia* that we know virtually nothing of the historical Socrates, and that Plato's Socratic dialogues are simply part of an entirely fictionalizing literary genre. See my reply to Kahn's line of argument in McPherran (3) and his response (3).

37. In Vlastos's most recent and extensive description of his interpretive strategy in (12) and (14), chaps. 2 and 3, he tells us that he makes the fundamental assumption that Plato's dialogues record the development of Plato's (not Socrates') mind, with a sharp change of direction in his way of thinking marked by the *Meno* and followed by the middle dialogues. This line of thought begins, however,

> with Plato still under Socrates's spell after his death, still convinced of the essential truth of Socrates's teaching. Eager to understand it better himself and to make it known abroad, he starts writing Socratic dialogues. But . . . Plato's [aim] . . . is primarily philosophical [not biographical]. This purpose could be served as well by invented conversations, as by remembered ones. Hence Plato would feel no urgency to give the protagonist of his little dramas lines which would preserve verbatim, or even in faithful paraphrase, things he may recall having heard Socrates say. He would feel no hesitation in keeping out of his text what he does recall, if it had not struck him then, or does not strike him now, as the most effective way of formulating Socrates's basic insights and vindicating their truth. ([12], 100–101)

been on the issue at hand.[38] Thus, it is well within reasonable historiographic procedures to bring to the interpretation of the early dialogues the hypothesis that "authentic Socratic thought survives in Plato's recreation of it."[39]

Next, we can use Aristotle's testimony to nail down the distinction between the Socrates of the early dialogues ("SE") and the Socrates of the middle dialogues ("SM") in a way that makes sufficiently plausible the developmentalists' working hypothesis that the ideas of the historical Socrates survive in Plato's early dialogues and thus that the historical Socrates is preserved in the guise of the Socrates of the early dialogues.[40] Some commentators, however, are unimpressed with Aristotle as a witness and as a historian of philosophy, holding that his testimony derives entirely (or almost entirely) from his knowledge of Plato's dialogues and possibly other Socratic testimonia. On this view Aristotle is thus but the first reader of a long line of readers (including Vlastos) "taken in" by the "optical illusion" created by Plato's masterly fictions.[41]

However, I do not think we have yet been given sufficient reason for rejecting the general reliability and independence of Aristotle's witness (especially where it is paralleled by Xenophon). For whatever sympathy the preceding general evaluation of Aristotle *qua* historian may elicit, it is (arguably) off the mark in the particular case of Socrates; and although Aristotle may violate modern historical standards by explicitly summing up the ideas of his predecessors in very much his own terms, we are often in a position to make reasonable allowances for it.[42] In his portrayal of Aris-

---

38. Cf. Kahn (5), 36.

39. Vlastos (12), 108.

40. Vlastos's (12) and (14), chaps. 2 and 3, are virtuoso performances of this approach, which finds ten key trait-differences between SE and SM; e.g., SE is exclusively a moral philosopher, disavowing knowledge and possessing no theory of separated Forms or a complex account of the nature of the soul, whereas SM is a philosopher of wide-ranging interests (including epistemology and metaphysics), confident that he has found knowledge, knowledge backed by a theory of separated Forms and of the tripartite structure of the soul. Irwin, too, relies on Aristotle to aid him in making the distinction between SE and SM ([4], 198–199, 291; [5], 195).

41. Kahn (4), 97, 100–101; (5), 34; (1), 310 and n. 13. Kahn's persistent and primary criticism of Aristotle's testimony is that he had "no taste or talent for the history of philosophy" ([1], n. 13; cf. [4], 100, and his recent [8]); also, disagreeing with the majority of scholars, cf., e.g., Vlastos (12), n. 86; E. R. Dodds (4), 209; and Guthrie (1), Kahn finds the alleged Pythagorean influence on Plato's development of the theory of Forms "extremely doubtful," thus impugning Aristotle's testimony to it ([1], n. 13). See now also Beversluis (3) and Nehamas (3) who criticize Vlastos's approach because of its reliance on the assumption that Aristotle is an independent witness; my reply—McPherran (1)—is in progress.

42. Cf. Guthrie (3), 3:357, and (7).

totle as the first "historicist," for example, Charles Kahn simply assumes that Aristotle is a naive, *uncritical* reader of the dialogues, who has (therefore) learned everything he attributes to the historical Socrates from those dialogues. But there are reasons to reject both these claims: (1) Aristotle is a most discerning and discriminating reader of the dialogues, testifying fairly unambiguously to the difference between SE and SM; willing, for example, to criticize only SE's moral psychology, not SM's (*EN* 1145b23 ff.; *EE* 1216b2 ff.), while even explicitly praising Plato's (*MM* 1182a15 ff.); crediting Plato, not Socrates (and not SE), with a doctrine of separate Forms (*Met.* 987a29 ff., 1078b12 ff., 1086a37 ff.); and (2) there are many items of Aristotle's testimony that seem unlikely to be due to his having been the artless victim of Plato's dramatic legerdemain, since there is nothing in the texts to suggest them (at least a third of the testimonia in Th. Deman seem to be of this sort).[43] Next, this sort of view overlooks Aristotle's own classification of the Σωκρατικοὶ λόγοι as imitation (μίμησις/ *mimêsis*) of a special sort, a sort to be distinguished from pure literary fiction (*Poetics* 1447a1 ff.). In the case of a Socratic dialogue that imitates a historical personage, poetic imitation must—on Aristotle's own account (1454a24–25)—be a reasonably faithful representation of Socrates' character and practice of philosophy. Finally, the fact that Aristotle was a critical reader who was also well acquainted with other Σωκρατικοὶ λόγοι *and* continually in contact with people who had known Socrates in their youth, should make the case for his general reliability. Rather than undermining the historical worth of Plato's early dialogues, then, Aristotle's reliance on them testifies to his confidence in them as a source of Socratic thought, where Plato "is speaking for Socrates, recreating Socrates's search."[44]

The foundational texts of this study are thus Plato's *Apology* and his early dialogues. I also presume that genuine Socratic thought and traits are captured in Xenophon's Socratic reminiscences and, in a much less direct way, in Aristophanes' *Clouds*. Unfortunately, it seems likely that both sources are heavily tainted by the quite different agendas of their authors: Xenophon by his desire to clear Socrates' good name of the various accusations made against him (especially that of impiety), Aristophanes by his intention to use Socrates as *inter alia* the basis for constructing a parody of the nature philosophers and Sophists of his day. I therefore use Xenophon primarily as a corroborating source, thinking that his agreement with

---

43. Deman (2). Cf. Vlastos (12), 102–108; Guthrie (3), 3:355–359; Beckman, 17–18; all the former following W. D. Ross, in, e.g., (3). But again see Beversluis (3), esp. 300.

44. Vlastos (12), 105.

Plato (and Aristotle where possible) adds somewhat to the evidence for the reliability of the attribution. Because of the richness of Xenophon's testimony on the subject of Socratic religiosity, however, I sometimes depart from this procedure, but where this occurs readers will usually find some attempt at a justification in the text and/or notes.[45] My quite limited use of Aristophanes follows the same scheme.

In my use of this interpretive method readers may on occasion (be it only that!) detect a certain arbitrariness of reading. This, I think, is the unfortunate, unavoidable sin that all interpreters must commit. Vlastos, for example, provides us with one plausible ordering of the early dialogues and employs it to produce an interesting and coherent account of Socratic philosophy,[46] yet others give us various other equally plausible orderings and derive from them different but nonetheless fruitful accounts—fruitful, again, on what will probably always be in part rather shaky criteria of what it is to be fruitful. That such a plurality of accounts should still stand after all this time is not surprising. There is really nothing quite like Plato's literary-philosophical creations—ancient or modern—and so nothing to compare them fairly to. We remain woefully ignorant of the "canons of the genre" of Plato's day and are in no good position to identify with any security the dialogues' intended audiences. Were the dialogues, for example, aimed at a sophisticated general public as advertisements for the Academy or were they for the philosophically advanced members of that body? Without knowing such things it is hard to know, for instance, whether some Platonic enthymeme marks an oversight or a maieutic philosophical challenge.[47] Given that, and given the opacity natural to all texts, the interpretation of the dialogues is bound to remain a perennial task.

This view, and the present interpretive situation, will prove disappointing to those hard souls happy only when they grasp the one true grail of certitude. But it should perhaps be enough of an achievement if we produce a limited number of plausible interpretations of the Socratic material arising from a limited number of diverse and plausible interpretive as-

---

45. For defenses of Xenophon as a source for the views of the historical Socrates, see, e.g., C. Bruell, D. Morrison, Ross (3), and P. Vander Waerdt (3), 1–22.

46. Vlastos's settled view (e.g., in [2], n. 30; [12], nn. 21, 79; [14], 46–47, esp. n. 4) is that the *Gorgias* is the last of the set of early "elenctic dialogues": *Ap., Ch., Cr., Eu., G., HMi., Ion, La., Pr., Rep. 1* (listed in alphabetical order). The other early, but transitional dialogues are *Eud., HMa., Ly.,* and the first third of *M.* (down to 80e). The *Menexenus* is an early but non-elenctic dialogue.

47. On the intended audience for the dialogues, see, e.g., M. Miller (2), esp. 15–25.

As for the "maieutic" reading of the dialogues, see, e.g., P. Friedländer, 1, 154–170; D. Halperin (1), 60–80, esp. 76–79; and K. Sayre, 93–109.

sumptions.[48] No doubt many of these interpretive flowers will bloom as a result of a longing for certitude. But that longing is perhaps more effectively channeled—and is perhaps more in line with Plato's own possible maieutic hopes for his creations—if it is tempered and informed by greater reflection on the import of Plato's well-known dream of being an elusive swan. Simmias the Socratic, at least, interpreted it as meaning that "all men would endeavor to grasp Plato's meaning; none, however, would succeed, but each would interpret him according to his own views" (Olympiodorus *In Alcibiaden* 2.156–162).

Let us imagine, then, that Plato was quite aware of the interpretive malleability of his work. If that should be right, then it would also seem true that *one* of Plato's intentions was to use his dialogues to goad us, as beginners in philosophy and taken in—as we almost always are—by the dramatic art of the dialogues, to seek to uncover the views of the historical Socrates (views which we are entitled to believe have been preserved for us there in living form). After all, some of Plato's early dialogues do seem intended to be *inter alia* defenses (and thus accurate re-creations in *substance*) of the characteristics, activities, and views of his master. Of course, as we seek out this Socrates, we must acknowledge that it was also perhaps Plato's further hope that we should begin to discover those elements in ourselves and the world that—projected onto the mirror of his texts—interfere with our attempts to grasp fully our long-gone swan (and his teacher). Moreover, and even after such discoveries are made, these texts will still serve as protreptic invitations to join in, say, the argument between Socrates and Euthyphro. They will always ask their readers to look for the unsupported assumptions and incomplete theories that need further thought on the way to the philosophical illumination Plato posits as the end of all our efforts and desires (*Seventh Letter* 341c–d). That, in any case, is the cage for our swan I adopt here.

1.3 The Religious Landscape

In order to make good sense of the religious dimension of Socratic thought we need to grasp how Socrates remained within Greek religious tradition and how he departed from it. It is important, then, to begin with some

---

48. And as T. Irwin (5), 199, notes: "It is an illusion to think we can find the right interpretive methods and strategies in advance of considering the philosophical merits of the conclusions they yield."

understanding of fifth-century Greek religion.[49] To this end, I include here an elementary sketch of the religious landscape of fifth-century Athens, a sketch that skirts many issues and saves many details for later discussion.[50]

Providing even a short introduction to this topic is not at all as straightforward as it might seem. To begin, notice that there is no Greek term "religion" (the root *religio* is Latin), indicating how the distinct phenomena this term designates for us was for the Greeks seamlessly integrated into everyday life, especially public, communal life: Greek religion did not comprise a unified, organized system of beliefs and rituals held at arm's length from the social, political, and commercial aspects of life we would term "secular." Rather, it was a complex tangle of practices and attitudes that pervaded every *polis*-member's life in a variety of ways. Even individual threads—such as the state-supported civic cult of Athens—are themselves composed of further, apparently disconnected or inconsistent elements, many of which do not bear an easily assimilated relation to the modern concept of religion, but rather, cut across the grain of our own conceptual boundaries.[51] It should prove unsurprising, then, to discover that Socrates' own religious expressions and thoughts[52] on certain topics are not to be found in a separate addendum to his rational consideration of them, but are simply interspersed among and integrated into those reflections.

We should perhaps first try to realize what Greek religion was not. First, it did not take as foundational any particular set of revealed religious texts: no text had the status of a Bible (including Homer's *Iliad* and Hesiod's *Theogony*). Neither was there an organized Church, a trained clergy, or a systematic set of doctrines enforced by such a clergy.[53] Thus, what

---

49. If—given the difficulty of this topic and the space available here—that is an unrealistic hope, it is at least essential that I briefly spell out the interpretation of Greek religion that serves as the backdrop for my portrait of Socrates.

50. Those familiar with the outlines of Greek religion are advised to skip over this last section. Good introductions to the subject include those by W. Burkert (2); Dodds (4) and (7); P. E. Easterling and J. V. Muir; A.-J. Festugière (1); Guthrie (2); J. Harrison (2); J. Mikalson (1); M. P. Nilsson (3), (4), and (5); R. Parker; J. Rudhardt (2); C. Sourvinou-Inwood; J.-P. Vernant (1) and (2); and L. B. Zaidman and P. S. Pantel (this last work served as the primary reference for the following synopsis).

51. See H. S. Versnel's introduction for an incisive discussion of the problem of investigating and understanding ancient religions (Versnel [2]).

52. "Religious," that is, since from our perspective his terminology (e.g., "gods") brings into play those categories we subsume under the term "religion."

53. See, e.g., Burkert (2), 8; Dodds (4), 140–144; Lloyd-Jones, 134; and Taylor (4), 15–16.

marked a city or individual out as pious (εὐσεβής)—that is, as being in accord with the norms governing the relations of humans and gods—was not primarily conformity of belief to a dogma or private pious sentiment, but correct, timely observance of ancestral tradition (τά πατρία) by maintaining and participating in a host of activities (e.g., contributing financially and otherwise to the upkeep of sanctuaries and the performance of sacrifices to various deities according to the calendar of festivals). As long as a state or individual scrupulously observed such practices—practices whose very institution was credited to the deities so honored—it could expect a measure of physical protection from those deities (both from the depredations of other humans and from the natural forces that could express the hostility of other deities). These rituals were plentiful and connected every day and every stage of life with the divine drama of gods and goddesses.

All Greek religious ritual centered on various forms of sacrifice, but typically included prayer (εὐχή) and other forms of expression.[54] Such sacrifices ranged from an individual's libation of wine at the start of a meal—pouring a bit on an altar or on the ground and consuming the rest while reciting a prayer that invoked the protection of a deity—to the great civic sacrifices of cattle held on the occasion of a religious festival, culminating in a communal banquet that renewed the ties of city-protecting deities with the citizenry through the mechanism of the shared meal (a portion of meat being set aside as a burnt offering for the gods; see, e.g., Od. 3.417–472).[55] Such rituals commonly involved either "rites of passage" (e.g., incorporation of a newborn into a household [οἶκος/oikos], purification after giving birth, enrollment into a phratry, entry into citizenship, marriage, and death) or constituted the focus of the religious festivals (ἑορταί) spon-

---

54. For examples of prayer, see Il. 1.446–458; Hesiod Erga 724–726, 465–468; Aeschylus Sept. 252–260, LB 124–151; and Thuc. 6.32. It is exceedingly difficult to say what feelings underlay many of these expressions, since there are so few pieces of textual evidence to guide us. Although there are indications that a person might experience a personal relationship with a deity akin to the sort a trusted servant might have for a kindly master (see, e.g., Eurip. Hipp. 948–949; Ion 128–135)—especially in the case of sects such as the Orphics and the various mystery cults (e.g., that of Eleusis)—the predominant popular sentiment seems to be that of distant respect; see, e.g., Dodds (7), H. S. Versnel (2), and Zaidman and Pantel, 13–15.

55. For surveys of sacrificial practice (and other forms of religious ritual), see, e.g., Burkert (2), chap. 2; Mikalson, chap. 11; and Zaidman and Pantel, 28–45. Some sects, such as the Orphics, set themselves apart from the civic religion by practicing bloodless sacrifice (motivated by a desire for the sort of ritual purity that would help them to recover their lost divinity); see Guthrie (4), esp. chap. 6.5.

sored by the city (as fixed by a sacred calendar, involving a procession, sacrifice, banquet, and competitions; e.g., the annual Panathenaia).[56] Besides such examples of what we might think of as "white" magic, however, we must also set those other rituals of "black" magic, which aim to harm, not help, others; in particular, curses (ἀραί/κατάραι) and other prayer-imprecations (see, e.g., Pin. Ol. 1.75 ff.; Il. 3.299–301, 9.456; Od. 2.134 ff.; So. Trach. 1239; Pl. R. 394a; Crit. 119e; and Laws 854b, 876e, 930e–932a, 949b).[57]

Whatever the ritual, sacrificial or otherwise, the actions composing it were typically aimed at a specific deity and were closely tied to the community, ranging from individual households—with their own altars, household divinities, and daily cult of Hestia (whose seat was the family hearth); cf. Eud. 302b ff.—to more complex groupings such as the deme (δῆμος), tribe (φυλή), and optional cult associations (paying cult to heroes, gods, or the dead [e.g., the cult of Asclepius]).[58] The most obvious organizing principle, however, was the overarching civic cult from which these smaller groups drew their structures. It was the city—in the form of religious officials and priests[59]—that exercised final authority over all religious functions and that oversaw the most prominent displays of public piety provided by the city's numerous festivals.[60] A city's typical mixture of temples, sanctuaries, and heroic tombs with buildings devoted to civic administration—as found, for example, in the Athenian agora—gives physical testimony to how religion and politics were mutually implicated for the Greeks.

A universal feature of this "polis religion" was its appeal to the pa-

56. See Zaidman and Pantel, chaps. 7 and 10.

57. See, e.g., G. Luck, chap. 1, and L. Watson, chap. 1. Watson, 3–4, notes that there was considerable blurring between the notions of praying and cursing in antiquity, since both were conceived of as requests (accompanied by sacrificial gifts) for a benefit to be granted the petitioner (or community) (e.g., harm to one's enemy). Note, though, that the priestess Theano declined the request of the Athenians to pronounce a curse on Alcibiades on the grounds that she was "a priestess of prayer, not of cursing" (Plut. Q. Rom. 275d; cf. Laws 801a–b, 931b-d; Alc. 2.143b). For further discussion of black magic, see Chapter 3.3 herein.

58. Associations whose generic term was "common" (κοινόν), and whose species included the phratry (φρατρία; e.g., that of Zeus Phratrios), genos (γένος; e.g., that of Athena Skiras), thiasos (θίασος; e.g., that of Dionysus), and orgeônes (ὀργεῶνες; e.g., that of Bendis); see Zaidman and Pantel, chap. 8, and Watson, chap. 1.

59. E.g., the elected hieropoioi (ἱεροποιοί) in charge of the major festivals, the appointed epimelêtai (ἐπιμεληταί) for others, the three senior Archons (esp. the basileus [βασιλεύς], on which, see Chap. 2, n. 7), sacred ambassadors (θεωροί), and appointed and hereditary priests and priestesses; see Burkert (2), chap. 2.6, and Zaidman and Pantel, chap. 5.

60. For a discussion of Greek religious festivals, see Burkert (2), chap. 2.7; P. Cartledge; and Zaidman and Pantel, 102–111.

tronage of a protector deity(ies): Zeus at Kos, and for Athens, Athena Polias ("Athena of the city") and Zeus Polieus (with whom Athena intercedes on behalf of the city's interests). Whether or not Athena did intercede, however, depended on a variety of things, the most important of which was—again—the proper maintenance of the friendship between her and the city *via* those communal meals and sacrificial rites dictated by tradition (preserved through the city's calendar of sacrifices). In addition, the Athenian Assembly and law courts concerned themselves with religious affairs (e.g., the consultation of oracles, pursuing damages against sacred olive trees, and so on), and officials of both were expected to maintain their family cults. Finally, the public religious oaths (ὅρκοι) and imprecations that ensured the order and honesty necessary for the operations of government, courts, and other institutions of civic life (e.g., the integrity of wills) involved swearing on the victims of a sacrifice, calling on the gods as witnesses and invoking their punishments on contract-breakers and perjurers (e.g., each meeting of the Athenian Assembly included a curse threatening utter destruction against any who might speak out of bribery or with the intent to deceive).[61]

In addition to the religion of family and state, there also existed more inclusive, Panhellenic institutions such as the sanctuaries, oracles, and sacred games of Delphi and Dodona. Here, besides the usual religious rites, one could receive through the mouth of Apollo's priestess, the Pythia, the god's predictions or advice in response to a question (see Chapter 4.2). Another important institution of this sort is the Eleusinian Mysteries, whose initiations—although controlled by Athenian officials—were open to any speaker of Greek whose hands were unpolluted by crime and which (for all the "secrecy" involved) served as a popular form of religious expression. A long period of preparation by candidates for initiation into the Mysteries (μύσται) included fasting, retreats, and a pollution-removing sacrifice of a "scapegoat" pig, culminating in the revelation of sacred objects inside the Hall of Initiation (τελεστήριον). For many, this apparently involved an emotional experience of contact with the divine and the vague promise of a situation in the afterlife superior to that of noninitiates.[62]

The preceding should help to indicate that the ancient Greek religious

---

61. Demos. *De Corona* 23.97, 19.70 (cf. 20.107, where we are told that Athenian democracy was founded on curses); Dinarchus 2.16; cf. *Laws* 871b; Ar. *Thes.* 349 ff. See also L. Watson, chap. 1, esp. 8–9, 18–22. Watson, chap. 1.6, notes that curses were widespread in the private sphere as well, protecting *phratries*, graves, wills, and possessions as small as an oil flask.

62. On which, see Burkert (1), 21–29. For further discussion of Greek attitudes toward death and the afterlife, see chapter 4.1 and its references.

"system" presupposed a notion of divinity rather different from the Christian, Jewish, or Islamic senses of it. In these traditions, the divine takes the form of an eternal, transcendent, omnipotent, omniscient God who has created the world and humankind. Although external in some sense to the world, this God can also become manifest in or to us and may respond to heartfelt prayer, with outward piety serving as a sign of an inner intimate relationship with the divine (a relationship that can hold the key to positive moral and psychological transformations). For a contemporary of Socrates, however, brought up on the picture of the gods' origins and natures drawn in the works of Homer and Hesiod, the gods did not create the cosmos or humankind, but rather, were themselves created. Their power was often gained through duplicity and violence, they were neither omniscient nor omnipotent nor eternal (but merely immortal and subject to fate), and they kept busy by constantly intervening in human affairs. Although they might exhibit an anthropomorphic appearance, possessing unique names, attributes, and adventures, they were also powers capable of differing manifestations, appearing even as natural phenomena (e.g., Zeus Keraunos [Zeus-as-Thunderbolt]).[63] Here on earth, then, there is no clear separation of the sacred from the profane or of the religious from the secular, and (thus) every human action, every facet of nature, had what we would call a religious dimension.[64]

Although for the Greeks the world was permeated by the divine, they also located its most potent expressions in beings distinctly different from perishable, mortal creatures, recognizing three primary forms of divinity: gods, *daimones* (δαίμονες), and heroes.[65] As seen above, the gods were, in

63. Although the Greeks sculpted anthropomorphic figures that were understood to be formulaic representations of the various divinities (e.g., Zeus holding his thunderbolt, Artemis holding her bow), these figures are best understood not as attempted *likenesses* of the gods, but rather, as figures that give human form to the formless, figures that use the human image to evoke the qualities of the divinity represented (M. Robertson; Zaidman and Pantel, 215–218).

64. Virtually "every stream, spring, plain, wood, or cultivated field was populated with divine powers whom it was wise to conciliate" (Zaidman and Pantel, 81). However, there are terms such as *hieron* (ἱερόν), *hosion* (ὅσιόν), and *hagion* (ἅγιον) that mark off things and practices as enjoying an especially close relation with the divine. Cults, cult acts, and sanctuaries are, for example, τὰ ἱερά, and sacred spaces (τέμενοι) for sanctuaries could be marked off from the surroundings by virtue of the special numinous qualities of the place. But something that can be helpfully sacred (e.g., sacrificial blood) can—depending on circumstances—also be dangerous (e.g., the blood of a murder victim; linked to ἅγιον *and* to pollution [μίασμα/*miasma*], on which see chap. 2, n. 10).

65. Δαίμονες (*daimones*) were sometimes thought of as "intermediary powers." However, "every god can act as *daimon*," and so the term is better understood as referring to the

turn, commonly instantiated in various guises and called by various epithets; e.g., Zeus Polieus was the presiding deity of the Dipoleia festival, but it was Zeus Meilikhios who received honors during the Diasia (Athena had at least fifty such epithets). Various pantheons of the most active gods existed, but the *polis* of Athens typically listed these twelve: Zeus, Poseidon, Demeter, Hera, Ares, Aphrodite, Artemis, Apollo, Athena, Hermes, Dionysus, and Hephaistos (with Hestia and Hades sometimes replacing Ares and Dionysus). More than just an assemblage of powers, the pantheon was a complicated system of relationships in which each deity was "part of a variegated network of associations with other gods. . . . The Hermes-Hestia couple, for instance, represents not only the complementary nature of two divine powers, the immovable goddess of the hearth and the mobile god of transitions," but also an intellectual category that organized the workings of institutions (e.g., these two were the deities who regulated marriage).[66]

Even though these ancient conceptions of divinity were not elaborated or enforced by an official theological body, religious education was not left entirely to chance or imagination (e.g., through haphazard exposure to the stories of childhood and the rites of the civic religion). Both Homer and Hesiod were universally heard or read, authors, who—while relying on a much older oral tradition—had established for the Greeks "a kind of canonical repertory of stories about the Powers of the Beyond."[67] It was on the basis of this repertory that "the elegiac, lyric, and tragic poets drew unstintingly while simultaneously endowing the traditional myths with a new function and meaning."[68] Thus, for example, the dramas of Aeschylus and Sophocles juxtapose some present situation against the events represented in Homeric religious myth, extending the mythology while also calling into critical question some facet of the human condition and contemporary society's response to it (see, e.g., Sophocles' *Antigone*). By the time of Socrates, some of this analyzing and probing of the traditional stories was influenced by (and also influenced) the speculations and discoveries of

---

"veiled countenance of divine activity" (Burkert [2], 180). A hero was a long-dead individual, about whom epic adventures might be told, usually tied to a specific locale that gave him cult (e.g., such as Theseus at Athens; although some—like Heracles—were widely worshiped). As much as any god, a hero had attained the status of divinity, and thus could respond to cult by providing protection, dealing out retribution, and so forth. On *daimones,* see Burkert (2), chap. 3.3.5; on heroes, see Burkert (2), chap. 4, and Zaidman and Pantel, 178–182.

66. Vernant (1), 277–278.
67. Vernant (2), 193.
68. Zaidman and Pantel, 144.

those thinkers working within the new intellectualist tradition "inaugurated" by Thales. These included "nature philosophers" such as Anaxagoras (those interested in the rational reinterpretation of divine phenomena like thunder) and professional teachers of rhetoric (Sophists) such as Protagoras (some prone to theological skepticism and—in a few cases—atheism). As a result, in the work of authors such as Euripides and Thucydides even the fundamental tenets of popular religion concerning the efficacy of sacrifice and prayer became targets of criticism.[69]

To conclude this section, it is probably helpful to sketch out the particular religious tensions that find their expression in the trial of Socrates. For—I contend—even if his prosecutors' charges of impiety should prove to be a smoke screen for concerns more personal or political, there is good reason to suppose that they borrowed some of their plausibility and punch from the ostensibly widespread religious concerns of the day. So—and without getting ahead of the details I need to bring into play at later textual and argumentative junctures—these "lines of tension" can be briefly illustrated by disentangling a few of the fifth-century threads mentioned above.

As I've portrayed the religious landscape of fifth-century Athens, there existed a recognizable, though informal, distinction between (1) the ritual-focused household and civic religion of the *polis* and (2) the story-focused religion of traditional poets like Homer. In addition, the populace had been exposed to (3) popular mystery cults such as that of Eleusis, (4) the sectarian practices and beliefs of groups such as the Orphics, (5) the Pythagorean blend of philosophy and religion, (6) the religious reflections of playwrights like Sophocles, and (7) the more critical probings of literature instanced by some of Euripides' characters, with the latter influenced by (8) the new and influential intellectualism of the natural scientists and Sophists.

Socrates' rationally derived moral theory—and the moral theology it determined—were influenced in various respects by factors (3) through (8). The end result was that although Socrates remained inclined to endorse the household and civic religion of the *polis* (1) (especially those features of it particularly open to philosophical reinterpretation, such as the function of oracles), he rejected and reinterpreted features of (2) the

---

69. For Euripides, see, e.g., *Bacchae* 216–220, *Trojan Women* [TW]1060–1080, and *Andromache* 1161–1165. For Thucydides, see, e.g., 2.8.2. The influence of scientific speculation on Euripides is generally acknowledged by reference to texts such as *TW* 884–888 (where some detect the influence of Diogenes of Apollonia).

religion of the poets, features that had helped to invigorate and motivate the actual practices of (1). The upshot of this was a unique, philosophical religion founded on a rationalist psychology and theology that devalued the old, publicly observable, external standard of piety that connected capricious all-too-human gods to humanity through the system of burnt sacrifice. In its place Socrates advocated an internal standard of virtue and human happiness that emphasized the rational purification of the soul through elenctic argument and a viewpoint that presupposed the existence of benevolent, rational deities who loved justice but were relatively indifferent to sacrifice. We will see how this rational reinterpretation of the ancestral religion entered into the trial that ended with his demise.

In Chapter 2, I elicit from the *Euthyphro* various pieces of Socrates' "theology," show how we can derive a partial, Socratically acceptable account of the virtue of piety from its second half, and then offer an initial sketch of Socratic religion as a whole. I devote Chapter 3 to understanding the charges against Socrates, to recovering items of Socratic theology from the text of the *Apology,* to delineating how Socrates' religious innovations both did and did not threaten Greek popular and civic religion, and thus to assessing his actual "guilt." In Chapter 4, I focus on the *daimonion* and other such sources of divination, in particular, the Delphic Oracle. In section 1, I argue for a solution to the epistemological puzzle of how Socrates could rely on extrarational monitions yet be commited to elenctic philosophizing. Next, I delineate the sources of Socrates' philosophical "mission," explaining how Socrates derived his duty to do philosophy from the Oracle's pronouncement that "no one is wiser" than Socrates and exploring the extent of that duty. In Chapter 5, I conclude by spelling out Socrates' stand on the immortality of the soul, his proof of god's existence (arguing we should accept Xenophon's attribution of this proof to him), and the relationship of Socratic religion to the influential religious views of his pupil Plato.

We can now turn to two encounters with Socrates: first, his grilling of a self-professed religious expert in the *Euthyphro;* next, his response to the charges of impiety leveled by his prosecutors in the *Apology.* That Plato would devote these two works—each a masterly expression of an intense literary labor—to clearing Socrates' name of accusations of civic impiety (and, arguably, also to demonstrating the nature of real, universal piety), helps to show that Plato and his contemporaries saw the issue of Socrates' relation to religion as central. This, I want to argue, is because while they all understood their teacher to be at the forefront of the new intellectualist investigations into argumentation and virtue, they just as clearly understood that the grist for this mill and the motivation for its use remained vitally linked to what they all recognized as the perennial, mysterious, "religious" dimension of life.

2
Socratic Piety in the *Euthyphro*

2.1 Euthyphro's Piety: *Euthyphro* 2a–11e

It is natural and useful to begin our study with Plato's *Euthyphro*. Its ostensible topics are the virtue of piety (εὐσέβεια) and pious behavior, and these are central concerns of traditional Greek religion and (as we shall see) a focus of Socrates' inquiry into the nature of the virtues.[1] The issues spotlighted by the dialogue, then, together with Socrates' own positive contributions to its arguments and the subtle interplay of those argu-

---

1. Since the Greeks had no word "religion," it is natural that the term εὐσέβεια (piety) carried a much wider sense than our English equivalent, emphasizing both proper religious conduct and knowledge of ritual (and so designated more than just correct belief about gods and ritual) (K. Dover [3], 246–254; J. Mikalson [1], chaps. 1, 8, 11). Εὐσέβεια takes as its field of concern not only one's immediate relation to the gods, but one's conduct toward parents, native land, and the dead and carries a sense of reverence for, even a certain fear of, the gods. One might thus be ἀσεβής (impious) in a variety of ways, by felling sacred trees or by giving offense to one's parents; see, e.g., W. Burkert (2), 270–275; Dover (3), 246–249; A. Momigliano (2), 565–566; and J. Harrison (2), 2–3. Note also that c. 430 the Athenians passed into law the decree of Diopeithes, which extended the scope of the crime of ἀσέβεια to include religiously offensive opinion; see Chapter 3.1.1. I assume, as most commentators do, that εὐσεβής is used synonymously with another term occurring in the *Euthyphro*, ὅσιος (piety as it designates that sphere of life allocated by the gods to humans), since to all appearances they are used interchangeably and unsystematically.

ments with its rich dramatic structure, make the *Euthyphro* a primary source for uncovering the religious dimension of Socratic philosophy.[2]

Not everyone will agree with this assessment: whether the *Euthyphro* is a source of positive Socratic doctrine or merely a peirastic inquiry is a persistent and much debated issue in this field.[3] Although a number of commentators have favored the former view and so have produced various reconstructions of the positive Socratic doctrine of piety they find implicit in the text following the aporetic interlude (11b6–e1),[4] a few prominent scholars have raised objections to this constructivist approach.[5] I contend that the anticonstructivists are wrong and that most of the interpretations the constructivists have offered involve the mistaken use of textual references that do not plausibly bear on the views of the historical Socrates and/or do not do justice to a reasonable understanding of Socrates' profes-

2. Although the *Euthyphro*'s date of composition has been the subject of the usual controversies, virtually all scholars place it within the set of early dialogues (see in particular L. Brandwood, xvii). I am especially inclined to put a good deal of weight on its direct dialogue form and its many dramatic connections to the events of the *Apology*, and hence, regard it as one of the earlier of Plato's early dialogues. But regardless of its exact chronological place, its connections to the *Apology* indicate that it was composed as (*inter alia*) a defense of Socrates' religious views in the spirit of the *Apology*. For further discussion, see R. E. Allen (1), 1 ff.; J. Beckman, 42; Brickhouse and Smith (6), 657–66; J. Burnet (3), 82–142; W.K.C. Guthrie (3), 4:101–102; W. Heidel, 169; and R. Hoerber, 95–107.

3. See W. Rabinowitz, 112–114, for a partial history of this issue, the discussion of which extends from Thrasyllus of Alexandria to the present (see, e.g., C.C.W. Taylor).

4. Among the constructivists are J. Adam; H. Bonitz, 233–234; Brickhouse and Smith (8), chap. 6.1, (12), chap. 2.5, and (6), 657–66; Burnet (3); S. Calef (1) and (2); P. Friedländer, 2:82–91; Heidel, 173 ff.; T. Irwin (4), 1–131; B. Jowett, 1:303–308; Rabinowitz; Reeve, 62–73; P. Shorey, 74–80; A. E. Taylor (1), 146–156; C.C.W. Taylor; Vlastos (14), chap. 6, and (18); and R. Weiss (4). For further references, see Rabinowitz, 113 n. 4, and L. Versenyi (1), 111 n. 4.

5. R. E. Allen (1), 67, for instance, taking Socrates' professions of ignorance (e.g., *Ap.* 21b) to heart, holds that the *Euthyphro* "bears its meaning on its face" and, thus, that it neither states nor implies a Socratic definition of piety (see also his 6–9); Beckman, chap. 2.1; G. Grote (2), 1:437–457. Curiously, Allen finds it easy to discover most of Plato's theory of Forms in a text that is perfectly coherent without such an attribution (employing universals [abstract qualities] instead of Platonic Forms). The very principles of interpretation Allen endorses (p. 9) sanction the constructive claim concerning piety I derive from the text; cf. Versenyi (1), 16. Lazlo Versenyi (1), 104–134, a kind of qualified anticonstructivist, argues rather more cogently that no definition of piety *involving reference to the gods* may be culled from the dialogue's explicit statements (contra most constructivists), and that in fact, the notion of piety toward which Socrates directs Euthyphro is a secular one that identifies it with the whole of virtue; cf. Calef (2), Versenyi (2), and C.C.W. Taylor. Beckman, 51–54, argues in a similar way that no definition of piety that involves the gods may be derived from the explicit statements of the text. Rather, he claims, Socrates argues implicitly that real piety is nothing but the whole of justice, for whose understanding and definition no gods are required. Irwin (4), 22, and Reeve, 64–66, seem to head in this direction as well.

sion of ignorance, his claims to be pursuing a god-ordered service, and the evidence of his somewhat traditional religious practices and beliefs.[6] As a remedy to these accounts, I offer here a cautiously constructive view of Socratic piety derived from the *Euthyphro*, a view consonant with a reasonable conception of the historical Socrates and the Athens of his time.

2.1.1 *Euthyphro* 2a–5c

The dialogue opens where Plato's *Theaetetus* ominously leaves off: Socrates has kept his appointment at the Porch of the King (the ἄρχων βασιλεύς), where he is to submit to a preliminary inquiry (ἀνάκρισις) concerning the counts of the writ (γραφή) of impiety against him.[7] But before this occurs, he is drawn into conversation with a certain Euthyphro, a conversation that quickly becomes a classic display of Socratic elenctic interrogation.[8] Typically, the grounds for these interrogations are provided by some interlocutor involving himself in a claim to expert knowledge of some virtue such as justice (cf. *R*. 331c ff., *Ap*. 21e–22e), which in turn incites Socrates to test this claim by asking for a definition of that virtue. In this case, the virtue at issue turns out to be piety.[9] But here, as elsewhere, the narrative that sets the stage for the introduction and pursuit of the Socratic definitional search into piety is not incidental to our concerns.

Five years prior to Socrates' encounter with Euthyphro, one of Euthyphro's farmhands killed a family servant during a drunken fit. Euthyphro's father had the murderer bound and thrown in a ditch, but before word arrived from one of the Athenian exegetes on the correct disposition of the case, the laborer perished from exposure. In response, Euthyphro now brings a suit for homicide (a δίκη φόνου) against his father, who is quite

6. A star instance of this is Heidel, 174, who defines piety as the "intelligent and conscious endeavor to further the realization of [Platonic!] Good in human society, as under God" (my insertion).

7. The specifics of these legal procedures are outlined by D. MacDowell (2), 56–65, 239–242. There were nine *archons* in Athens, with the ἄρχων βασιλεύς being charged with the oversight of public sacrifices and judicial cases involving the state religion (cf. *Pol*. 290d–e). See Burkert (2), chap. 2.6; J. Hoopes; MacDowell (2), 24–27; and Zaidman and Pantel, chap. 5, for an overview of his functions.

8. Whether this character is Plato's pure invention or is related to a historical individual (perhaps the [apparently] historical Euthyphro of *Cratylus* 396d2–397a1) is an open question; but see n. 16.

9. *Mem*. 1.2.37 also testifies that Socrates discussed piety (ὅσιον) with interlocutors.

old (4a), in order to cleanse both his father and himself of the religious pollution (μίασμα) that he sees attending this sort of unjust killing (4b–e).[10]

Socrates is understandably astonished by this story. By suing his own father, that is, by acting as though he is an aggrieved relative of his laborer, Euthyphro is proceeding contrary to all legal custom. Moreover, such aggression toward his father is an outrageous violation of the unwritten canons of filial piety (4d9–e1; and furthermore, he thereby brings shame to his entire family).[11] Hence, Socrates insinuates that it is only through the possession of a conception of piety superior to that of received tradition that Euthyphro could with confidence pursue such an unconventional and potentially damaging course of action on religious grounds: "Before Zeus, Euthyphro, do you suppose that you have such precise [ἀκριβῶς] knowledge about . . . pious and impious things that . . . you don't fear that by pursuing a lawsuit against your father that you may happen to be doing something impious?" (4e; cf. 4a–b, 15d–e). Without the least hesitation, Euthyphro swallows the bait by agreeing with Socrates' suggestion, grandly laying claim to a "precise [ἀκριβῶς] knowledge" of all such divine things.[12] The characteristic setup of a Socratic interlocutor has thus been successfully stage-managed. If Euthyphro has such an accurate and exact understanding of divine matters then surely—Socrates suggests—he can spell out just what piety is.[13]

From the outset of this story, Plato has plotted an implicit analogy: both Socrates and Euthyphro's father are old, and now both find themselves defendants in legal suits,[14] each of which presuppose on the part of their

10. On the precise legal, historical, and religious issues raised by this story, see Burnet (3), 82–107; W. Furley; I. Kidd (1); MacDowell (2), 109–132, 192–194; and Hoerber. On *miasma*—a pollution, a defilement, that can settle and spread like a disease and upon which disasters attend (indeed, *miasma* in its widest sense included disease) (Burkert [2], 147)—see R. Parker (2) and Soph. *Ant.* 775–776; cf. *Laws* 871b–e.

11. See M. Blundell, 41. Note too that Euthyphro apparently has no legal right to prosecute his father (R. Klonoski, 130–131). *Cr.* 50e–51a may provide additional evidence that Socrates endorsed the traditional authority of fathers and the virtue of filial piety; cf. *R.* 574a–c, *Mem.* 2.2.13, and *EN* 1163b18 ff.

12. As A. Gómez-Lobo, 27, points out, there is an implicit contrast here between Euthyphro's self-assured claim to exact knowledge with ordinary claims to know τύπῳ ("roughly," or "in broad outline").

13. It is a common theme of the early dialogues that the possession of knowledge of some concept confers the ability to give a Socratic definition of it; see, e.g., *Laches* 190c ff.

14. Euthyphro charges his father with a δίκη φόνου (4a–b), whereas Socrates is charged with a γραφὴ εὐσέβεις (2a–b); on these and the distinction between them, see MacDowell (2), 56–65.

young plaintiffs a knowledge of piety and "things divine."[15] But the parallels between Socrates and Euthyphro's father, and Meletus and Euthyphro, are not the only ones intended here. Euthyphro also makes a number of remarks to the effect that both he *and* Socrates share a common position insofar as they both possess an interest in and understanding of theological matters vastly superior to that of the "many," and that this has had the result of making the Athenians hostile to them both (3b–c). Euthyphro sees Socrates as a kindred spirit not only because of the laughter and envy they have excited within the *polis,* but because Socrates, like himself, is something of a diviner, a *mantis* (μάντις) (3e3):[16] While Euthyphro predicts future events for the benefit of the Assembly, Socrates is himself the privileged recipient of a predictive "divine sign" (the δαιμόνιον/*daimonion*) that warns him away from unbeneficial courses of action (see Chapter 4.1).

With the sketch of these parallels complete, Plato is able to indulge in a teasing, but instructive, punch before letting Socrates loose: Socrates proposes that since Euthyphro has such precise and extensive knowledge of the divine things, and since he, Socrates, has always had an interest in divine things himself and now stands accused of impiety concerning them, he should immediately become Euthyphro's student (5a–c; cf. 15e–16a). This would allow Socrates to turn the tables on Meletus by deflecting Meletus's charge of corrosive religious teaching, directing it instead against his own teacher, Euthyphro: if Socrates corrupts the youth concerning divine things, then it is simply because *his* teacher, Euthyphro, has corrupted *him!* The biting humor here is entirely lost on Euthyphro, however, who blithely imagines that he could very well assume the role of Socrates' instructor as a fellow—but superior—expert on religious topics. Indeed, he boasts, if indicted in the place of Socrates, he would thrash even Meletus himself in forensic combat (5b–c)!

15. Socrates stands accused by a certain Meletus of "making new gods and not recognizing the old ones," and thereby "corrupting the youth" (2c–3b; what these charges amount to, and what they might tell us about Socrates' deviations from traditional Athenian religious conceptions must await Chapter 3). Note also, e.g., Socrates' characterization of himself as but one of the "older ones" Meletus will soon "clean out" of Athens (3a), and Euthyphro's claim that Meletus is "beginning from the hearth" with his prosecution of Socrates (3a).

16. Cf., e.g., *Phd.* 85b4–6. This characterization provides good evidence that this Euthyphro is the same individual referred to in the *Cratylus,* whom Socrates credits with expertise in etymology, divine inspiration, and divine wisdom (396d2–397a1). See Guthrie (3), 4:102 n. 2., and Furley, 201–202.

But, of course, the teasing irony in all this is as inflated as Euthyphro's estimation of himself. It is Euthyphro, not Socrates or Meletus, who will shortly receive a lesson in religious thought and elenctic refutation, although we may relish in our imaginations the spectacle of his hypothetical indictment and trial (while we might simultaneously applaud the substitution). All this is driven home by the unremitting refutations of Euthyphro's pretentious and self-deceived claims to religious knowledge that follow: it is Euthyphro's "prosecution" by Socrates—not Socrates' by Meletus—that the ensuing "elenctic trial" of the *Euthyphro* turns out to be "much more about" (5c2–3).[17] And so one of the messages telegraphed by all this seems quite apparent: it is Socrates—indicted for his philosophical service to Apollo (*Ap.* 20e ff.)—who is truly pious and it is he who possesses the best measure of wisdom currently to be had concerning divine matters. Euthyphro, then, is no coreligionist of Socrates, for he is soon to be revealed as being as ignorantly confused about divine matters as Socrates' prosecutors and other opponents are. I suggest then, that we read this text as it has often been read before: as one of Plato's defenses of Socrates, a companion piece to the *Apology,* which—instead of adumbrating a direct, forensic defense—displays the realities of Socratic piety against the backdrop of Euthyphro's all-too-common hubristic and dangerous illusions. Naturally, those who stand convinced that the dialogue is purely aporetic will be skeptical of this interpretive agenda. I shall address their skepticism as I proceed.

There is another traditional view I also need to begin to undermine: some of those who agree with the apologetic reading of the *Euthyphro* make sense of that interpretation by taking Euthyphro to be a mouthpiece for traditional Athenian religion.[18] This reading, however, is very much mistaken.[19] As we shall see, Plato gives us a number of reasons for supposing that this role is instead played out in the background by Meletus and his fellow Athenians (2b–3e), one reason being the setting—the portico of

---

17. Note also, for example, the subtle undermining of Euthyphro's claims to be an expert *mantis:* at 3b he tells Socrates that he has never been mistaken in a prophecy, and then at 3e, in response to Socrates's flattery that the outcome of his trial is unclear to all "except you diviners," Euthyphro foretells that Socrates's lawsuit will go according to Socrates' wishes, as will his! The *Euthyphro* thus seems to mark the first of Plato's several attacks on fraudulent and/or unjust divination and "magic" (see, e.g., *R.* 364b–c; *Laws* 908c–d, 909b).

18. See, e.g., R. E. Allen (1), 9; Cornford (3), 311; M. Croiset, 179; Grote (2), 322; R. Guardini, 9, 26; Heidell, 165; and Jowett, 3:61.

19. Those who agree to this include Burnet (3), 85–87; W. Furley; Hoerber, 95–98; Hoopes; Klonoski; F. Rosen, 105–109; and A. E. Taylor (1), 147. See also L. Strauss (2).

a most important Athenian religious official.[20] On my view, Euthyphro is a strange sort of Homeric sectarian[21] whose primary literary function is to serve as a religiously hubristic patient for Socrates' therapeutic *elenchos* (but see n. 23). For although Euthyphro clearly endorses traditional Greek religion in many of its respects, unlike any sort of traditionalist he is willing to prosecute his own father (cf. *Nu.* 1303–1453),[22] takes Socrates' side in the accusations against him (including that of "making new gods"), sympathizes with him as a fellow "heretic," finds nothing impious in Socrates' *daimonion* (despite his recognition of its potential threat as involving religious innovation) (3b–c), and is willing to accept—with a quite nontraditional presumption—Socrates' imputation of wisdom to him (4b). Indeed, if one disregards Plato's rhetorical intentions in the direction of *contrasting* Euthyphro with Socrates (*via*, e.g., his self-deceived ignorance, his lack of philosophical ability, his odious suit, and so on), it is striking how many similarities between Socrates and Euthyphro Plato hints at. Hence, it seems that Euthyphro's literary function is twofold: (1) he serves not only as a nontraditionalist patient for the *elenchos*, but also (2) as a dark doppelgänger of Socrates, a lesson in what Socrates is *not*.[23]

20. See Klonoski; H. Newmann, 265; and Rosen, 105–109.

21. Euthyphro fits Theophrastus's category of the "superstitious man," a man who—like Euthyphro with his prosecution—always acts alone (Mikalson [1], 88).

22. It is thus part of the parallel that Plato draws between Socrates and Euthyphro that a prosecution *against* Euthyphro on a γραφὴ κακώσεως γονέων (a suit for ill-usage of parents; see Ar. *Constitution of Athens* 56.6; Xen. *Mem.* 2.2.13; and Klonoski, 129–131) would not be out of the question. Cf. *Laws* 717b–718a, 869a–b, 931a.

23. First (1), and again, although Euthyphro endorses the Homeric tradition (e.g., believing in Zeus, the quarreling Olympians, and sacrifice; fearing the μίασμα resulting from his father's deed), he is willing to prosecute his own father, takes Socrates' side against the Athenians, accepts—as a fellow "diviner" (3b–c)—that the *daimonion* is harmless, grants Socrates' imputation of wisdom to himself (4b), and implicitly appeals at 5e–6a to the Socratic-Sophistic principle that the standard of morality for the gods is the same as for humans (against the tradition of a divine double-standard; cf. *R.* 378b). As for (2), Plato points to a number of similarities between Socrates and Euthyphro: e.g., he has Euthyphro claim that his imagined court discussion would "turn out to be much more about him [Meletus] than about me" (5c2–3), a typically Socratic claim, and just as Euthyphro claims to know with precision an uncommon amount about divine things, so Socrates likewise regards such knowledge as an important matter (5a) to which he also makes a similar claim (though modest in extent; cf. 6b). Socrates, after all, seems to know "with precision" that he has been commanded by the gods to do philosophy (*Ap.* 33c), and both Euthyphro and Socrates regard the divine as a source of conviction on matters of virtuous conduct—one proceeding to prosecute his father on ostensibly religious grounds, the other proceeding to his trial and death for the sake of what he takes to be his religious duty. Moreover, both believe that one should proceed against those who do injustice, even if they are close relatives (4b–c, 5d–e). Although Euthyphro is portrayed as mildly chastising Socrates for seeming to believe otherwise, this is a

Relying on this reading of the *Euthyphro*, I now want to extract from each of the dialogue's argumentative episodes those elements that help to identify the religious views of Socrates.

2.1.2 *Euthyphro* 5c–11d

Euthyphro's first proposed answer to Socrates' request for instruction in "what the pious is" (5c–d) follows a pattern seen in other early dialogues devoted to the pursuit of virtue-definitions (see, e.g., *La.* 190e–191e, 192b; *M.* 71e–77a): After agreeing with Socrates that in every pious action there is but *one* self-same universal characteristic responsible for its piety (5d1–6 [cf. 6d9–11]; or impiety in the case of impious action), Euthyphro announces:

> **P1**   The pious is just what I am doing now: proceeding against whoever does injustice such as murder or theft of sacred things, or does a wrong in any other such matter, whether it happens to be a father or mother or anyone else; and not to so proceed is impious. (5d–e)

Euthyphro even offers a "great proof" (μέγα τεχμήριον [5e2–3]) that this correctly captures the unwritten law (νόμος/*nomos*) of piety: Everyone agrees that Zeus is the best and most just of all the gods, yet that Zeus also imprisoned *his* father, Kronos, for the injustices Kronos committed against his father (Ouranos) and Zeus's siblings.[24] Therefore, he concludes, those who complain that Euthyphro acts unjustly by prosecuting his father contradict themselves, for they cannot hold that Zeus is just for prosecuting

---

Socratic principle (*Eu.* 8d–e; *Cr.* 49b8; *Ap.* 28b; cf. *G.* 480a–d); but see n. 25. Cf., e.g., R. E. Allen (1), 23; Burnet (3), 3, 23, 113; W. Furley, 202–204; Hoerber, 95–107; J. Tate (5), 77–78; and A. E. Taylor (4), 16 n. 1, 149.

24. Hesiod and other later poets tell us that Kronos castrated Ouranos at the urgings of his mother Gaia (earth) in her pursuit of vengeance for Ouranos having hid her newborn children. Kronos's other injustice is that he swallowed his own children at birth because of the prophecy that one of them (Zeus, as it turned out) would overthrow him (*Theogony* 132–182, 453–506, 617–819). Although Kronos's castration of his father is characterized as punishment for evildoing in Hesiod, no such warrant is produced for Zeus's overthrow of his father. That is Euthyphro's addition.

wrongdoers irrespective of familial ties but that Euthyphro is unjust for doing likewise (6a5).[25]

Euthyphro's argument (and his agreement that there is but one sort of piety) confirms that he is no hidebound traditionalist. Only someone with an unorthodox theology would simply presuppose—as Euthyphro does with his "proof"—that there is but one canon of virtue *for both gods and human beings,* since the common view had generally held there to be two standards of behavior, one for humans and another for the gods.[26] That Socrates passes over this clear presupposition in utter silence—together with his introduction of the notion that there is but *one* overarching property of piety—indicates that he too thinks of piety as a universal, unitary, and univocal concept/property.

Socrates' response to Euthyphro's "proof" is, instead, entirely prompted by Euthyphro's conventional assertion that among the gods there exist many disagreements and battles similar to that experienced by Kronos and Zeus (6b5–6, 6c5–7); and to *this,* Socrates's reaction appears to be swift incredulity (6a–c).[27] Indeed, he indicates that whenever anyone has said such things about the gods he has responded with a disbelief so unmistakable that he speculates that public awareness of this disbelief may be what has prompted his indictment on charges of impiety (6a6–c4).[28] I shall have

25. Weiss (4), 264–265, is correct to observe that the leading motive in Euthyphro's action is not a high-minded devotion to impartial justice, but fear of the μίασμα that only a member of the household or a relative can inspire (regardless of whether the slain person is οἰκεῖος or ἀλλότριος [4c1–2]). However, she neglects to take into account 5d–6a—which in two different places (one cited above) emphasizes the idea that *any* wrongdoer, relative or not, ought to be "proceeded against"—and 8b–e, where the same point is made. Hence, and contrary to her claim, Euthyphro *does* advocate prosecuting "just any unjust killer" (265), but places the prudentially based responsibility for doing so on the wrongdoers' relations. Hence, contra Weiss (n. 9), we should also see Euthyphro as appealing to Zeus's impartial justice as evidence of his own impartial justice at 5e–6a; cf. R. E. Allen (1), 23.

26. See, e.g., Guthrie (6), 121–124, and Lloyd-Jones, 176–179. This is true despite the fact that the gods were generally understood to underwrite a code of just conduct for humans; see Thuc. 5.104–105 and Chapter 3.2 herein.

27. Of course, rather than play the dogmatic, Socrates makes his typical confession at 6b2–3 that he *knows* nothing about the myths of conflict; that is, he is unwilling to affirm as *certain* that they are true or false, or how it is that they are true or false.

28. Euripides (or at least many of his characters) is another adamant critic of divine immorality (e.g., *Hera.* 1340–1346). In his *Hippolytus* (433–481) he also points out that the gods might be invoked to excuse or sanction human immorality in the way Euthyphro does by having Phaedra's nurse excuse her illicit passion with a reference to the example of Zeus and Eos, conquered by the power of Aphrodite; cf. Aeschylus *Eum.* 640. Plato makes the same point, in a clear reference to the *Euthyphro* (*R.* 377e–378e; cf. *R.* 391d–392a; *Laws* 886c–d). Note too that even a critic of the new intellectualism like Aristophanes sees this same

more to say about this speculation in Chapter 3.3 on the formal charges against Socrates. Here I simply claim that we can now extract two initial postulates of Socratic religion: by presupposing without restriction in his definitional search that the *definiens* of piety must apply to *every* pious action (5d; and *per* his tacit acceptance of Euthyphro's point concerning the scope of Zeus's justice)—and given his apparent rejection of divine enmity and violence—Socrates is committed to the claims (1) that there is but one universal canon of justice and piety for all beings, gods and humans alike, and (thus) (2a) that the gods are perfectly just and good, and so (2b) they experience no moral disagreements among themselves. Confirmation that Socrates is in fact committed to these propositions—and an examination of what they entail—will be found in later sections.[29] For the moment, the important thing is to recognize their presence in the argumentative arena, since both play important roles in the discussion immediately following this little interlude (6a–c).

Socrates gets his examination of Euthyphro back on track beginning at 6c8 by allowing Euthyphro to entertain the denial of (2b) for the sake of the definitional quest. He then offers as a response to Euthyphro's first attempt at a definition (P1) his typical challenge to definitions of P1's kind (cf., e.g., *M.* 69e–77a). Euthyphro, Socrates asserts, has not taught him "sufficiently" what the pious is on the grounds that his response is formally incorrect. This is so because P1 claims, in essence, that piety just *is* prosecuting the religious wrongdoer, and this sort of answer fails to take into account other clear cases of pious action (6d6–7). Socrates reminds Euthyphro that he was not looking for the citation of merely one or two *instances* of piety (6d9–11) (i.e., either individual action-tokens such as Euthyphro's prosecution, or action-types such as "prosecuting the religious wrongdoer"), but rather, he seeks an account of the *one eidos* (εἶδος) of piety: That unique, self-same universal characteristic by which *all* pious acts are pious, which Euthyphro had earlier agreed was the object of their

---

foists it onto the intellectuals, not the traditionalists (correctly so, since it is they who are responsible for advocating a unitary conception of justice); e.g., in the *Clouds* he has Wrong Argument advocate using the example of Zeus to excuse one's own adulteries (1079–1084; cf. 904).

29. As will become clear, although Socrates and Euthyphro agree that there is but one standard of justice and piety, they employ this principle in converse fashions. Euthyphro uses it to derive moral principles *for humans* by appealing to the traditional tales of the gods, whereas Socrates uses it to justify his placing Socratic, elenctically derived moral principles on (even) the gods.

search (cf. *La.* 191d, *M.* 72c).[30] This *eidos* is a *pattern* (παράδειγμα), and possessing a complete account of it would put its possessor in a position that (together with other factors) would allow him or her to recognize reliably actions that are pious as such and to distinguish them from those that are not. Such an account would furnish one with a completely accurate *measure* for determining the piety or impiety of any action.[31]

Readers familiar with other Socratic dialogues will recognize that with this clarification the search for a Socratic definition of the virtue-concept "piety" has now begun in earnest. What the formal conditions of such definitions are—what precisely they must spell out to be complete—is a somewhat thorny issue.[32] However, Socrates generally seems to be after (ideally) a definition of the form "F is(=) D," where there is a relation of mutual entailment and extensional identity between the definiendum F and definiens D, and where the definiens gives a complete *explanation* of why any individual action or thing x is F, an explanation that will put one in position to recognize any F-instance x as being an F-instance.[33] Such an account would provide Socrates with at least most (if not all) of the knowledge of piety that he has jokingly credited to Euthyphro and which he now seeks instruction in. This elaborate a story of what Socrates is really after would, of course, be news to Euthyphro, but on his next attempt he nonetheless manages to offer Socrates an answer of the requisite *form:*

P2 Piety is(=) what is loved by the gods [προσφιλὲς τοῖς θεοῖς] (and impiety is what they hate). (6e10–7a1)

Socrates expresses pleasure that Euthyphro has answered "just as I was seeking for you to answer" (7a2–4), but we may conclude—given the elenctic refutation of this definition which shortly follows—that what Soc-

---

30. On the structure and problems of the typical initial answers Socrates receives to his "What is F-ness?" questions, see Benson (2), and Nehamas (1).

31. Brickhouse and Smith (8), chap. 2.5, have made a strong case that while for Socrates knowledge of virtue-definitions is *necessary* for the sort of moral wisdom that would allow one to judge correctly *every* instantiation of virtue, many other factors (e.g., the ability to reliably know the particulars of each case) are also necessary.

32. On Socratic definitions and the abstract universals (e.g., piety) they concern, see, e.g., Benson (2), 97–135; R. Kraut (2), 209 n. 38; R. Robinson (3); and G. Santas (1).

33. Socrates gives an example of the sort of thing he has in mind at *Meno* 76a, where a satisfactory answer to the question "What is figure?" is said to be "the limit of a solid." On extensional identity (every F-item names a D-item and vice versa), see Santas (1), 106–115.

rates approves of is its form, not its content.[34] Euthyphro has, at least, grasped more-or-less that a Socratic definition will have its definiendum connected by an "is" of definitional identity to a definiens that purports to be completely general in scope, covering all instances of piety.

The elenctic examination of P2 begins with Socrates' obtaining agreement that piety and impiety are not the same but opposites (ἐναντία), and then reminding Euthyphro that the Olympian gods he recognizes are prone to quarrels and disagreements (7a–b). Socrates next asks after the nature of their disagreements: What exactly do they quarrel about? His roundabout tactic for helping Euthyphro to answer this is to first consider what it is that human beings quarrel about. Disagreements about numerical quantities and the amounts and weights of things are offered as candidates, but these are rejected for a quite suggestive reason: we humans possess decision procedures in each of these cases that allow us to resolve our disputes quickly and easily; namely, calculation, measuring, and weighing (7b–d). So, Socrates leads Euthyphro to agree, they must be topics other than these that bring us into real, unresolvable, long-lasting conflict; and the best candidate seems to be the domain of moral and value judgments. Hence, since such judgments—including those concerning the piety of actions—are the most common source of disagreement among *us*, it is probably the same for Euthyphro's quarreling gods (7d–e).

One implicit part of this argument that escapes Euthyphro's attention, but which Plato must surely intend us to see, is that the key reason *we humans* fall into moral conflict and long-lasting enmity is because of our lack of moral intelligence and conceptual clarity, our failure to have thoroughly reliable, agreed-upon procedures for adjudicating moral disagreement. Hence, one message of the text is that it is not just Socrates with his epistemic modesty who must confess that he lacks knowledge of the *eidos* of piety he seeks from Euthyphro, but all humans—thus, even Euthyphro, despite his pretentious claims and audacious suit. In addition, while Euthyphro's willingness to infer what is acceptable behavior for humans from the behavior of Zeus, and what the gods quarrel about from what mortals quarrel about, again indicates that he shares with Socrates a unitary conception of morality, his agreement with Socrates about the nature of the gods' quarrels threatens the very coherence of his own position.[35] For by

34. Socrates' approval of the form is also indicated by his telling Euthyphro that his answer is "altogether noble" (7a2).

35. Note also Socrates' "unitarian" claim that "no god *or* human being dares to say that the doer of injustice ought not to pay the penalty" (8d11–e1; cf. 8c9–d2).

conceding that moral disagreements stem from a lack of moral knowledge and adequate decision procedures, Euthyphro implicitly affirms that *his* quarreling gods must then not possess an adequate method of adjudicating moral disputes: apparently even *they* lack complete knowledge of the standards (εἰδή) of piety and justice and how to apply them! And if it should turn out that even the gods lack moral knowledge, then again surely Euthyphro must lack it as well (once more undercutting his legal case).[36] Moreover, his own definition P2 must then also fail, since if his gods do not all possess an ability to agree on the piety of things in a reliable fashion, then their loves and hates can provide no guide at all to what the pious and the impious really are.[37]

Socrates, however, does not formally draw this last conclusion here, since as subsequent discussion shows, he sees that Euthyphro may at least escape the implication (above) that the gods *completely* lack agreement on the *eidos* of piety by limiting the scope of the gods' disagreements to the piety of individual actions: we may suppose that they do not disagree on whether wrongdoers should "pay the penalty" or on what piety *is,* but only on whether certain actions are or are not pious (8b–e; still, though, this means that Euthyphro's gods lack complete knowledge and practical wisdom). Moreover, at this juncture Socrates is in a position to make a much simpler *elenchos* concerning P2. He points out that Euthyphro's commitment to P2, to gods that can disagree and quarrel, and to the proposition that the pious is not the same as the impious, are mutually inconsistent. If P2 were true, then since some act could be found to be just by one set of gods (and thus loved) but unjust by another set (and so hated), the same act would be both pious and impious, something that had been implicitly ruled out earlier on with their agreement that piety is one unique characteristic (with impiety its opposite) (5d, 7a). In any case, Socrates notes, while on his own account Euthyphro's prosecution may be an act loved by Zeus or Hephaestus, that same thing might also be hated by Hera and other gods, in which event he cannot easily claim divine sanction for his actions. Hence, this prosecution of his, according to his own conception of piety (P2), may well be just as impious as it is pious (7d–8b).[38]

---

36. Socrates thus (again) nicely turns the tables on Euthyphro: Euthyphro begins by arguing from the justice of Zeus to that of his own actions, and Socrates then uses the unitary conception of justice this relies on to argue from the human sphere (what we disagree about) back to the divine to make Euthyphro's Zeus useless as a moral standard.

37. Cf. Weiss (2), 441, and (4), 263–264.

38. Such conflicts are a persistent theme of Greek popular religion and, thus, an inextrica-

But at this point (8b), as we saw above, Euthyphro is able to counter with the suggestion that the gods are at least all in agreement that unjust killers must pay the penalty for their injustice. However, it quickly becomes clear that Euthyphro is somewhat confused in this response. What he needs in the context of Socrates' last objection—where attention has been focused on the individual case of Euthyphro's father—is to somehow show that the gods do not differ concerning *his* case at least. Instead, Euthyphro is shown that while humans and gods may be unanimous in holding the general view that wrongdoers ought to pay the penalty for their crimes, Euthyphro's gods—given their past history of disagreement—may still differ (as do humans) on the facts of a particular case; especially on whether an individual act was just or not. So once more, Socrates challenges Euthyphro to show that according to P2 his particular prosecution is pious by showing that *all* the gods love and approve of it (9a–b).

Euthyphro's response is sheer bluff: demonstrating that all the gods love his proposed legal suit is "no small work" (9b4–5), he claims, but nonetheless it is a task well within his power. But rather than press Euthyphro into further embarrassments on this issue, Socrates pursues the more philosophical course by noting that even if Euthyphro *could* somehow (miraculously) reveal the unanimous endorsement of his plans by the gods, he still would not have replied to the challenge of defining piety (or—the implication seems to be—to the challenge of showing the piety of his suit). For again, the agreement of the gods could be entirely contingent, perhaps even unrelated to the facts or "actual piety" of the case. It still remains possible with P2 (and Euthyphro's still-unreformed, still-quarreling gods) that other acts could be loved by some and hated by others, and so both pious and impious, something Socrates has already shown to be at variance with Euthyphro's commitments (9c2–8).[39] At this juncture Socrates could also point out that Euthyphro's previous concessions saddle him with gods who, since they can disagree on the justice of particular cases, cannot be fully wise and knowledgeable, something quite at odds with that aspect of the traditional view that held otherwise (e.g., Homer *Od.* 4.379,

---

ble feature of Euthyphro's quasi-fundamentalist "theology"; father-punishing, for example, might well be dear to Hephaestus, since Zeus once cast him down from heaven (*Il.* 1.586–594), and hateful to Hera since it would threaten her husband. This passage also contains an allusion to the battle between Hera and Hephaestus; cf. *R.* 378d.

39. As Weiss (2), 440–447, and (4), 263–264, notes, Socrates' characterization of Euthyphro's gods as always prone to disagreement about *some* things (at both 9c2–8 and 9d1–5) predicts in advance the failure of Euthyphro's upcoming attempt to define piety by reference to what *all* the gods love.

20.75–76; Hesiod *Erga* 267, *Thg.* 886–900).[40] Moreover, they cannot be thought to love or hate wisely, and so their loves and hates cannot be useful in determining what is really pious. Nevertheless, Socrates is willing to rephrase Euthyphro's attempted definition in light of the previous difficulties (9c), by universalizing on Euthyphro's view that all the gods love his prosecution. Euthyphro is thus now willing to posit:

P3 Piety is(=) what *all* the gods love (and impiety is what they all hate). (9e1–3)[41]

Socrates prepares Euthyphro for an investigation of this third attempt by asking whether or not they ought to be content with mere assertion, or instead, should demand a careful scrutiny of such claims (9e). Euthyphro is still confident of his knowledge and so affirms (and thus invites) the latter. Socrates then asks his famous question of Euthyphro's P3:

Q Is (a) the pious loved by [all] the gods because it is pious or (b) is it pious because it is loved [by all the gods]? (10a2–3)

The complexities implicit in Q and the elenctic refutation of P3 it fuels (10a–11b) have attracted the attention of many scholars, and justly so. Among other things, the profoundly insightful argument that follows (leading to P3's rejection) is the ancestor of most criticisms of "Divine Command Theories" of morality.[42] Here, however, I do not require that we pursue the intricacies of that argument. I rely instead on a summary interpretation of Socrates' argumentative strategy and presuppositions.[43]

40. And note that this is at odds with Euthyphro's later rejection of piety involving service (θεραπεία) to the gods on the grounds that the gods have no need of improvement (13c). Discussion of the tradition that the gods (or at least Zeus) are wise follows in Chapter 3.2.

41. And, as Socrates stipulates, any acts loved by some gods but hated by others will be considered either both pious and impious or neither (9d).

42. See, e.g., the example provided by J. Rachels, 49–50.

43. For a classic treatment of this argument, see S. M. Cohen; the following account is also influenced by Irwin (1), 75–78. Here is a bare-bones version of the argument: Euthyphro agrees that (1a) the pious is loved by the gods because it is pious and that (1b) it's not that the pious is pious because it is loved by the gods (b). He also agrees that—as with the examples of seer and seen thing, carrier and carried thing, lover and loved thing—(2) a god-loved thing is god-loved because the gods love it, and (3) it's not that the gods love a god-loved thing because it is god-loved. But if P3 were true (viz., that the pious = the god-loved), then by substitution from P3 into (1a), it would be true that (4) the god-loved is loved by the gods because it is god-loved, and by substitution from P3 into (2) it would be true that (5) a

In response to Euthyphro's request for some clarification of Q's alternatives, Socrates provides a series of examples ("being seen" versus "seeing," "being loved" versus "loving") that display the agent-dependent nature of passive properties, with the analogy to the "god-loved" clearly implying that this too is an agent-dependent passive property; that is, something only comes to possess the property "god-loved" by being loved by some god(s). Once Euthyphro recognizes this, he is able to see that proper explanations of the possession of such properties must make reference to the agent-cause of the property in question and thus, ultimately, what initial property it is in the object of the agent's attentions that elicits the agent-response (10c); for example, it is because something loves x that x has the property of being loved, while it is not the case that x is loved by something because it has the property of being loved, but because x is perceived to possess some other (lovable) property y. Given this account, Euthyphro readily agrees that choice (a) in Q is the correct response: Any and all acts x loved by all the gods are loved by them because they are pious; hence, it is their piety that is the initial explanatory property for their being loved (10c–d).

With this choice, however, Socrates moves quickly to show that P3 must be rejected, essentially on the grounds that it is inconsistent with Euthyphro's agreement with alternative (a). If P3 *were* true, then (b) ("the pious is pious by being loved") would have been the correct answer to Socrates' question Q, since (b) spells out precisely what is implied by P3 (insofar as *that* attempt represents a stab at Socratic definition); namely, that "loved by the gods" is the *explanatory property* for anything's being pious. But Euthyphro has rejected (b), and rightly adopts (a). Choice (b) must be rejected, since it asserts that being loved is the explanatory property for something's being pious, and that would be analogous to asserting that the explanation for something's being seen is that it is a seen thing, which explains nothing.[44] So likewise, the agent-dependent passive property "loved-by-gods" cannot explain x's being pious: Whatever sort of prop-

---

pious thing is pious because the gods love it. However, (4) contradicts (3), and (5) contradicts (1b). Thus, (1a), (1b), (2), and (3) cannot be jointly affirmed while also affirming P3 (resulting in P3's rejection).

44. For those needing more graphic and congenial analogues, note that as attempted definitions of "polemical argument" or "beer," the phrase "loved by McPherran" tells us nothing very useful about what polemical argument or beer *are*. To attempt to use either of these—or "loved by the gods" in the case of piety—as practical definiens for identifying instances of their definiendums would involve trying to follow either McPherran or the gods around in hopes of identifying their loves.

erty the piety of a pious action may turn out to be upon further inspection, a Socratic definition of it must *explain* why the gods' reaction to it is one of love, what it is about it that evokes that response. Option (a), then, is the right choice, since to explain why anything evokes the response of love by a lover *p* to some *x* thereby giving *x* the property "loved-by-*p*," we need to appeal to some explanatory property *y* that inheres in *x*, the property to which the lover responds.[45] In this case, what evokes the response of love on the part of the gods, Euthyphro holds, is always and only whatever unitary quality it is that makes pious action pious; and if so, then P3 is not an acceptable Socratic definition since it fails to *explain* the response of the gods, but instead, only notes it.

Socrates clarifies this last point by indicating that Euthyphro had failed to distinguish P3—which claims that the essential nature and explanatory property of piety is its being loved by the gods—from

P3'   All and only pious things are loved by all the gods. (11a–b)

Assuming the truth of P3', it is true that "piety is what all the gods love," but only so long as we recognize that the copula "is" here is that of predication and not that of definitional "essence-stating." "Loved by all the gods" is not what piety *is*(=) in its nature (οὐσία [11a7]), although it may be agreed that "loved by the gods" is an ever-present property of pious action (a πάθος of it [11a8]).[46] In our search for Socrates' religious commitments, then, can we credit him with P3'? I think so, since to begin with, Socrates never challenges Euthyphro's implicit commitment to P3', and moreover, he leaves the claim in place throughout the dialogue (see n. 54). Second, Socrates says that "whether it [the pious] is loved by the gods or however it is affected—for *we won't differ about this*" (11b3–4). Finally, P3' is supported by the numerous passages in Xenophon where Socrates emphasizes the appropriateness of honoring and *pleasing* the gods (e.g., *Mem.* 4.3.17). Thus, given this apparent agreement with Euthyphro, we may ascribe P3' to Socrates.[47] Further support for this follows, and

45. Euthyphro must accept the presupposition at work here that piety is an objective feature of acts, given his earlier concession that there is but one quality in every pious action that explains its being pious (5d).

46. On these distinctions (and the philosophical progress they mark), see, e.g., Allen (1), 40 ff.

47. As does Friedländer, 2:87. Weiss (4), n. 12, disagrees, seeing in Socrates' command to "say what the pious is, whether it is loved by gods, *or however it is affected*—for we won't differ about this" (11b2–3), a lack of commitment on Socrates' part to piety's having "loved

later I shall show precisely how much Socratic theology may be gleaned from P3', but for the moment we can see that it allows us to credit Socrates with a belief in the existence of gods, gods who also retain at least some of the characteristics assigned to them by tradition. Given P3', for example, the gods of Socrates will have attitudes that take into account the activities of mortals. This is to be expected, but also receives support from Socrates' earlier assurance to Euthyphro that the gods *listen* to us (9c1).

Nonetheless, there is an implication to be noted here that is quite non-traditional: the naively voluntaristic view that piety is defined by reference to the love of the gods has been rejected in favor of the view that piety is loved by the gods because it *is* pious; hence, that the pious is constituted by a *god-independent property* that evokes the gods' love in response to it. This view subtly undermines the authority of the gods as divine legislators and thus, potentially, the conventions (νόμοι/*nomoi*) underwritten by that authority. For under the traditional conception of the gods as modeled after the aristocratic rulers of Homer's world, justice and piety *are* in a sense defined simply by reference to whatever these rulers command out of their own selfish motives, or even in an arbitrary and irrational fashion.[48] What trips Euthyphro up in his defense of P3 is his desire to retain both this traditional conception of the gods as capricious, disagreeing rulers and his thought that they might also behave in a uniform, rational, and standard-setting fashion (e.g., that Zeus displays a standard of justice we should adopt and imitate [5e–6a] and that the gods might all of them have a rational love for the same thing). But then once Euthyphro insists on this latter idea and is thereby forced to concede that the piety of an action is thus ultimately justified by reference to god-independent standards of virtue, the authority of the gods and their commandments must be acknowledged as derivative: one obeys the commands of the gods not because they come from more powerful beings that one ought to fear and placate, but rather, because as wholly good and virtuous beings the gods—more so than any human—must themselves behave (and thus speak) in a fashion consonant with the universal dictates of virtue (cf. *Ap.* 28b, 28d). But as we shall see later on, these dictates are only (for the most part) revealed

by the gods" as a πάθος. This apparent *possible* lack of commitment here, however, seems only that in light of Socrates' earlier agreement with Euthyphro that "*we* agree that the pious is loved [by the gods]" (10e2–3). Weiss also concedes (n. 13) that "perfectly rational and moral gods would love the holy." She is right to observe, though, that Euthyphro's agreement to P3' is at odds with his own imperfect gods, who might well be imagined to love some non-pious things or hate some pious things.

48. See Guthrie (6), 124–125, and Chapter 3.2 herein.

and grounded for human beings through philosophical investigation; even traditional, pragmatically sound *nomoi* must, for Socrates, be able to pass the test of the Socratic *elenchos*. Thus, for Socrates, reason—not revelation or appeals to authority—forms the bedrock of the virtuous life (see Chapter 4.1). This, together with Socrates' rejection of divine enmity, constitutes a direct challenge to the moral authority of Athenian culture, and as we shall see, poses a profound threat to many of the motivations underlying the popular practice of religion.[49]

With the abandonment of Euthyphro's third attempt at definition, we reach the "aporetic interlude" (11b–e): Euthyphro is frustrated by his previous definitional failures and is momentarily unwilling to provide Socrates with any further grist for his elenctic mill. He likens Socrates to Daedalus—sculptor of moving statues—for he seems able to make the speeches of others "move about" (i.e., Euthyphro is constantly giving up one proposition for another; cf. *La.* 187e). Socrates concedes that "as is likely" (11d5), he is able to do this, but he does so with regret, for he desires more than anything to find those claims that will "stand still," claims, that is, that will resist every hammer-blow of the *elenchos* because they are rooted in the truth. To that end, Socrates now offers to take an "eager part" in aiding Euthyphro to teach him about the nature of piety (11e).

2.2 Socrates' Piety: *Euthyphro* 11e–16a

Following the aporetic interlude, Socrates offers renewed and substantial assistance to Euthyphro in his search for a definition of piety (11e3–5). Socrates begins by raising the question of whether justice (δικαιοσύνη) and piety (εὐσέβεια) are coextensive concepts (such that all and only just acts are pious acts) or whether justice is a broader concept than piety such that piety is then a "part" of justice (where pious acts are a subset of just acts [11e4–12d5]). Subsequent to his careful explanation to Euthyphro of these alternatives, Socrates secures Euthyphro's free assent to the second proposition that piety is a part of justice. Socrates' explanation of these alternatives, and his illustrative use of the relation of odd-numberedness to

49. Cf. S. M. Cohen, 175; Nehamas (2), 302–304; Nussbaum (2), 235; Reeve, 66; and Vlastos (14), chap. 6.

number (12c6–8), make it fairly clear as well that both he and Euthyphro accept that as a consequence there may exist just acts that are neither pious nor impious.[50]

2.2.1 Pious Justice

With this established, the search then begins for the characteristic that differentiates pious justice from the secular remainder. Although Euthyphro's claim that piety is the part of justice having to do with our service to the gods (θεραπεία θεῶν [12e5–8]) is shortly defeated (12e1–13d4), it seems evident that the proposition primarily (or only) fails on Socrates' view because of the problems ("one little point" [13a1]) he raises for Euthyphro's use and interpretation of the term θεραπεία (*therapeia*). Socrates says, for instance, that if Euthyphro identifies for him the part of justice that piety is, he will then be able to understand adequately (ἱκανῶς) what piety is (12e3–4),[51] and after having made this attempt, he *congratulates* Euthyphro for having "spoken well" (καλῶς φαίνῃ λέγειν [12e9]).[52] This much, then, seems a Socratically acceptable (though not completely definitional) claim about piety:

> **P4** Piety is that part of justice having to do with the relation of humans to the gods. (12e5–8)

There are many additional reasons for attributing a belief in P4 to Socrates. It is Socrates himself who introduces the view that piety is a part of justice, and claims to do so as an *aid* to the definitional search (11e3). It is also significant that P4 retains the Socratically acceptable form of P2, that it is explicitly nonvoluntaristic and so in line with the previous rejection of P3, that Socrates keeps the form of P4's answer constantly before Euthyphro for the remainder of the dialogue,[53] and that it remains unrefuted

---

50. Cf. Vlastos (9), 231 n. 25, 435–436, who accepts this interpretation.

51. Vlastos (9), 228 n. 17; Rabinowitz, 114.

52. See the Vlastos-Irwin dispute over whether this is to be read as an endorsement of Euthyphro's attempt (Vlastos [9], 224–228; Irwin [4], 301 n. 57).

53. Noted by Rabinowitz, 115. Observe also that P4 retains P1's connection of piety with justice, a connection possessing popular, endoxic warrant.

throughout the dialogue (see esp. 15d6–8).[54] Socrates might wish to mislead Sophists at such length, but not, one would think, such a confused soul as Euthyphro. This would seem to be especially true where there exists a real possibility of some harm ensuing (viz., to Euthyphro's father) if Euthyphro comes to perceive himself to be a victim of mere eristics. In any case, it would be odd to view this section of the dialogue as an attempt to reduce Euthyphro to a state of *aporia,* since Euthyphro has already confessed his confusion in the aporetic interlude.[55] Socrates does not generally pursue trickery for simple enjoyment, and it is hard to see how an insincere Socratic commitment to P4 throughout the dialogue would be of any pedagogic value. Finally, it is of some further significance that P4 *follows* the aporetic interlude. A familiar feature of Plato's dramatic style is for positive doctrine to be suggested following such breaks in the discussion (e.g., *Protagoras, Phaedo, Phaedrus, Theaetetus*).[56] With all this, then, we have compelling internal evidence that Socrates holds P4 to be true.[57]

Scott Calef has objected, however, that although "piety is a part of justice" may be introduced by Socrates as a definitional aid, Euthyphro is *also* offered as an equally acceptable choice the alternative that "all that is just is pious" (11e7).[58] On this account, Socrates is really offering Euthyphro two possible choices: (1) "all that is just is pious" (although this is compatible with justice being a part of piety or justice and piety being coextensive) or (2) piety being a part of justice, with (1) marking "a good first step" toward the Socratic view that piety is identical to justice.[59] I find this reading implausible simply because Euthyphro's immediate agreement with Socrates' "eager" suggestion that "all the pious is just" (11e4–6) rules out his accepting the view that justice is a part of piety. Hence, (1) is not itself being held out as a live alternative. Rather, Socrates' question

54. I do not, however, think that *every* unrefuted claim in a Platonic dialogue represents positive doctrine. Hence, by making this point I am not endorsing the mistaken (I believe) "Bonitz principle" that whatever remains unrefuted in Platonic text represents positive doctrine (Bonitz, 233–234; cf. J. Adam [1], xxi, and Heidel, 171). For criticisms of this principle, see Allen (1), 6, and Versenyi (1), 111 n. 3.

55. Brickhouse and Smith (6), 661.

56. As noted by Rabinowitz, 114. This and several of the points made above are at least obstacles to Allen's claim (1), 5, that no substantive issue in the interpretation of the *Euthyphro* turns on its dramatic structure. C.C.W. Taylor, 112, observes that other dialogues contain clear hints of conclusions not explicitly drawn (e.g., *Ch.* 174d–175a). On the connections of the *Euthyphro* with the *Theaetetus,* see Allen (1), 7.

57. Cf. Santas (1), 97–135.

58. See S. Calef (2), my reply (13), and his riposte (1).

59. Calef (2), 8.

"And is all the just pious?" (11e7) can only intend coextensiveness. It is because his and Euthyphro's agreement with "all the pious is just," is compatible with either the view that in addition "all the just is pious" (where piety and justice are coextensive), or with the view that piety is but a part of justice, then, that Socrates asks whether "all the just is pious" (contrasting this with the view that "the pious is all just, while the just is not all pious but part is pious, part something else" [11e7–12a2]). Now, then, given that this is the choice at issue—between coextensiveness and (2) piety-as-part-of-justice—it seems clear that in the clarification passage that follows (12a–d) Socrates is encouraging Euthyphro to adopt the piety-as-part-of-justice thesis.[60]

Calef maintains that in the clarification passage Socrates is trying to "clear up Euthyphro's confusion so that he can answer the question put" (n. 26), but since the "question put" is whether piety is coextensive with justice or but a part of it, if Socrates is being perfectly impartial on the issue we should find the sorts of clarifying analogies Socrates gives to be offered impartially as well. However, what we find is Socrates emphasizing the part-of-justice relation: awe as part of dread, odd as part of number, where Socrates asserts it incorrect to hold that where dread is there too is awe or where number is there too is oddness (thereby discounting both the coextensiveness option and the already rejected idea of justice being a part of piety). Next, when Socrates goes on to refer back to his initial presentation of choices (12c10–d3), there is one mention of the previously seen (11e7) coextensive analysis ("where 'just' is there too is 'pious'"), but he concludes with two mentions of piety as a part of justice, followed by "shall we say so, or does it seem otherwise to you?" It is best, then, to understand Socrates' presentation as rhetorically designed to lead Euthyphro to agree with his final suggestion that piety is a part of justice (12d4).

I think it especially telling that Euthyphro's agreement to the part-of-justice thesis is followed by his claim that "you appear to me to speak correctly" (12d4), a reference to the mutual agreement to piety's being part of justice Socrates has just suggested. This means, I think, that Euthyphro clearly perceives Socrates as having been arguing *via* his examples for the part-of-justice view because he regards that view as Socrates' view. We would also expect Socrates to challenge Euthyphro's interpretation of his "shall we say so?" question as a rhetorical endorsement of the part-of-

60. Accepted by Weiss (4), 267.

justice view, were Socrates really interested in keeping to the sort of elenctic neutrality the above counterinterpretation requires.

Finally, the attribution of P4 to Socrates has additional support external to the *Euthyphro*. Both P4 and 12e5–8 show that while piety is a form of justice concerned with the relation of humans to the gods, there is another distinct part of justice concerned with the relation of humans to other humans. This division of justice into two kinds of just relations by reference to two different sets of relata is also suggested by *Apology* 32d3 ("no unjust *or* impious deed"), *Crito* 54b–c, *Laches* 199d–e, and especially *Gorgias* 507a–b, where Socrates asserts that a person doing what is appropriate toward other *people* acts justly and doing what is appropriate toward the *gods* acts piously.[61] Furthermore, Socrates' division of the virtue wisdom into two sorts, human and divine, suggests that he would also divide another virtue such as justice into two parts on the basis of their respective domains of concern: human-to-human versus human-to-god (cf. *Ap.* 20e, 23a–b). Finally, Xenophon (*Mem.* 4.6.2–5) represents Socrates as analyzing legal conduct into two subclasses, where pious persons are defined therein as those who know what is lawful towards the gods (in contrast to what is lawful toward humans).[62] This again supports the view that Socrates would have found it natural to divide justice into two subclasses, human secular justice and divine justice (piety). Whether to trust Xenophon on this is a live issue, but considering the other evidence presented it would be odd if it did not have credibility, especially given the widespread, if unclear, traditional connection between being just and being pious.[63]

---

61. As C.C.W. Taylor, 110, notes: "Ordinary Greek idiom would naturally appropriate the term *dikaiosunê* as the name for the virtue of social relations with human agents, and it is in accordance with that usage that the good man is described at G. 507b as one who would do right by men. . . . It is unnecessary to suppose any difference of doctrine between that passage and the *Euthyphro*."

62. Pious acts, on this view, would be those we ought to perform, doing so in accordance with the laws governing the relations of men and gods.

63. See Dover (3), 247–248; A.W.H. Adkins (4), 133; and J. Mikalson (2), 178–179. Dover notes that "the formal conjunction of *hosios* with *dikaios* was sometimes augmented by reference to 'both gods and men,' as if recognizing a distinction between divine law and man-made law" (247–248), and Mikalson claims that "the evidence from tragedy seems to confirm Socrates's proposition, and nothing in the popular sources contradicts it" (178–179). Irwin (4), 22, points out that piety had a well-established association with justice for Hesiod, Solon, and Aeschylus, among others; cf. C.C.W. Taylor, 110.

I should note that despite the strength of the case for P4, there is one serious objection to it.

2.2.2 Piety: Therapy or Service?

Statement P4, as we saw, was derived from Euthyphro's first attempt (12e5–8) to specify the nature of the relationship between humans and gods that would constitute just relations. That first attempt can be represented as:

> **P5**   Piety is that part of justice that is our tendance (θεραπεία) of the gods.

Socrates attempts to clarify the term θεραπεία[64] by means of a craft analogy that compares those who would tend the gods to those who tend horses, dogs, and herds (13a–d). Θεραπεία, it is shown, can imply a kind of expert craft knowledge whose practice aims at the substantive improvement of that which is tended. This in turn implies that the subject to which tendance is given lacks both self-sufficiency and excellence, and that the agent is superior to that subject in some aspect of power or knowledge. These implications, however, are incompatible with Euthyphro's conception of the relative powers of gods and humans, which, in accord with popular belief, represents the gods as vastly superior to humans in respect of knowledge, power, self-sufficiency, and enjoyment. It is on these

---

P4 differentiates pious justice from non-pious justice, and yet at *Pr.* 331a6–b8 we find Socrates claiming that "justice is pious" (seemingly meaning that there is no non-pious justice). Much is made of this difficulty by those who subscribe to T. Penner's view, 35–68, that the unity of the virtues is a thesis asserting their identity: e.g., Calef (2); Irwin (4), 22; and C.C.W. Taylor, 116–118. In defense of that view, they reject any constructivistic interpretations of the text that employ the substance of P4 (Taylor, however, tries to retain a sense of P4 by maintaining that piety is virtue "under a certain aspect"). Vlastos (9), 224–228, on the other hand, utilizes the evidence of the Socratic commitment to P4 as partial grounds for the rejection of Penner's interpretation. An adequate discussion of this dispute goes far beyond the practical limits of this work. Nonetheless, the weight of the evidence for P4 we have seen, together with the observation that the dialogue seems primarily interested in the piety of *acts* (noted by I. M. Crombie, 1:211, also n. 34) leads me to endorse the Vlastos solution to this apparent incompatibility. In brief, this solution allows us to analyze *Pr.* 331a6–8 as asserting that someone is a just *person* if and only if he/she is a pious person—and likewise for the other virtues (Vlastos [15], 418–423; cf. [10] and [21]). On the other hand, P4 should only be taken to claim that while all pious *acts* are just, a just act (of any sort of person) need not also be a pious one (e.g., repaying a small loan; see Vlastos [15], 421 n. 5, [16], and [18] on the concept of virtue's "parts"; cf. Brickhouse and Smith [8], chap. 2.5.5–6; P. Woodruff [4], 101–116; and M. Ferejohn).

64. Which can simply mean the correct treatment of any class of beings; see Burnet (3), 135, and Versenyi (1), 100.

grounds that Euthyphro rejects P5.[65] In addition, Socrates gives some indication (13c–d) that he too would find P5 objectionable for the same reasons.[66] Later in this study we shall see additional evidence that Socrates does in fact agree with this much of popular theology concerning the gods' powers.

By the replacement of the objectionable term θεραπεία (a "little" matter, says Socrates at 13a1–2) with ὑπηρετική—a term that does not imply the possession of a craft knowledge that improves a subject—Euthyphro produces (13d3–8) a candidate for a definition of piety much more consonant with (I shall argue) both traditional and Socratic belief:

> P5′   Piety is that part of justice that is a service (ὑπηρετική: along the lines of servants to masters or assistants to craftsmen) of humans to the gods.

Both Socrates and Euthyphro are portrayed in the craft-analogy sequence that follows (13d–e) as reasoning by analogy (naturally enough) from the fact that many human ὑπηρεσίαι in the assistance of some work (ἔργον/ergon) produce some end result, to the implicit conclusion that all human services aim at helping those they serve to achieve the result that defines the professional activity of those helped; e.g., a servant's service to a shipbuilder is the service that aids his master in building a ship. With this general principle before him, Euthyphro is then asked to specify precisely the nature of that "most beautiful work" (πάγκαλον ἔργον) in which the *gods* utilize our assistance (13e–14a). But Euthyphro tenaciously avoids answering this question (which, significantly, is asked three times)[67] and instead declares:

> I told you a little while ago, Socrates, that to learn precisely how all these matters stand is a rather lengthy work. I will, however, simply tell you that if someone has knowledge of how to say and do things pleasing to the gods by praying and sacrificing, these are the pious things. And such things preserve private families as well as the com-

65. Which again illustrates his confusion, given his earlier implicit concession that his gods are no better than humans at settling their moral conflicts.

66. Socrates does not press P5 upon Euthyphro and would have found it "surprising" for Euthyphro to maintain it. Note also that in Xenophon (*Mem.* 1.4.10) Socrates holds that it is the gods that give θεραπεία to humans, not vice versa.

67. As Rabinowitz, 115, has noted, the fact that Socrates is pressing Euthyphro to produce the gods' *ergon* constitutes evidence of Socrates' commitment to something like P6 (following).

mon interests of cities. The opposites of the things pleasing to the gods are impious, and they upset and destroy everything. (14a11–b7)

Socrates responds clearly and emphatically that with this reply Euthyphro has now "turned aside" at the very moment he was *close* to giving a *briefer* answer (than he did), one that would have given Socrates all the information he needed about piety (14b8–c6). Many scholars have found this powerful evidence for ascribing to Socrates a belief in something like the following:

P6   Piety is that part of justice that is a service [ὑπηρετική] of humans to gods, assisting the gods in their work [ἔργον], a work that produces some good results.

To this we should add the claim that Socrates also believes that pious acts are loved by (and please) the gods. For as we saw, the claim P3' was left in place at 9e and was apparently accepted to capture a *pathos* of piety at 11a, and is thereafter left unrefuted.[68] Notice too that at 9e4–7 Socrates seems to hint that a statement allowed to pass through the discussion unchallenged would be one accepted by both of them. Finally, it is Socrates who implies (11a6–b1) that Euthyphro *has* (in fact) identified an attribute of piety.[69] The anticonstructivists wishing to deny this and P6 to Socrates are thus left with the task of reconciling the Socrates who insists that people state what they truly believe with the deceptive Socrates their anticonstructivism would at this point force on them.[70] Moreover, there are several other considerations that support our attributing P6 to Socrates.

2.2.3 Additional Evidence

To begin, all the evidence in support of P4 serves as support for P6, whose form it preserves and from which it derives. Like P4, for example, P6 is left unrefuted at the end of the dialogue (see nn. 54, 68). As distinct from P4,

68. Again, no endorsement of the Bonitz principle is intended; see n. 54.
69. Cf. *R.* 612e, where Plato (at least) maintains that justice is dear to the gods, while injustice is hateful to them.
70. The "say what you believe" dictum is a familiar feature of Socratic *elenchos*; see, e.g., *Eu.* 9d; *Cr.* 49c–d; *Pr.* 331c–d; *G.* 500b–c; Brickhouse and Smith (8), chap. 1.2.3, and (6); Irwin (6); and Vlastos (16).

and constitutive of P6's improvement over P4, P6 makes use of the concept of a service assisting a work that produces something good. Such a motif is a typical methodological model of Socrates, characteristic of his teleological outlook and use of craft analogies.[71] Socrates later emphasizes that this question of service to the gods is of the greatest importance to him (14d4–7)[72] and, significantly, urges Euthyphro to specify the nature of our service to the gods no fewer than six times between 13e6 and the end of the dialogue.[73] Plato also credits Socrates with conceiving of our relation to the gods as being a kind of master-slave relation (*Ion* 53e; cf. *Phd.* 62d–63d, *Parm.* 134d–e) as does Xenophon (*Mem.* 1.4.9–12). This represents, as well, what the Greeks usually had in mind when discussing a θεραπεία θεῶν.[74] Nonetheless, this evidence remains at best suggestive until we see its confirmation by the touchstone of the *Apology*.[75]

A few of the many connections between the *Euthyphro* and the *Apology* have been previously noted (n. 2) and more observations of that sort will follow. Here I want to simply point out that the dramatic settings and internal remarks of both combine to present a historically continuous characterization of Socrates. The *Apology* emphatically portrays in careful detail a Socrates who both conforms in many ways to traditional religious practice and belief and conceives of himself as obligated to pursue his philosophical mission because of various divine commandments (*Ap.* 30a). This mission is thus a service to the god(s) (τὴν ἐμὴν τῷ θεῷ ὑπηρεσίαν [*Ap.* 30a6–7; cf. 23b–c]) producing good results (*Ap.* 30a5–7), such as the improvement of those who are persuaded by Socrates to care for their souls and do what is right (*Ap.* 30a–b, 36c–d; *Cr.* 47d–48d; cf. *Eu.* 14e11–15a2).[76] Finally, it is clear that Socrates/Plato (and Xenophon

---

71. Brickhouse and Smith (6), 660–661; see also Guthrie (6), 136–139.

72. Rabinowitz, 115. Although this remark as a whole has some flavor of irony to it, that is explicable on the grounds that by this point in the dialogue it is quite reasonable to portray Socrates as becoming bored with Euthyphro's avoidance of the question of the gods' *ergon*. Socrates, giving up hope of eliciting a useful answer from Euthyphro, is perhaps playfully needling him on his pretensions to divine knowledge.

73. *Eu.* 13e6, 13e10–11, 14a9–10, 14d6, 14e9–15a4, 15a7–8.

74. *Od.* 11.225; *Erga* 136 (as noted by Versenyi [1], 102).

75. On the status of the *Apology* as a "touchstone," see Chap. 1, nn. 4 and 34, and, e.g., Burnet (3), 143–46, and Brickhouse and Smith (12), chap. 1.1–2.

76. In the *Apology* Socrates often refers to his service to the god as a λατρεία, but like ὑπηρετική, this term connotes the work of, among other things, a servant for a master (λατρεία especially connotes the work of a prophetess or temple employee for its god; see Burkert [2], 273). Note also that although the term κελεύω at *Ap.* 30a5, commonly translated as "command," does have several other possible translations, it is this sense of the term

in his *Apology*) emphasize the religious dimension of Socrates' philosophical mission to the Athenians in order to emphasize the piety of that mission (as a rebuttal to the charges of impiety). It would, thus, be hard to produce stronger evidence that Socrates in fact believes P6 to be true. Nonetheless, as Socrates himself sees, by failing to identify the work and produce of the gods, P6 is not yet definitional of piety and is left incomplete by the conclusion of the discussion.

There have been numerous interpretations attempting to make good P6's deficiencies by characterizing the work and produce of the gods, thereby allowing an inference to the nature of our service to them (see n. 4). Unfortunately, these attempts either impute Platonic doctrine to Socrates, or ignore Socrates' ambivalence concerning the precise work and nature of the gods, or discount the claim that piety is but a *part* of the justice mentioned in P4 and P6 (or some combination of these). In the next section I will suggest and defend a hypothetical completion of P6 that I think Socrates endorsed.

Returning to the text, it remains to discuss Euthyphro's "wrong-turning," which introduces the conception of piety as a kind of knowledge or craft of proper giving to (which is again a kind of service; ὑπηρεσία) and requesting from the gods (a kind of ἐμπορία [14b2–7, 14c4–15b5]). This section I think we should see as primarily a transition to a somewhat different matter which Socrates is forced to follow—as he suggests (14c3–4) —by the rules of elenctic discourse,[77] but whose course he shapes in pursuit of the unresolved issue of P6; that is, the nature of our service to the gods and the chief product we help them produce. Here the service is identified as a "giving" to the gods of prayerful praise and sacrifice, for which we may hope to receive the good things we request. Though Euthyphro concedes that there is nothing *artful* in giving someone what they do not need, he nonetheless maintains (rather inconsistently) his earlier position (13b13–c2) that while our gifts cannot *benefit* the gods, they can still *please* them (which would not seem to be a *need* on their part). With this answer, Socrates concludes that they have returned to the definition of piety rejected in the first portion of the dialogue: piety is just doing what the gods love (at 10e9–11b5).

---

which should be preferred, given Socrates' likening of his situation to a man's being on station at a military post (*Ap.* 28e–29a).

77. Not to mention Plato's artistic considerations: This is the move that finally leads the discussion full circle, back to Euthyphro's earlier rebuffed claim that piety is what is loved by the gods.

The logical details of this section deserve careful treatment, but here I will only contend that it represents a digression in the discussion. As evidence of this we have the reluctance of Socrates to pursue Euthyphro's new definition and Euthyphro's own apparent inconsistency mentioned above. In addition, Socrates only helps to advance Euthyphro's definition in order to clarify Euthyphro's own initial reply to his quest for the completion of P6. Since Euthyphro is not portrayed as having any philosophical acumen, the dialogue does not then seem to argue for Euthyphro's approach to the identification of piety.[78] Furthermore, this section has moved—by Euthyphro's casting his "wrong-turned" answer in terms of the know-how pious people would have—from a consideration of the nature of pious *acts,* the dialogue's primary concern,[79] to that of the *knowledge* pious *persons* would have. This is not to imply that genuine piety will not be characterized in terms of knowledge or that some of that knowledge will not include knowledge of appropriate religious practices. Socrates would affirm both these claims, and the dialogue makes clear that Euthyphro's attempted definition has only been rejected on the grounds that it is incompatible—taken as a *definition*—with the earlier rejection of the same sort of claim (i.e., that piety *essentially* involves pleasing the gods).[80]

78. I. M. Crombie, 1:211; but now see Calef (2).
79. Note Crombie's observation, 209:

> There are two ways of expressing an abstract noun in Greek; firstly one can use the definite article with the neuter of the appropriate adjective ("the holy"), and secondly one can use a noun formed from the adjective ("holiness"). It is natural to use the first form for the thing-abstract and the second for the person-abstract, and this the *Euthyphro* does. Socrates begins by asking for a definition of the thing-abstract; the primary subject of the dialogue is the quality attaching to objects and actions which makes them holy.

The evidence for this view includes the fact that the dialogue begins with a concern over whether or not Euthyphro's *act* of prosecuting his father is pious (4e–5a, 5d–6a, 8a–e) and the charge that Socrates has *acted* impiously by "making new gods and not believing in the old ones" (2a–3e, 12e). In addition, Socrates requests that Euthyphro state what piety and impiety are with reference to the *act* of murder and all other cases (acts), specifying whether "the holy [is] always one and the same thing in every action [πράξει]" (5c9–d2), and what the form of holiness is that is found in every holy *action* (6d9–e1). This latter concern continues right up to the aporetic interlude (11b–e), which is followed by a concern over what sort of acts of service to the gods would constitute pious *action* (12e–14a). Socrates then turns the discussion of piety as a kind of knowledge back to a discussion of what sort of *actions* this knowledge calls for (14d–15b). The dialogue then concludes by returning to the topic of whether or not Euthyphro's *act* of prosecuting his father and Socrates' *actions* are pious or not (15c–16a).
80. Weiss (4), esp. 273–274, now argues that Socratic piety is unique among the virtues in that it *cannot* be characterized as a form of knowledge. This is so, since it involves a form of

It is interesting that Socrates *never* doubts in this section that pious action involves a virtuous relationship of humans and gods, with benefits accruing to the worshiper (cf. 14e11–15a2) and pleasure accruing to the gods.[81] Indeed, Socrates' remark at 14e11–15a2 adds one more piece to the puzzle of Socratic religion (to be employed later): there we find that he positively affirms that "there is no good for us they [the gods] do not give." It is also left open for Socrates to affirm at this point that although *full* and *certain* knowledge of piety would necessitate a knowledge of *how*

---

nonexpert, servile service (ὑπηρετική), something that precludes our assisting the gods in a knowledgeable fashion. This is why Socrates *must* reject Euthyphro's notion of piety as a knowledgeable art of commerce (14d1, 14e6). My own view is partly sympathetic to this (see below), since I agree that our service to the gods (as ignorant mortals) cannot involve the possession of the expert moral knowledge of the virtues that Socrates disclaims. Nevertheless, Weiss seems to be confusing knowledge of piety with the knowledge of how to give the gods the nonknowledgeable service implied in piety's definition P6. There is no reason piety cannot be—like all the virtues—a form of knowledge; namely, knowledge of piety is knowledge of *how* (i.e., the ways in which) humans should—as a matter of justice—serve the gods (in a subordinate fashion) to accomplish their chief (known) end. That allows the gods to know piety (though they cannot, of course, *be* pious any more than knowing courage they can be courageous) and still leaves us humans in a position to acquire the sort of nonexpert knowledge that will allow us to aid the gods in a *useful* fashion; cf. Weiss (4), 274; and Chapter 4.1.4 herein. After all, it would seem that without possessing *some* knowledge (or beliefs tantamount to the possession of some practical knowledge) of how to assist a craftsman, a craftsman's assistants are as likely to botch the product as to help produce it (e.g., and contra Weiss [4], 269, assistants to shipwrights must possess *some* of the same craft-knowledge possessed by their masters relevant to the product they *jointly produce;* see n. 104).

81. I want to agree with Weiss (4), 266, and n. 22, that this should not lead us to think that Socrates thought of the gods' gifts as a *direct* response on their part to the actions of humans (i.e., that every pious action is immediately or always rewarded), or that he endorsed the idea that such gifts should serve as the sole motivation for performing pious actions. It doesn't follow from that, however, that the god's gifts are not *"in any way* a response to what human beings do," or that piety doesn't involve acting to please the gods and that so acting doesn't please the gods or give benefits to us (esp. intrinsic ones). Weiss also goes too far in thinking that this is so because for Socrates "there is nothing that human beings can offer the gods that equals or approximates in value the gifts the gods give them." Clearly, for Socrates human beings can offer the gods instances of just service (e.g., risking one's life for the sake of soul-improving, justice-producing philosophy) that are more valuable than the external goods (e.g., good looks) a god might confer on some mortal. Next, any decent Greek would have thought it obligatory to *try* to repay those (esp. *gods*) who had lavished gifts on one, no matter how paltry the return (see n. 133). Finally, as an instance of virtue, pious action must for Socrates be productive of happiness, a divine benefit if there are any; and on Socrates' view, everyone wants to possess the εὐδαίμων life [e.g., *Ap.* 25d, *Cr.* 48b, *Eud.* 281d–e, *G.* 499e]) and that requires doing what is right (*Ap.* 28b, 28d, 30a–b; *Cr.* 48b, 48c–d; *G.* 507d–e, 469b–c). Although this happiness may not be the direct result of a god conferring a benefit *in response to* being pleased by a pious action, it remains true (because of the nature of virtue and the human soul) that benefits accrue to the pious as a result of their aiming to please a god (see Chapter 3.4).

our acts of sacrifice, prayer, and obedience to their desires *are* a service to those gods (*what* about them is pleasing and how they contribute to their work), no human may possess knowledge so extensive or certain. Nevertheless, he may claim, there *are* practical standards to guide us in the performance and identification of pious acts. P6, he could claim, gives us a general foundation that will allow us to derive rationally what pragmatic knowledge we *need* (what we could be content with [14c2–3]) for the pious conduct of our everyday lives. It is this view, I contend, that the discussion surrounding P6 intimates and which Euthyphro—shrouded in his eccentric religious dogmatism—has failed to appreciate. I will also show how this view bears on Euthyphro's justification of his prosecution of his father on the grounds of its piety (3e–6a), and later, its connection to Socrates' rejection of the common motivations underlying the traditional cult. Before doing so, however, it will be helpful to defend P6 against four anticonstructivist challenges.

2.2.4 Four Anticonstructivist Challenges

1. J. Burnet, R. E. Allen, and L. Versenyi have each argued that nothing like P6 can be attributed to Socrates, since it is not possible in the context of the dialogue to specify an *ergon* (and product) that piety serves.[82] Versenyi takes this line of argument further by claiming that the reason for this is that the gods, being perfect, cannot be conceived to have any *ergon:* "If the gods are already as good as possible and possessed of all that is good for them, then. . . . They can have no ends still outstanding . . . and thus no rational motivation for action."[83]

This contention misses the mark. Although the perfect gods of Versenyi *are* no doubt incompatible with P6, there is no evidence that the gods of either Socrates or the majority of his fellow Greeks were understood to be perfect beings of this quasi-Epicurean sort. One can import *Platonic* text (e.g., *R.* 381b–c, *Sym.* 202c–d) to the contrary (as Versenyi, surprisingly, does),[84] but such a tactic is not even helpful for conclusively establishing *Plato's* views. In the *Phaedrus* (247a), for example, each god is said to

---

82. As will be seen, my own position relies on the notion that although we cannot (with certainty) specify the *ergon* of the gods, that does not prevent us from attributing P6 (as specifying a *pathos* of piety) to Socrates.

83. Versenyi (1), 110. He derives this line of reasoning (122) from *M.* 77c–78b.

84. Versenyi (1), 109. This is surprising because of Versenyi's condemnation of those constructivists who import Platonic, rather than Socratic, doctrine into their theses (107).

have his own *ergon,* and in the *Laws* (885b ff., 888c, 948c ff.) Plato actively condemns those who hold that the gods "take no thought for human affairs." In any case, there is good evidence that Socrates believed in divine activity (e.g., that they listen to us and give us commands and gifts [*Ap.* 33c, 41d; *Eu.* 9c1; *Mem.* 1.4.10–16]).[85]

Aside from all this, Versenyi's argument contains a confusion. Although perfect gods themselves may be incapable of improvement in their own natures, from this it follows that such gods are inactive only if we suppose them to act solely out of rational *self*-interest so as to have already satisfied all their desires. But it is possible that it could be in the rational interest (self-regarding or otherwise) of the gods to have left *some* of their ends outstanding. The accomplishment ("improvement") of *these,* unlike the improvement of their natures, we *could* well be in a position to help achieve (e.g., they could have left the world and/or our souls unfinished and in need of betterment).[86]

2. Versenyi has also argued against the coherence of our performing a service (ὑπηρετική) to the gods (as in P6) along lines similar to those above.[87] Such a service implies that those assisted by us are benefited, yet Euthyphro rejected the previous definition of piety as a θεραπεία θεῶν (P5) precisely on the grounds that the gods could not be benefited and thereby improved. The notion of a ὑπηρετική is thus just as incompatible with the gods' self-sufficiency as was that of a θεραπεία θεῶν.

If the above is correct, it is then very curious that Socrates should *not* have leapt upon this repetition of a previous "wrong-turning" rather than pursue (as he does) for a full Stephanus page a much more obscure point (viz., the identity of the gods' *ergon*), or does not at least return to drive home what—on Versenyi's interpretation—would be a very simple *elenchos.*[88] Such neglect (on this account) is made all the more malicious by

85. See also *Phdr.* 229e and *Mem.* 1.3.2. At *Mem.* 1.4.10 we see Socrates opposing Aristodemus, a man who holds that the gods are too great to give humankind any thought. Even the gods of Aristotle, after all, have an *ergon* (viz., *noesis*), sublime though it may be (*EN* 1178b9–30). Cf. Guthrie (2), 231.

86. This latter task is C.C.W. Taylor's specification of the gods' *ergon*, 113: "There is one good product they can't produce without human assistance, namely, good human souls." Cf. Vlastos (14), 175, and (18), 233–234. See below for my response to this idea.

87. Versenyi (1), 104–111.

88. In fact, Socrates cannot, since as the discussion of piety conceived of as ἐμπορική reveals (14b–15b), Euthyphro has become educated on this matter, and thus does not allow himself to be interpreted as suggesting that we can further the excellence of the gods (by giving gifts).

Socrates' remark that Euthyphro was close to a satisfactory answer by his pursuit of the question concerning the gods' *ergon*. Versenyi's argument, then, has the effect of portraying Socrates as an ineffective and deceitful teacher. Worse than that, it renders him guilty of impiety, since in the *Apology* Socrates claims (under the threat of impious perjury) to be pursuing a service to the god (e.g., 22a, 23b, 30a).[89] Irrespective of this, Versenyi's objection fails on grounds similar to those in point 1 above.

Socrates' rejection of θεραπεία seemed to rest on two implications of that term: that the gods lack in their nature self-sufficiency and excellence, and that humans are superior to them in some respect (the respect in which it is that *humans* may improve the gods). The concept of ὑπηρετική clearly lacks the second implication, and so Versenyi is apparently claiming that the only service we could perform for the gods would be a service that would (*per impossibile*) improve the nature of the gods. But it does not follow from the concept of ὑπηρετική that by assisting the gods in their work ("their functioning") that we thereby improve their capacity to function (their nature, as θεραπεία was taken to imply), "and thus their very being."[90] It is quite within the realm of Greek religious conceptions that the gods should delegate to us the performance of some beneficial and god-pleasing service they are quite able to do themselves, but from which they abstain (as a parent might—for various reasons—allow his child to mow the lawn; consider, e.g., the Labors of Heracles).

3. Taking ὑπηρετική to imply a "slavish, ignorant, and utterly submissive" kind of service, Versenyi argues that accepting something like P6 would thereby undercut Euthyphro's and Athens's claim to know—and thus prescribe—pious behavior; it would also, he implies, undercut our having *any* knowledge of piety at all.[91] On the other hand, if we *can* have knowledge

89. Socrates insists at *Ap.* 35d that perjury is impious. Socrates also testifies that he has a service to the gods, but by crediting Socrates with the additional belief that such service is incompatible with the nature of the gods (since Versenyi would hardly think that Socrates is missing his own point), Versenyi—very implausibly—must then discount all of Socrates' talk concerning his divine mission as ironic ([1], 111–112 n. 7). Thus we see his motivation for doing so; viz., to avoid just the sort of objection to his rejection of ὑπηρετική I have given above.

90. Versenyi (1), 109.

91. Versenyi (1), 104, 107–108. I say "implies" because Versenyi does not clearly assert this, but requires it for his dilemma (107–108) to be formally valid. Weiss (4), 268–274, on the other hand, does clearly assert this. She argues that ὑπηρετική refers to unskilled labor, a form of assistance that precludes the agent from possessing craft knowledge; on which, see n. 104.

of the gods' *ergon,* and that *ergon* is the fostering of goodness in human life (say through philosophical activity), then any references to the gods in the definition of piety (as in P6) are gratuitous. This is so, Versenyi claims, because of the lesson of the first half of the dialogue we are supposed to have learned: that to know what is pious is to know what is just in human life, and that knowledge one can have independently of and without reference to the gods or their love. Piety, on *this* view, is then not a part (as in P6), but the *whole* of moral virtue, for whose performance we all have the necessary intrinsic motivation, and which is what it is whether or not the gods even exist.[92] This secular account of piety is furthermore inconsistent (according to Versenyi) with the notion of serving the gods in the subordinate fashion of ὑπηρετική. By serving human justice we serve ourselves, and this is a relation between equals (in fact, he says, if the gods' work is realizing the good in human life, then that seems to make them *our* servants!).[93]

To this tortured line of reasoning Socrates can (and would, I shall later argue) respond that it is precisely Euthyphro's and his city's claim to know with certainty what pious actions *are* that he wishes to undercut, and that if the ὑπηρετική of P6 has this effect, so much the better. Indeed, such an undercutting is the thrust of the entire dialogue. It also perfectly accords with Socrates' constant confession that he lacks divine wisdom and can only reasonably hope for *human* (fallible) wisdom. In comparison with the knowledge of divine things we are indeed ignorant (cf. *Ap.* 23a–c), but this need not imply complete ignorance about piety, as Versenyi suggests. For if we understand P6 as it stands, and it is true, then we understand something about piety.[94]

The remainder of Versenyi's argument is based on the supposition that

92. Versenyi (1), 86, 104–110; see also Beckman, 51–54; S. Calef (2); and C.C.W. Taylor, 113–118. Reeve, 65, appears to join this camp by claiming that for Socrates piety is nothing other than the knowledge of good and evil.

93. Versenyi (1), 104–109. Some might follow Versenyi, thinking that ὑπηρετική cannot yield a Socratically acceptable definition of piety, since while *p*'s service to a craftsman produces a product beneficial to *others* (and not to *p* or to the craftsman), piety-as-a-part-of-*justice* must (for Socrates) benefit *p*. But this is clearly wrong, since *p*'s service to a craftsman can easily be imagined as bringing direct or indirect benefit to *p*; cf. Weiss (4), 269–70, and my n. 104.

94. If we assume that the gods are much more knowledgeable beings not of this world (as both Socrates and Versenyi would), then that does suggest that we cannot fully know the reasons (ends) of the gods, which on P6's model suggests that we cannot fully understand the piety of actions. By analogy, servants might not be in a position to fully know the reasons of their masters, and so not fully understand the nature of their service. But that need not keep them from knowing enough to recognize and perform particular acts that are "master-pious." Cf. *Mem.* 1.4.4. and Geach, 381.

the gods' *ergon*—if they had one—would be the accomplishment of the good in *human life*. Versenyi provides no argument for this crucial supposition, which arbitrarily delimits the class of the gods' good acts to those in the merely human sphere. Further, this supposition, by identifying piety with the whole of human justice, also contradicts all the evidence for P4 and P6, since both P4 and P6 imply that some just acts need not be pious as well. And of course, if (more plausibly) the gods' *ergon* is simply the establishment of good in the *universe,* the possibility remains open that some of the tasks involved in helping them to attain that end might simply be a matter of following the gods' orders without knowing their reasons. In such a case, any remotely clear notion of piety must involve reference to the gods.

Next, even if we suppose the *ergon* of the gods to be simply the establishment of the good in *human* life (and we can thus serve the gods' ends by means of a virtue-knowledge that involves no reference to them), it does not follow that an attempted *definition* of piety may ignore these gods. For example, although my father may not wish for anything but *my* good, and although the acts of filial piety he sanctions are only those acts productive of such good, that does not entail that "filial piety" *means* "the son pursuing his own good." Rather, an act of filial piety would seem to crucially involve an *intention* to satisfy parental desires. Analogously, the difference between a piously just act and one that is merely secularly just would simply seem to be that in the former case one acts with the *intention* to please and honor the gods.[95] Finally, I take Versenyi's last point to be a *reductio* of his own position. Since making piety the whole of virtue on Versenyi's account *would* suggest a relation to the gods of equality or superiority, we ought not to make such an identification.[96]

95. I derive this point from Geach, 381. Of course, then, on this account any one act could be *both* secularly just and pious (or secularly unjust and impious); e.g., intentionally damaging a just state out of a god-disregarding and self-aggrandizing desire will, for Socrates, naturally be a case of secular injustice, and—since such an act does not aim to help but to harm the good-promoting projects of the gods—will be impious as well. It is also incorrect to think that since "the gods love the pious because it is pious" (i.e., that a pious action is pious irrespective of the gods' attitudes toward it) that piety is definable without reference to them (Calef [2], 25). After all, if a pious action is pious because it promotes (intentionally) the gods' chief *ergon*, it does so irrespective of the gods' love of that action. Cf. Brickhouse and Smith (8), chap. 2.5.5–6.

96. Reeve, 64 n. 74, argues that my attribution of P6 to Socrates ("P3" in McPherran [14]) "cannot be right" along similar lines, since "Piety is simply knowledge [the knowledge of good and evil]," and, hence (65), the whole of virtue. He also claims there that "service to the gods" cannot be part of a Socratic definition of piety, since that would be inconsistent

4. Versenyi recognizes that the conclusion of the first part of the dialogue—that "the god-loved" is not definitive of piety—still leaves open the possibility that all and only god-loved acts are those which are pious (P3′). I have argued above that this claim would probably be acceptable to Socrates. In order to preclude the attribution to Socrates of even so minimally a positive claim as this about piety, Versenyi presents an argument that when generalized, would falsify virtually all of the statements of the *Euthyphro* concerning the relation of humans and gods.

On his account, both the early and middle dialogues,[97] and especially the *Lysis,* make it clear that love (as a desire for what is lacking) is irreconcilable with perfection, and that therefore the (perfect) gods cannot love anything. Furthermore, if they cannot love anything, and since all rational activity is rooted in rational love, they cannot act at all, be pleased by (for this implies lack) or care about anything, or thus be the givers of what is good to us humans.[98]

Socrates, however, clearly believes that the gods act and have given human beings many good things (cf., e.g., *Ap.* 21b, 28e, 31a, 33c; *Eu.* 14e–15a). Versenyi has also not established (again) that Socrates's gods *are* perfect, or that he had any beliefs entailing this, or that (having such beliefs) he was aware of that entailment, or (being so aware) that he would have seen Versenyi's inference.[99] It is also doubtful that Versenyi may es-

---

with Socrates' claim that it is the *ergon* of the gods that "holds the key to the definition he seeks" and is at odds with the claim that Euthyphro's account of piety at 14b1–7 could have been much briefer than it was. My argument in the main text addresses Reeve's first contention. Although I share the view that for Socrates piety is (a kind of) knowledge and that the essence of piety is the same as the essence of the other virtues, piety may nonetheless be differentiated from them by the intentionality of the pious person and by piety's concern for what is good and evil with respect to the gods; see McPherran (3), 120–122. Reeve's remaining objections are non sequiturs: first, by the point that the specification of the chief *ergon* of the gods becomes an issue, it has already been agreed that its identification will tell us what sort of service it is that aids them in producing their main product. Second, it is precisely part of my account that the answer Socrates seeks to his quest for the chief *ergon* of the gods is a brief one. But, I argue, that brief answer is that "we can't know" the *ergon* of the gods. Reeve's own suggestion—that Euthyphro is supposed to say "knowledge"—simply won't work (despite its brevity), since by specifying the gods' *ergon* to be knowledge Euthyphro will not have given Reeve's answer that "*piety* is knowledge" (65; my emphasis) and will not have provided the response that Socrates was willing to call "sufficient" (14b8–c6), since such an answer fails to spell out what the knowledge that piety *is* is *of.* For a similar, but more recent attack on my attribution of P6 to Socrates, see Calef (2).

97. Viz., *Lysis* 221–222a, 217a–218c, 214e–215b, 210c–d; *Sym.* 200b–e, 202b–d, 203e–204a; *R.* 334c.

98. Versenyi (1), 120–123.

99. Or, seeing it, that he would not have rejected one of his other entailing beliefs to save

tablish such claims on the basis of middle dialogue text, which on the whole is not directly relevant to issues concerning *Socratic* belief. As for the *Lysis,* it is commonly regarded as a *late* early dialogue, and so what positive doctrine it contains is much more likely than the material of the *Apology* (in which the gods have desires) to import Platonic doctrine into the Socratic portrayal.[100] The *Lysis* is also aporetic and refuses to make it clear whether or not Socrates *believes* that perfection and action are irreconcilable. In fact, by the end of the dialogue, Socrates has consciously led Lysis and Menexenus by the nose to conclude not only that "those who are already good are no longer friends to the good" (214e–215b: one of Versenyi's pieces of evidence), but also its contradictory, that "none are friendly with the good but the good" (222d).

2.2.5 Piety and the Work of the Gods

With the preceding, then, the claim that P6 represents a Socratic belief emerges unscathed. It remains to be seen whether and how Socrates himself would characterize the nature of the gods' *ergon* and our service in its behalf. To address this, let us ask what answer would have satisfied Socrates when he asked Euthyphro to specify the πάγκαλον ἔργον of the gods. Close inspection of the text at this point (13e–14c) might suggest that Socrates uses a false analogy to mislead Euthyphro. While it is true that different human professions have a *chief* (κεφάλαιον) result, it does not follow that the gods *qua* gods must then also have a single characteristic product. Indeed, as a somewhat twisted variety of Homeric fundamentalist, Euthyphro should persist in his initial answer (13e12) that they produce *many* fine things (being many different gods, after all). However, when pressed by Socrates, he does not insist on this, but goes on to another, quite traditional conception of our relations with the gods: one of *do ut des* ("I give so that you will give") barter (ἐμπορία [14a–b]; on which see Chapter 3.3–4).[101] Why, then, does Socrates press this point, and why does Euthyphro not repeat his earlier answer? Because, as the earlier

---

the gods from being thought indifferent and inactive. In any case, I do not see how Versenyi makes his attribution of a belief in perfect gods compatible with the statement of Socrates' alleged agnosticism (*Crat.* 400d), which Versenyi (1), 123, calls "the most likely candidate" for an accurate account of Socrates' religious beliefs.

100. See, e.g., Brandwood, xvii, and Vlastos (14), 46–47.
101. Burkert (2), 66 ff.

discussion of 6d–10a has indicated, Socrates believes—and has now convinced Euthyphro to believe—that piety is one thing the gods must *all* agree about if piety is to be an objective feature of acts measurable by a single moral standard. If, then, piety is a service that helps (as in P6), there must be at least some project commonly agreed upon by the gods which pious actions serve to promote.

What then is this "chief" πάγκαλον ἔργον, the "chief part" of P6 outstanding on Socrates' view (as he puns)? The answer to this question should be, I submit, that *we cannot have complete or certain knowledge of it* (though we must concede that whatever it is, it is good). This—and not some elaborate constructivistic speculation—is just the answer that would satisfy a man who claims not to have any wisdom of things "more than human" (*Eu.* 6a–b; *Ap.* 20e) had only by gods (*Ap.* 23a), and who is quite conscious of this shortcoming (e.g., *Ap.* 20d).[102] By such nonhuman "divine wisdom" I interpret Socrates to mean a kind of *infallible* and *complete* craft knowledge, where its possessor is made able to reliably perform, judge, and explain all pious actions correctly.[103] Such a certain and complete understanding of piety would include certain knowledge of the definition of piety, a definition that contributes to a *complete* explanation of why instances of piety are pious. Such a definition would require a specification of the gods' *ergon*, and yet the complete specification of that *ergon*

---

102. Calef (2), 12–18, offers his own constructivist thesis that the long-winded answer Euthyphro gives at 14a11–b7 contains a Socratically acceptable answer to the question of the god's πάγκαλον ἔργον: it is the preservation of families and states (with piety the knowledge of how to help them do this). After all, this is brief and Socrates told Euthyphro that had he wished it, he could have told him "much more briefly" (14b8–9) the main point of what he was asking about. But clearly, in context "much more briefly" is a complaint about the long-windedness (not partial correctness) of Euthyphro's answer, since on the analogies of generals and victory, farmers and food (14a1–7), he should have said something consisting of a few words. Calef's thesis is also made improbable by Socrates' claim that with his answer Euthyphro "turned away just now" at "the very point at which *if you had answered,* I would have learned piety *sufficiently*" (14c1–3; my emphasis). Also, note that even Euthyphro never suggests that the preservation of families and states is something that the *gods* desire and wish to promote, and when Socrates goes on to characterize Euthyphro's understanding of piety as a commercial τέχνη (14e6–8), he shows that he thinks that Euthyphro means that *we* pray and sacrifice primarily in order to get something *we* want, not in order to assist the gods. Finally, Euthyphro's suggested "product" seems primarily intended by Plato to be a piece of humorous irony: after all, how are we supposed to take seriously a person who suggests that pious action preserves families when that very same person is busy prosecuting his own father on the grounds of piety? (Klonoski, 134). For further criticism and discussion, see my (12) and Calef's (1).

103. See Brickhouse and Smith (8), chap. 2.

would seem a prerogative of the gods: only *they* can know with completeness and certainty what their *ergon* is.[104]

This profession of ignorance is also what we should expect Socrates to be attempting to elicit from such a person as Euthyphro, whose claim to know things more than human and to be guided thereby in the performance of serious actions leaves Socrates in "awe" (*Eu.* 4a–5d). Euthyphro is even so presumptuous that he thinks that actions permissible for Zeus—a being who *does* possess complete moral wisdom on some accounts—are straightforwardly permissible for him.[105] But since Euthyphro *is* ignorant of piety, it is then part of Socrates's mission to force him to concede that—like Socrates himself—he lacks infallible and even fallible knowledge of the gods' *ergon*.[106] Next, this response would be in accord with Socrates' claim that a satisfactory answer would have been much briefer than the one Euthyphro offered (14b8–c1). Finally, Socrates presents a subtle *modus tollens* for the view that piety is not completely known (or knowable) by using the evidence of Euthyphro's own ignorance: he states that if

104. Again, I think Weiss (4), 269–274, is mistaken in locating all of piety's unknowability in the meaning of ὑπηρετική (without bringing in the identity of the gods' chief *ergon*), since although it is true that a servile assistant will not *qua* servile assistant possess all the expertise of a craftsperson, he or she can possess all sorts of helping-skills relevant to the direct production of the product (contra Weiss, 269–270, he or she can produce the products the expert does and need not merely possess an "expertise of obedience"; e.g., those who assist shipwrights [e.g., carpenters and caulkers] have *some* craft knowledge). By relentlessly pursuing Euthyphro on the topic of the gods' chief *ergon*, rather than pressing him on the precise nature of our service to them, Socrates' point would seem to be that without knowing *what* project it is that the gods—and thus we as their assistants—are engaged in (are we here to help to produce ships, healthy bodies, or healthy souls?), we cannot fruitfully use whatever share of expertise we *do* possess. A Socratic sense of ὑπηρετική, then, asks that we imagine it possible that besides the existence of all the many unreflective "helpers of the gods" who unconsciously assist them in their work (e.g., those, say, who help in the production of moral virtue in an ordinary way by, e.g., being good parents), that there can exist *reflective* servants (like Socrates), who aim to achieve a portion of that knowledge of piety that would allow them to grasp (if only in a general way) what it is the gods are aiming at and, thus, how one might go about assisting them to achieve that end in a more efficient fashion (e.g., by doing philosophy?).
105. Cf. R. Holland, 3. Again (see n. 23), Euthyphro is portrayed as agreeing with Socrates that there is but one standard of justice for both gods and humans, and thus appears forward-thinking (see Tate [5], 78), but in his case it may be that his agreement is due not so much to philosophical reflection as to his characteristic attraction to arrogant and precipitous religious dogmatism.
106. As Weiss (4), 270, notes, it also seems to be Socrates' aim to turn Euthyphro from self-centered conceptions of piety (e.g., saving himself from the harmful effects of *miasma*) toward Socrates' altruistic conception, where piety involves service to the gods so as to achieve benefit *for others;* cf. Vlastos (14), 176–178.

anyone knows what piety is, it is Euthyphro (15d2–3). Thus, by having repeatedly demonstrated Euthyphro's ignorance, Socrates is here informing us that *no person knows* (completely and infallibly) what piety is.[107]

2.2.6 A Last Constructivist Challenge

At this point, however, there is a constructivist challenge to be met: both C.C.W. Taylor and Gregory Vlastos have held that since "there is one good product they [the gods] *can't* produce without human assistance, namely, good human souls," the *ergon* of the gods is this very production (my emphasis).[108] Hence, the one way in which we are truly able to serve the gods is by attempting to improve the moral state of our souls *via* Socratic self-examination. Now while neither Taylor nor Vlastos provide any evidence for attributing this claim to Socrates, their view might be thought plausible on the grounds that it is hard to see how anyone could *make* another person morally good—implanting the right moral beliefs into them—and thus to suppose that the gods could do this (if they wished) is to credit the gods with unimaginable, miraculous powers. Moreover, if Socrates had thought that the gods *are* able to improve human souls, then he is faced with an ancient version of the Problem of Evil: Why would perfectly good gods leave us humans in such bad (moral) shape if they are—according to Socrates—givers of everything good?

My response is this: *if* Socrates holds that the gods created and implanted our souls, then he would probably hold that they have the power to radically affect the structure and contents of our souls. Does he hold the antecedent of this conditional? It would be natural for him to, unless his previous acknowledgment of the gods' existence is based on the unlikely belief that the gods are Versenyi's perfect, noninterfering, Epicurean-style gods. But it seems much more likely (given the preceding examination) that Socrates would not have held the gods so powerless in any sphere of activity. Rather (he would think), the gods have left our souls unfinished in terms of knowledge and goodness for whatever reasons they have, although it is still within the scope of their power to produce such good human souls. In any case, Xenophon credits him with the above anteced-

---

107. For the reasons given above, I interpret Socrates' remark to be more than just an ad hominem attack on Euthyphro.

108. C.C.W. Taylor, 113; Vlastos (14), 175, and (18), 233–234.

ent (e.g., *Mem.* 1.4.13–14), and *Euthyphro* 15a1–2 ("There is *no* good for us they [the gods] do not give") strongly suggests it. Xenophon also allows Socrates to suppose that the gods can put beliefs "into" people, however it is that they accomplish this (*Mem.* 1.4.16), and at the conclusion of the *Meno* (99b–100c) we see Socrates suggest (rather gratuitously) that the only way virtue can come to a human being is through divine dispensation.[109] Finally, given Socrates' frequent disavowals of wisdom, we ought not to expect him to be committed to a theory of *how* the gods are able to do any of this and why they have left so many of us "unfinished." Thus it seems likely that he would leave it open that they could—if they wished—put the right moral beliefs into someone and eliminate others, thereby improving his or her soul. For Socrates, it is simply not within the grasp of "human wisdom" (*Ap.* 20e–23c) to understand why the gods refrain from improving our souls (more than they may have already; see, e.g., *Mem.* 1.4.13–14). And just as we cannot expect Socrates to have well-developed, elenctically tested views on every theological issue (e.g., on how many gods there really are), so we cannot expect him to venture an opinion here, except that our unfinished state is for the best in some way.[110]

2.2.7 Euthyphro's Prosecution

Returning to the text, we can now see that besides having discredited Euthyphro's claim to a complete understanding of piety, Socrates has also thereby undermined Euthyphro's justification of his attempt to prosecute his father. That is, since Euthyphro does not understand what piety is, its relation to the gods, or the precise nature of the gods, he cannot justify his action by simply appealing to its evident piety or to the alleged behavior of the gods (5d–6a). Furthermore, by having acknowledged that (as in P6) piety is but a part of justice concerned with our relation to the *gods*, Euthyphro can no longer straightforwardly claim that the prosecution of his father for an act concerning another *person* is just by reason of its piety

109. It is also a common theme in Greek religion that the gods can implant mental states in humans; see, e.g., Zeus's infusion of *atê* into Achilles (*Il.* 19.86ff.) (E. R. Dodds [4], chap. 1). On the end of the *Meno*, see E. Snider.

110. Note, however, that Socrates may hold that we are *by nature* intellectually deficient *and* that the gods do no evil, hence, that the causes of our deficiencies are intrinsic to the realm of becoming; see Kraut (2), 208, and, e.g., *R.* 379a ff. See also Chap. 5.2, n. 96, on Socrates' "problem of evil."

and the danger of religious pollution (4b–5a). Rather, the case now appears to be a matter whose merits can only be determined on the grounds of *secular* justice.[111] It is thus probably more than just an attempt at an ironic parallel that Plato presents both Euthyphro and Socrates as involved in court cases whose crucial concern (from the Socratic/Platonic perspective) is pious action.[112] The implicit message intended by tying these two cases together (see esp. 15c–16a) would seem to be this: since we as mere humans cannot complete P6 and so do not have complete knowledge of what acts serve the gods (nor a precise assessment of the intentions of any person), we should be extremely hesitant in judging someone's acts to be pious or impious (especially when the actions predicated on those judgments contravene conventional morality). Hence, just as Euthyphro ought not to prosecute his father for a crime against another man out of a concern for *miasma* and on the assumption that his prosecution is pious (or that a failure to prosecute would risk impiety), neither should Socrates be charged with impiety.[113] Such a charge is unwarranted, given our very fallible and incomplete understanding of the gods, and especially in view of Socrates' claims elsewhere that (in accord with P6) rather than acting impiously he is in fact operating under a divine mandate (see Chapter 4).

111. This, however, is not provided for by Athenian legal practice, which, as seen by Burnet (3), 83, "only took cognizance of homicide in so far as it created a religious pollution." This explains Socrates' remark at the end of the dialogue that it would be unthinkable for Euthyphro to initiate a prosecution of his father for murder without knowing what piety is (*Eu.* 15d). That is, it would be unthinkable for someone like Euthyphro, who seems to agree with Athenian legal practice and whose apparent primary justification for his prosecution is the danger of religious pollution posed by a failure to prosecute (4b–c). The question of whether or not Euthyphro's father still ought to be prosecuted on nonreligious grounds is thus left open (note that there is some question whether or not Euthyphro's father even committed the act in question [*Eu.* 4d]).

112. Strictly speaking, of course, it is Euthyphro's father and family who have introduced the issue of the piety of Euthyphro's prosecution, since from Euthyphro's perspective the issue concerns *miasma* and justice, thus his prosecution using a δίκη φόνου (see nn. 10 and 11). Socrates assimilates his own prosecution on a charge of impiety (a γραφὴ εὐσέβεις) with Euthyphro's prosecution of his father by implicitly agreeing with Euthyphro's family that a son's prosecution of his father (esp. out of a concern for *miasma*) raises an issue of impiety.

113. Socrates, Plato seems to be telling us, is especially unjustly charged with impiety if the basis of those charges lies in Socrates' doubts (6a–d) concerning the sorts of quarreling gods Euthyphro ignorantly appeals to in justification of his legal case. The stories of the gods' quarrels may well have been doubted by other Athenians, and if so, that is one reason for thinking that the charges against Socrates are unfairly brought (see Chapter 3.3–4 and Adam, xviii–xix). All this accords with and helps to explain the common judgment that the *Euthyphro* was written with more than Plato's usual degree of apologetic intent; cf. e.g., Versenyi (1), 153.

However, whether or not this moral is implied by the *Euthyphro*, my primary thesis remains unaffected: given that the implicit answer of the dialogue is that P6 is true and yet cannot be fully completed by mortals, then neither the constructivists nor anticonstructivists have been correct. I will now adduce further evidence in support of my view and offer a brief account of the pragmatic guidelines to pious action Socrates understands P6 to warrant. This will provide the canvas on which to draw a more detailed and better justified portrait of Socratic religion in later sections.

2.2.8 Socratic Piety and Philosophy

Given Socrates' commitment to P6 and the preceding discussion, we may credit him with the beliefs that (1) pious acts are a species of just acts, (2) whose performance is a service to the gods (which pleases them), (3) which assists them with their work productive of a good result, and now, (4) that all these elements exist in the context of a limited agnosticism that precludes their specification in full detail. An elaboration of (1) through (3) and a mapping of the *extent* of Socratic agnosticism must await our further investigations, but this is the most plausible account of the evidence gleaned to this point. In Socrates we find what might be called a species of theist who believes that there *are* gods, but that our understanding of their nature and relation to us is extremely limited. Full knowledge of the gods is simply not within the power of finite human understanding (as it is currently constituted) to achieve. Nonetheless, we can and should acknowledge the great morality, knowledge, and power of the gods, and doing so is a sign of that proper intellectual humility which is partially constitutive of pious wisdom, that is, a recognition that our relation is in fact analogous to that of servant/assistant to great unseen master/craftsman. Because of their excellence, the gods—who for Socrates may be addressed by their traditional names (*Eu.* 4e4; *Ap.* 35c–d)—do not bear all their traditional descriptions. They are, for instance, wholly moral and—unlike the gods of Greek tradition—do not quarrel (*Eu.* 6b–d, 7c10–9e3; cf. *R.* 379b, *Phd.* 62c–d). Socrates would hold that acts of traditional sacrifice performed with the correct intentions are pious, but do not constitute the whole of proper religious practice as he conceives it, since piety above all requires that we engage in the practice of philosophy. Thus, for Socrates there is no radical split between the life of philosophy and that of true religion. Both call for virtuous acts and the care and tendance of the soul that only rigorous, elenctic self-examination can provide (on which, see Chapter 3.2–3 and 4.2).

Socrates is also somewhat traditional in belief. He holds that we do receive goods from the gods, that they therefore deserve our gratitude and honor, that we owe obedience to their commands, and that pious acts are productive of good things. Furthermore, and just as the tradition held out as an important practical good to be had from the gods, there are occasions on which our human knowledge may be supplemented by divine and nondiscursive sources of information such as dreams, divinations, and divine voices (e.g., the *daimonion*).[114] These sources are not, however, to be regarded as providing standard methods of philosophical inquiry (see Chapter 4.1). Finally, I would hypothesize that all the elements above are fully integrated in the thought and practice of Socrates, and thus in his belief in the unity of the virtues; e.g., to the extent that we understand the nature of pious relations between humans and gods, we likewise understand the nature of right relations between humans.[115]

Socratic agnosticism is founded on the distinction between human and divine wisdom, where it is only the former sort which we might properly lay claim to (*Ap.* 23a). The field of human wisdom comprises the knowledge that we lack divine wisdom (23b3–4) and may include our partial and fallible knowledge of virtue; it does not extend to the full and infallible apprehension of divine objects such as gods, or facts such as whether or not dying is *certainly* good (*Ap.* 20e), whether the life of philosophy *certainly* achieves something (cf. *Phd.* 69d), or what names the *gods* apply to themselves (cf. *Crat.* 400d). Rather, Socrates endorses Heraclitus's claim that "the wisest of men is like a monkey compared to the god in wisdom, fineness, and everything else" (*HMa.* 289b3–6).[116] Thus neither does human wisdom extend to the complete and infallible understanding of the definition of piety, since that would require a complete and infallible

---

114. Such prophetic information was traditionally obtained from an oracular shrine (e.g., Delphi), from seers (μάντεις/*manteis*) who read the omens revealed in the entrails of sacrificial animals, and from the books of prophecies carried by oracle-mongers (χρησμολόγοι). The questions typically put to such sources were of a particular and practical nature; e.g., Will my wife have children? Will it be advantageous to keep sheep? Is that child mine or another's? See R. Parker (1), 261.

115. This is in essence the interpretation of the doctrine of unity of the virtues favored by Vlastos (21) (cf. [10] and [15]) and Brickhouse and Smith (8), chap. 2.5.5–6. See my n. 63.

116. See Brickhouse and Smith (8), chap. 2.1, and Reeve, 33–37, on the human/divine wisdom distinction.

knowledge of the gods' *ergon*. To strive after such knowledge in the hope of actually obtaining it is futile. Socrates, for instance, castigates the Sophists and natural philosophers for attempting to be "wise in a wisdom more than human" (*Ap.* 20e), an attempt he has given up (cf. *Ap.* 20e, *Phd.* 97b–101a, *Mem.* 1.1.11–16, *Phdr.* 229e).[117] Lacking such knowledge (e.g., of future events) we should pray for no specific thing, since we cannot reliably know if the fulfillment of our prayer would be a good for us or not (*Mem.* 1.3.2). This is so, since divine wisdom is a property of the gods (*Ap.* 23a–b; *Mem.* 1.1.6–8, 1.1.9, 1.1.13) and we must thus be content with the investigation of human matters (*Mem.* 1.1.9, 1.1.16), for to do otherwise is ridiculous and irrational (*Phdr.* 229e–230a; *Mem.* 1.1.8–10).[118] Socrates has such human wisdom, as the Delphic Oracle has testified (*Ap.* 21a), and he demonstrates it by recognizing the worthlessness—that is, the incompleteness and lack of explanatory power—of human wisdom as contrasted with divine wisdom (*Ap.* 23b). The pursuit of this wisdom—that sort which is practically obtainable—is not to be denigrated, however, for it is the wisdom proper to fallible humans. In some cases, of course, the pursuit of human wisdom will amount to an effort to obtain the most complete and most fully justified knowledge about divine matters which is humanly possible (human wisdom), but this effort should be conducted with the recognition that we cannot obtain complete and

117. Socrates would seem at *Ap.* 20e to be referring not only to Sophists such as Gorgias (mentioned at 19e) but also to those who inquire "into things below the earth and in the sky," who, due to the portrait of him in Aristophanes' *Clouds,* he has been confused with (*Ap.* 19b–c); e.g., the nature philosopher Anaxagoras, who does have a theory about a thing "in the sky," viz., the sun (Ap. 26c–e). Socrates has "no disrespect for such knowledge, *if anyone really is versed in it*" (*Ap.* 19c5–8). See also *Phd.* 97b–101a for Plato's portrait of Socrates' disappointments with Anaxagoras's theories; note especially that as far as Socrates was concerned Anaxagoras was not as well versed in the knowledge of divine things as he claimed, and that his theories failed to provide a knowledge of the proper ends of human—not divine—action (i.e., he did not possess human wisdom). Although the *Phaedo* is a middle dialogue, this section clearly purports to give us a relatively accurate picture of a period in Socrates' youth (cf. e.g., *Eu.* 5a, which supports the attribution to Socrates of a youthful—and now past—interest in the "divine things" of the nature philosophers). See also Chapters 3.1–2 and 5.2 herein.

118. While I appeal to middle dialogue text both here, above, and below in this initial characterization of Socratic piety, I have been careful to use it only to supplement citations from early dialogues (esp. the *Meno* and *Euthyphro*) and/or Xenophon's *Memorabilia.* My use of the *Memorabilia*, in turn, has been limited, mentioning supporting points which are independently corroborated by material from the Platonic *corpus.* In those few cases where this is not true, the citations generally corroborate a previously supported point, or the point is not crucial to my thesis.

certain (divine) knowledge of these matters.[119] Such incomplete knowledge is constitutive of the human wisdom and knowledge Socrates seeks to gain by means of the *elenchos*.

To this point the characterization of Socrates' theism has been negative. What kinds of gods are those we serve in accordance with P6? An initial appraisal of the evidence indicates that Socrates' claims concerning the gods were to a large extent compatible with the Greek religious traditions of his time. Socrates apparently believes that real gods exist (*Ap.* 35c–d, 42a; *Cr.* 54e; *Phd.* 62b) and that they may be called by the same names as the gods of the state (*Ap.* 26b–c; *Eud.* 302c;[120] *Mem.* 1.1.10–11). These gods are thoroughly wise and therefore completely virtuous (and so never lie [*Ap.* 21b6–7; *R.* 379a ff., 389b–c; *Phd.* 62d–63c]),[121] knowledgeable (*Cr.* 54c; *Ap.* 42a; *Mem.* 1.1.19, 1.4.18), and are in complete harmony with one another (*Eu.* 7c10–9e3), and so cannot be described as being identical to the gods of the popular and civic religion as they were commonly understood (see Chapter 3.3–4). Again, though, since Socrates subscribes to a dualist epistemology of divine versus human wisdom that emphasizes our weak epistemological powers, the gods ought not to be

119. Since, on Socrates' view, the gods presumably know everything with certainty by virtue of their possessing divine wisdom (*Ap.* 23a; *Mem.* 1.1.9) and we in turn may know some facts concerning the gods (e.g., that they have awareness, that P6 is true), the difference between human wisdom and divine wisdom would not seem to lie primarily in there being different objects of knowledge (human and divine) appropriate to each sort of wisdom. Rather, it is the degree of completeness (of generality) and epistemic reliability which distinguishes the two: a person may only hope for knowledge about any state of affairs that will at best remain fallibly warranted relative to the infallibly warranted knowledge had by the gods. In certain cases, however—like that of the *ergon* of the gods—the explanation for the impossibility (or difficulty) of having certain knowledge is to be specifically found in the fact that the gods are divine metaphysical entities that, as such, are not as easily known as are, say, facts having to do with material objects and the practices of human society (e.g., horse training). Also, the differentiation of human wisdom from divine wisdom for Socrates seems to be connected with his emphasis on the importance of the pursuit of human ethical wisdom, whose human subject matter takes precedence for him over questions concerning the nature of the divine objects (e.g., the sun) studied by the nature philosophers (complete and certain knowledge of which would be a kind of divine wisdom [*Ap.* 20e; *Mem.* 1.1.11–16]). Cf. Brickhouse and Smith (8), chap. 2; Reeve, 33–37, 53–62; and Vlastos (13), on Socrates' disavowal of knowledge and his account of human wisdom.

120. This passage provides evidence that Socrates had his own altars and family prayers, from which it seems reasonable to infer that he prayed to the gods of the state at least in name; but see n. 131 below.

121. They must be completely moral, since we saw it admitted that the gods cannot themselves be improved (*Eu.* 13c–d). This view is also suggested by Socrates' remarks concerning the behavior of the traditional gods at *Eu.* 6a–d. See Chapter 3.2–3 for a full account of Socrates' moralizing reformation.

confidently described in detail. Thus, and because they are beings who perform actions, who can be pleased, and who love, they also should not be identified with the deified metaphysical principles of the nature philosophers (*Mem.* 1.1.11–13; Chapter 5.2 herein).[122] Hence, Socrates should be said to plot a course between the confused traditionalism of his day and the overconfident intellectualism of the Sophists and nature philosophers. Instead of denying belief in the gods, it appears that Socrates renders them *more* believable by eliminating their nonsensical squabbles while simultaneously emphasizing the role reason plays in our shared moral life. It is, again, part of Socrates' goal to show that people like Euthyphro may not invoke traditional divine behavior to justify their courses of action.[123] This is so, since aside from the belief that the gods are good, the specifics of divine behavior (including their chief *ergon*) and their nature are not fully accessible to us. Rather, we must admit our inability to obtain divine knowledge and search for the human knowledge of what constitutes just behavior between humans.

Socrates is not simply a purified traditionalist, however. The formal charge of introducing "new divinities" (*Ap.* 24b; cf. *Eu.* 3b–d), for example, indicates that Socratic religion also sanctions an unusual and notorious divine sign, the *daimonion*. This sign (*Ap.* 31c–d) is negative in its advice (dissuading rather than prescribing)[124] and gives a counsel that is primarily personal, practical, and particular (*Ap.* 41c–d, 40a; *Eud.* 272e; *Phdr.* 242b–d; *Tht.* 151a; *Mem.* 1.1.4–5). Thus Socrates may add to P6 his agreement with Euthyphro that he at least receives many fine things from the gods; viz., advice on certain occasions. It is clear that Socrates does regard this advice as useful (*Ap.* 31d) and good (*Ap.* 40c–d), and subject to rational explanatory confirmation. For instance, it can be so confirmed when it advises against a life of politics (*Ap.* 31c–33b) and claims that Socrates is the wisest of humans (*Ap.* 21a). On the whole it serves Socrates as a source of personal conviction in pursuing courses of action and may be supplemented by philosophical reflection.

Such information, which may include that gained by divination and po-

---

122. On which, see Chapter 3.2.2–4. Of course, given Socrates' youthful attraction to Anaxagoras's "cosmic" Mind (*Nous* [*Phd.* 97b–98a]), it is possible that Socrates might have been willing to entertain as a hypothesis that it is *Nous* which is named by all the traditional names of the gods. This would depend, however, on how confident Socrates was in his use of the plural "gods" (cf., e.g., *Phd.* 62b–c), on which see Chapter 5.2.

123. See Tate (5), and Chapter 4.1 herein.

124. Although if one follows Xenophon without restraint—as I am not inclined to do— the *daimonion* also prescribes (see, e.g., *Mem.* 1.1.4).

etic inspiration (cf. *Ap.* 20e ff., 33c; *Ion* 534e; *Meno* 99c; *Mem.* 1.1.2, 1.1.6–10, 1.4.16) should be considered a form of human knowledge, for although it comes from a nonhuman source, it is often empirically confirmable.[125] Furthermore, Socrates would hardly find such information useful or consoling, as he does, if he considered it mere conjecture or a hunch, and not a source of knowledge. Also, since Socrates conceives of the gods as our masters (who, again, never lie; see, e.g., *Ap.* 21b), it is reasonable for him to expect those gods to aid those who serve them—both himself and others (*Mem.* 1.4.15–19)—by sharing their knowledge and offering us good advice (cf. *Il.* 2.484–92).[126] This good advice in turn may be expected to contribute to the attainment of our principal good, the improvement of our souls, by providing us with information and encouragement relevant to the making of good moral judgments (*Mem.* 1.4.18–19) (for further discussion, see Chapter 4.1).

Socrates believes that we receive more than gifts of knowledge from the gods; he also believes that the gods care for us and demonstrate that care by providing us with all and only good things (*Eu.* 14e11–15a2; *Ap.* 41c–d; *R.* 335b2–e6, 379b1–c7; *Mem.* 1.4.5–19), including well-designed bodies and the very precondition of our moral excellence and happiness: the best type of soul (*Mem.* 1.4.13–14).[127] Again, however, such care should not be identified with the chief *ergon* of the gods, since—as we have seen—its precise specification is a task for which human epistemic powers are not adequate.

Having observed that for Socrates there *are* gods, gods whose *ergon* is good, and who give us many good things, we come to the task of specifying the nature and requirements of our service (ὑπηρετική) to the gods. In accord with this sense of service—that we are servants to masters of quite another station and unable to specify their *ergon*—we may not state with certainty what final end our service helps the gods to achieve (beyond the fact of its goodness). Nonetheless, Socrates is able to spell out what the practical guidelines of that service are and what goods redound to us from

---

125. It should be noted that just before *Ion* 534e Socrates says that the "inspired" poet is "out of his mind" and that "intelligence is no longer in him." In the *Meno* Socrates also says that those who are "inspired" "don't understand anything they say" (99c). Nonetheless, keeping in mind how the pronouncement of the Oracle served as a source of knowledge for Socrates—once properly interpreted by philosophical investigations—the ravings of the poets might also serve as sources of information for others; on all this, see Chapter 4.1.

126. See Reeve, 183.

127. The claim that these citations from Xenophon accurately represents Socratic doctrine has been disputed; see, e.g., W. Jaeger (3), 167, and my response in Chapter 5.2.

conforming to them. The texts indicate that he understands this service to include acts of traditional sacrifice and prayer and especially obedience to the gods' commands, all of which, as we saw, please them in their performance (cf. *Mem.* 4.3.17). Socrates, for instance, obeys a divine command to philosophize (*Ap.* 28d–e, 23b, 29b) taking precedence over all others, which helps the cause of the god (*Ap.* 23b–c; with no implication that what it achieves is somehow beyond the power of the gods to effect).[128]

As for the evidence that Socrates thought traditional sacrifice and prayer to be a pious service, we have a clear instance of sacrifice at *Phaedo* 118a (a request that a cock be offered to Asclepius; note also the libation and hymn at *Sym.* 176a; cf. 220d), while *Phaedo* 61b shows us a hymn to the gods (see also *Eud.* 275d).[129] Nonetheless, we cannot conclude from this relative lack of testimony that Socrates did not sacrifice or pray on a regular basis. Indeed, we may infer from Socrates' modest mode of life and Xenophon's explicit claims, that Socrates' sacrifices were humble (*Mem.* 1.3.3). If so, we need not expect Plato to have dwelt on the matter.[130] In any case, *Euthydemus* 302c–303a (cf. *Ap.* 35d), *Menexenus* 243e–244b, *Phaedrus* 229e, and numerous references in Xenophon's *Memorabilia* (1.1.2, 1.1.19, 1.3.64, 4.3.16–17, 4.6.4–6; cf. *Apol.* 11–12) all testify to some extent to Socrates' orthodox religious behavior.[131] Although Xeno-

---

128. Socrates also obeys the exhortation of a recurring dream (*Phd.* 60d–61c), and such dreams he regards as containing the commands of a god (cf. *Ap.* 33c).

129. See B. Jackson on the prayers of Socrates (twelve in Plato), and Chapter 3.4.6, n. 203.

130. There is no need for testimony to this effect in the *Apology* either, for the charges against Socrates concern an alleged lack of orthodoxy (and of teaching to that effect), not a failure to sacrifice. Plato would also not be likely to think that such testimony would be a philosophically relevant matter to bring up in the *Apology*, just because of its irrelevance to this issue of one's possessing the correct intellectual attitude to the gods. Plato surely recognizes that truly impious people may still sacrifice. Xenophon, on the other hand, should not be expected to distinguish clearly between practice and belief, and in his zeal to defend Socrates before everyone, to emphasize his sacrificial practice. This is just what we find in the *Memorabilia* (e.g., *Mem.* 1.3.1–4). See Chapter 3.3–4 for further discussion.

131. A mode of life that would have been encouraged through youthful attendance at sacrifices and similar occasions (see *La.* 187d–e). It must be conceded that the ancestral cult objects referred to at *Eud.* 302c–d merely come with the *oikos* and certify one's membership in the phratry and other civic bodies and, hence, have minimal religious significance; see Aristotle *Ath. Pol.* 55.3, and W. K. Lacey, 25 ff. Nonetheless, in the same section of text (302d) Socrates declares that as much as any Athenian he has family prayers and altars, and that the gods associated with these—e.g., "family Apollo" (Ἀπόλλων πατρῷος) and "court-yard Zeus" (Ζεὺς ἑρκεῖος)—are not only his ancestral gods, but his *masters* as well, thus indicating genuine belief in the gods associated with the cult objects and giving weight to the idea that Socrates engaged in cult practice.

phon's claims may well exaggerate the extent of Socratic orthodoxy out of apologetic fervor, he nonetheless seems to confirm a degree of traditional practice independently testified to in Plato (note, for example, the stage-setting of the start of the *Republic* [327a], where Socrates has traveled down to the Piraeus in order to pray to Bendis and observe her festival).[132]

Finally, the philosophical justification for the performance of honorific sacrifice *and* the following of divine commands is implicit in P6: Socrates would have endorsed the moral imperative of filial piety (including gifts and praise), and thought it a species of human justice. By analogy, then, we are obligated to perform acts of respect, gratitude, and obedience to our heavenly ancestors and masters (though we cannot know what benefits they derive from it [aside from pleasure]). Beyond this, what makes our obedience a matter of *justice per* P6? The early dialogues do not address this issue, but in Xenophon Socrates argues that we are obligated to be pious on the principle of just reciprocity that since we receive many gifts from the gods we owe them in return what it is ours to give (e.g., sacrifices and obedience [*Mem.* 4.3.15–17]). Although this is again Xenophon, it seems just the sort of argument Socrates might offer, for it parallels the argument in the *Crito* (48d–54d) where Socrates attempts to establish our obligation to our civil "master," the laws of the state. Socrates may argue on such lines that since we have received many blessings from the gods since birth, we have thereby entered into an implicit contract with them to obey their commands.[133] Furthermore, as servants, we are the *property* of the gods (*Phd.* 62a–63a): Therefore, the gods have a claim on our service as the right of property owners (cf. *Ap.* 29b). Finally, we have prudential grounds for satisfying our obligations, given that the gods are both moral and omniscient.[134]

This analysis also shows how piety is a virtue and provides the basis for showing why Socrates conceives of philosophy as a pious duty: given that

132. This is at least evidence that Socrates attended religious festivals and thus that he had something of a traditional side to him. Based on the state of the evidence, however, we are not in a position to establish a specific motive for Socrates wishing to pay cult to Bendis in particular. On Bendis and her introduction into Athens c. 432 (as an exotic, Thracian Artemis), see Garland (3), 111–114, and Versnel (1), 111–113.

133. The expression of gratitude is also a fundamental tenet of the Greek ethos. It was thought an evil not to reciprocate a good for a good (Demos. 20.6), and if no material return was possible, one repaid a gifted good with honor, esteem, and loyalty (*EN* 1163b10–14). See Blundell, 33–34, for further evidence (and discussion) of this.

134. None of these considerations imply that our service to the gods is a kind of straightforward *emporia* (ἐμπορία), which Socrates seems to ironically discount (*Eu.* 14e–15a).

we have entered into an implicit contract with the gods, since it is virtuous to keep our contracts it is virtuous to be pious. As a virtue, pious activity naturally gives good results; just those which the gods give us and whatever end is served by our service. Beyond that, there is the good for ourselves and others we accomplish by the practice of right philosophy. Socrates is convinced, after all, that his service to the gods is one of the greatest gifts Athens could have been bequeathed (*Ap.* 30d–31c), and that there is no good greater than the moral wisdom philosophical self-examination promotes (*Cr.* 47e–48a; *Eud.* 281d–e; *G.* 512a).

One might get the impression from reading the *Apology* that Socrates sees the practice of philosophy as a special—not general—obligation imposed in his particular case by an order of the god. However, while he does see himself under special, divine orders, other passages indicate that he also views philosophy as a task everyone ought to undertake, for it improves us and makes life worth living (*Ap.* 29e–30b, 36c, 38a). Does Socrates then think that philosophy is a pious activity only for himself, whereas for others it is a matter of nonpious prudence? I think not, and for somewhat different reasons than are usually derived from the *Euthyphro* to show that philosophy is a pious obligation. Such arguments usually simply identify the *ergon* of the gods as the attempt to instantiate goodness in the world, then suppose that philosophy is the service that does this, and so conclude in uniformity to P6 that piety is nothing other than philosophy.[135]

Now I think that Socrates would have found it a likely and worthy belief—one that has withstood or would withstand repeated testing by the *elenchos*—that an *ergon* of the gods is to promote the establishment of goodness in the world, and that as an activity which helps in this, philosophy is surely a pious activity. Nonetheless, he would object to those arguments (such as the one above) which presuppose as (1) an item of infallible knowledge that (2) the establishment of goodness in the world is the (only or chief) *ergon* of the gods. As I have already argued, Socrates would find it presumptuous to identify with certainty the nature of the gods' chief *ergon*. Furthermore, doing so in the manner of the argument above undercuts P6, for if our *pious* service is *simply* to help instantiate the good in the world, then there would not seem to be any nonpious just acts (contra P6),

---

135. E.g., Heidel, 174, and C.C.W. Taylor, 113–118. Reeve, 65, heads in this direction as well.

and as Versenyi argues, any reference to the gods in P6 then begins to appear superfluous.

Thus it seems to me that Socrates may well have held philosophical activity to be the primary (though not sole) form of pious activity for reasons additional to those which involve a hypothetical identification of the gods' *ergon*. One such reason might be that since the gods are wholly good, it is a compelling hypothesis that they desire our virtuous happiness (εὐδαιμωνία/*eudaimonia*). Since philosophical activity in both its constructive (i.e., truth-establishing, belief-warranting) and destructive (i.e., elenctic, inconsistent-belief-showing) modes aims at the production of this,[136] and since our service to the gods would seem to call for us to satisfy their desires, philosophical activity is pious.[137] Moreover, it is only possible to be a pious person by having a fallible human knowledge of piety; that is, a nondogmatically held claim to a knowledge recognized to be fallible that one would therefore always be willing to submit to the *elenchos*. This knowledge of piety involves the belief *that* P6 is true *and* not completable in this mortal life, a tentative claim why that is so, and elenctically tested beliefs concerning which rules of pious action ought to be endorsed. I have briefly explained what those pragmatic rules are and what it is in P6 that might justify them. But given the above requirement that we understand that P6 cannot be completed in this mortal life, it follows that the practice necessary to know this is then pious itself on derivative grounds. This practice is simply the elimination *via philosophy* (in its destructive mode) of the epistemological conceit possessed by most humans. That is, again, the conceit that we mortals might possess the certain knowledge of divine things (e.g., the gods' chief *ergon*), which *would* complete P6, whereas all that is vouchsafed to us is fallibly warranted knowledge.

Philosophical practice in its constructive mode is in turn the justification by means of the *elenchos* of those beliefs—such as the belief that P6 is true and not completable—constitutive of human wisdom.[138] This activity is pious, as I suggested, because it is productive of the virtuous happiness which good gods desire for us. Insofar as this is likely to be a matter of concern to the gods, this constructive aspect of pious philosophical activity

136. See, e.g., *Ap.* 38a2–6 and Chapter 4.2 herein.

137. Brickhouse and Smith (8), chap. 2.5, esp. 2.5.5, now argue that Socrates believes piety to consist in "the knowledge of how to give aid to the gods in promoting wisdom in other human beings." My account includes this specification, but would add "and oneself, and in promoting those ends constitutive of the gods' chief *ergon*."

138. However, recall again that the idea that knowledge is obtainable *via* the *elenchos* is hotly disputed; see Chap. 1, n. 14.

demands that we serve the gods by putting our faith only in those beliefs which we have rigorously tested *via* the *elenchos*. Additionally, we should always regard such bits of human wisdom with a humility and caution that will always consent to their retesting by elenctic procedures.[139] This active humility and caution are called for, since as Socrates' practice of the destructive mode of the *elenchos* has repeatedly demonstrated (*Ap.* 21b–23b), humans are constantly in danger of supposing that they have certain knowledge of both divine and human matters, and that they are thus in no need of improvement. Euthyphro serves as a paradigm case of this danger. Such an attitude is impious and is therefore to be guarded against because (again) it represents a lack of knowledge concerning the truth about piety (that P6 is not completable by mortals) and because it impedes humans from serving the (likely) desire of the gods that we improve souls and produce virtuous happiness.

It is thus part of the preceding account that it is impious to suppose—contrary to the correct understanding of piety—that we mortals may possess divine wisdom. Hence, in the *Euthyphro* it is precisely Socrates' pious activity to attack the impiety underlying Euthyphro's presumptuous claims, which take divine things to be possible objects of certain knowledge for mortals and a reliable source of moral justification. Philosophy on the Socratic model is then a prime case of pious activity designed to reveal the real epistemic state of affairs between humans and gods. This anti-hubristic activity returns us to a state of human wisdom and the correct appraisal of what that activity is epistemically worth. Piety is also linked to the rest of the virtues by philosophy. That is, the human understanding of the virtues sought by Socratic philosophy is only possible by performing a pious activity, which, if performed correctly, results in the proper understanding of piety.[140] Socrates, it seems, offers us a theistically mitigated skepticism in the service of a skeptically mitigated theistic commitment.

Socrates' methodological skepticism emerges from the preceding as the expression of a piety more "true to the facts" of human epistemic weakness (at least, as Socrates sees it [*Ap.* 35d]) than most expressions of conventional Greek piety, which naively presuppose a more extensive knowl-

---

139. Socrates even subjects the pronouncement of the Oracle that "no one is wiser [than he]" to an exhaustive examination: the god has said something Socrates finds mysterious and paradoxical (*Ap.* 21b), and since anything a master might say to his servant could conceal a demand for some sort of service on the slave's part, Socrates conceives it to be part of his pious obligation—a religious duty—to discover the meaning of the god's claim. For my account of Socrates' interpretation of the Oracle, see Chapter 4.2.

140. Cf. the accounts of Reeve, 21–32, 62–73, and K. Seeskin, 77–81, 90–91.

edge of the gods. It is also an activity grounded in faith in the power of the *elenchos* to win for us some measure of human wisdom, as well as a faith in that divine certainty by which the fallible worth of human knowledge is recognized. Socrates, therefore, emerges from the *Euthyphro* as not only a hero of critical rationality, but of a kind of religious faith as well. We might even say that by rejecting more than most Athenians, he "out-believed" them all.

Of course, religious innovators and their reforms are rarely received by their communities with open arms, and the fate of Socrates is a famous case in point. So the obvious place to turn next in pinning down the nature of the Socratic "faith," its relationship to Greek religion, and its connection to Socratic philosophizing is Socrates' defense to the Athenians of his religious and philosophical mission.

3
Socrates and His Accusers

3.1 The "First Accusers": *Apology* 17a–24b

In Chapter 2 I characterized Socrates as a proponent and exemplar of a quite demanding standard of piety and justice; the natural effect of this is to make it problematic that such a man should have ever been hauled into court on charges of impiety and atheism. As one of Socrates' own associates put it: "I am amazed . . . how the Athenians could have been persuaded that Socrates was not temperate regarding the gods (Xen. *Mem.* 1.1.20). This characterization also makes it strange that Socrates failed to achieve an acquittal, especially in view of the eloquence and forensic power of his defense speech (assuming that the *Apology* derives a good deal of its cogency and force from the historical original).[1] Why, then, was Socrates indicted, and why was he indicted on a charge of *impiety*? Why in 399 B.C.E.—after forty years of playing the irritating, marketplace gadfly—and not long before?[2] And why, once indicted, was he convicted?

The number and variety of responses to these questions are legion, but many of them advocate a common strategy of reducing the ironic tension between Socrates' piety and his conviction by emphasizing the nontradi-

---

1. On this and related issues, see Chap. 1, n. 34, and Brickhouse and Smith (12), chap. 1.
2. Libanius raises just this question in defense of Socrates (*Apol.* 10.2.36).

tional aspects of that piety and thus Socrates' guilt of the formal charges.[3] On this view, Socrates did not in fact sufficiently acknowledge (νομίζειν/ *nomizein*) the gods of Athens and/or did make religious "innovations," and thus was just the sort of threat to the traditional civic cult his prosecutors said he was.[4] Proponents often arrive at this view by finding fault with Socrates' own *apologia*. Given his tremendous intellectual and rhetorical abilities, it is said, the many seeming logical failures of his defense speech, together with his final conviction, are telling indicators of his actual guilt.[5] Others hold as well that even what direct and effective defense we do find is laced with insincerity: Socrates may *speak* of his having a god-given mission to the Athenians (e.g., *Ap.* 29d–31d), but such talk is just the disingenuous dissembling all too typical of Socrates.[6]

Here I resist such interpretations. I contend instead that in the *Apology* we can find that—within the constraints imposed by Athenian trial procedures and Socrates' own moral principles, especially his commitment to telling the truth (e.g., *Ap.* 18a5–6, 20d5–6)—Socrates attempts to persuade the jury of his innocence by providing a sufficient defense against the formal (and informal) charges brought against him. I will also show how it is that in a strict sense Socrates is actually innocent. Doing so will involve a close examination of the charges, his reply to them, and his own explanation of the motivations behind his indictment. Among other things, the results will extend and buttress the previous sketch of Socratic piety elicited from the *Euthyphro*. Nonetheless, we shall also find that there are

3. A great number of other scholars reconcile Socrates' evident piety with his conviction by viewing the religious charges as simply masking the real, primary, *political* motivations underlying Socrates' prosecution (viz., that Socrates was antidemocratic, sympathetic to the cause of Sparta, and taught his pupils accordingly, including those such as Critias who later became members of the Thirty Tyrants); see, e.g., J. Burnet (3), note on 18b3; Chroust (3), 26, 164–197; Seeskin (2), 75–76; and Vlastos (4). Although such readings do have some ancient backing, they do not come adequately to terms with how both Plato and Xenophon treat the religious charges as primary. For a detailed and effective reply to this line of interpretation (a line most recently popularized by I. F. Stone's *The Trial of Socrates*), see Brickhouse and Smith (12), chap. 2.4, and (4), chaps. 5.3–4, 6.1.1; see also T. H. Irwin (7).

4. R. Garland (3), 151, for example, argues that "according to the letter of the law he [Socrates] indubitably was [guilty of the formal charge of nonrecognition of the civic gods]." On the meaning of νομίζειν, see below, and E. Derenne, 217–223; K. Dover (1), 203; W. Fahr; W.K.C. Guthrie (2), 237; J. Tate (1), (2); and H. Yunis, 63–66.

5. E.g., R. E. Allen (2), 4; G. Grote (1), 7:157; and R. E. Taylor (1), 156–167, and (4), 30.

6. Based, for example, on the alleged rhetorical parody he employs in his opening address (*Ap.* 17a–18a), where he denies being a clever speaker (Allen [2], 5–6) and having knowledge of forensic diction (Burnet [4], 67), but proceeds to demonstrate both; on which, see Brickhouse and Smith (12), 48–59, and Reeve, 4–9.

factors at work in the prosecution and conviction of Socrates—some only indirectly related to the charge of impiety—which in all probability contributed to his conviction (or which at least had the potential for doing so) and which show him to be a genuine threat to traditional piety (and so— in a manner of speaking—guilty of the formal charges). To what extent Socrates might have been aware of these factors and to what extent he shaped his defense in response to them are issues to be taken up as we proceed.

3.1.1 The Charges

Socrates' appearance in court is precipitated by the indictment (γραφή) brought against him by Meletus.[7] According to the report of Diogenes Laertius (D.L. 2.40) and Xenophon (*Mem.* 1.1.1), and as Socrates himself recounts at 24b8–c3 (cf. *Eu.* 3b–d), the writ of impiety (γραπὴ ἀσεβείας) consisted of three distinct charges:

1. Socrates does not recognize (νομίζειν) the gods recognized by the state.
2. Socrates introduces new divinities (καινὰ δαιμόνια/*kaina daimonia*).
3. Socrates corrupts (διαφθείρων) the youth.[8]

Instead of mounting an immediate reply to these formal charges, however, Socrates sees the need to respond to various long-standing allegations—the "*first* false charges"—of engaging in various harmful activities, which had been circulated by an assortment of individuals he terms "the first accusers" (18a7–b1). Socrates is sure that many members of the jury have heard these specious stories and, as a result, have been left deeply prejudiced against him (18a8–18e4, 24a1–4, 28a4–b2). Indeed, Socrates regards these "charges" as more dangerous than even the quite threatening formal ones (18b3–4), since they have received greater elaboration and

7. Meletus was supported in this by Anytus and Lycon (*Ap.* 23e3–4, 36a7–9). On the identity of these men, see Brickhouse and Smith (12), 27–30. On the issue of whether this Meletus is the same individual who prosecuted Andocides on a charge of *asebeia* (which seems likely), see W. R. Connor, 51.

8. See below for an analysis of these charges. For the argument that the charges are historically accurate and authentic, see Brickhouse and Smith (12), 30, and Versnel (1), 124 n. 122.

repetition, have been promulgated for a much longer time, have made an impression on some of the jurors during their youthful, formative years, have spread unhindered by any response on his part, and cannot be defended against by producing and cross-examining any specific individual (with the possible exception of Aristophanes [18d1–2]). Moreover, it was the influence of these accusations that led Meletus to bring the formal charges themselves (19b1–2, 23e3–24a1), and they and their corrosive effects are what will, in the end, be the chief cause of his conviction (28a2–4).[9]

These "first accusations" are reported three times, with the second formulation put in the style of a legal indictment:

> There is a certain Socrates, a clever man [σοπὸς ἀνήρ], a thinker about the heavenly things, who has inquired [ἀνεζητηκώς] into all the things under the earth, and who makes the weaker argument [λόγος] the stronger. (18b6–c1)

> Socrates does injustice [ἀδικεῖ] and is overly curious, by inquiring into the things under the earth and the heavenly things, and making the weaker argument [λόγος] defeat the stronger, and by teaching others these same things. (19b4–c1)

> The young who follow me . . . imitate me, and in turn attempt to examine [ἐξετάζειν] others. . . . Thereupon, those examined by them are angry at me, not at themselves, and they say that Socrates is someone most disgusting and that he corrupts the young. And whenever someone asks them, "By doing what and teaching what?" they have nothing to say but are ignorant. So in order not to seem to be at a loss, they say the things that are ready to hand against all who philosophize: "the things aloft and under the earth" and "not believing in gods" and "making the weaker argument the stronger." (23c2–d7)

The substance of these charges is clear: As the popular caricature has it, Socrates is an investigator of natural phenomena, for example, the sun

9. Socrates' claim that the slander and envy that will convict him has convicted others in the past and will do so in the future (28a8–b2) indicates that his specification of this chief cause is quite general; that is, it is not limited to the specific ill will created by the "first accusations" against him, but also includes whatever elaborations and distortions those early rumors may have generated among the populace of Athens.

(26d4), and a crafty practitioner of sophistical argument, and teaches others his results and methods. Where lies the danger posed by these alleged—and at first glance seemingly legal—activities? The first formulation of these charges in the text is followed by the answer: Socrates regards these rumors as especially dangerous because, as popular belief has it, "investigators (φροντιστής) of these things" also "do not recognize the gods to exist" (οὐδὲ θεοὺς νομίζειν) (18c2–3). This connection is then made an explicit part of the informal charges in the third account of them. In this same section of text Socrates also informs us of a further important "first accusation": lads of leisure and wealth have taken to imitating Socrates' practice of elenctic examination on various Athenians, and the anger of these elenctic targets is now being directed against the apparent teacher of these youths *via* the charge that Socrates corrupts them. What form of corruption? Socrates is alleged to corrupt them by *teaching* them about "the things aloft and under the earth" (i.e., the views of the new natural science), how to "make the weaker speech the stronger" (i.e., sophistical argumentation), and to "not recognize gods" (i.e., atheism).

Socrates' estimation of the danger posed by the informal allegations is clearly warranted. As we shall see, popular opinion directly connected the activities of natural scientists such as Anaxagoras with atheism, and although the teaching of sophistical argumentative technique was apparently no longer criminally actionable in 399—as it seems to have been under the rule of the Thirty (*Mem.* 1.2.31)[10]—the charge would nonetheless have carried great prejudicial weight. Note in particular the hostility Socrates' future prosecutor Anytus shows toward the Sophists at *Meno* 89e–95a. These men who go about claiming to teach others how to become "virtuous" (i.e., successful in personal and public life), he asserts, are the "ruin and *corruption*" of anyone who makes their acquaintance (91c) and they are an evil influence upon those cities that allow them free rein (92a–b; cf. *Pr.* 316c–d).[11] Worse yet, the link between sophistical reasoning and legally culpable atheism was a natural one to make. For as Socrates makes plain, although the "investigators of heavenly things" he has in mind are

10. Note that according to Xenophon this prohibition was aimed specifically at Socrates by Critias (and in addition, Socrates was prohibited from conversing with the young [*Mem.* 1.2.32–33]). The overthrow of the Thirty in 403 was followed by a reinscription of the laws, and no law or decree of the Thirty of this sort is likely to have been retained (D. M. MacDowell, 46–47).

11. For further evidence of the popular hostility toward the Sophists—a hostility that cut across political boundaries to include both oligarchs and the supporters of the newly restored democracy—see G. B. Kerferd, 15–23, and M. Ostwald, chap. 5, esp. 229–250.

primarily those intellectuals who study natural phenomena, the class also includes those who teach "how to argue with equal success on either side of an issue" (i.e., Sophists).[12] Hence, it is implied, anyone persuaded by the first accusers that Socrates is some sort of natural philosopher—a *phusiologos*—after the likes of Anaxagoras (cf. *Ap.* 26d), *or* a "virtue"-teaching Sophist (especially after the likes of those with a reputation for atheism; e.g., Diagoras of Melos, Prodicus of Ceos [*Ap.* 19e3], or Protagoras), or both, will also be persuaded that Socrates is an advocate and teacher of atheism and, thus, is guilty of at least the first and third of the formal charges. Atheism, then, is the black thread that links the popular caricature with the formal legal condemnation.[13]

But this is not the end of the troubles posed by the rumors of the first accusers. The charge that Socrates has been *teaching* (and not just inquiring) about the heavens and earth puts him into direct conflict with the provisions of the decree (ψήφισμα) of Diopeithes. We are told by Plutarch that around the beginning of the Peloponnesian War "Diopeithes brought in a decree providing for the impeachment of those who did not recognize [νομίζειν] the gods or taught doctrines about the heavens, directing suspicion at Pericles by means of Anaxagoras" (*Pericles* 32.1).[14] Although this unprecedented decree may have been specifically aimed against Anaxagoras and was another of the decrees annulled by the amnesty of 403/2,[15] the *substance* of its proscription would have still been legally actionable under the new constitutional law governing impiety (a broad and flexible law, as we shall see).[16] The attitude captured by this decree, its implicit

12. At the time, little distinction was made between the *phusiologoi* and the paid teachers we call the Sophists (Guthrie [2], 228).

13. It should be noted here, however (and see below), that at the time in Greece "atheistic" (ἄθεος) had a broad range of usage. It could be used to described those who—committing a religious offense such as disclosing the secrets of the Eleusinian mysteries—were thus said to be "without God" or "God-forsaken" (the earliest meaning of ἄθεος), those who were said to diverge significantly from the accepted understanding of the gods of tradition (e.g., Xenophanes, Anaxagoras), those who were said to be agnostic (e.g., Protagoras), and those who were said to reject the existence of non-naturalistic gods altogether (unqualified atheism of the sort attributed to Diagoras of Melos and Democritus; cf. *Laws* 888a–890a). On this, and ancient atheism and atheists, see A. B. Drachmann; H. D. Rankin, chap. 8; and L. Woodbury (1); cf. Sextus Empiricus *Ad. Math.* 9.55–57.

14. J. Mansfeld ascribes the decree to 438/37.

15. Following the overthrow of the Thirty Tyrants and the restoration of the democracy, an amnesty clause was included in the peace treaty between the supporters of the Tyrants and their democratic opponents that barred vindictive actions by either party; see, e.g., M. Ostwald, 497–509.

16. The historical accuracy of Plutarch's report of this decree has been disputed (notably

connection of naturalistic investigation with atheism, the strong possibility that legal actions based on its sentiments had been directed against a series of philosophers such as Anaxagoras and Protagoras, once again confirms Socrates' worries about the effects of the "standard charges" that have gathered about him. They suggest that if Socrates is some sort of quasi-Anaxagorean scientist and educator, then he is an atheistic teacher and, thus, is guilty of impiety and corruption.

Socrates' first line of defense against these long-standing calumnies is the traditional—and traditionally ineffective—response: he repeatedly denies them outright as being simply false and slanderous (διαβολή) (18a–b, 18d2, 19a1, 19b1–3, 19c8–e1, 20c5, 20d4, 23a2, 23c–24b; cf. 17b–c). However, he also attempts to weaken the hold of these allegations on the jurors by offering up an exculpating explanation of their origin (αἰτία [24a7–b1]), according to which they have arisen from the sorts of all-too-human motives and misunderstandings familiar to everyone. This explanation is hindered by the fact that Socrates is short on time (19a1–2, 37a6–7) and is able to identify only one of these first accusers by name, "a certain comic poet" (viz., Aristophanes [18c–d]). Hence, Socrates is in the difficult position of "fighting with shadows and refuting with no one to answer" (18d6–7). Nonetheless, beyond citing the general resentment and misunderstanding that motivate the allegations of his first accusers (18d2–3), Socrates is able in the course of his defense to characterize those opposed to him on the basis of their various mistaken and often malicious responses to his activities. Some have been aroused by envy, mistaking Socrates' elenctic examination of others as evidence of his having expertise on the topic of his conversations (22e–23a), some by anger at the humiliation they suffer when—at his hands and those others who imitate his elenctic method—their pretensions to wisdom are shown to be no more than that (21b–22a, 22e–23d), and some are moved against him by ambition (23d), here making a not-too-disguised reference to his formal prosecutors (23d–24a).[17] This etiology of the informal charges also explains what it was that fueled them, keeping them alive over these many years: Socrates and the

by Dover [2], 39 ff.), but it has not been discredited for most scholars; see Brickhouse and Smith (12), 32–33; Vlastos (14), 295 n. 167; and esp. Versnel (1), 127–130.

17. Note also how Socrates, with his description of the three classes of people he angered—the politicians, poets, and craftsmen (21b–22e)—humorously and rhetorically prepares his audience for his reply to the formal charges. For, as it turns out, his three later accusers are of just those three classes (23e–24a; with Meletus representing the poets, who Socrates tells us turned out to be "know nothings") (A. S. Ferguson, 170).

students who imitate him have, by their pursuit of elenctic philosophy, continually fed the flames of anger and jealousy by undermining the pride of the know-it-alls they examine. Most important, in the course of this account, Socrates is able to directly and specifically reject the dangerous implication of the informal charges—that he does not believe in gods—by describing how it was that he came to engage in his elenctic "mission" to the Athenians: he is driven, he says, by a divine commandment from "the god" of Delphi (a fairly unambiguous reference to Delphic Apollo)[18] to pursue philosophy (20e–23c; reaffirmed at 28e, 29a, 29d, 30a–b, 30d–31b, 33c), and this is an unmistakable repudiation of the allegation of being a *global* atheist, the sort who recognizes no gods whatsoever.

3.1.2 Aristophanes: First Accuser

Socrates' first direct response to the informal charges follows his second "legal" formulation of them (19b4–c1) and is prefaced by a wish to "proceed in whatever way is dear to the god" (19a6), a subtle initial reminder of—and defense against—what he takes to be the underlying atheistic thrust of those charges. As it happens, the one first accuser whose identity Socrates and most Athenians are sure of—the comic poet Aristophanes—has portrayed in his *Clouds* a character bearing the name of Socrates who appears guilty of all the informal accusations and their atheistic implications (19c3–5). This "Socrates" seems at first glance to be a generic type-portrait of a fifth-century scientist-Sophist, an investigator of natural phenomena and heavenly things (171–173) who disbelieves in Zeus and the other traditional gods, replacing them instead with "new divinities" (*kaina daimonia;* e.g., the Clouds) (360–430). He also runs a formal school, a "thinkery" (φροντιστήριον; [94]) where he trains students in not only these blasphemies, but also the "immoral speech" of how to "make the weaker argument defeat the stronger" (112–118). The Socrates of the *Apology* even encourages the jury to think of this Aristophantic Socrates as incorporating all the informal charges against him (19c); and thus, although we cannot know with precision what other malicious gossip might be laid at the doorstep of the first accusers, we can be confident that the *Clouds* captures the most worrisome substance of their allegations.

As an initial rejoinder to the popular prejudice that Socrates sees the

18. Whether the reference is to the Apollo of tradition or to some sanitized, Socratic version going by the same name is discussed below.

Clouds as having fostered, he declares that "such things"—knowledge of natural phenomena and topics of Sophistic education—are entirely foreign to his interests, that he values such knowledge (if anyone should have it [19c5–7]), but categorically denies that he has had any "share" in it (οὐδὲν μέτεστιν [19c8]), or has ever discoursed (διαλεγουμένου) about such things, much or little (19c7–d7), or has ever taught it, especially as a fee-earning professional (19d–20c). I think that we shall find sound reasons for giving these denials a great deal of credence. But to see this—and to determine the degree of belief they warrant—we need to ask how such a confusion about Socrates could have arisen in the first place. After all, it seems hard to believe that Aristophanes could have been so thoroughly ignorant of Socrates that he foisted nothing but the most blatant and grave falsehoods on him. It is also hard to believe that his portrait is pure malicious invention, since he could not have reasonably hoped that his parody would succeed with his audience unless the stage-figure he presented bore a recognizable and substantial affinity to the Socrates they knew from the marketplace.[19] But what makes it plausible to suppose that the *Clouds* is *parody* and not utter fiction? While saving the interpretive work of eliciting the telling *philosophical* similarities between the Socrates of the stage and that of the *agora* for the next section, I think we can assume as a best interpretive bet that the caricature of Socrates found in the *Clouds* makes unmistakable, intentional reference to the historical figure recollected by the *Apology* and the other early dialogues—and so is not primarily a stand-in Sophist—simply because both individuals share a number of physical similarities and personal idiosyncrasies.[20] Moreover, the stereotyping view of the *Clouds* does not square with the amount of attention Xenophon and Plato devote to refuting Aristophanes' portrait and its implicit allegations. Naturally, the figure parodied is also being used to represent the new intellectualism that had taken root in fifth-century Athens, and it is precisely this stereotyping to which Socrates objects in the *Apology*.[21]

19. See M. Nussbaum (1), 48; Reeve, 19–20; and P. Vander Waerdt (1), 57–58. On the serious function of Aristophantic comedy, see J. Henderson.

20. E.g., they both go about shoeless (*Nu.* 103, 363), unwashed (837), are apparently undernourished (175, 185–86, 416, 441), live in poverty (175), and cast sidelong glances (362–63), and both have a pupil named Chaerephon (cf. Xen. *Mem.* 1.6.3; cf. 1.2.1, 3.5, 6.2; Pl. *Sym.* 174a, 220b); see Nussbaum (1), 71–72; Brickhouse and Smith (12), 69; and Vander Waerdt (1), 58–59. See also K. J. Dover (4); L. Edmunds; Havelock (3); H. Neumann; and Nussbaum, (2). Note too that later Socratics never denied that the figure depicted in the *Clouds* was Socrates.

21. Dover (1), xxxiv ff. On this intellectual development, see, e.g., E. R. Dodds (1), 179–206; Guthrie (7), chap. 3; G. B. Kerferd, chap. 3; Ostwald, chap. 5; and B. S. Strauss.

Before we can assess his blanket denials, however, we need to consider at length the Socrates his jury recalled from the stage. By paying close attention to this fictional figure we can also, I think, discern something of the reality lurking behind him.

3.2 The "First Accusers" and the Socrates of the *Clouds*

The *Clouds* opens with Strepsiades, an old farmer forced into Athenian residence by war, lamenting the financial burdens that his aristocratic wife and playboy son have inflicted on him.[22] Strepsiades is a man of the "old school," naively trusting in the dictums of traditional religion and morality, but—and as a sign of the times perhaps (see below, 3.4.8)—his self-interested motives are no longer entirely held in check by the other-regarding virtues of that tradition. Under the press of debt, he plans to escape the claims of his creditors by having his son, Pheidippides, receive instruction in the sophistic "wrong argument that prevails" so that Pheidippides might cheat them out of their due (112–118, 239–246, 882–885). As it happens, this very subject is part of the special educational fare taught at the nearby "Thinkery," a school headed up by a certain "Socrates." This teacher and his students are also deeply involved in pursuing the new science of nature: Socrates is described as a "new Thales" (180) and investigates the jumping of fleas (145), the physiology of the gnat (156–65), and the motions of the moon (171–72), while his students pursue "the things under the earth" (188), astronomy (193–195, cf. 201), geometry (177–179, 202–203), geology (187–188), and geography (202–216).

Pheidippides himself is ripe for corruption. He is a young aristocratic playboy, little molded by the old forms of education and the values of either familial or civic piety, chiefly motivated instead by a desire for pleasure.[23] His encounter with the sophistical rhetoric of the Thinkery and its replacement of the old gods with new ones thus easily strips him of the last vestiges of restraint which the traditional values of *nomos* (human law,

---

22. This section was completed prior to the appearance of P. Vander Waerdt's "Socrates in the *Clouds*," (1) which argues in a similar way that "the *Clouds* . . . illuminates the pre-Socratic stage in Socrates' philosophical development" (51). I have, however, attempted to take account of his paper in this chapter's notes.

23. Nussbaum (1), 68–69.

custom, convention) had previously imposed. Preferring what he takes to be the *phusis* (φύσις; natural reality) revealed by the new, hair-splitting sophistic logic to the established *nomoi*, he learns to "argue down" conventional justice (887–888, 1336–1339), the existence of Zeus, traditional artistic judgments, the authority of fathers, and ends up endorsing both father and mother beating (1325–1475).[24] The play closes with Strepsiades reverting to the old values, embracing Zeus, and disavowing the new deities of Socrates (the Clouds and Vortex), and—in righteous anger at the corruption of his son (1464–1466)—he puts the Thinkery to the torch (1472–1510). In the final scene we hear Strepsiades exclaim (as he beats Socrates' associate Chaerephon): "Why then did you blaspheme the gods? What made you spy upon the moon in heaven? Thrash them, beat them, flog them for their crimes, but *most of all because they dared to outrage the gods of heaven!*" (1506–1509).

The real danger of the new intellectualism targeted by Aristophanes' lampoon then seems to be the same danger that popular opinion associates with the charges of the first accusers. In both instances, it is claimed, rationalistic investigations into nature and argumentation go hand-in-hand with the destruction of the traditional *nomoi*, the introduction of strange new "gods," and the consequent corruption of society (cf. D.L. 2.20). In particular, such investigations threaten the greatest danger of all by undermining the traditional conceptions of the gods to the point of fostering outright atheism. For as popular opinion had it, these nature philosophers were materialistic mechanists who replaced the divinities of sun and moon (and other celestial phenomena) with mere stones and earth (*Ap.* 26d).

3.2.1 Socrates and the Socrates of the *Clouds*

At first glance it may be hard to see how Socrates—at least the one we know from the early dialogues—could have served as all that plausible a reference point for Aristophanes' stage version. First, it is made clear by virtually all the early dialogues (and Aristotle *Met.* 987b1–1) that Socrates is no teacher of the sort of training in argument Strepsiades sends his son

24. The terms *nomos* and *phusis* became catchphrases of the fifth century for the popular discussion of what might be "true by virtue of human artifice and custom" (*nomos*) versus what is "true by nature" (*phusis*), and in discussion were treated as opposed to each other; e.g., while it is "true by nature" that we desire food, what specific food we eat (say, grain and not insects) is "true by convention." See Guthrie (7), chap. 4, and Kerferd, chap. 10.

to receive.[25] What we see instead is the informal elenctic practice of Socrates, focused primarily on moral issues, grounded in a eudaimonistic moral theory and "taught" only by example and without charge. Formal, professional training in argumentation and speech-making is the business of Sophists such as Gorgias (*Ap.* 19e) and Euenos (*Ap.* 20b–c), not Socrates.[26] Likewise, should a student desire instead some exposure to the new natural science and its methods, all our other sources make clear that he or she should turn not to Socrates, but to "investigators" like Anaxagoras (or his books; see, e.g., *Ap.* 26d).

Despite the non-Socratic elements Aristophanes' portrait suggests, it manages to capture and critique a number of threats to moral value and religious tradition present in the methods of Socrates.[27] There is no doubt, for example, that Socrates is an intellectualist opponent of the traditional education and its methods. Even in the section of the *Apology* we are currently considering (and later again at 24c–25c) he trots out one of his usual craft analogies, holding that one ought to send children (as with horses) to an *expert* for training, rather than leaving it—as tradition would have it—as a task for the uninformed many who are conversant in the ways of conventional *nomoi*.[28] And although it appears that Socrates wishes to preserve most of the *content* of popular morality—grounding it in a philosophically tested moral theory not prone to the incoherencies he finds in the former—his methods threaten that very aim.

Socrates' elenctic examinations of moral experts, for example, can appear to be premised on the view that such inquiry will be productive of moral knowledge and that such knowledge will guarantee right action.[29] But Plato portrays this search in a highly ambiguous light. For the most part, he produces instances of elenctic examination of "experts" that lead to only their refutation (and often flight from the elenctic arena, as in Euthyphro's case), not knowledge, and the intellectual acumen this pro-

25. Note, however, that Aristophanes clearly parodies Socrates' philosophical method, having his protagonist use a proto-*elenchos* at 385–393 and showing him concerned with "character" at 478–480: see also 740–742, 137–140, and Vander Waerdt (1), 59.

26. The character "Wrong Argument" of the *Clouds* (889–1114) is not a Socrates, but rather, a kind of Thrasymachus (*R.* 336b–354b), and close to being a Callicles (*G.* 481b–527e) (Nussbaum [1], 65). Note too that Aristophanes himself acknowledges that there is also a Right Argument taught at the Thinkery (112 ff.). See also Reeve, 19–21.

27. Nussbaum (1) has very much influenced the following account.

28. See, e.g., *Cr.* 47a2–48a11; *R.* 342c4; and *Mem.* 4.1.3–4. On the traditional education, see *Pr.* 325c–26e; *G.* 483e–484b; *Soph.* 229e–230e; F.A.G. Beck; and I. Marrou, chap. 4.

29. See, e.g., *Ap.* 29–30a, 38a2–6; *Cr.* 46b–48d; and *G.* 506a; cf. Vlastos (13), (17).

cedure seems to require of its practitioners is—if not superhuman—at least beyond the powers of the mass of the citizens enjoined by Socrates to do philosophy (on this, see Chapter 4.2). Worse yet, when Socratic philosophizing *is* productive of positive moral reform, the results seem only to confirm the claim that Socrates "makes the weaker argument the stronger." What, after all, could be more upside-down relative to established morality than his view that no one should return evil for evil (*Cr.* 49c–d)?[30] Thus, it is understandable that Socrates should fear the informal charges of practicing and teaching sophistic logic despite their actual falsity: he may not engage in deceptive rhetorical reasoning or take money for instruction in that subject—he may be, that is, no friend to the Wrong Argument personage of the *Clouds* (889–1114)—but his methods and its effects can easily appear to be dangerously close to both.[31] As Socrates even freely confesses in the *Apology* (23c–d), he has his young imitators who are able to overturn the inadequate moral concepts of the day, but having done so they do not appear to have gone on to replace the traditional *nomoi* with any enduring *phusis* of expert moral knowledge. So, then, how could this not be corruption?[32] Note too that in later life, Plato's own educational reforms—which limit philosophy to the qualified few—appear to be founded on a recognition of the moral danger posed by the purely purgative use of the *elenchos* (see esp. *R.* 538c6–539a3; cf. Chapter 5.3 herein). Particularly threatening, however, is the association popular opinion will have made between those who practice and "teach" the new argumentation and those who avow atheism, on the grounds that several of those individuals labeled "Sophists" were thought to have been skeptical of the gods of the civic religion (e.g., Protagoras).[33] If Socrates could be plausibly associated with such men, then despite the conceptual niceties distinguishing Socrates from them, Aristophanes would not be utterly off-base in characterizing Socrates as "a wise man [σοφὸς ἀνήρ]" (18b8) who does not acknowledge the gods. More on this shortly.

In contrast to the difficulty Socrates' jurors might have had in distin-

---

30. Vlastos (14), 179–190; cf. M. W. Blundell, 56.

31. Nussbaum (1), 67–79; Reeve, 166–169; see H. Benson (3), on the distinction between eristic and the *elenchos*.

32. Reeve, 10, notes that Socrates must spend a good deal more time defending himself against the charge of practicing and teaching sophistic argument (19d–24b) than teaching natural science. For although Socrates is not known to discourse on the latter, like a Sophist he frequently talks in public about virtue and becoming virtuous (*Ap.* 30e–31a, 36c, 38a).

33. And also Gorgias, Prodicus, Euenos (*Ap.* 19e, 20b), Critias, and Diagoras of Melos; see A. B. Drachmann, 22–45; Guthrie (7), 226–249; Kerferd, 163–172; and Woodbury (1).

guishing the man before them from Aristophanes' caricature on the two counts of practicing and teaching sophistic rhetoric, Socrates' disavowal of scientific interests, again, ought to have been comparatively easy to establish. The early dialogues, for example, do not testify to any interest on his part in scientific inquiry during his later life, and that absence is underscored in the *Apology* by Socrates' insistence that every one of his jurors (several of whom must have been of his own age and older) may serve as a witness to the fact that they have never heard him discoursing on such topics (19c1–d5; see also 20c, 23d2–9, 24a, 26d1–e2; cf. *Phdr.* 229c6–230a6). There is also a good deal of positive evidence, provided by the most reliable of our sources, that Socrates stood aloof from the investigations of the *phusiologoi,* and—neglecting all other branches of study as well—directed all his energies to ethical inquiry.[34] Aristotle is confident enough of this that he contrasts Plato's interests with those of Socrates in parenthetical fashion: "But Socrates, occupying himself with ethical questions, *and not at all with nature as a whole* [τῆς ὅλης φύσεως]" (*Met.* 987b1–2). Xenophon too, testifies (albeit, perhaps, overenthusiastically) to Socrates' disdain of natural science, representing him as having never speculated—like so many other intellectuals (σοφιστῶν)—about the nature of the universe (περὶ τῆς τῶν πάντων φύσεως). Rather, we are told, Socrates warned his compatriots against an interest in the secret, necessary causes (τίσιν ἀνάγκαις) of heavenly things on the ground that they are undiscoverable by humans, holding Anaxagoras before them as an example of the insane pride one risks by becoming an advocate of physical theories (*Mem.* 1.1.11–15, 4.7.6–7, 1.1.14). His conversation, as distinct from that of such puffed-up professors, "was always of human things" (viz., investigating the typically Socratic questions of "What is just?" and "What is pious?" [*Mem.* 4.1.16]).[35]

By contrast with all this, the Socrates of the *Clouds* is a jumbled crypto-*phusiologos* and Sophist, the head-polymath and experimental investigator of all varieties of natural and supernatural phenomena, part Thales (180) and part Prodicus (361): a "high-priest of poppycock" (358–361, 833–839). Introducing the scientific, experimental side of the Think-

34. Recall the ancient tradition that it was Socrates who "first called philosophy down from heaven . . . and compelled her to investigate life and customs, good and evil" (Cic. *Tusc.* 5.10–11). On all this, see A. R. Lacey, 27; Reeve, 18; Vander Waerdt (1), 48; and Vlastos (14), 159–162.

35. Note, though, that the question of what piety is is counted as a human thing; see Reeve, 16, and n. 17, and esp. my Chapter 5.2.

ery, Aristophanes shows us Strepsiades discovering (behind the privacy of the school doors) Socrates and his students measuring the jumps of fleas by means of waxen Persian booties, determining the orifice by which gnats buzz, fixing the revolutions of the moon, engaging in geological and geographical study, and (more ominously) practicing a kind of geometrical theft (143–218). Although such interests hint that this Socrates, at least, has some positive doctrine of *phusis* with which to replace the elenctically toppled *nomoi* of the masses, it soon becomes clear that whatever those doctrines are, they will not vindicate Socrates of the related charge of atheism. Again, the popular connection between natural science and blasphemy testified to by Socrates in the *Apology* is just as evident here.[36]

At the outset of Strepsiades' introduction to Socrates the point is hammered home that this Socrates does not recognize the existence of the Olympian gods. Indeed, he sneers at them (226–228, 423), finds references to them an empty, merely verbal coinage (247–248), accepts without a murmur Strepsiades' rejection of traditional sacrifice and prayer (425–426), and flatly denies the existence of Zeus (367, 1232–1241). In place of a traditionalist Socrates, we are given an ascetic high priest (833–839) and servant of powerful divinities, deities he introduces to Strepsiades in the manner of one leading initiates into the Mysteries of some quasi-Corybantic cult (250–292; cf. 140, 143, 198–199).[37] These, then, are the only true divinities (250, 264, 365): Chaos, Clouds, Tongue, and Vortex (424, 364, 380).[38] Tongue proves to be a minor deity compared with the Clouds, for Tongue is but an aspect of the Clouds, deities who give eloquence and

36. Cf. Nussbaum (1), 76.

37. Nussbaum (1), 73 and n. 58, writes that the fact that Aristophanes' Socrates makes education analogous to initiation into a mystery religion complete with initiation rites (140), oaths of secrecy (143), and monastic seclusion—a most uncommon sort of analogy to make—gives us reason to believe that Aristophanes had accurately noted Socrates' use of initiation language in connection with philosophy (*Cr.* 54d; *Eud.* 277e; *Meno* 76e; *G.* 497c; *Phd.* 69c, 81a; *R.* 378a [cf. *Tht.* 155e; *Symp.* 209e–212a; *Phdr.* 249e ff., 250c–d]); cf. Dover (1), xli; A.W.H. Adkins (1); R. H. Epp; R.S.W. Hawtrey; Reeve, 17; and G. J. de Vries. Adkins (1) argues that Aristophanes' attribution of bogus mysteries to Socrates was tantamount to charging him with blasphemy; this has been effectively responded to by de Vries.

38. Burnet (4), xxxix–xlii, and Vander Waerdt (1), 66–75, make a compelling case for the view that Aristophanes' Socrates is represented as an adherent of the theories of Diogenes of Apollonia (with Vander Waerdt showing their presence in the youthful scientific interests of the Socrates of the *Phaedo*). Note also that this part of Aristophanes' portrait lends informal support to the formal charge of introducing new divinities, especially that aspect of the charge concerned with the nature of Socrates' *daimonion*. Cf. also the "divinities" Air and Aether (263–264).

rhetorical power to all indolent Sophists (316–318).[39] We are also told that the universe is a kind of vast Cosmic Oven (95–96), and it seems as though we are to conceive of it (that is, insofar as Aristophanes may be attempting to attribute to Socrates anything close to a consistent cosmology) as enclosing a Chaos (Space), wherein the Clouds swirl according to the mechanistic dictates of Vortex (379–381).[40]

We need to ask then—despite all previous evidence to the contrary— whether and how there might have been a credible basis for Aristophanes' implied charges that (1) Socrates is in some sense a *phusiologos-cum-*Sophist (2) who (thus) rejects the existence of the traditional gods, and why popular opinion linked (1) and (2) in this way.

3.2.2 Natural Philosophy and Greek Religion

The relationship between Presocratic science and Greek religion is exceedingly complex, but one can simplify it as follows: starting (more or less) with Thales, a line of "investigators of nature" (*phusiologoi*) began to quietly transform the inherited conceptual landscape by searching for *inter alia* a rational account of the nature and function of the "source of all things" (the ἀρχή). (Thales asserted, for example, that the ἀρχή is water.) This was, of course, an activity confined to the sophisticated few. Although it was widely conceded that figures like Thales were wise or clever in some way, the great mass of Greeks were not well informed on these developments. Rather, most were semiliterate (at best), deriving the bulk of their ideas, especially their religious ideas, from an oral tradition backed by a ritual practice whose origins were shrouded by time and imagination. Prior to the work of the *phusiologoi*—and long after it as well—this traditional approach to religion had fostered a conception of divinity that was, for all its benefits, profoundly at odds with itself: that patchwork of popular religious conceptions which has been termed the "Inherited Conglomerate."[41]

To recall our earlier preliminary sketch (Chapter 1.3) and the initial results of Chapter 2.2, we can say that this outlook took as essential the idea that there exists a radical split between the realm of the gods and that of humanity. The human world is the one of experience as it is revealed to

---

39. See Dover (1) and C. Segal.
40. Dover (1), 106–107, 149, 265; W. Arrowsmith, 136–137.
41. G. Murray in Dodds (4), 179.

us through our senses, that world to which we as perishable creatures of finite intelligence and power are confined, flourishing or fading in response to natural rhythms that are fundamentally indifferent to our desires and other psychological attitudes. The other, divine realm is one populated by mysterious beings—gods and other divinities—possessed of an altogether better estate. Although they, like us, are individuals with varied personalities and whims, they vastly exceed us in knowledge and power.[42] This power is so great that they are imperishable, thus "divine," and in every other way they commonly fall outside the causal constraints that bind us. Hence, while we cannot enter their realm at will, they can if they so desire effect the profoundest changes in ours for good or ill and with relative disregard for what we would call the regularities of nature. In ways and for reasons an average Greek would not hope to fathom, these supernatural personalities might cause any manner of disaster: droughts, barrenness, financial ruin, epidemics, military defeats, or shipwreck (Hes. *Erga* 242ff.; *Il.* 1.5, 9.456). Even more commonly, they can intervene internally in our affairs by filling our hearts with lust or envy, or—at night—by filling our heads with dreams (e.g., *Il.* 19.86ff., 9.376, 12.254ff.).[43] Thus, these deities can and do directly manipulate most aspects of our world. In recognition of their intimate involvement with the human sphere, Greek popular religion included as tenets the claims that the gods take some thought for humans and that they can be appeased and influenced by propitiatory sacrifices, prayers, and curses (and sometimes without strict regard for the rules of human morality).[44] Finally, through the authority of poets such as Homer and Hesiod, these deities were often credited with behavior that would be deemed immoral or illegal in humans; e.g., the adulteries of Zeus, the thefts and deceits of Hermes, the jealousy of Hera, and other seemingly malicious and vengeful fits.

This popular view of the gods may be explained in part genetically by postulating that "in the beginning" of Greek religion Zeus and the Olympians were conceptualized *via* analogical, anthropopsychic comparisons to the chief visible powers of this world, kings and the nobles of their courts.[45] Like an earthly king, Zeus was credited with an overall plan of how to

---

42. Even lesser divinities like the Muses are sometimes said to know everything humans wish to know (*Il.* 2.485–486; cf. Alcmaeon, DK 24 B1).

43. See, e.g., Dodds (1), 1–27; Dover (3), 133–138.

44. H. Yunis, 34; see also Chapter 3.3–4.

45. See Guthrie (2), 27–109; H. Lloyd-Jones, 176; M. Nilsson (5), 38–75; and Murray, chap. 2.

accomplish his interests, and given his status as the divine strongman, this was thought to be a plan that in the end he could force his divine underlings to submit to.[46] Chief among Zeus's interests, it was thought, was his desire to secure from all beings of lesser rank that foremost of all Homeric goods, honor (τιμή/*timê*). Humanity, conceived of as a kind of indentured peasant class—and so reliant on the judicial functions of their rulers—would then naturally speak of Zeus's justice and appeal to it against the transgressions of both other humans and lesser deities (with cult then an extension of the Homeric practice of gift-giving, aimed at maintaining harmonious relations between unequals).[47] However, on this same picture Zeus and his divine compatriots do not govern the universe in the interests of humans, but in their own, and so "the justice of Zeus" is not always to be understood by finite mortals and cannot be counted on to coincide with their own moral presuppositions and assessments.[48] The gods, for example, might well fulfill a *prima facie* unjust curse imprecation or—while responding to a just one—pay back a wrongdoer with a misfortune far in excess of what the ancient law of retributive justice (the *lex talionis*) would call for (e.g., wiping out an entire family line because one member of it defaced a tomb [*IG* 3.1423.7–13]; cf. Eur. *Pho.* 66ff.).[49]

This picture, when extended to the governance of the cosmos, was bound to breed contradiction.[50] On the one hand, to think of the gods as humanized superiors is to portray their actions as willful *incursions* into the familiar natural and moral order of *this* world, and when subjected to the categories applicable to human superiors these acts will often have appeared haphazard and *unjust*. As such, these actions could even be explained as resulting from a *lack* of power and knowledge (as, e.g., resulting from the necessary, Zeus-independent operations of the "fates" [*moira:*]; see *Il.* 16.431–461, 22.167–185, 23.115–119; Irwin [1], 16–17). Hesiod, for example, is willing to describe Zeus as at one point *deceived* by Prometheus (*Erga* 48; cf. *Il.* Bk 6; *Mem.* 1.1.19) and—as we saw admitted in the

---

46. Lloyd-Jones, 174–184.

47. Sophocles, for example, mentions Ζεὺς ἀραῖος "Zeus who listens to curses" (*Phil.* 1183) and makes Heracles threaten Hylus with θεῶν ἀρά, "the curse of the gods" if he fails to obey his father (see also *Il.* 9.456; *Laws* 931b–c, 854b); see L. Watson, chap. 1.11–13.

48. Lloyd-Jones, 179.

49. L. Watson, chap. 1, esp. 1.12. On the *lex talionis*, see Blundell, chap. 2, and my discussion to follow.

50. Note Euthyphro's use of what must have been a well-recognized moral tension—employed, for example, in the *Clouds* (904–905)—when he affirms that "human beings themselves believe that Zeus is the best and most just of the gods, while at the same time they agree that he bound his own father" (*Eu.* 5e5–6a2).

Euthyphro—some gods may *misjudge* the correctness of some action. Furthermore, the very practice of invoking the gods' justice in making a curse imprecation presupposes that the gods lack full awareness of our world (viz., that some situation requires their assistance for just redress to be accomplished).

The other side of this coin, however, is that part of the popular conception of the gods (esp. of Zeus) emphasized the idea that—just as with any set of superiors who have an interest in maintaining the flow of goods from below—they would put up with only just so much misbehavior from their chattel. Oaths, for example, were essential to the binding force of life's major transactions (e.g., marriages, treaties), transactions without which there would be no *polis* and thus no *polis*-cult. Hence, one common epithet applied to Zeus was "Zeus of Oaths": Zeus in his oath-overseeing role (a being who ensures that oathbreakers or their offspring suffer severe punishment).[51] Existing side by side with the Conglomerate's conception of divine unpredictability, aloofness, and immorality, then, there was a hope that could blossom into weak conviction that behind all the apparently willful and seemingly chaotic actions of the gods there existed an all-knowing Zeus, a deity who from the start of things possessed a scheme of cosmic justice. On this rough picture, the interferences of the gods in human affairs are not miraculous violations or suspensions of natural law but part of a larger, coherent plan that obeys in some sense the necessary laws of one overarching scheme of justice.

It was this idea that helped to provide a conceptual foundation for the work of Thales and the other *phusiologoi* who followed.[52] One general accomplishment of these men was to quietly ignore (and so suppress) the anthropopsychic and dualistic aspects of the Conglomerate's notion of divinity, emphasizing instead the supreme power of a thoroughly rational Zeus overseeing a *unified* and law-governed cosmos. Thus, for example, when Anaximander announced that the one principle (ἀρχή) of existing things—including the heavens—is the Indefinite (τὸ ἄπειρον), he offered an account that treated *all things* as parts of *one*, seamless whole, a whole governed by impersonal principles of necessity.[53] At the same time, however, he was able to characterize the prime principle of things as "divine,

---

51. R. Parker (1), 256–257; L. Watson, chap. 1.

52. Lloyd-Jones, 82, 172–173; Irwin (1), 14, who draws attention to *Il.* 1.8–52, 6.297–311, 21.210–252, and 24.33–76; but cf. Vlastos (20), esp. 114–117.

53. See, e.g., G. S. Kirk, J. E. Raven, and M. Schofield, 105–122; Vlastos (14), 159–160. Irwin (1), 16–19, sees the "fates" as suggesting the impersonal aspect, with "Zeus" designating the intelligent moral order.

since immortal and indestructible" (Ar. *Phys.* 203b7), and connect it with a cosmic Justice (*Dikê*) not unrelated to the *Dikê* of Homer's Zeus.[54] Hence, even without offering an explicit critique of the anthropopsychic conceptual confusions of traditional religion, the *phusiologoi* exploited aspects of the tradition to emphasize the concept of a nature that encompasses all there is, even "divinity" and, thus, created "a new conception of the universe as a cosmos, a realm of all-encompassing, 'necessary' order whose regularities cannot be breached by interventionist entities outside it because outside it there is nothing."[55] So the quiet revolution of the *phusiologoi* had been accomplished with little said about its divine victims. If all is governed by the dictates of rational, necessary laws of nature (and possibly by chance), there is no room left for the operations of capricious miracles or willed, human-regarding reciprocal responses to our actions. Instead, one encounters only the naturalized, necessary actions of Zeus . . . or—even more ominously for a traditionalist—the motions of Vortex (*Clouds* 379 ff.; cf. *Laws* 886d–e, 889a–c).

Despite the inclination to think that "Zeus" in this scheme now serves as merely a *façon de parler* for the laws of nature, most *phusiologoi* cannot be thought of as having been out-and-out atheists. Rather, there was still room in their accounts for orderly and rational divinity. Xenophanes, for example, holds that all things are moved without toil by the omniscient thoughts of one being, a being he quite confidently calls god.[56] Indeed, in the surviving fragments of the *phusiologoi* few words are more frequent than "god."[57] Nonetheless, impersonal, law-obeying deities such as the one god of Xenophanes and the one Logos of Heraclitus were seriously at odds with the traditional polytheism and anthropopsychism of both mythology and the civic cult and were almost no longer sufficiently similar to traditional conceptions of divinity to be called Zeus or to serve as the subjects of sacrificial cult. This development is, naturally, a precondition for the progress of science, since there is little hope of understanding the "divine plan" and mechanisms of the cosmos so long as that plan involves the workings of hidden personalities and wills that exert mysterious actions at a distance. However, once stripped of such anthropopsychic qualities, "Zeus" also no longer designates a being with personal motivations

54. Lloyd-Jones, 80–83; L. Gerson, 14–17.

55. Vlastos (14), 159; cf. (12), 215.

56. DK 26 + 25, Simplicius in *Phys.* 23, 11 + 23, 20; Kirk et al., 169–170. See esp. Gerson, 17–20.

57. Vlastos (20), 97.

and a will that would be worth one's while to attempt to sway with sacrifices and prayer: one might as well make burnt offerings to the Law of Gravity in hopes of getting it suspended.[58] In confirmation of this, we find no *phusiologos* attempting to connect his conception of divinity with the public cult.[59] Once apprised of this development, any traditionalist *would* have to suspect such thinkers of endorsing a form of atheism. For although many of the cult practices that constitute proper piety might be rendered compatible with accounts that have been purged of the old honor-hungry, curse-enforcing gods, such traditional activities—the practical bedrock of Greek religion—would surely begin to seem superfluous without them (consider, e.g., the attitude of "the many" presupposed by R. 364b–365a; *Laws* 889 ff., 908c–d, 909b). Aristophanes provides evidence that the average man seems to have sensed this, for when Strepsiades is converted to the new deities of "Socrates" he exclaims: "I absolutely will not talk to the other gods, not even if I meet them on the street; I will not sacrifice, nor pour libations, nor offer frankincense to them" (425–426).

With all this, the lack of a clear distinction between atheism and the purified theism that underlies the ambiguous religious stance of the *phusiologoi* can now be seen to explain why Socrates couches the inference from (1) being a *phusiologos*-Sophist to (2) being an atheist (of some sort) at 18a–d in the way he does; namely, speaking only of what others believe, not what he himself understands the theological implications of natural philosophy to be. Rather than make explicit the worry driving the formal charges (viz., that Socrates does not recognize to exist what popular opinion holds to be the gods of the state) by stating that the *phusiologoi* and Sophists do not believe in the deities *of the state,* he claims that "people" believe *phusiologoi*-Sophists do not recognize gods *simpliciter*. This leaves the statement of the informal charge "not believing in gods" ambiguous between "not believing in any gods whatsoever" (on which count public opinion would be incorrect about many *phusiologoi* and Sophists) and "not believing in the Homeric and/or civic gods." This loose formulation we will find paralleled in Socrates' later treatment of the formal charges, and now here we can perhaps spy his motive: Socrates is clearly not guilty of outright atheism, calling nothing "divine" what-

---

58. As Plato perceptively puts it in the *Laws:* "It is the common belief that men who busy themselves with such themes [i.e., natural philosophy] are made infidels by their astronomy and its sister sciences, with their disclosure of a realm where events are shaped by stringent necessity, not by the purpose of a will bent on achievement of good" (967a1–5).

59. Vlastos (20), 104.

soever—no more so than the majority of *phusiologoi*. But like them, though, he may be plausibly charged with encouraging the view that the gods lack the full complement of Homeric/Hesiodic anthropopsychic qualities (thereby recognizing instead nonstandard deities, deities loosely specified by the *kaina daimonia* phrase of the second formal charge). So his most prudent but undeceptive defense is to do just what he does: leave the interpretation of "does not believe in gods" to the jury, who will most likely take to its first meaning, understanding it to refer to the completely cult-denying, atheistic position held by the worst sorts of *phusiologoi* and Sophists, which will then allow him to deny being *that sort* of outright atheist. Doing more than that would require Socrates to employ his customary elenctic methodology at great length—for which he has no time (18e5–19a2)—and might unnecessarily reveal the way in which he *is* in some sense a genuine menace to certain aspects of conservative tradition (aspects to be addressed shortly).

3.2.3 Presocratic Science and Socrates

So, then, it seems likely that if the first accusation of having engaged in natural philosophy were to prove true, Socrates' jury would have had strong *prima facie* evidence that Socrates harbored atheistic or at least quite unconventional inclinations, inclinations that posed a threat to the sort of reciprocity presupposed by the traditional cult.

There are a number of reasons why Aristophanes might have thought he could make Socrates a plausible target for a parodic accusation of being a *phusiologos*. One source that is commonly cited is the story Socrates tells at *Phaedo* 96a6–99d2 of his now-past youthful interest in natural philosophy:[60] "When I was young . . . I was remarkably keen on the kind of wisdom known as natural science; it seemed splendid to know the reasons for each thing . . . examining questions such as . . . what happens in the heaven and the earth" (96a6–c2). One hypothesis, then, is that Aristophanes is either unaware or does not care that this interest is no longer current (*Phd.* 99d4–5), and so extends the sins of Socrates' youth into his

60. See Vander Waerdt (1), 68–75, for a full catalog of other such items (e.g., *Symp.* 7.4, which gives evidence of Socratic curiosity about natural phenomena).

maturity.[61] But there is a difficulty with this speculation: the story of Socrates' youth is told by the same Socrates who connects those youthful investigations into natural science with the discovery of Plato's middle-dialogue theory of Forms, and this may seem to make the testimony of the *Phaedo* worthless as Socratic testimonia.

This response, however, is simplistic and extreme. The *Phaedo*—notwithstanding its interest in Platonic Forms—is also just as interested in portraying Socrates' last day on earth. It is on virtually all accounts a *patchwork* of Socratic memorabilia and Platonic metaphysics, with the metaphysics harnessed to the dramatic engine of Socrates' martyrdom.[62] So the problem is to keep the Socratic and Platonic strands apart. I think it fair to assume here that the story up to the introduction of the Forms at 99a preserves a kernel of the truth concerning the youthful interests and dissatisfactions in the intellectual life of Socrates. The first half of that kernel is this: Socrates did take a youthful interest in the work of many of the *phusiologoi,* one that included reading and critically examining their views (e.g., those of Anaxagoras [*Phd.* 97c]).[63] The bulk of the evidence for Socrates' denial that he "shares in" or discourses on the theories of the *phusiologoi,* then, constitutes merely a denial that *in his maturity* he continues to possess an interest in natural science or possesses such views of his own (the *point* of *Ap.* 20e and 26d–e). Moreover, nothing in the *Phaedo* says that Socrates even in his youth either laid claim to any knowledge of naturalistic facts or discussed his investigations with others.[64] Fi-

61. It would be natural for Aristophanes to make a sinister connection here with a rival playwright: Euripides studied under Anaxagoras (Strabo 14) and Aristophanes blames Socrates for the corruption of Euripides (*Nu.* 1369–1373; fr. 376); hence, he may well suppose that Socrates was himself corrupted into the ways of the *phusiologoi* by his study of Anaxagoras. However, Socrates makes it clear that the result of his investigation was skepticism on these topics, not his own private theory (*Phd.* 96c1–6, 99d4–5). See Dover (4), 67–68, and Guthrie (6), 103–104. Vander Waerdt (1), n. 9, provides reasons for thinking that Socrates' interest in *phusiologia* may have extended well into his middle age.

62. See Reeve, 15 n. 15.

63. Note, too, the tradition recorded by Theophrastus and others that Socrates was a disciple of the successor of Anaxagoras at Athens, Archelaus (DK 2, 46; D.L. 2.16, 2.19, 10.12, and esp. 2.23), and that the scientific doctrines mentioned in Socrates' account of his youth were current in the mid fifth century when Socrates was about twenty years old. For all that, Archelaus does not seem to have been a significant influence on Socrates; see L. Woodbury (2), 299–309; Brickhouse and Smith (12), 18. For a balanced discussion of the controversy over the value of this section of the *Phaedo* for the study of the historical Socrates, see R. Hackforth (3), 127–132.

64. Indeed, the passages (e.g., *Phd.* 96c) testify to the idea that Socrates ended up even more skeptical on these topics than before.

nally, although the *Phaedo* testifies that Socrates investigated the same sorts of issues addressed by the *phusiologoi,* the straightforward sense of the passages is that unlike typical nature-scientists whose investigations were grounded in a commitment to certain mechanistic assumptions, Socrates conducted his exploration without any such fixed commitments, afterward turning all his attentions to ethical inquiry (for further discussion, see Chapter 5.2).

So we may assume that just as Socrates' report of the informal charges alleges, there were rumors—plausible rumors—that Socrates had once followed out the naturalistic line drawn by others. And how else could he have intelligently denied in the *Apology* having a share in the views of the *phusiologoi* (especially at 26d6–e2) if he had not at some point become acquainted with their doctrines? And besides whatever credence one gives this evidence, it seems most likely that his active intellect would have led him to acquaint himself with the accounts of these thinkers. However, even if this helps to explain the rumors underlying the allegations of natural philosophy and his innocence of those charges taken in a literal, straightforward fashion, it does not clear him of the accusation that like some *phusiologoi* he replaces old gods with new. One need not trade in physicalistic speculations to perpetrate theological ones, and since no hard and fast distinctions between astronomy or cosmology and theology existed in this period, forward-thinking theological innovations could have been used by Aristophanes and his audience (and thus Socrates' jury as well) as evidence of Socrates' holding concealed scientific tenets.

On this issue, consider again the "biographical" portion of the *Phaedo.* Here we find the second half of our "kernel" in Socrates' revelation of what led to his initial youthful attraction to the views of Anaxagoras (and to his ultimate disillusionment with the *phusiologoi*). As someone read from one of Anaxagoras's books, Socrates heard that it is

> [Νοῦς/*Nous*] that orders and is the reason [αἰτία] for *everything.* Now this was a reason that pleased me. . . . I thought that, if that's the case, then Intelligence . . . must order . . . each individual thing in the best way possible. . . . On this theory, a person should consider nothing else, whether *in regard to himself or anything else,* but the best, the highest good. . . . Reasoning thus I was pleased to think I'd found, in Anaxagoras, an instructor to suit my own intelligence in the reason for the things that are . . . and I supposed that in assigning the reason for each individual thing, and *for things in*

general, he'd go on and expound . . . what was *the common good for all.* (97c1–b3; trans. Gallop)[65]

But Socrates had his hopes dashed. He did not find accounts of the sort he had been lead to believe he would encounter, but rather, only purely mechanistic explanations. Instead of hearing about the sorts of moral and political reasons that would warrant his decision to remain in Athens, for example, he found a view that would specify the physiological inertia of his sinews and bones as a "reason" for staying (98b–99b). What does all this indicate concerning what it is that he *had* hoped to find? It seems clear that he had hoped to discover an entirely general account that subsumes all phenomena under one universal, all-embracing *moral* yardstick: the one principle of goodness that would account for the existence and role of individual things, explaining even the goodness of acts that otherwise might be viewed in their particularity as locally evil (see Chap. 5.2, n. 96). Socrates, then, seems to have possessed the presupposition of an all-embracing morality that we saw testified to in the *Euthyphro* even in his youth. For him, all things, even those we must call divine, are encompassed by the necessities of one moral law. Thus, being superlatively wise and knowledgeable (*Ap.* 23a; *Mem.* 1.4.17–18), the gods do not have moral disagreements, always do what is morally correct, and thus do not, and cannot while remaining divine, lie or do other evils. But what connection does this have to the parodic intentions of Aristophanes?

Simply this: Socrates comes to both the investigations of his youth and the elenctic arguments of his last days with a presupposition profoundly analogous to the universalist presuppositions of the *phusiologoi.* Both he *and* they approach their quite disparate investigations—physical phenomena for the scientists, moral phenomena for Socrates—with the very same all-encompassing view that what is true of this realm must hold as well in the realm of divinity.[66] So just as the *phusiologoi* undermined Olympus by placing bonds of necessity on the *physical* interventions of the gods, so (I

65. Some would find the teleological point of view represented here as utterly foreign to Socrates. The issue of Socratic teleology will be addressed in Chapter 5.2; but in the meantime, see *Mem.* 1.4.2–19.

66. Note in particular (and again) the evidence that the Socrates of the *Clouds* attempts to explain all natural phenomena by reference to material causes and constituents in a way that is both consistent with the young Socrates represented in the *Phaedo* and in a way that suggests he held a position close to that of Diogenes of Apollonia (see, e.g., the use of air [the single source of all other beings for Diogenes; DK B2] at *Nu.* 223–234); cf. Vander Waerdt (1), 66–75.

think) should Socrates be regarded as a similar innovator of the moral dimension, imposing the yardstick of virtue on both gods and humans alike. And if justice binds both gods and humans, and justice is to be understood Socratically, then it might naturally become apparent that one can no longer satisfy or evade the demands of morality and real piety as readily as before (e.g., *via* sacrificial propitiation). It is easy to imagine, therefore, that—seeing something of this and for these very reasons—Aristophanes has portrayed Socrates as a *phusiologos*.

3.2.4 The Socratic Reformation

The key move of the Socratic religious reformation seems to be this: whereas the Ionians and their brethren had tamed the gods, making them rational and naturalizing them physically within a unified realm called cosmos, Socrates put the gods under the reign of reason by bringing them completely into line with the universal demands of morality, demands that constrain them within norms applicable to both humans and gods.[67] What makes this especially revisionary, however, is that Socrates' unified moral scheme does not simply draw all its tenets from the accepted *nomoi*, but instead, takes as primary those comprised by the *innovations* of Socratic moral theory. The most important of these is his rejection of the rule of retaliation.

From Homer on, Greek popular thought assumed as a fundamental principle that justice consists in reciprocation, in repayment in kind: a gift for a gift, a loss for a loss, an evil for an evil.[68] Even among the gods this principle of *lex talionis* is assumed as basic (e.g., at *Il.* 4.40–43, Hera offers Zeus her favorite cities in return for his abandoning Troy; cf. Soph. *Ajax* 79).[69] Tied to this idea as its most prominent corollary is the moral

67. See Guthrie (2), 231, and Vlastos (14), 159–162.
68. Cf., e.g., Hes., fr. 174; Aesch. *Choe.* 306–314, *Ag.* 1564; and Ar. *EN* 1132b21–27, *Top.* 113a2–3, *Rhet.* 1367a19–20. See Blundell, chap. 2, and Vlastos (14), chap. 7, for additional citations and analysis.
69. Hence, here is an instance where the common view recognized a *shared* view of justice that applied to requesting or receiving the aid of the gods (unlike those cases where common opinion saw humans and gods subject to different standards of behavior); so, e.g., a god's aid put one in the debt of a sacrifice (cf., e.g., *R.* 331b).

imperative, "Help your friends and harm your enemies."[70] Here, we need to be clear, we are not encountering the view that those who do evil should be *punished* (as a moral therapy or so as to deter them and others from future wrongdoing). Rather, this idea holds that it is fitting to exact a revenge against personal enemies that is motivated by hate and by a desire to relieve one's feelings of resentment (e.g., *Il.* 21.423, Thuc. 7.68.1f, Ar. *Rhet.* 1370b30). True, the *talio* is a norm of *justice* in some sense, since without its notion of repayment *in kind* there would be no moral constraints at all on the methods and amounts of harm one might visit upon a hated enemy (cf. Eur. *Ion* 1046–1047; Demos. 23.69). In practice, however, it could be used to justify helping a friend to win an unjust lawsuit (e.g., Isae. 1.7; Hyp. 1.10) or to sanction savage civic actions; e.g., the proposed execution of all the males of Mytilene, selling their wives and children into slavery (Thuc. 3.40.7; cf. 3.38.1).[71]

Regarding this venerable principle, it seems clear, Socrates must be ranked a self-conscious moral revolutionary (*Cr.* 49b–d).[72] For as he sees it, since we should never do injustice, we should never do evil, and from that it follows that we should never do an evil in return for even an evil done to us (*Cr.* 48b–49d, 54c; cf. *R.* 335a–d).[73] As Plato makes clear, an average Athenian would have been astonished and troubled when confronted by this innovation: to forgo the pleasures of fully despoiling one's enemy (including, say, the infliction of physical harm on his innocent relatives) in favor of the intellectual pleasures of doing the just thing probably seemed like an unlikely, inverted way of looking at things. As Crito wonders (*Cr.* 45c–46a), for example, by failing to inflict a harm on an opponent aren't we doing to ourselves that very thing which the opponent wishes done to us (viz., "unjustly" depriving ourselves of goods)? Thus, as

---

70. See, e.g., *M.* 71e; *R.* 332d; Pi. 2 *Pyth.* 83–85; and Eur. *Medea* 807–10. For extensive documentation and discussion of this corollary, see Blundell, chap. 2, also Vlastos (14), chap. 7, esp. 180–190.

71. Vlastos (14), chap. 7, 181–190; Blundell, 50. Although Mytilene escaped this sort of fate, Scione, Torone, and Melos did not. Blundell, 55, notes that enmity and revenge were accepted as natural motives for lawsuits, and that revenge could be endowed with respectability if it was argued that revenge was being sought on behalf of the *polis* (e.g., Lys. 1.47).

72. However, for references to possible precursors of Socrates's rejection of the *talio*, see Blundell, 56 n. 146.

73. On this inference and its connections with the rest of Socrates' moral theory, see, e.g., Vlastos (14), chap. 7. Vlastos (14), 195 n. 52 (and also, e.g., [8], 2), understands Xenophon's Socrates to endorse the ancient help-friends-harm-enemies ethos (at, e.g., *Mem.* 2.6.35). For a cogent response, see Morrison, 16–18 (and cf. *Mem.* 4.8.11).

we consider Socrates' moral cleansing of the gods below (and especially its consequences), it will be important to remember that Socrates' gods do not merely operate according to a universal standard (as we saw, after all, even Euthyphro can live with *that,* so long as Zeus remains a "father basher"), but are "socratized" as well. For Socrates, not even Zeus (rather, least of all Zeus) can return one injury for another.

The details of how Socrates went about clamping moral restraints on beings such as Zeus, beings still—given his somewhat nonscientific point of view—anthropopsychic in several ways (e.g., still conscious repositories of wisdom, still capable of being pleased by our actions) are obscure (but see Chapter 5.2). However, Socrates' principles appear to moralize the gods in this fashion: it is simply a given that the gods are perfectly wise, especially in comparison with human beings (*Ap.* 23a5–b4; *Mem.* 1.1.19; cf. *HMa.* 289b). But because of the unity of the virtues (see, e.g., *Pr.* 361b, 329e ff.; Chap. 2.2, n. 63), wisdom entails the possession of virtue (in a god as much as a person, since there is but one moral domain). Hence, the gods are supremely virtuous (*Mem.* 4.4.25). But since the most virtuous persons—knowing the good as they do—can only do good and can never cause evil to anyone, and since there is, again, but one moral domain, the gods too must be the causes of only good and never evil (*Eu.* 15a1–2; *R.* 379b–c; cf. 379c2–7).[74] It should be clear, then, that although Socrates' gods were probably thought by him to be free of at least some of the constraints the *phusiologoi* placed on divinity (e.g., Socrates allows that they can love), his gods have been brought under a rule of necessity potentially just as threatening to the popular religion of the man in the street as were those that were endorsed by the devotees of Mind and Vortex.[75] For,

74. Cf. Vlastos (14), 162–165; Brickhouse and Smith (8), chap. 6.2.1. The latter perceptively note (n. 6) that Vlastos, 163–164, is incorrect to think that the gods' goodness does not simply follow from their perfect wisdom, since for Socrates no one can know the good and fail to do it (e.g., *Cr.* 49c; *Pr.* 352b–d, 358c–d; *R.* 335a–d; Xen. *Mem.* 3.9.5, 4.6.6; Ar. *EN* 1145b25).

Note that Reeve finds Socrates' reliance on extrarational indicators to be justified by "the elenctically established goodness of the gods" (70). But we never see Socrates offer elenctic arguments for the goodness of the gods; rather, to all appearances he simply *assumes* this, or derives it from their having wisdom in the above fashion. The attribution of wisdom to them, in turn, is either simply assumed or is derived (perhaps) from "the very meaning of what it means to be a god." See McPherran (6) and N. Smith (2), 401–402.

75. Note, too, for example, that θέμις in Socrates' claim that "it is not sanctioned (θέμις) for the god [Delphic Apollo] to say something false" (*Ap.* 21b5–8) is a term that commonly refers to a law or ordinance, in some cases one binding on even the gods. The goddess Themis

again, how will one enlist the assistance of gods such as these in one's affairs, especially one's shady affairs? Will Socrates' thoroughly just Zeus, any more than Anaxagoras's Mind, respond to burnt offerings, showering goods on one's friends and calamities on one's enemies?

Whether or not Aristophanes had actually discerned dangers of this sort in the views of Socrates himself, however, he will have seen it in the views of the *phusiologoi* and Sophists. And if one or more of them were thought to bear a strong similarity to Socrates, then Aristophanes and others might understandably make an inference by analogy, type-casting Socrates as a *phusiologos* and Sophist. This would not be good philosophy on anyone's part, but it could make for effective drama and devastating courtroom insinuations.

Consider the figure of Xenophanes, then. In one of his best known fragments, he testifies that "Homer and Hesiod have attributed to the gods everything that is a shame and reproach among humans, stealing and committing adultery and deceiving each other" (Sextus *Ad. Math.* 11.193).

Aristophanes—and the more educated members of his audience—would in all likelihood have been acquainted with Xenophanes and his attacks on aspects of popular mythology.[76] But if so, then given the sorts of similar anti-anthropopsychic remarks we saw Socrates making at *Euthyphro* 6a–c, putting the gods under the same moral yoke as ourselves and denying them enmities and deceptions (see also *Ap.* 21b; *R.* 377e–382e, 389b–c), Socrates would have immediately been associated with at least this much of Xenophantic thought and those of the Sophists who followed a similar revisionary line.[77] Moreover, it was common to associate such rejections of the immoralities of the myths with the *phusis-nomos* discussions engaged in by Sophists, and those discussions were linked in turn with the investigations into *phusis* pursued by the *phusiologoi*. Thus, criticism of popular religious myth on moralistic grounds could be used as the basis for a guilt-

---

is also well connected to Delphi; see J. E. Harrison (1), chap. 9. See *R.* 381e–382c, and Chapter 4.2, esp. p. 224, on why socratized gods do not lie.

76. "Of all the Pre-Socratics it is Xenophanes who might be credited with 'moralizing divinity'" (Vlastos [14], 164 n. 32).

77. Note too that a probable contemporary of Socrates, Democritus, declared that the gods are the source of all good and that man is responsible for the evils that he suffers (DK B 175). Again, both Sophists and Socrates assume that laws of morality must apply with consistency to both gods and humans; but Socrates, rather than using divine immorality to do away with conventional human justice in a *modus ponens* inference, appears to reason *modus tollens* that since it is wrong, say, to injure your father, then the story that Zeus imprisoned Cronus must be false.

by-association charge of atheism, especially when linked to other suspicious activities, such as elenctic argument.[78]

One indication in the text of the *Clouds* that the audience is in fact supposed to make this sort of connection is seen in the morally based argument "Socrates" uses to convince Strepsiades that it is the Clouds, not Zeus, that send lightning: if Zeus were its source then we would have to think that he punishes trees for oathbreaking; but since that notion is absurd, Zeus is not the cause of lightning (395–405). Another, more direct, hint at the association occurs when Aristophanes has Socrates explain that the Clouds are like the clouds of our experience: they can take on the shapes projected by their viewers, resembling wolves, for instance, when confronted with a wolfish personality (346 ff.). It was just this sort of point—that if lions had gods they would resemble lions—that Xenophanes and others had used to argue against the anthropomorphism of the popular understanding of the gods, holding that such conceptions were merely true by convention (*nomos*), not nature (*phusis*).[79] Finally, it was generally thought that those who dwell on the tales of immorality among the gods either undermine the authority of the gods or popular morality or both, and at *Clouds* 904–906 we see just this sort of reaction in Right Argument when the Wrong Argument of Socrates' Thinkery adduces divine immoralities to disprove the existence of Justice.[80]

Next, and as we saw, there was at least a rumor that Socrates had an interest in the monotheistic "deity" of Anaxagoras as well, an inclination that might again be immediately traced back to Xenophanes, whose constructive theology featured as a radical innovation a unitary non-anthropomorphic deity that like Anaxagoras's *Nous*, "shakes without toil all things by the thought of his mind."[81] Finally, in Xenophanes we find a skepticism reminiscent of Socrates' own, one that similarly employs the traditional doctrine of divine omniscience contrasted with human intellec-

78. See *Laws* 889a ff., and Kerferd, chap. 10.

79. Clement *Strom.* v, 109, 3. Aristophanes could also be telling us that anthropomorphism is something we cannot escape, but that the *Clouds* are insufficiently human-like to make them effective, useful gods.

80. The inferences drawn from the "unhappy tales of the poets" by Euripides (*Hera.* 1317–19; cf. *Ion* 442–451) show how common such arguments were; see Tate (5), 77. Cf. also *Frogs* 1491 ff., where Aristophanes explains Euripides' fondness for the unsavory parts of mythology by citing his association with Socrates.

81. See Kirk et al., 169; it is also significant that one of Socrates' own pupils, Antisthenes, arrived at a similar doctrine according to which there is but one god, dissimilar to any image we are acquainted with (Philodemus *Peri eusebeias* [p. 72, T. Gomperz]; Cic. *De nat. deor.* 1.13.32).

tual limitations; and so again, given that Socrates' disavowal of knowledge was a common theme of his mission to the Athenians, it becomes extremely plausible to hold that in Socrates Aristophanes thought he had seen a second Xenophanes (or similarly, an antinomy-hawking, god-doubting Sophist like Protagoras) (see also Chapter 5.2.3, esp. n. 120).

One sign that Aristophanes also recognizes the skeptical, agnostic side of Socrates and his elenctic method is found in the main deities he has his Socrates worshiping in place of the gods of tradition: the Clouds—intellectuals like Socrates always have their "heads in the clouds" (331–334, 219–234). But instead of providing fixed, eternal beings to underwrite the *phusis* of a new morality that will replace the overturned *nomoi,* these are foggy, ever-changing, misty wisps of air (285–300) that—like the shifting arguments of the Sophists (331; cf. 316–318)—take on the shape of whatever approaches them (340–355).[82] So as Martha Nussbaum puts the matter: "Insofar as the Clouds are symbolic of Socratic teaching, they display it as elenctic and negative, imparting no insight into anything but the interlocutor's own defects, leaving beyond the structure of the *elenchos* only a formless nebulosity."[83]

Given all the above, then, Aristophanes' ascription of physicalistic interests and unorthodox religious leanings to Socrates should be seen as natural. Socrates might well have been viewed as a "likeness" of Xenophanes, a moralistic theological reformer, and as such would have been *believed* to be a *phusiologos:* a man possessed of theories concerning the heavens, the roots of the earth, and the materialistic sources of "all that comes to be."[84] Aristophanes is even more on the mark in his association of Socrates with the intellectualist criticisms of the traditional gods made by various Sophists. In fact, it seems probable that it must be this sort of intellectual that Socrates at *Apology* 18c fears he will be associated with, for several of these teachers seem to reject not only the anthropomorphic gods of the state, but all gods, and at least one of the Sophists Socrates disassociates himself from by name—Prodicus (19e)—was in all probability an outright atheist.[85]

---

82. See Reeve, 18.

83. Nussbaum (1), 76. Vander Waerdt (1), 59–60, notes that the Socrates of the *Clouds* is unlike the typical sophist by "avoiding rhetorical set pieces, . . . preferring to argue dialectically on the basis of his interlocutor's premises." Note also the possible reference at 137–140 to Socrates' reputed midwifery, only delivering the ideas of others and never giving birth himself; on this, see D. Sider.

84. Cf. Kirk et al., 163–180.

85. See Guthrie (7), 274–280.

The preceding also makes clear that Socrates' criticism of the poetic tradition's portrait of the gods on moral grounds was not fully original. Besides Xenophanes' critique, there had also been the similar attacks by Pindar (fr. 201 B) and Heraclitus (DK 5; Aristocritus *Theo.* 68).[86] Moreover, in his own day, Socrates was joined in being scandalized by the old stories of divine theft, seduction, and deceit by the characters portrayed in the plays of Euripides. Heracles, for example, is made to declare that "I do not believe that the gods take pleasure in unlawful intercourse, nor . . . load each other with fetters. . . . God, if he be truly god, lacks nothing. These are the wretched tales of poets" (*Heracles* 1340–1346).[87]

Whether this sort of criticism was enough to provoke legitimate charges of impiety within the context of the state religion of Athens must await the explorations of the next section, but the real worry Socrates pinpoints with his specifications of the informal charges against him is this: others who had raised these same kinds of problems, tying them to anti-anthropomorphic arguments, had often been led into endorsing agnosticism or atheism. So if theological reformation leads to (or by itself, constitutes) such outcomes, the ordinary Athenian might think, why not Socrates too? Socrates, like Protagoras, had confessed that he lacked all wisdom, so it would be legitimately wondered whether he had not drawn the same agnostic conclusion (for which Protagoras may have been prosecuted)[88] that "concerning the gods I am not in a position to know either that (or how) they are or that (or how) they are not, or what they are like in form" (D.L. 9.51–52; DK 80 B4).[89] Another thinker, Diagoras of Melos, beginning out of moral concerns like Socrates, had ended up with a reputation for blasphemy by focusing on the phenomenon of unpunished wrongdoing.[90] This association must in fact be intended by Aristophanes when he calls Socrates the "Melian" (830).[91] Last, we find that Prodicus is explicitly associated with Socrates by Aristophanes (361) and (therefore) Socrates actively attempts to disassociate himself from Prodicus in the *Apology* (19e). Here it seems Aristophanes is simply relying on the plausibility of associating overintellectualism with atheism. Both a Sophist and nature philosopher,

86. See, e.g., Dodds (1), 33, 180–182; Kirk et al., 209; and Lloyd-Jones, 146.
87. For a close examination of Euripides' criticisms of Greek religion, see Festugière (2); Yunis, part 2; and M. Lefkowitz (2); cf. Irwin (2).
88. See Dover (2) and C. W. Mueller.
89. See Guthrie (7), 234–235, and Kerferd, 164–167.
90. Rankin, 139–140; Woodbury (1), argues that the attribution of complete atheism to Diagoras is a development of the fourth century.
91. Dover (1), 200–201; Guthrie (7), 237; Woodbury (1).

Prodicus was notorious for his atheism, explaining belief in the gods as being rooted in our natural feelings of gratitude for the gifts of nature.[92]

We can now appreciate why, despite the real implausibility of the informal case against Socrates, Aristophanes need not be found to be guilty of utterly malicious distortion. Although in all probability Socrates did not engage in or teach active, committed physical investigation or theorizing during his later maturity—playing little with fleas, maps (Anaximander), or magnets (Thales), giving no lessons in the new sophistic, and never finding atheism attractive—he had exhibited enough of an interest in the new science, seemed connected to one (possibly two) noted figure(s) in this field (Xenophanes, Diogenes) and any number of Sophistic anti-anthropo-psychics to make a charge of guilt by association not entirely unreasonable. And of course, given that it is not to the comic purposes of Aristophanes to spend any amount of time carefully distinguishing the various new intellectuals, it is natural for him not to be too concerned to represent the position of Socrates with complete accuracy. As Socrates himself suggests, he is simply the target of the standard criticisms brought out against any philosopher (*Ap.* 23d). His defense consists in asking the jurors to confront these prejudices with their actual knowledge of him gained in the twenty-three or so years since the first production of the *Clouds*.[93] But as both Socrates and Aristophanes realize, what is most menacing to common religious opinion is not Ionian physical experimentation and speculation per se, but the heretical conclusions they invite, and on this count, Socrates' gods (or god) and his agnosticism are almost as problematic as Vortex. For while Socrates may preserve something of the old dichotomy between gods and humans that allows his gods to continue both to play an interventionist role (as with, e.g., the *daimonion*) and to serve as a caution to epistemological hubris, they nonetheless *appear* to be nontraditional, moralized innovations that could conceivably threaten traditional belief and cult, offering in their stead only the superintellectual, rootless search of the *elenchos*.

Socrates, then, is entertaining no diversion when he takes up and denies the informal charges. Those who saw the *Clouds* performed and those who were influenced by the kinds of rumors it traded in may have written

---

92. Note too that the Eleatic philosopher Melissus declared that it is impossible to have knowledge of the gods (D.L. 9.24); see Guthrie (7), 236–238. Note too the atheism attributed to the new intellectuals Critias, Gorgias, Euenos, and Hippias (Guthrie [7], 235–247; Kerferd, 163–172; Drachmann).

93. Dover (1), lxxx; Reeve, 20.

off the Thinkery's investigator of fleas and gnats, but not the teacher of religious innovations as well. Socrates is fully aware that the charge of being a new intellectual paints its target with a broad brush, and that insofar as it puts him in the tradition of Xenophanes it is not entirely in error. He may be able to deny with ease that he is an atheist, but how might he reply to the charge that his thoroughly moralized gods are not the gods of the Athenian state, that for him those civic gods are only *nomos* to the real *phusis* of things, just "an out-of-date coin" (*nomisma* [*Nu.* 248])? To discover an answer to this, we must turn to Socrates' defense against his formal indictment.

3.3 The "Later Accusers": *Apology* 24b–35d

We have seen how the forces underlying the indictment and conviction of Socrates began to take form many years in advance, as various rumors— some slanderous, some dangerously close to the truth, and thus plausible and *persuasive* (πιθανῶς λέγοντες) (23e1–2)—began to circulate (18c8– d2). Again, Socrates tells us that what fueled them was his uninterrupted career as the elenctic gadfly of Athens. His continual practice of "examination" and his many refutations of supposed experts (and those performed by his young followers) bred a reputation for possessing and teaching "wisdom," and all this fostered resentment, anger, and envy. Athenians so affected were then naturally led into making and believing slanderous misinterpretations of his activities (cf. 20b–24b).

Socrates thus comes to trial before a jury deeply infected by the prejudices and fears the informal accusations spawned; and whatever their own opinion of the matter may have been, Meletus and the other formal accusers brought charges tailor-made to exploit those prejudices.[94] For as the ensuing interrogation reveals, Meletus bases his "corruption of youth" charge on the same kinds of accusations Socrates sees tied by popular opinion to the informal charges of engaging in natural science and sophistry; namely, the accusations of both holding and teaching novel religious views that undermine conventional religion (and thereby corrupt). Considering everything we have seen so far, together with the atheistic reputations of Socrates' infamous former "pupils" Alcibiades and Critias (and

94. Cf. Brickhouse and Smith (12), 111–112.

without considering other aspects of their moral and political reputations), such accusations as these would have had great prima facie plausibility.

3.3.1 Socrates' Formal Defense

One of the reasons Socrates gave for fearing the first accusers more than the later ones was that because of the anonymity of the former he could not use his standard method of investigation to cross-examine (ἐλέγξαι) them (18d5), but that difficulty is removed with these later accusers. Thus, Socrates chooses to conduct much of his defense against the formal charges by interrogating the official instigator of those charges, Meletus. As we shall see, Meletus fails miserably in his attempt to maintain the coherency of his allegations in the face of Socrates' elenctic probing. Socrates' tactics and Meletus's failure have caused a good deal of scholarly controversy concerning the legitimacy of the charges, the sincerity of Meletus's motivations, and the historical accuracy of the *Apology,* as well as the cogency of Socrates' defense. It has appeared to some, for example, that Socrates attempts only an ad hominem evasion of Meletus and not a direct refutation of the charges against him.[95]

I am going to presume for my purposes that such concerns have been effectively addressed by two recent studies of the *Apology.*[96] These works make it clear that the weight of evidence shows that all the parties to the case understood the indictment to specify important, legally actionable crimes that required of Socrates a serious, thoughtful reply. For, among other things, the items composing the formal indictment directly parallel the insinuations of the first accusers (insinuations that Socrates clearly takes seriously), capture the sensibilities of conservative religious tradition,[97] were sufficiently plausible to persuade the ἄρχων βασιλεύς to forward the case to a large group of paid jurors, a majority of whom in turn were sufficiently convinced to vote for conviction, and show every appearance of being a legitimate application of the law proscribing impiety.[98]

95. See, e.g., Beckman, 61; Burnet (3), notes on 24c9, 26a4, 26d4; Ferguson, 170; Hackforth (2), 104; and Taylor (2), 100.
96. Brickhouse and Smith (12), 112–117; Reeve, 82–87. See also Brickhouse and Smith (8), chaps. 5 and 6.1.
97. See, e.g., Isocrates *Areiopagitikos* 7.29–30.
98. On the nature of impiety (ἀσέβεια/*asebeia*) as a legal charge, see D. Cohen (2); MacDowell, 197–202; and Versnel (1), 123–131.

It is especially telling that Socrates never attempts to dispute the general legality or morality of raising such charges in the abstract (but only their application to his own case), something we would expect if he had doubts on this score, especially in light of his scrupulous insistence on proper legal procedure during the trial of the ten generals (32a–c).[99] Although Socrates adamantly holds that the formal charges—like the informal charges—are utterly false (17a–b, 23d, 28a2–4) and is convinced that Meletus at least is in reality (if not consciously) insincere in his pursuit of the case (24c–d),[100] he conducts his defense as though such charges might be appropriately brought against others and explains the injustice of his conviction as the fault of men, not the laws or institutions of Athens (Cr. 54c; cf. 50a–52). Finally, Socrates is himself obligated by his own moral principles and declarations to do more than merely rhetorically evade or "entrap" Meletus; rather, he must do his utmost to offer a truthful and thorough response to the actual charges against him (as he implies at 19a2–4), and this, he concludes at 28a2–4, is just what he has done.[101] To do otherwise would be to contravene his many promises to tell only the truth (18a5–6, 20d5–6, 22b5–6, 28a6, 31e1, 32a8, 33c1–2), and would convict him of the very charges he has been brought to trial on: sophistry if he only befuddles Meletus, impiety if he says anything that persuades the jury unjustly (35c–d) or that violates the oath he would have made at his pre-trial hearing (ἀνάκρισις).[102]

---

99. See Cohen (1), 213–216, who also notes that Socrates' comments at Eu. 3b–c and 5e–6d support the view that he has no objections to laws forbidding impiety per se. Note, also, the commitment to the rule of law Socrates exhibits at the end of the Apology (34b–35d; cf. Crito, esp. the suggestion [50a–54d] that one ought to do what one can to repeal those laws one disagrees with or—failing that—obey them; see Kraut [2], chap. 3). Allen (2), 15–19, is one of the few who thinks unorthodox belief was not culpable under the Athenian law proscribing impiety.

100. It has been suggested by Ostwald, 494–495, for example, that one of Meletus's motives in prosecuting Socrates is to rehabilitate himself politically, to distance himself from the tyranny of the Thirty in which he had played a leading role; cf. H. Blumenthal and Mac-Dowell (1), 208–210. It also seems that Meletus was one of those previously shown to be an ignorant "know nothing" poet through elenctic refutation (most probably by one of Socrates' young followers) (23d–24b, 22a–c; cf. 19b1–2). Some scholars have identified Meletus with the Meletus who prosecuted Andocides, thus suggesting he is some sort of religious zealot (e.g., A. E. Taylor [1], 110), and thus—contra Socrates—sincerely religiously motivated in bringing his charges (e.g., Reeve, 98–99). But see the arguments against this view in Brickhouse and Smith (12), 27–29.

101. Cf. Brickhouse and Smith (12), 112 n. 6, and (8), 185.

102. See MacDowell (2), 240–242, and Mikalson (1), 85, 94.

3.3.2 The Formal Charges

Socrates takes up the three formal charges in reverse order, considering the corruption charge first: "[Socrates] also wrongs the youth by corrupting them" [ἀδικεῖ δέ καί τοὺς νέους διαφθείρων]. Socrates' initial response to this charge is to offer two arguments which purport that attempting to corrupt youth is something that he does not do, or at least, would never willingly do (24c–26a; cf. 37a). These arguments are in themselves important and revealing, and I shall touch on them later. But for the purposes of determining Socrates' relation to popular religious conceptions, I turn straight to his defense against the other charges. Another reason for postponing consideration of this third charge is that it is based on the other two. For when pressed for clarification of the precise manner in which he is alleged to corrupt the youth (26b2–6), Meletus vigorously affirms (26b7) that it is *teaching* youths the notions specified by the other two charges that constitutes the charge of corruption (a reduction paralleled at *Euthyphro* 3b1–4).[103] So, according to Meletus, if Socrates can show the religious charges to be false he will thereby establish the falsehood of the corruption charge.[104]

Before we turn to these two charges, it is important to note that in the Athenian legal system there was no "letter of the law," no set of formal definitions of such crimes as impiety.[105] Rather, the legally effective definition of a crime was simply the one "inherent in the collective consciousness of the community as manifested through the 500 or so judges who happened to be sitting on a particular day to hear a particular case."[106]

---

103. Contrary to the view of some commentators (e.g., Stokes [2], 66), who see the corruption charge to encompass "dubious moral teaching." See Reeve, 75–76, on Hackforth's, (2), 105, objection to this view (cf. Reeve, 96 n. 35). Because of the rumor of atheism provided by the first accusers, the charge of nonrecognition of the civic gods does not appear to be an *inference* from the καινὰ δαιμόνια charge (contra A. E. Taylor [4], 8 n. 1).

104. As noted below, Socrates is only required to defend himself against the prosecutor's *interpretation* of the formal charges; no other interpretations (e.g., someone's view that Socrates corrupted youth in some other fashion) are legally at issue before the court (Brickhouse and Smith [12], 119; Reeve, 79, 84–87). Also, I will be presupposing on the basis of *Ap.* 26c–d that Socrates and Meletus understand that whatever Socrates "teaches"—that is, asserts as true to students—is what he believes, and hence, that a good defense against a charge of, say, corrupting by teaching atheism will involve arguing that one does believe in gods of some sort.

105. Again, cf. Garland (3), 151, who argues that Socrates was clearly guilty "according to the letter of the law."

106. D. Cohen (2), 698, and see (1), 207–210; cf. Vlastos (14), 294.

Hence, what will be of paramount importance in our analysis of the formal charges and our assessment of Socrates' "guilt" will be our judgment of how the prosecutors and (following their lead) the jurors would have interpreted each charge; in particular, those jurors who voted for conviction. Note also that where we might see evasion or irrelevance in the conduct of a defense speech Athenians might have seen relevance, for since there were no rules of evidence in such proceedings and because any trial presented an opportunity to address old grievances (no matter how irrelevant to the actual charges they might be) it was taken for granted that the conduct of one's entire life was at issue. How then are to we to understand each formal charge, what is the nature and adequacy of Socrates' response, and in what ways might he be judged innocent or guilty of each count against him?

The first charge reads: "The gods the state recognizes, [Socrates] does not recognize" [οὓς μέν ἡ πόλις νομίζει θεοὺς οὐ νομίζων]. There has been a lengthy controversy over the meaning of this phrase in part because of the unclarity of the term θεοὺς νομίζειν.[107] Does Socrates' alleged failure to "recognize" (νομίζειν) the civic gods mean that he is charged with nonconformance to the religious practices overseen by the Athenian *polis* (e.g., not "recognizing" gods like Athena Polias by not paying appropriate cult to them) or is he charged with not believing them to exist (i.e., not "recognizing" their very existence)?[108]

The best gloss on νομίζειν is, arguably, one that captures its essential link to νόμος. Assuming that linkage, then, νομίζειν bears the broad meaning "to accept (or "treat," "practice") as normal."[109] On this reading, the expression θεοὺς νομίζειν should be understood to mean "to accept the gods in the normal way," indicating that both customary religious behavior *and* the set of attitudes that are conventionally taken to underlie such behavior are implied. Hence, the first formal charge on its face may be interpreted by the jurors to concern "the gods of the state" in matters of belief or practice (or both). We do not possess a transcript of the prosecution's speech and so we have no way of really knowing whether Socrates' observance of cult practice might have in fact been an explicit issue of his trial. However, Socrates himself never addresses such concerns during

107. For overviews of the history of this debate and its scholarship—as well as judicious treatments of the problem—see Brickhouse and Smith (12), 30–34; Fahr; and Yunis.

108. See, e.g., Burnet (3), 184, who makes the first charge out to be "one of nonconformity in religious practice, not of unorthodoxy in religious belief."

109. Yunis, 65; Dover (1), 203; Fahr, 15–17, 107, 138–139.

the course of his defense. That fact, together with his focus on the identity and nature of his *beliefs* and what he purportedly *teaches*, suggests at the very least that the primary *aspect* of θεοὺς νομίζειν at issue in the case of Socrates is its attitudinal, intellectual component, one that assumes above all that the Athenian gods in question *exist* (which implies a sincere belief in their power, as well as genuine "fear" of them; cf. *Ap.* 26b8–d5, 29a1–4, 35d2–5).[110]

Although the law against impiety at the time of Socrates' trial was vague, there is every reason to suppose that this sort of charge of heterodoxy—interpreted during the preliminary hearing and trial as a particular extension of that law—would have been seen as legally appropriate.[111] Socrates' long reply to the first accusers also makes little sense if the charge is not one concerning improper *belief*. Xenophon, as well, indicates that the charges against Socrates involved atheism, not solely or mainly failure in orthopraxy (*Mem.* 1.1.2–5, esp. 1.1.5). Greek law may have emphasized correct religious behavior over belief on the whole, but the average Athenian would surely have seen the threat to traditional practice posed by instances of theoretical atheism (or those views that imply it) and would have had little tolerance for anyone who advocated atheism no matter how irreproachable their observance of cult might have been. Rather, it was understood that proper religious practice required a minimal set of religiously correct attitudes, especially an intellectual commitment to the existence of those to whom ritual is directed.[112] So, then, the first formal charge accuses Socrates primarily of not believing that "the gods of the state" *exist*.[113]

Nevertheless, failure to observe proper cult practice may have been an issue for *some* jurors, since, among other things, they might have recalled that the Socrates of the *Clouds* seemed to accept a rejection of the standard cult (425–426), sacrificing *solely* to the Clouds (*Nu.* 365). Socrates' actual behavior would have also been thought to have an important bear-

---

110. Yunis 39, 63–66; Fahr, 153–157; Brickhouse and Smith (12), 31; Connor, 50 n. 10; Versnel (1), 125. E. Derenne, 217–223, has convincingly argued that for a great number of passages in Plato the interpretation "not believe in the *existence* of the gods [in the way it is traditionally done by the *polis*]" is the correct gloss of θεοὺς οὐ νομίζων. Reeve, 78, also argues that νομίζειν θεούς gets cashed-out throughout the *Apology* as νομίζειν θεοὺς εἶναι.

111. MacDowell (2), 184–186, 199–200, 240–242; Brickhouse and Smith (12), 33.

112. See, e.g., Yunis, 39.

113. Contrary to the majority of recent interpreters, Garland (3), 14, 142–144, has suggested that the real issue posed by the first charge is non-conformity to traditional religious practice, but he provides no arguments for adopting this suggestion.

ing on determining his real intentions and the potential threat to the civic cult posed by his beliefs. Thus we will have to take up the issue of Socrates' observance of traditional religious practice in the next section (3.4).[114] Finally, we will also need to ask what the phrase "the gods acknowledged by the state" is supposed to refer to. This question is more complex than it may seem. As an initial identification, however, it is fair to say that the phrase denotes those gods whose cults received *polis*-wide political, economic, behavioral, and emotional support; gods such as Athena Polias, Zeus Polieus, and Apollo Delphinios. These are the civic deities tied to the identity and protection of the entire *polis* and whose sacred enclosures were geographically, politically, and socially at the center of Athens.[115]

Socrates begins his response to the first charge by cross-examining Meletus, initially requesting that he clarify—"before the gods about whom we now speak" (26b8–9)[116]—that allegation: Does Meletus mean to charge that (1a) Socrates believes that there exist gods *of some sort* (εἶναί τινας θεούς) who are other than (ἑτέρους) the gods believed to exist by the city of Athens and does not believe that the gods of the city exist (thus charging Socrates with "local" but not *complete* atheism) or does he mean to charge Socrates with complete atheism (1b), that is, with believing in *no gods at all* (26b9–c6)? The response from Meletus is immediate (26c7) and is reaffirmed (26e3–5) after a brief discussion. Implicitly joining forces with the atheistic implications of the "first accusations," Meletus now means to charge Socrates with being a complete, "global" atheist (τὸ παράπαν οὐ νομίζεις θεούς; cf. *Mem.* 1.1.5, Aris. *Rh.* 1419a8–11). Since, as we saw, the prosecution's interpretation of the formal charges is what—more than anything else—*defines* those charges for the purposes of the trial, complete atheism (1b) is what Socrates must now defend himself against before the jurors, not merely nonrecognition of the civic gods.[117]

114. Note that Xenophon defends Socrates by stressing the idea that *both* his utterances *and* his behavior were truly religious (*Mem.* 1.1.20); see Ostwald, 137, and Cohen (1), 200–217.

115. C. Sourvinou-Inwood, 307–309. Greek cult was almost always directed to the aspect of a deity rather than the deity in the abstract—e.g., Athena Polias, protector of Athens, rather than Athena *simpliciter*—and each such aspect could be regarded as virtually an independent deity (ibid., 300, 307; Mikalson [2], 10; Garland [3], 144, 151).

116. This seems pretty clearly not to be a reference to the divinities behind the second, καινὰ δαιμόνια charge (hence, not a reference to his *daimonion*), but an affirmation that he, Socrates, also acknowledges (in at least some sense) the existence of the gods of the state.

117. Brickhouse and Smith (12), 117–119, and (8), 182–189; Reeve, 78–79, 84–87. Cf. Allen (2), 22–32; Bonner and Smith, 2:123; Dover (2), 41; and MacDowell (2), 43–46, 60.

This interpretive choice has the effect of eliminating the second charge of religious innovation from further independent consideration,[118] recasts the corruption charge as one of teaching atheism, and instantly opens up to Socrates a most effective rebuttal.

Socrates first reminds Meletus of the second accusation, that of "introducing other, new divinities" [ἕτερα δὲ καινὰ δαιμόνια εἰσηγούμενος] (27a5–6; cf. 27c4–8). Next, he extracts from him the admissions that if one believes in *daimonia* (δαιμόνια, "divine matters") one believes in *daimones* (δαίμονες, "divinities") (27c1–2), and second, that since divinities are themselves either gods or children of gods (27c10–d3), one who believes in them must believe in gods (27d10–e3). Socrates then concludes that Meletus's accusations are contradictory and senseless (27a1–7): Meletus is charging him with both believing and not believing in the existence of gods.[119]

In view of the ease with which Socrates is able to derive this devastating contradiction, and because it gets Socrates off the hook of having to address the second charge, many interpreters have been puzzled by how Meletus interpreted the first charge.[120] Some even see Meletus as the victim of entrapment, lured into his atheistic interpretation by the sweet prospect of making "Socrates' wickedness more astounding."[121] But this is implausible: Socrates has given Meletus the clearest of choices between theistic innovation (of some sort) and complete disbelief in divine beings.[122] So then why did Meletus not take the first option, the interpretation that our discussion of the informal charges and Meletus's own worries about Socrates' replacement of the civic gods by καινὰ δαιμόνια would argue as coming much closer to the truth?

The answer to this question is necessarily speculative, and it must be distilled from a number of indicators. First, given Socrates' own characterization of the "first" accusations seen above, we may suppose that the

---

118. I see no reason to agree with Reeve's claim that "Meletus does not simply charge Socrates with teaching atheism. He charges him with teaching atheism by teaching belief in *daimonia* (26b8–c7)" (95).

119. See Reeve's more formal version of this argument, 93; cf. Aristotle's report (*Rhet.* 1419a10), and see *Mem.* 1.1.4 for echoes of this same argument.

120. Cf. Allen (2), 6–7; Garland (3), 143; Grote (1), 7:152–163; and Hackforth (2), 104. See Reeve, 82–83, 94.

121. Taylor (4), 9; cf. Brickhouse and Smith (8), 184, who hold that those like myself who see a threat to cult in Socrates' conception of the gods will see Socrates as "carefully avoiding" the formal charge (1a) by "getting Meletus to construe the charge as one of atheism."

122. Phillipson, 306–311; Reeve, 84.

popular prejudice against nature philosophers and Sophists (and their connection with atheism) with which Socrates had long been associated was something Meletus would have been well aware of. So he may have been blindly taken in by those prejudices *per* Socrates' allegation (19b1–2), and even if not, he may have thought that they were so pervasive and deep—and the distinctions between the various degrees of religious nonconformity held by the new intellectuals sufficiently murky to the jury (see, again, *Ap.* 23d)—that a charge of complete atheism would be the best tactical choice.[123] Moreover, if Meletus were to choose to pursue Socrates on the first interpretation, under which Socrates would then be much more recognizably religious in some sense, he could then no longer rely on the much more deeply felt popular animosity toward complete, global atheism to make his case (thus risking an acquittal).[124] Hence, if Meletus thought he could count on most of the jurors believing that typical intellectuals reject all recognizable, genuine divinities (meaning, especially, the kind that respond in expected ways to material propitiatory cult) and, in addition, intended (perhaps) to show that Socrates' καινὰ δαιμόνια are no *real* divinities either, then his hope of convicting Socrates on a count of global atheism would be reasonable.

That Meletus does in fact think his charge is reasonable is indicated by his vigorous, negative response when he is asked by Socrates (in clarification of the charge of compete atheism) if he, Socrates, does not believe—as other human beings generally do—that the sun and moon are gods (26d1–3). Meletus's adamant denial of Socratic theism (26d4–5) and his attribution to Socrates of the doctrine that the sun is stone and the moon earth—a doctrine famously associated with Anaxagoras[125]—also shows us that

123. Brickhouse and Smith (12), 123, and (4), 185, favor the explanation that Meletus settled on his charge of atheism because he had been blinded by the prejudices bandied about by the first accusers.

124. Brickhouse and Smith (8), chap. 6.2.4, argue that since Socrates' belief in moral gods is so evident (even during the trial), that if it threatens disbelief in the cult-respecting gods of the state (on a *strict* interpretation)—that even a dimwit like Meletus would have been able to make that threat clear, and so would have pursued (1a) rather than the charge of atheism (1b). However, it should be clear by this point (or at least by the end of this chapter) that for Meletus to even discern—let alone actually demonstrate convincingly—how Socrates' own moral theory undermines certain aspects of cult (and only that, while also requiring philosophy of us)—and to do so without risking an even more devastating elenctic demonstration of confusion than the one he actually received (26b–27e)—is a task beyond his abilities (or is, at least, a much more difficult task than simply charging Socrates with atheism).

125. Who may have been tried some years before on charges of impiety; see D.L. 2.12–14 and Plutarch *Pericles* 32. Dover (2), 27–32, has questioned whether this prosecution actually

Meletus seriously expects to persuade the jury that Socrates is an atheist and holds it reasonable to suppose that most Athenians will find Anaxagoras an atheist, despite his advocacy of cosmic Mind. Such newfangled explanatory principles like this, even if they might be *called* gods, are not what most Athenians mean by the term (for such "gods" do not seem to require or respond in expected ways to sacrificial cult).[126] Of course, Meletus's interpretive choice may also have resulted from a lack of quick intelligence, a failure to anticipate the possibly obscure point that belief in divinities implies belief in gods, a momentary confusion abetted by religious fanaticism, and/or (perhaps) darker, self-interested motives.[127]

Whatever Meletus's motivations were, his hope of substantiating a charge of atheism was audacious. After all, by this point in the trial Socrates has already denied having the sort of wisdom nature philosophers like Anaxagoras lay claim to, and implicitly—but directly—has denied that he is an atheist before (19a, 20e–23c) and after Meletus's "clarification" of the charge (26e3, 28d–31a, 33c) by invoking "the god" (Apollo) and Zeus and by declaring himself to be the dedicated servant of a *god* (Apollo Pythios, a god possessing civic cult; see n. 161). Further, Socrates gave clear and pointed notice that the youth of Athens hardly have need of plagiarized instruction in doctrines found in texts that can be picked up for a mere drachma (namely, Anaxagoras's text [26d9–e2]). Socrates' remarks at this point (26d1–3) also have the rhetorical effect of attesting *to* a belief on his part that the sun and moon *are* in fact gods of some sort,[128] and as

---

took place, but (nonetheless) *Ap.* 26d6 can be understood to strongly suggest it; see also Yunis, 66–72.

126. See L. Woodbury (1), esp. 208; Fahr, 15–17, 107, 138–139; and Ostwald, 525–536.

127. Garland (3), 143, suggests the first point; Reeve, 94, the second.

128. "Do I not even believe, then, that sun and moon are gods, *as other human beings do?*" Socrates' prayer to the sun in the *Symposium* (220d) gives some additional evidence that he would have accepted the divinity of the sun; see B. Jackson, 14–17. So does Plato's recognition of the sun and moon as gods at *Laws* 821b, 886d–e, and 887e, and his instituting a sun cult in the *Laws* (945b–948b). Mikalson (4), 98, notes that Socrates' choice of gods is puzzling, since if Socrates wanted to address the charge of nonrecognition he could have chosen a god(s) with an official cult (which to the best of our knowledge Helios lacked). However, Garland (3), 144 n. 7, speculates that Socrates may have picked Helios with an eye to turning the tables on Meletus and the court: hinting with his choice that since the jurors themselves customarily pray to Helios (Hesiod *Erga* 339; Soph. *Ajax* 823 ff., esp. 846, 857; *Laws* 887e) they too are guilty of the second charge by worshiping a deity that has never been formally "licensed" by the state. It seems to me that Socrates may also be defending himself against Aristophanes's implication (*Nu.* 225–234) that Socrates does not recognize the divinity of the sun.

we saw, he ends by convicting Meletus of a seemingly malicious contradiction premised on a charge thereby shown to be "hubristic, unrestrained, and rashly conceived" (26e) (one to which we see no response). Of course, this turns out to be a Pyrrhic victory, since a sufficient portion of Socrates' jury is apparently so thoroughly prejudiced against him that they convict him despite his elenctic mauling of the prosecution.

Readers of the *Apology* are thus commonly left with the impression that Meletus has bungled what could have been a much more decisive attack, noting for example that Socrates never himself asserts the premises of his refutation of Meletus (e.g., that he actually *believes* in the existence of *daimones* traditionally conceived) but only proceeds elenctically, purely on the basis of Meletus's own concessions. But even if Socrates did not believe every one of the premises driving his refutation, his defense is not thereby reduced to prevarication or a mere ad hominem attack: showing that the case of the prosecution is incoherent ought to be sufficient to convince any clearheaded juror that the entire set of charges is unlikely. Moreover, in this case Meletus—as the initiator of the γραφή—is *also* a prosecution "witness," and so it is quite to the point for Socrates to undermine this witness.[129] It is nevertheless frequently suspected that Socrates' tactics left a number of his jurors with misgivings about his own positive religious commitments, and so perhaps some number of them voted for conviction on some revised interpretation of the first charge (and the others) against which Socrates had no real defense.[130] What other argumentative options, then, were open to the prosecution?

3.3.3 Meletus's Options

Suppose, first, that Meletus had maintained his choice (1b) to convict Socrates of outright atheism, pressing on to elicit Socrates' own religious views. In order to avoid falling into contradiction with his second charge of religious innovation, Meletus would need to show that at least one of the following premises of Socrates' *elenchos* against him is not held by Socrates or himself:

129. Reeve, 86, 105–106.
130. E.g., Allen (2), 7.

1. Anyone who believes that there are (νομίζειν) divine matters (δαιμόνια πράγματα) of any sort must believe in the existence of divinities (δαίμονες) in the same way (just as those who believe in "horse matters" must believe in the existence of horses). (27b3–c10)
2. Anyone who believes in the existence of divinities (δαίμονες) must also believe in the existence of gods (θεοί), since δαίμονες are either gods or the offspring of gods (just as someone who believes in the existence of horse-children must believe in horses). (27c5–e3)
3. If one believes in the existence of and/or teaches (sincerely) about divinities (the second charge), one must believe that there are divine matters (δαιμόνια) of some sort. (27c5–8)[131]

As it happens, however, none of these propositions could reasonably have been denied by Meletus or shown not to be held by Socrates (and most other Athenians), and furthermore, we have good reasons for thinking that both he and Socrates would endorse all three.

1a. Meletus himself must agree on grounds of common Athenian good sense and in view of the several compelling examples provided by Socrates (viz., human, horse, and flute matters [27b3–8]) that a belief in divine matters implies a belief in divinities. And it seems eminently plausible to suppose that Socrates is himself persuaded by his own examples to believe that if an activity is defined by reference to the actions of an entity, and one recognizes the existence of that activity under that description, that then one must hold that entity to exist. The fact that Socrates in response to the question of whether *anyone* would reject various instances of (1), immediately answers in the negative for Meletus (who exhibits an initial reluctance [27b8–9]) and the jurors also indicates a Socratic commitment to (1). Why, though, does he not simply *affirm* that he *does* hold (1)? The answer to this and the explanation for the entire ad hominem structure of his argument lies, I think, in Socrates' own legal strategy and his commitment to the value of the elenctic method (and its proper conduct). As Socrates sees it, his task at this point is to show that Meletus's charges are

131. Cf. Brickhouse and Smith (12), 121–124. Reeve, 76–78, argues that the καινὰ δαιμόνια of the second charge (and so δαιμόνια here) refers to divine "doings." However, "matters" seems the preferable translation because it seems that the prosecution intends for the charge of innovation to cover the informal prejudice that Socrates believed in unconventional *entities;* e.g., deities like Aristophanes' Clouds, Anaxagoras's Mind, and the god or δαίμων whose voice is the *daimonion.*

confused, and the most rhetorically effective way to do that is not to simply affirm 1 through 3, but rather, to show that the main author of the charges against him cannot coherently interpret those charges in a way that avoids contradiction. In addition, by using the "say what *you* [Meletus] believe" principle of the Socratic *elenchos*, Socrates is able to simultaneously undermine the charges while *also* displaying by example (rather than engaging in simple denials) his innocence of the "corruption" charge. Just as he maintained in his reply to the first accusers, he might say, he now *shows* that he does not *teach* any doctrines (let alone atheism), not even such obvious claims as (1), but rather, goes from one individual to another exposing *their* presumptions of wisdom (*Ap.* 33a1–b8).[132]

2a. Meletus himself could hardly deny that he holds that a recognition of δαίμονες sensibly requires a recognition of θεοί: someone who initiates a prosecution on impiety charges simply could not put himself in the position of denying a standard religious belief of the day. Neither should we see in the options Socrates builds into (2) any uncertainty on his part concerning its truth. Common usage allowed δαίμων the flexibility to refer to any manifestation of divine power: it could be used to designate Aphrodite (*Il.* 3.420), but could just as well indicate the unnamable occult power that watches over an individual.[133]

Although the attribution of this second proposition to Socrates has excited the greatest resistance of the three,[134] there is simply no evidence that anyone at the trial, including Socrates, would have accepted the existence of δαίμονες but rejected that of θεοί (and although the view that δαίμονες are gods or children of gods is stated hypothetically at 27d9–10, it is simply affirmed at 27c10–d1).[135] Moreover, the second formal charge against Socrates, of introducing καινὰ δαιμόνια (of any sort, and thus θεοί) appears to have stemmed in part from Socrates' well-known, self-confessed belief in his *daimonion*, a belief that Meletus (at least) is unlikely to deny (see *Ap.* 31c7–d2, *Eu.* 3b5–6, and below).[136] Finally, the attribution of (2) to Socrates is supported by the fact that he affirms in the strongest possible

132. See Reeve, 160–166.
133. See Chap. 1, n. 61, and Burkert (2), chap. 3.3.5; cf. *Sym.* 202e–203a.
134. See, e.g., R. Guardini, 43; Seeskin (2), 84; and T. G. West, 146–147. Also, Socrates might interpret the proposition metaphorically.
135. Cf. Reeve, 94 n. 31.
136. Reeve, 76–77, 84 n. 14, 97, however, goes overboard in thinking that Meletus targets only the *daimonion* with his καινὰ δαιμόνια charge: if that were correct, then Meletus would not have used the plural δαιμόνια.

terms throughout the *Apology* his belief in gods of some sort (see esp. 35d5–7).

3a. For these same reasons it would be difficult (to say the least) for Meletus to deny at this point that Socrates holds that belief in divinities implies belief in some variety of "divine matters"; and in any case, Socrates clearly does believe in "divine matters." However, given that Meletus must here work under the self-imposed burden of showing that Socrates is a *complete* atheist, he might attempt to show that the divinities lurking behind the καινὰ δαιμόνια rubric that Socrates would sanction are not real, genuine divinities. But such an attempt faces insurmountable difficulties. The first and most devastating of these is that there does not seem to be any plausible evidence that Socrates is such an atheist. Rather, Socrates directly and indirectly affirms his belief in gods and divinities, referring to his *daimonion* as a divine voice of god.[137] Thus, only by producing evidence that Socrates has held otherwise can Meletus convict him of insincerity in those theistic professions. But when Socrates later produces witnesses against the corruption (*via* irreligion) charge—noting that Meletus has produced no such witnesses himself—and then invites anyone to produce a witness that he has corrupted some youth, the clear implication of all this is that Socrates has never taught atheistic doctrine and, hence, that no such evidence exists (33d–34b; cf. *Apol.* 19–20). In any case, even if Meletus could have engaged in some fancy theological footwork, attempting to persuade the jury that the gods of Socrates (including the one responsible for his "sign" [40b1]) are somehow similar to the mechanistic, pseudodivine Vortex of the *Clouds,* Socrates could at least still revert to his defense against corruption; he can request that witnesses be produced and can point out that if it should turn out that Socrates believes and teaches what is false, the correct course of action is not punishment but instruction (24c–26a). Given the preceding, then, it is evident that once Meletus chooses to prosecute on a charge of atheism he becomes guilty of pressing false charges—or at least an unsound argument for them—upon Socrates. That Meletus is nonetheless successful in winning his case verifies Socrates' estimation of the weight of the ancient prejudices ranged against him.

In order to understand better the nature of these prejudices, and in order to clarify Socrates' religious views further, it is important to consider how

137. See, e.g., *Ap.* 40b1 and 31c8–d4 and Chapter 4.1.3 herein.

the trial might have gone had Meletus stuck with his original charges. This is not simply an exercise in imaginary forensics: regardless of Meletus's reformulation of the formal charges under Socratic examination, the initial accusations would stand in the mind of at least some jurors as still requiring rebuttal (especially in view of the long-standing biases against Socrates and the natural impression among some perceptive jurors that Meletus has blown his case under elenctic badgering). So then, what if, contrary to fact, Meletus had stuck to the sense of his original case and charged Socrates with not believing in the civic gods but in divinities other than those "recognized by the state" (and, hence, that *per* the second charge he believes in and pays cult to new divinities)? This, I will show, would have been a somewhat more legitimate route to take, and possibly more productive of votes to convict, since there are indications that Socrates did harbor suspect religious views. So the question becomes: Could Meletus have used Socrates' alleged nonstandard religious beliefs to obtain a conviction that was true (or truer) to the facts of the case?

3.4 Was Socrates Guilty?

It seems clear that if Meletus had in fact pressed his initial charges he could still have made use of the support provided by the first accusers. For as we saw, the threat of heresy implicit in those charges is ambiguous. The popular religious implications of being a "new intellectual" were equivocal between outright atheism and revisionary theology. Thus although Meletus might no longer attempt to connect Socrates with atheists like Prodicus or Diagoras directly, he could still associate Socrates with the intellectualist rejection of the poetic tradition that the jury will have associated with less extreme, though recognizably theistic, thinkers (e.g., Xenophanes and Diogenes of Apollonia). And this rejection some jurors might still find worthy of legal censure in itself, or at least insofar as they might find it productive of atheism or heterodox belief in "new deities," or—worse than either—devaluation of traditional cult.

What, then, might Meletus have adduced as formal evidence of Socrates' guilt on the first charge of heterodoxy and, thus, the second charge of innovation? The most likely sources of such evidence would be the various rumors that connect Socrates with the moral transformation of the civic gods into nonstandard deities (to the detriment of the civic cult), instanced—it might be argued—by his frequent references to his mysterious *daimonion*. Of course, Socrates' acceptance of the *daimonion* is compatible with his innocence of the first charge, but it would be a natural source of suspicion on the issue of what kinds of divinities one sanctions. The *daimonion* is, however, directly connected to the second, less-specific charge that Socrates introduces new "divine matters," which covers gods other than the civic gods, other new *daimones,* new cultic practices, or some combination of these, where all such introductions were potentially legally actionable.[138] Let me turn first, then, to an examination of the second charge, that of introducing καινὰ δαιμόνια.

3.4.1 Introducing New Divinities

Socrates seems to have been the first person in the history of Athens to be formally accused of this sort of crime.[139] Despite the lack of precedent, however, there is every reason to think that the charge is legally permissible. The Athenian *polis* took an active role in overseeing and funding all religious activity; in particular, it had the power to exclude or allow forms of worship, and those wishing to introduce new cults into Athens sought official sanction.[140] As the influx of foreign deities such as Bendis into Athens increased during and after the life of Socrates, there even seem to have been a number of prosecutions for failure to meet the requirements for proper religious innovation:[141] A foreign prostitute by the name of Phryne was charged with "introducing a new god" *c.* 350 (Euthias fr. 1 Muller = Ath. *Deipn.* 13.590d–591f; cf. Hyperid. fr. 60T), the orator and politician Demades was fined for "introducing Alexander as a god" in 324 (Ath. *Deipn.* 6.251b; cf. Aelian *VH* 5.12), and we hear of the execution of

138. P. Ciholas has argued for the view that since *Eu.* 3b–c recounts the formal charge as one of "*making* new gods," foreign importation of already recognized gods is not the issue, but rather, the deification of things formerly *not* thought to be gods. But this interpretation of what it is to "make" a new god ought not to be preferred here, given that this accusation is also allowed to encompass the *daimonion* without objection from Socrates (the *daimonion* being, probably, for Socrates the "sign" of a recognized civic god, Apollo).

139. Garland (3), 136, 146; Versnel (1), 127.

140. On this, see, e.g., Burkert (2), 176–179; Derenne, 224 ff.; Nestle, 79 ff.; Nilsson (3), 91 ff.; Sourvinou-Inwood, 297; Yunis, 23; and esp. Garland (3), 14, 19, 137, 149. Cf. *Laws* 738b–739a.

141. Dodds (2), 23; Garland (3), 149. Strabo (10.3.18) famously praises the Athenians' hospitality that includes tolerance toward even foreign gods: "For they welcomed so many of the foreign rites [viz., Bendis and Sabazios] that they were ridiculed by comic writers."

the priestess Ninos in a case that used a law against "introducing a foreign god" (Demos. 19.281; Josephus, *Apion* 2.267–268; cf. Servius *ad* Verg. *Aen.* 8.187).[142]

What were the requirements in Athens for proper religious innovation— in particular, the introduction of a new god by an Athenian—at the time of Socrates' trial? Typically, the "candidate-deity" first signaled his or her readiness to become a member of a *polis* by enlisting the help of a human representative through some sort of epiphany.[143] The Egyptian god Sarapis, for example, declared to the priest Apollonios in his sleep that a Sarapieion would have to be built on Delos (*IG* 9.4 1299.14–18), while the introduction of the instantly popular physician-god Asclepius was probably due to his having healed his sponsor, Telemachos (or a relation of his), at the mother sanctuary in Epidauros.[144] Subsequent to such manifestations, it was then up to the god's representative to drum up popular support for the deity's incorporation into the life of the *polis*, defending the accuracy of the epiphany, the goodwill of the god, and his or her past and potential largess to the *polis*, aiming, finally, to petition the *Boulê* and *Ekklesia* for implementation of the required changes (e.g., purchase of sanctuary land, inclusion in the religious festival calendar). Since such representations to the *polis* implied privileged access to the divine, were in the last analysis (at least in a primary sense) unverifiable, presented economic and devotional competition to the established cults, and could easily be based on self-interested (especially political) motives, a significant burden of proof would have been borne by the petitioner. If that burden was met, the final step prior to the implementation of the new cult was to secure its approval

142. Derenne, 224 ff., followed by O. Reverdin, 208–217, make the case for the existence of a fourth-century law forbidding the introductions of new gods. Versnel (1), 102–130, reviews the "foreign gods" of Athens (Adonis, Cybele, Bendis, Kotys, Sabazios, and Isodaites) and the cases of *asebeia*-by-importation cited above, arguing that although these cases and much other evidence postdates the execution of Socrates, there is ample reason to believe that there was a precursor of the law that sanctioned these trials (coming into existence between the decree of Diopeithes and the trial of Socrates) or an improvised precursor of the law used to prosecute Socrates; see also Derenne, 168 ff.; Garland (3), 150; Mikalson (1), 65–66, 92; MacDowell, 197; Reverdin, 213; and Rudhardt (1). Reverdin, 217, notes that Plato did not generally deviate from existing Attic law, and then observes that R. 427b–c rejects private cults on the grounds that it is difficult to introduce new cults and gods without making mistakes.

143. Another route would be for foreign residents to request the right to found a temple for their god. They were required to secure the formal permission of the Athenian Assembly to acquire a piece of land *and* permission to build the temple on it (Mikalson [1], 92–93).

144. On the introduction of Asclepius into Athens in the late 420s by Telemachos, see Garland (3), chap. 6.

by a relevant god (or gods) *via* an oracle. For Athens this typically meant consulting Apollo Pythios through his oracle at Delphi (*R.* 427b–c; Demos. 21.51; cf. *Laws* 828a).[145] Even then, however, "new gods and their sponsors were by no means assured of a warm welcome when they petitioned for entry into a Greek community."[146]

In view of all this, and given the interpretive flexibility of legal definition noted earlier, it appears that all the prosecution would need to do to persuade the jury of Socrates' guilt of the second charge is convince the majority of the jurors that the source of Socrates' *daimonion* (the deity whose "sign" and "voice" it is)—be it god or δαίμων—has not been formally licensed by the state.[147] Naturally, if they can also show that this being is harmful to Athens or an unreal delusion, so much the better, but this is not required.[148] Of course, to ensure victory Socrates' prosecutors would also want to obtain a conviction on the first count of nonrecognition, but they would probably not wish to attempt the very difficult task of showing that recognition of one's "unlicensed import" implicates one in practices or beliefs that undermine recognition of the existence of the gods of the state (and is thus a source of corruption).[149]

3.4.2 The *Daimonion* and New Divinities

There are a number of reasons for taking the view that the *daimonion* was directly connected with and central to the καινὰ δαιμόνια charge. Primary among these is Euthyphro's suggestion—to which Socrates does not ob-

145. See Garland (3), 1–20, 137, 149, and Sourvinou-Inwood, 303–304. Versnel (1), 103–123, cites several cases where the road to acceptance of the new deity was fraught with conflict; e.g., although Cybele was officially received into Athens and accorded a sanctuary (c. 450), the objectionable appearance and behavior of her more extravagant devotees fueled fierce resistance.

146. Garland (3), 146. Versnel (1), 121, writes: "The very nature of the notion 'foreign' [e.g., god] evoked various unpleasant associations: The smell of magic and profit-making, connotations of license or ecstasy, revelry and sexual promiscuity."

147. Cf. Burkert (2), 317: "From the legal point of view the introduction of new gods was the actionable fact." See also Garland (3), 149, and Reverdin, 228–231.

148. Contra Brickhouse and Smith (12), 34, who think that Socrates' prosecutors *must* show that his καινὰ δαιμόνια are not *real* divinities. In addition, Garland (3), 149, notes that there would have been significant disincentives for attempting this: the prosecution would risk retaliation by the contested δαιμόνια and would be hard-pressed to provide any kind of convincing evidence, given the flexibility of the concept of divinity at the time.

149. Contra Taylor (4), 7–9, esp. n. 1; cf. Burkert (2), 317, and Reeve, 75 n. 1.

ject—that Socrates has been called before the ἄρχων βασιλεύς because "you [Socrates] assert that the *daimonion* comes to you on occasion. So he [Meletus] has brought this indictment, claiming that you are making innovations concerning the divine things, and he is going into the law court to slander you, knowing that such things are easy to make slander about before the many" (*Eu.* 3b5–9; cf. 5a7–8). Xenophon also claims that the second charge derives from Socrates' talk of the *daimonion* (*Mem.* 1.1.2–3; *Apol.* 12), and the Socrates of Plato's *Apology* reports that "Meletus wrote about it in the indictment" (31d1–2).[150] Add to this the fact that Xenophon feels the need to defend Socrates against this sort of understanding of the charge (*Mem.* 1.1.3–4; *Apol.* 12–14; cf. *Mem.* 4.3.12–13) and we have solid grounds for supposing that Socrates' *daimonion* was indeed its primary target.[151]

Again, however, this charge may also be intended to accommodate other allegations and rumors of religious invention.[152] Since both the first and later accusers attempt to portray Socrates as a crypto-*phusiologos*-Sophist similar to the Cloud-worshiping Socrates presented by Aristophanes, and since the later accusers may well suspect that Socrates rejects various traditional anthropopsychic qualities associated with the gods, then whatever god or gods it could be thought had been left over after his theological cleansings will have served as a potential source of suspicion to the court. History, after all, is filled with cases where reformation was confused with heretical revolution.[153] In addition, given Plato's willingness to picture Soc-

150. So contra Brickhouse and Smith (12), 124 n. 22, Socrates *does* show an awareness that the *daimonion* might have concerned the jury; cf. Ehrenberg, 378.

151. Contra Taylor (4), 10 ff. See, though, Brickhouse and Smith (12), 35, and n. 125. Later writers also took the same view of the second charge. Josephus, for instance, writes that "Socrates was condemned . . . because he . . . claimed—surely a joke as some say—that something daimonic gave signs to him" (*Ap.* 2.263). Mikalson (1), 66, seems correct to hold that the prosecution used "new δαιμόνια" rather than "new gods" in formulating the charges precisely in order to target the *daimonion*. Others who hold that the *daimonion* must have played an important part in the second formal charge include Derenne, 153ff.; Dodds (4), 202 n. 74; Ehrenberg (1), 367 ff.; and esp. Ferguson, esp. 158, 169–175.

152. Which, again, explains the use of the plural form δαιμόνια, rather than the singular δαιμόνιον (Brickhouse and Smith [12], 35–36; Burnet [3], 180–185; Hackforth [2], 70).

153. This worry may explain the version of the second charge found at *Eu.* 3b, where Socrates tells us that he is accused of being a *maker* (ποιητής)—as opposed to being merely an introducer—of new gods. Again, this connects up directly with the rumors originating with Aristophanes' *Clouds*, where its Socrates says that "the gods have no currency here" (247), denies the existence of Zeus (366), calling the Clouds instead "our divinities" (252). As we saw too, natural scientists replace old gods with new divine powers (e.g., Anaximenes in Cic. *Nat. D.* 1.10.26).

rates as having close ties with Pythagoreans (*Phd.* 59c1–2), there may also have been gossip tying Socrates to this and other nontraditional religious movements that was sufficiently plausible for the prosecution to use it to intimate, if not actually establish, that Socrates acknowledged the "new," unlicensed divinities of those groups.[154] Thus, Socrates' formal accusers could use the plural, generic, interpretatively flexible allegation of introducing καινὰ δαιμόνια and the new gods they imply to incite within each juror their own individual set of rumors and favorite prejudices—conjuring up for each some "new god" or other—and so convict Socrates on the count of illegal religious importation.[155]

Putting all this aside for now, let us ask how the *daimonion* might have been used to convict Socrates of introducing καινὰ δαιμόνια. As the quotation from the *Euthyphro* indicates, the *daimonion* possesses aspects that could be used to arouse the natural suspicions Athenians had concerning foreign and new theological imports and to manufacture religious misrepresentations.[156] There are at least three areas of potential danger: (1) the source of the *daimonion* may be an unlicensed deity to whom Socrates pays unlicensed cult; (2) his characterization of this sign puts him on special, private terms with a deity; and (3) this sign and the deity behind it may be illusory or the deity may have hostile intentions toward Athens.

The first concern (1) is the explicitly actionable one. Socrates' epistemological modesty about the source of the *daimonion*—always scrupulously avoiding any explicit specification of the god whose sign

154. For the extreme version of this, see Taylor (4), 17–30. L. Robin, and A. S. Ferguson, however, provide compelling arguments for rejecting Taylor's suggestion that the "new divinities" charge focused on Socrates' alleged introduction of Pythagorean/Orphic deities; cf. Brickhouse and Smith (12), 20, and n. 64. There is, contrary to the expectations of many, little reliable evidence for the view that Socrates was a member of—or was heavily influenced by—the views of the Pythagoreans (cf., e.g., my chap. 5, n. 114).

155. Versnel (1), 127, 129, comes to the same conclusion, holding that "this part of the accusation was deliberately phrased in such vague and ambiguous terms precisely in order to shelter a complex of unexplicit imputations." This reading is supported by Xenophon's Socrates when he makes it a point to note that no one had ever seen him "sacrificing to strange gods [καινοῖς δαίμοσιν] nor swearing by or acknowledging other gods" (*Apol.* 24); cf. *Mem.* 1.1.2–4, 3.1, 3.4; *Apol.* 10–11; *Anab.* 3.4.1–8; Plato *Ap.* 21b, 33c; and *Phd.* 60b–61b.

156. Versnel (1), 121–122, notes that foreign cults tended to be associated with private rituals, which in turn fostered all sorts of suspicions. He also persuasively shows through a survey of cult-introduction in Athens (102–131) that "in addition to the negative connotations of *foreign* cults . . . there is also a marked resistance to the *novelty* of nontraditional gods and cults" (130): a resistance to change of *ta patria* that extends back to Hesiod (fr. 322) and which shows up in Xenophon's advice from Delphi to "follow established custom" (*Mem.* 4.3.16). Thus the *daimonion* could represent to some Athenians the worst possible religious threat: not only a foreign import, but a new one to boot!

(σημεῖον) or voice (φωνή) it is—and its unique attachment to Socrates (*R.* 496c) makes it natural that others might understand it to be the communication of some "uninvited" deity.[157] Although the *daimonion*'s visitations resemble the epiphanies of "solicitation" Athenians expect of a god who wishes to join the *polis,* the jurors will have known—and are even reminded of the fact by Socrates during his defense (31c–d)—that the "voice" has been coming to Socrates since childhood. Some jurors, then, may take this to show that Socrates has been carrying on a private cult for many years, one that would typically be interpreted as a form of new, private rites (cf. *Laws* 909e), rites that Socrates has clearly never attempted to share with the *polis* by obtaining official sanction for a "cult of *daimonion.*"[158] Although most Athenians would hold (on pain of impiety) that several previous foreign religious importations had been a great boon to their city, they would not allow that to excuse someone from the legal obligation of having to subject their enthusiasm for a new god to the critical scrutiny of the *polis* (cf. *Laws* 909d–910d).

Despite all these worries and their direct connection to the laws governing religious importation, however, this threat would not have been as useful to the prosecution as it might seem. For one thing, Socrates' failure to specify the source of the *daimonion* is quite in the spirit of Greek religious tradition, which denies that mere humans can know the identities of every genuine divinity.[159] Moreover, as Xenophon's version of Socrates' defense against the second charge shows, it would have been quite easy for Socrates to have claimed that the *daimonion* is a sign of essentially the same sort as that received by traditional and legitimate diviners (*Mem.* 1.1.2–4; *Apol.* 12–13). He might also have pointed out that there is no evidence of his sacrificing or making oaths to any new gods or δαίμονες (*Apol.* 24–25). Moreover, new cults, even private ones, require new sacred precincts and shrines, but it is completely contrary to Socrates' characterization of the *daimonion* to suppose that there ever was or could sensibly be a Socratic "shrine" to it.[160] Further, the wide-ranging referential possi-

157. Cf. Reeve, 95–96.
158. Yunis, 48–49, and n. 26. Note too Xen. *Apol.* 24–25, which indicates that *sacrificing* to new deities to the neglect of the old, established ones is a legal concern of Socrates' trial.
159. Lloyd-Jones, 85; Sourvinou-Inwood, 303; and note that Xenophon's Socrates is unsure of whether there are two goddesses "Aphrodite" or one (*Symp.* 8.9; cf. Pl. *Sym.* 180d).
160. Jurors might have thought, though, that if the *daimonion* is some kind of δαίμων, then since such things do not normally have cult (Mikalson [1], 65), the *daimonion* would not have it either.

bilities for the use of δαίμων are even further exceeded by the diminutive, elliptical substantive δαιμόνιον; thus, so as far as anyone—including Socrates and Meletus—can accurately determine, the sign comes from any one of the true Olympians.

Nevertheless, since Socrates characterizes himself as the servant of the god of the Oracle at Delphi (20e–23c) and the *daimonion* as the sign of the god that aids him in his mission (40b1), that makes it fairly plain that Socrates thinks that the most likely source of the sign is Delphic Apollo, a god with official Athenian cult.[161] No doubt it would have been best if Socrates had made this connection vividly explicit, but given all the above and the failure of the prosecution to stick to the original charges, it is not unreasonable for Socrates to think that his characterization of the *daimonion* at 31c–d as simply a voice that forbids but doesn't command behavior is sufficient to show that its occurrences are quite different from the typical epiphany of some god seeking official Athenian cult. There are, finally, additional elements implicit in Socrates' defense speech that he might expect jurors to take as further indicators of his innocence: the origin of his mission with the Delphic Oracle would suggest that the key step in sanctioning a "cult of *daimonion*" (even supposing there were such a thing)—namely, obtaining Delphi's approval—has already been met.[162] Socrates may also have hoped that by using the moon and sun as examples of gods he claims most (or all) humans believe in (26d1–3; cf. *Laws* 812b, 886d–e, 887e), the jurors will be prodded to notice that they too are just as guilty (or rather, just as innocent) of the second charge by recognizing an "unlicensed" deity (see n. 128).

I want to argue, then, that the real threat to Socrates posed by the second charge lies in its previously mentioned extralegal dimensions (2 and 3), each of which can be understood to generate the sort of envy, hatred, and slander that Socrates cites as the true causes of his conviction (28a). First, envy (and fear as well) is precisely the reaction that must have been generated by Socrates' unusual claim to be continually receiving without benefit of oracle or priest the guiding voice of a god (2). After all, even Euripides' character Ion, devoted servant of Apollo, must go to the temple

161. Sourvinou-Inwood, 309. Indeed, the Athenians considered their Apollo Patrôos the equivalent of Apollo Pythios; see, e.g., Demos. *De Cor.* 18.141, who calls upon Apollo Pythios as Apollo "who is Patroos to the city" (C. Hedrick, 200–201). Note too that seercraft was the province of Apollo (Garland [3], 141). Given Apollo's well-known and unmistakable preference for the Spartans during the Peloponnesian War (Thuc. 1.118), however, Socrates' characterization of himself as a servant of Delphic Apollo may have only inflamed some jurors' prejudices (Garland [3], 111).

162. Sourvinou-Inwood, 303–304; cf. *R.* 427b–c.

to inquire of the god (*Ion* 1547) and frequently even the sons of the gods are not as well informed of the divine will as is Socrates.[163] Such a source of private and unerring information implies great intimacy with—and thus benefit from—the divine (*Mem.* 1.1.9, cf. 1.1.4–5, 4.3.12; *Symp.* 4.47–49), and this is sure to arouse jealous hatred and fear in others (*Apol.* 14). Even more troublesome, however, (3) is that there exists no device others can use to verify the veracity and wisdom of Socrates' internal voice, and some may think it the voice of delusion (*Mem.* 4.8.1; *Apol.* 14), or worse, that of an evil δαίμων, perhaps one of those involved in "black magic" (e.g., those involved in the functions of curse tablets).[164] Socrates must have only deepened such fears in some of his jurors when he made the shocking confession that it was the *daimonion* that kept him from entering public politics (*Ap.* 31d–32a), something commonly thought to be obligatory for any Athenian citizen (Thuc. *History* 2.40).

As Socrates must fully realize, he is not in an ideal position to soothe these sorts of reactions to his *daimonion*. The time he has been allotted is inadequate to the formidable task of removing by reason what are primarily emotional, nonrational responses (cf. *Ap.* 18e–19a).[165] Socrates cannot deny that the *daimonion* gives him a unique advantage in life over everyone else in Athens, and other sorts of denials unaccompanied by proof (or adequate proof) are all he has time to offer in response to the charge that his voice offers evil counsel (e.g., by noting that its content is always dissuasive, never prescriptive [31d]). Moreover, once Meletus opted for his charge of complete atheism, Socrates was obliged to focus most of his defense against that allegation, not all the other allegations that the jury might still be weighing against him. Thus, here in the second charge I think we find one potent source that Meletus might have called upon in pressing a nonatheistic attack and one source for the jury's actual vote for conviction: Meletus's invocation of the *daimonion* may well have significantly inflamed—albeit illegitimately—the prejudices of the jury, leading a good number of them to vote for his conviction on the charge of introducing καινὰ δαιμόνια.

---

163. M. Lefkowitz (1), 245; Garland (3), 18, 149.

164. Yunis, 48–49; Burkert (2), 181. Versnel (1), 117, notes that "black magic" was generally associated with foreign cults (e.g., Sabazios and Cybele) and that the same accusation against Socrates of "making religious innovations" is leveled against a sorceress in a fable by Aesop (no. 112). It might even be the case that some would have connected Socrates' elenctic prowess with *daimonion*-provided magical powers (as Plato has Meno warn Socrates at *M.* 80b).

165. In the *Theaetetus* (172d–173a; 201a–b) Plato contrasts the length of time required for adequate philosophical discussion with the inadequate amount found in the law courts.

Again, though, this is not the end of the second charge. Meletus might still have attempted to use it to convict Socrates *legitimately* by showing that—quite apart from the *daimonion*—what Socrates calls gods, divinities, and divine matters (out of sincere belief or not) do not in fact warrant that appellation by right-thinking Athenians, or if they do, that they (again) have not been properly, legally introduced into Athens. The prosecution's evident desire (given Meletus's interpretation of charge 1 as outright atheism) to insinuate that Socrates is some sort of nature philosopher-Sophist along the lines of the Aristophantic portrait of Socrates—a devotee not of Zeus, but of the false god Vortex (a divine name for a materialistic force)—as well as Socrates' characterization of the first accusations, suggests that this line of attack is an implicit part of both the charge of atheism and that of introducing new divinities. Naturally since on Meletus's view many of the genuine divinities in existence are those recognized by Athens, whatever evidence could be produced that would show that Socrates is guilty of the nonrecognition charge would also implicate him—given his frequent talk of gods—in the charge of introducing new divinities. Hence, it is best at this juncture to investigate how Socrates might have been thought guilty of the charge of religious nonconformity.

3.4.3 Recognizing the Gods of Socrates

As we saw earlier, the first charge that Socrates "does not recognize [νομίζειν] the gods recognized by the state," concerns primarily belief, but may extend to behavior. I need, then, to map out the extent to which the gods Socrates endorses might be thought not to be those of Athens. Using those results—together with a consideration of Socrates' own religious behavior—we may then investigate the implications of Socrates' theology for traditional Athenian religious practice (with an eye to determining whether those implications could have played a significant role during Socrates' trial).

First, then, what does it mean to believe in the existence of the civic gods of Athens? What are the core beliefs one must have in order to be in agreement with the everyday "belief-demands" of Athenian *polis*-religion? At a minimum, it is clear that one must believe (1) that there exist gods denoted by the names of those gods who enjoy publicly funded cults (e.g., Athena Polias), (2) that these gods pay attention to the affairs of humans (e.g., taking notice of oathbreaking, curses, sacrifices, and murders), and (3) that there exist relationships of reciprocal exchange between humans and these gods such that—among other things—they will recognize the need to respond to prayers and sacrificial offerings (i.e., are gods with a *do ut des* [I give so that you will give] cult).[166] Where, then, does Socrates stand on these three commitments and the gods they imply?

It seems quite likely that Socrates satisfied condition (1), believing in some genuine sense that the civic gods of Athens *exist* (and so, again, is innocent of the charge of global atheism). For first, the rhetorical effect left in place by Socrates' invocation at 26b8–9—"before the gods about whom we now speak" (a remark made prior to any clarification of the charge of not recognizing the gods of the state) and his many positive references to "the god" who speaks through the Pythia at Delphi (a clear reference to Delphic Apollo) who has stationed and ordered him to philosophize with the Athenians (disobedience to whom *would* convict him of religious nonconformity [29a]) provide good *prima facie* evidence that Socrates has an intellectual commitment to the existence of the gods of Athens. In addition, and as we saw, Socrates possesses the household shrines required of Athenian citizens (e.g., Apollo Patrôos; *Eud.* 302b–d; cf. Arist. *Ath. Pol.* 55.3; Chapter 2.2) and would have taken any number of civic oaths during the course of his life, all of which call the civic gods as witnesses: the ephebic oath (to maintain the fatherland, to obey reasonably established law, to honor the ancestral sanctuaries, and so on), those taken as a juror (supposing he had once been one [as is likely]), and those taken as a member of the *Boulê* (*Mem.* 1.1.18) and as a litigant at the ἀνάκρισις of his own trial.[167] These observations, the probability that Socrates conceives of the *daimonion* as the voice of Apollo, and Socrates' conception of piety as involving service to a god of Athens, all testify to a Socratic belief in the existence of the civic gods. Pretty clearly, the above—in addition to the evidence I presented in Chapter 2.2—also give good support to his holding the view that (2) the gods pay attention in some way to human conduct.

---

166. These are taken from Yunis, 42–45, 50–58, who provides extensive textual support for them.

167. JACT, 158; Mikalson (1), 85, 94; Rhodes, 36; P. Siewert; Yunis, 26, 43, 52; L. Watson, 8. Note, however, Kraut (2), 152 n. 1, who argues that although the ephebic oath was given to military recruits in the second half of the fourth century, the silence of the Laws in the *Crito* on the topic shows that it was not required of every citizen in the fifth century—and that probably Socrates did not take it. For if Socrates *had* verbally agreed to obey the Laws, why do "they" (i.e., Socrates as he speaks for them) not mention this quite relevant detail?

It is with the final core belief—the relationship of reciprocity—that we encounter significant difficulties. Besides popular recognition of the sort of human and divine "commerce" that best exemplifies this relation—the sacrifice of goods with the hope (and, often, the expectation) of thereby maintaining or obtaining divine favor (the *emporia* of *Eu.* 14e)—it was also thought that the gods provided moral reciprocity by visiting retribution on those who violate various norms of behavior (e.g., oathbreakers).[168] But this view encounters problems that were indicated earlier and which must now be faced head-on in some detail: while it seems clear that Socrates' thoroughly moral gods are *compatible* with gods who serve this latter role of moral enforcement, how can they also be squared with the popular portrait of the gods as capricious rulebreakers who can be influenced to "help friends and harm enemies" by means of imprecations and material sacrifice? Can Socrates' perfectly moral gods really be *entirely* identified with the sacrifice-responding gods of the civic *do ut des* cult?

3.4.4 Socrates' Moral Gods

In the *Euthyphro* we learn of a possible motive for the formal charges against Socrates: "Is this, Euthyphro, why I am a defendant against the indictment: that whenever someone says such things [e.g., that Zeus bound his father] about the gods, I receive them somehow with annoyance? Because of this, *as is likely* [ὡς ἔοικε], someone will assert that I am a wrongdoer" (6a6–9).

There are, as we saw above, very good reasons for reading this passage in context, and in light of other passages in the *Euthyphro* and elsewhere, as a confession by Socrates that he is firmly committed to the proposition that the gods—"if they be gods"—must do only good, never evil, and are thus always in moral agreement with one another. Could this piece of theology *in and of itself* (irrespective of what it might imply) be sufficient warrant for convicting someone of not believing in the existence of the gods of Athens but in καινὰ δαιμόνια instead? According to Brickhouse and Smith, this pretrial musing of Socrates in the *Euthyphro* is "not an informed one," and so they join John Burnet, A. E. Taylor, and others in holding that Socrates' confession of skepticism concerning the traditional

---

168. Lloyd-Jones, 156–164; cf. chap. 1.3, herein.

tales of conflict contains "nothing to shock Athenian sentiment."[169] However, other scholars have held that such a blanket moralizing of the gods
would be tantamount to a complete rejection of the old myths, something
that would surely outrage the vast majority of Athenian citizens.[170] On this
view, Socrates is a true "religious radical" out to "clean up the Augean
stables of the Olympian pantheon," who now suddenly finds himself on
trial in a situation not unlike that of a "free-thinking radical Christian
preacher, . . . defending the bona fides of his gospel before a church-court
packed with Bible-belt fundamentalists."[171]

To adjudicate a resolution on this important issue necessarily involves a
degree of speculation, but I think that there are sufficient resources to
make a probabilistic decision possible. First, we need to recall that Greek
religion was far more tolerant of what we would call heterodoxy than
later, belief-focused religions (and a far cry from Christian fundamental-
ism). Again, Greek religion had no revealed texts with the status of the
Bible (not even the *Iliad* played such a role), no systematic doctrines enforced by a trained clergy, and no organized Church.[172] Although it was
the expected custom for the citizens of a Greek state to observe various
sacrifices and other religious duties, they were not required by written stat-
utes to subscribe to any set creed in order to maintain a pious standing.
Thus, as long as customary religious observances were commonly met, and
it was admitted that there do exist gods, an individual's private beliefs
could vary considerably from those of his neighbor without significant difficulty.[173] A Pindar could speak plainly of "Homer's lies" (*Nem.* 7.23)

169. Brickhouse and Smith (12), 125–126, and n. 23; (8), chap. 6.2; Burnet (3), 115;
A. E. Taylor (3); Reeve, 84 n. 14. Brickhouse and Smith (12), 126, and (8), 183, use as one
justification for this claim the fact that Euthyphro expresses no shock at Socrates' view. But,
in response, we need to remember that Euthyphro is Plato's creature—shock would not allow
the dialogue to proceed in the way that it does. Plato's argumentative strategy requires that
Euthyphro be committed to quarreling gods, and having him express shock would turn the
dialogue's discussion to a topic that it is not designed to explore explicitly; viz., the explanation for Socrates' rejection of the myths of conflict (note too how Socrates *forestalls* Euthyphro's attempts to demonstrate the truth of his own strange stories [*Eu.* 6c8–9] so as to get
on with the definitional quest). Moreover, Euthyphro is an unusual fellow—not an archetype
of traditional piety and so not at all likely to be shocked by the views of another "fellow
religious innovator" (and in any case, he may see no way to convince Socrates of the error of
his ways and the truth of his [Euthyphro's] views).
170. Vlastos (14), 165–167; Tate (3–5); Nilsson (5), 275; Beckman, 41.
171. Vlastos (11).
172. Burkert (2), 8; Dodds (4), 140–144; Lloyd-Jones, 134; Taylor (4), 15–16.
173. See Zaidman and Pantel, 11–13. As Parker (1), 255, notes, "Religion was not a
matter of innerness or intense private communion with the god . . . piety (*eusebeia*) was

without incurring—so far as we know—any legal sanction, and we have no evidence of anyone ever being prosecuted for disbelieving the stories found in Homer or Hesiod, such as the adultery of Ares and Aphrodite (*Od.* 8), or Zeus's deception of Metis (*Thg.* 872–906).[174] Again, with their exposure to the works of Hesiod, Sophocles, and Aeschylus, Athenians of a wide variety of social standing were acquainted with affirmations of the gods' justice, and we hear of no one demurring at these expressions.[175] Even among the nonintelligentsia it was frequently admitted that the doings of the gods are difficult to ascertain and that their behavior cannot be subsumed under our moral categories, and hence, even in common opinion there existed a defense for one's particular skepticisms.[176]

Among most Athenians of the middle to the end of the fifth century, anyway, it would have been no great shock to hear expressions of doubt or outright denial concerning the poets' tales of divine immorality. They had been exposed to such criticisms for years by thinkers such as Hecataeus, Solon, Pindar, Xenophanes, Euripides, and Heraclitus, with Heraclitus even attacking the cult of prayer-images (saying that it was like talking to a man's house rather than its owner [DK 5]), and many intellectuals seem to have thought that this sort of skepticism and the naturalistic accounts that sometimes accompanied it were compatible with more sophisticated forms of theism.[177] It is also noteworthy that none of these particular thinkers appears to have suffered from religiously based persecution.[178] Again, we learn from the *Phaedrus* (229c) that doubts about the stories from the poetic tradition were not uncommon in Socrates' day, and there also existed many affirmations of the justice and morality of the gods, gods with such appellations as "Zeus Meilichios" (kindly Zeus), "Zeus Xenios" (Zeus the guardian of strangers and oaths), and "Delphic Apollo who cannot lie" (and who is foremost among the gods to encourage the notion that the gods underwrite just behavior among humans).[179]

Perhaps the best explanation for the apparent popular conflict over the

---

literally a matter of 'respect,' not love, and even the warmest relationship would quickly have turned sour without observance of the cult."

174. Lloyd-Jones, 134; Burnet (3), 114; Dodds (4), 141–143; Kerferd, 167; Momigliano (2), 566; Taylor (1), 147; Yunis, 39.

175. Lloyd-Jones, 109.

176. Lefkowitz (1), 243.

177. Burkert (2), 246; Lloyd-Jones, 79–85; Vlastos (20).

178. Lloyd-Jones, 130.

179. See Lefkowitz (1), 244; Burkert (2), 246–250, 273; Mikalson (1), 3–5, 64; Nilsson (5), 34; and Yunis, 55–56 nn. 40, 43.

moral status of the gods, then, is the view that during this period two religious threads coexisted in dynamic tension: on the one hand, the creative, flexible, and popularly accepted theology of the traditional tales of divine enmity—as well as those of the poets and dramatists—none of which demanded adherence (with the poets and dramatists analyzing and probing both popular belief and the efforts of other thinkers); on the other, the theology of the *polis* and its cult practices, which did demand adherence and which provided the foundation for *polis*-justice by assuming its sponsorship by just, *lex talionis*-respecting gods.[180] This view and the foregoing discussion argue that we should side with those scholars who hold that Socrates' tenet that the gods are thoroughly cooperative and good would not have been seen as impious or as directly undermining belief in the gods of the state. The worries that Socrates expresses in the *Euthyphro* are thus primarily only that: worries offered as one hypothesis for his indictment that simply focus on an allegation that by itself and at worst would have incited only a minority of Athenians.

3.4.5 Socrates and Cult

The preceding tale of tolerance is, however, only half a story. Religion for the Greeks was, again, much more a matter of request and ritual, even pre-Homeric ritual, than intellectual theory. These rituals included, moreover, practices akin to magic—including the "black magic" of curse-imprecation—practices often tied to the agricultural calendar and deriving much of their psychological dimension from the numerous and diverse mythological stories of the deities. For example, in each of the three great religious festivals of the Greeks—the Diasia, the Thesmophoria, and the Anthesteria—the Olympian deities appear to be late additions to ceremonies that centrally involved an atmosphere of magical dread and the sacrificial appeasement of various spirits of the underworld. In particular, the sacrifices of the Diasia, though nominally connected with Zeus, were not of the sort where—after the manner of a communal feast cementing mutual

180. Hence, the works of the tragedians both reflect popular culture and use it to explore creatively the latent tensions of the inherited tradition (Burkert [2], 246; Mikalson [2], 3–6). On this, Yunis, 75, writes: "In the life of the *polis*, religious forms . . . enjoyed a clear primacy over unchanneled, interior religious beliefs; only those circumstances in which personal belief jarred with accepted forms would pose problems of directly sensible consequences for the religious institutions of the *polis*."

friendships—a portion of the sacrificial victim was divided between the god and worshipers. Rather, the victim was entirely consigned to a holocaust of flames in order to placate the unpredictable, chthonic powers of the dead beneath the earth.[181] Furthermore, for most Greeks the most significant divinities are those tied to one's immediate situation, those heroes and lesser gods with more local, partisan interests than the Olympians, who served as helpers in the struggles of everyday life: Hephaestus for the blacksmiths, Asclepius and Heracles for everyone in time of trouble, and numerous others.[182] Even the Olympians themselves, however, were thought to be involved in the centrally important task of fulfilling curse imprecations: Either Zeus (So. *Phil.* 1183) or all the gods (Soph. *Oed. Tyr.* 269) could be called upon to fulfill one's retaliatory aims (although there was, apparently, a preference for seeking the help of the gods of the Underworld; e.g., Hades, Hecate, Persephone, and [esp.] the Erinyes).[183]

Traditional religious practice, then, often centered on prayers to a god or gods for a *particular* (not general) good or harm. As tradition also commonly saw it, however, these supernatural "helpers" needed to be put in one's debt first in order to be enlisted in one's cause (or "gifted" subsequent to their services). Thus it was unusual not to accompany a prayer of request with an offering of some sort designed to establish a claim on the helper: a farmer should offer wine and incense to the god before he calls on his or her aid, and having sacrificed richly he could remind the god that something was now owed to him in return. As we saw Euthyphro confess to Socrates (*Eu.* 14c–15a), this *do ut des* conception of reciprocity between gods and humans is rather like an art of commerce (ἐμπορική) involving a material gift accompanied by a petitionary prayer (14c).[184] But this same passage suggests that Socrates finds such a notion distasteful (at least in some aspect of it), and that possible distaste may be connected with his rejection of the gods' injustice and communal conflict. If that is correct, then we can see how such a rejection *could be seen* as an indirect—but quite worrisome—threat to the *practical* (hence, most important) basis of everyday Greek religion.

To ask after the fate of Socrates in this respect, then, we need to characterize Socrates' gods and discover what interpretation the court would

181. See G. Murray, 28–34; Parker, 257; and Zaidman and Pantel, 37–38.
182. Dodds (7), 153–154.
183. See L. Watson, chap. 1 (esp. 1.14); Mikalson (4), 84–85.
184. On the ancient self-interested attitude toward cult, see Dodds (7), 144–155; Dover (3), 246–249; and Vlastos (14), 176–177.

have put on the phrase "gods of the state." It needs to be emphasized again that—for the moment—the issue is not so much how *Socrates* might have interpreted this phrase: given the legal procedures previously noted, his practical, legal guilt or innocence before the court on the nonrecognition charge is a matter of the meaning the prosecution (and jurors) place on it. If Socrates believes nothing at variance with the gods of Athens *under the description placed on them by these individuals* then he ought to be found innocent, but if he disbelieves key attributes taken by them to be referentially essential, he is guilty of the charge (so construed). As we saw, both Socrates and the rest of the court probably understood what the phrase "gods of the state" meant to *most Athenians*. Despite its flexibility of reference, custom dictated as falling under this locution the gods to whom the rituals of the civic cult were directed, in particular, Athena Polias ("she who rules over Athens") and Zeus Polieus ("Zeus of the City").[185]

Now although religious reformers often begin with theological reformation and then infer on the basis of their new canon what changes in moral theory and actual behavior must then be made, it appears (as we saw) that Socrates reversed this procedure. Since he is more a moral philosopher than a speculative theologian, his revolution is directed first to the moral domain. In particular, again, he insists against traditional morality and its foundational *lex talionis* conception of justice (such that justice is "helping your friends and harming your enemies") that since it is never just to inflict evil on another or to aid the cause of injustice, at least the negative side of retributive justice ("evil for evil") and the use of barter of favors (*do ut des*) contrary to justice must be rejected as coherent features of true justice.[186] So again, since Socrates demands that the principles of true justice extend to even the gods, his "socratized" gods are not simply good and just in a traditionally recognizable way, but are also in complete accord with one another, are forbidden from exacting *lex talionis* retribution against one another and humans, and cannot respond to *do ut des* petitionary sacrifice *irrespective of the demands of Socratic justice*. To what extent, then, do these aspects of Socratic moral theology put Socrates at odds with the gods of Athens and the civic cult?

Again, there is no reason to think that disbelief in divine enmity per se would put one at risk of disbelief in the civic gods even as popularly understood. Although the previously cited passage from the *Euthyphro*

---

185. Contra Brickhouse and Smith (12), 119. Cf. Dodds (7), 153–154; Nilsson (4), 7–8; Zaidman and Pantel, 82, 177–78; and Yunis, 42.
186. See Vlastos (14), chap. 7.

shows Socrates to reject the substance of the scenes depicted on the festival robe offered to Athena Polias (*Eu.* 6b–c; *R.* 378b–380c, 381e–382e), this "Battle of the Olympians and Titans" is not an article of required civic belief, but simply one tale of the poets with which anyone might disagree with relative safety.[187] It is, rather, with the rejection of the negative side of the *lex talionis* and some of the propitiatory *do ut des* aspects of cult that Socrates' doctrine of divine justice presents a genuine threat to the civic religion of Athens.

Gregory Vlastos, again, provides the extreme version of this threat by portraying Socrates' conceptions of piety and justice as demanding *only* that we serve the gods through the improvement of our souls, gods who are by their very nature "relentlessly beneficent" since completely good.[188] As he sees it, this thoroughly undermined the bulk of popular Greek religion, founded as it was on the notion that the gods can be petitioned and "bribed" with sacrifices to help oneself or one's friends by doing some "good which without that gift their own will for good would not have prompted them to do."[189] On these same grounds Socrates' gods cannot be enticed in any way to harm one's enemies. Rather, the gods do the good that they must and pay no heed to sacrificial curses or imprecations. To determine the extent to which this captures Socrates' relation to traditional religious practice we need to ask first, then, the extent to which its core presupposition of divine reciprocity included the notion that the gods can be reliably influenced to do our wills for *both* good and ill.

As with so much of Greek religion, the evidence seems contradictory, suggesting that the Greeks were of two minds concerning the susceptibility of the gods to petitions. On the one hand there are passages that support the idea that the gods can be counted on to respond to material requests, even irrespective of the justice of the *talio*. At *Iliad* 9.497–501, for example, Phoenix assures Achilles that the gods' wrath *can* be diverted by means of sacrifice. Note also Plato's account of Chryses' imprecation for revenge to Apollo, where Chryses uses his past sacrifices as establishing a basis for a return of favors from the god (*R.* 394a; cf. *Il.* 1.375–385). Likewise, Euripides' Medea feels confident that she can exact "just repayment with God's help" (*Medea* 803) against Jason (and even though that means his just "repayment" for infidelity is three innocent lives taken "impiously" [796]). Next, at *Republic* 364b–c we learn that there were wan-

187. See Tate (3), 144.
188. Vlastos (14), 176.
189. Vlastos (14), 176.

dering priests and soothsayers who promised to expiate past wrongdoing or to harm enemies—justly or not—by means of sacrifice; and the following section (364e–366b; cf. 419a) indicates that there are some who might believe those poets who hold that the gods can even be "swerved" from punishing wrongdoers by getting a "cut of the take" (i.e., offered sacrifices purchased through unjustly acquired gains). Along the same lines there is the anonymous Athenian's mention at *Laws* 885b–e of those many people who require proof that the gods are "too good to be diverted from the path of justice" by gifts (cf. 888a–d, 908e–909d), which strongly suggests that such requests were common (perhaps even as part of public cult).[190] At *Laws* 948b–948e he even claims that the creed of the *majority* is that "if they pay the gods a trifle in the way of sacrifice and flattery, they [the gods] will lend their help in vast frauds and deliver the sinner from all sorts of heavy penalties" (948c4–7). There is, finally, a clear instance of retributive civic religion to be found in the opening ceremonies of the *Boulê*. There, before each meeting, a herald would recite a prayer that included a curse on those who plotted evil against Athens, requesting that such enemies meet a miserable end.[191] These examples all suggest that it was common to think that one's sacrificial requests for good things—and especially curses on others—were likely to be fulfilled, even irrespective of justice.[192]

But against all this, however, one must set the well-entrenched tradition dating from at least Hesiod which emphasized that the size and splendor of a sacrifice is only of use in displaying and advancing one's social status and is thoroughly *irrelevant* to the gods.[193] We hear, for example, of a man from Magnesia who came to Delphi and—after offering a lavish sacrifice—asked the Pythia who of all men most pleased the gods with sacrificial honors, assuming (naturally) that *he* would be named. As is common to such stories, however, the priestess named another, much more obscure man, who—though his sacrifices were modest—never neglected the proper

190. Note also the prayer cited in Parker (1), 258: "Protect our city. I believe that what I say is in our *common interest*. For a flourishing city honors the gods" (my emphasis).

191. Rhodes, 36–37. And here, of course, the curse need not have been always thought just, since it might be acknowledged that it could be just to *oppose* Athens on some policy.

192. See L. Watson, chap. 1 (esp. 1.7). Mikalson (4), 83, makes the point that in the corpus of Greek tragedy one finds relatively few prayers which are not granted by a deity.

193. Burkert (2), 274; Mikalson (1), 100–102; Parker (1), 259; Yunis, 51; Hes. *Erga* 336; quoted in *Mem.* 1.3.3; cf. *Alcibiades II* 149b and Arist. *EN* 1164 b 5 ff. Connor, 53, is thus too extreme when he holds that Socrates' view that the size of a sacrifice is irrelevant to the gods is threateningly *non*traditional.

rites (Porphyry *Abst.* 2.16). In addition, it is important to note that a good deal of sacrificial activity was not aimed so much at obtaining specific goods or evils as it was for simply maintaining an ordered relationship with the gods and ensuring their goodwill, a will that—it was generally agreed—could not be *reliably* influenced by such activity.[194]

So what emerges from this brief consideration is a sense that there existed side-by-side with the more material, amoral, mercantile aspects of Greek religion another strand that emphasized the worshiper's inner motivation, his or her determination to carry out the traditional rites in a timely and scrupulous manner, and so a reciprocity based on one's inner propriety and justice, not on one's pocketbook.[195] In view of the human (and surely Greek) propensity toward self-aggrandizement in almost everything, however, this nonmercantile attitude was in all likelihood an intermittent, minority phenomenon. For most Athenians, gods who exist but who do not eventually and in some concrete fashion *respond* "to sacrifices fulfilled or oaths forsworn" (and sometimes without a strict regard for justice—especially when conceived Socratically) are "no gods at all."[196] The question then becomes whether and to what extent Socrates' views support or undermine the notion of reciprocity in both mercantile and nonmercantile senses.

This question is not too difficult to answer. As we have begun to see (e.g., in Chapter 2.2), the evidence indicates that Socrates is committed to a rejection of the *purely* mercantile and amoral/immoral senses of sacrificial cult. His gods cannot care for any material sacrifice per se, and curse imprecations, in particular, would seem ineffective (or might even "backfire") on his account. He is, however, able to retain the internal, nonmercantile dimension of the tradition, emphasizing the petitioner's intentionality over his or her material gift-offering. Thus Socrates can admit of reciprocity between gods and humans, sanctioning our *requesting of* the gods, demanding that we *honor* them (in *some* fashion, and with a divine response quite possible; see Chapter 2.2.8), while not making it a strict *requirement* of piety that the honoring involve a material sacrifice. He also revolutionizes the traditional notions of piety and "honoring," recasting

194. Mikalson (1), 89; Parker (1), 259; Mikalson (4), notes the few unanswered prayers and vows in the Homeric literature, observing that a common feature—as in tragedy—is the impiety of the petitioners.

195. Yunis, 54–55. Although the primary term for offering a sacrifice is θύω, one often also sees τιμάω or τιμή, which carry the sense of paying honor to the gods.

196. Yunis, 43; 54 n. 35; cf. Vlastos (14), 166, and Connor, 56.

them in terms that emphasize the priority of acting justly and engaging in philosophical "soul therapy" (as kinds of pious "honoring") over petitionary prayer and material sacrifice. Socrates is thus not—contra Vlastos—a *wholesale* threat to the actual *practice* of cult, but to the inner, narrow self-aggrandizing motivations of many of its practitioners: those who give priority to *material* sacrifice in the cause of external gain and neglect the form of "belief-sacrifice" ("self-examination") mandated by Apollo ("caring more for bodies and money than for the improvement of the soul" [*Ap.* 30a–b]; cf. *Phdr.* 279b–c). For certain jurors then—jurors who could not embrace a religious life informed by motivations beyond their usual ones—Socrates could have been recognized (by those with eyes to see) as a genuine threat to cult *as they conceived of it*. Let me elaborate on these claims and provide evidence for accepting them.

According to Socrates, from perfectly good gods we have nothing to fear (*Mem.* 4.3.5–7) and many goods they will simply give to us at the right moment, actively requested for or not (*Ap.* 41c8–d2; *Eu.* 15b1–2; *Mem.* 1.4.5–18, 4.3.3–17; cf. *Alc. II* 149e3–150b3). Moreover, and when it is consistent with the demands of Socratic justice, they may reward and aid us (e.g., by sending us a "sign") *in response to* the justice and piety of our souls (though not to the size or kind of any material offering [*Mem.* 1.3.3, 2.1.28]).[197] The gods, of course, *need* nothing from us (e.g., *Eu.* 13c; *Mem.* 1.6.10), and since they cannot be at odds with one another *or* with justice, they cannot be magically influenced to serve as vengeful *lex talionis* helpers against the forces that oppose our wills, especially when our plans involve the commission of injustices (cf. *R.* 364a–c, *Laws* 905e).[198] Nevertheless, there is room here for Socratically acceptable and "effective" petitionary prayer and a modified, positive *do ut des* conception of human-god reciprocity.

Although Socrates would not seem to consider traditional cult practices such as prayer or sacrifice to be *essentially* connected to the virtue of piety (as seen in Chapter 2.2)—or to have any particular bearing on the intellectual recognition that gods exist—the operations of prayer and sacrifice are nonetheless compatible with his view of piety. Just as the tradition holds

197. See also *Mem.* 1.1.19, 1.4.10–18, 4.3.13–14; *Symp.* 4.48–49. Note that Aeschines of Sphettus, a close friend of Socrates and an author of Socratic dialogues, ascribes this same view to Socrates (see G. C. Field, 149) as well as the view that "the fine and good get a better deal from the gods because of their greater piety" (Dittmar, Fr. 8, lines 61–62; Reeve, 67–68 n. 80).

198. Were it otherwise, piety would be the rejected ἐμπορία of *Eu.* 14e6–7, and the gods mere "evil moneylenders" (*Alc. II* 149e4–5); cf. Reeve, 68.

(cf. Eur. *Hipp*. 7 ff.), we should reciprocate the gods' gifts by *honoring* the gods in fitting ways through performing acts with the inner intention to so honor them (acts which are also virtuous [*Mem*. 4.3.17]; cf. Chapter 2.2). While, again, serving the gods *via* philosophy has pride of place in providing such honors, honorific actions can include god-honoring/thanking prayers and material sacrifices.[199] Such actions serve the gods in an indirect fashion: they help to align our souls (and those of others) in the ways of justice—thus producing good in the universe—by habituating us to return good for good (and not evil for evil). Hence, it seems that while Socrates rejects the negative half of the *lex talionis/do ut des* conception of piety—forbidding the return of evils for evils—and rejects Euthyphro's notion that the gods can be bartered with in a material, commercial way (14e), he accepts the idea that we should return goods for goods, though without expecting to establish a claim on any deity that would give us a right to expect any *specific* return.

In fact, Socrates would appear to think that since the gods aid those who do what is virtuous, and since god-honoring/thanking prayers and sacrifices are virtuous (pious), that virtue-assisting favors will be returned to us for such efforts in some fashion (though not necessarily in the fashion we would choose for ourselves [*Mem*. 1.3.2, 2.1.28]).[200] Xenophon, at any rate, represents Socrates as accepting the view that he receives goods from the god(s) (viz., portents such as his *daimonion*) *because*—apparently—of the virtue of his mission to the Athenians.[201] Socrates also has a very developed and conservative sense of obligation to the written and unwritten *nomoi* of Athens; thus, we can expect him to enjoin and practice those rituals required or expected by such *nomoi* (*Mem*. 1.3.1, 4.3.13,

199. *Mem*. 4.3.13, 16. Here we see the importance of the *intention* to please the gods (who desire honor), which in Chapter 2.2 was postulated as a *differentia* of the species "piety" from the genus "justice." Cf. *Laws* 716–717 where Plato makes clear that he approves of ritual *veneration* of the gods.

200. As N. Smith points out to me, the account of friendship in the *Lysis* seems to show that Socrates had no problem with a moral notion (friendship) being based on a mutual exchange of benefit. Also, Socrates' eudaimonism implies that to do good is merely to pursue benefit (though of a primarily nonmaterial kind).

201. *Mem*. 1.1.9, 1.1.19, 1.3.3, 1.4.15–19, 4.3.16–17, 4.8.11; *Symp*. 47–49. Note especially how at *Mem*. 4.3.12 Socrates does not demur when Euthydemus claims that the gods must be very friendly with him—more friendly than with others—because *even when they are not asked* they reward him. Also, at 2.1.28 Socrates asserts that to acquire *the favor* of the gods you must worship them. However, this passage includes the claim that the gods give nothing good to man without toil, and this seems at odds with the view that all good things come to humanity from the gods (even when they go unasked and unworshiped; e.g., *Eu*. 14e–15a).

4.3.16, 4.4.25; cf. *Cr.* 48d–54d).[202] Even Plato—despite his reticence on the topic of Socrates' cult practice—is willing to put twelve prayers into the mouth of his Socrates.[203] Finally, all the evidence we saw earlier (esp. in Chapter 2.2) suggests that Socrates himself engaged in religious ritual and cult. But again, although for Socrates the gods are always pleased in some sense by the honor such sincerely motivated practices display toward them, they—quite unlike the gods entertained by some Athenians—are not responsive to either the material basis of the sacrifice (e.g., its *size*) or the specificities of the request (since any particular item requested might not be conducive to our real good [*Mem.* 1.3.2; *G.* 511c–512b]) or to Socratically unjust petitions (cf. Aristophanes *Peace* 363–425).[204]

In Chapter 2 we saw indications that Socrates also reinterprets the concept of cult in a way that includes the practice of elenctic, self-examining philosophy, and that such a cult is a kind of ritual purification of the soul which is not only compatible with Socratic piety, but positively demanded by it (see Chapter 4.2). For those jurors disposed to hear things his way, Socrates gives eloquent and emphatic testimony that he is—just as Xenophon later said he was—the most conspicuous and constant acolyte of the gods to be found in Athens. He may even claim to be among the most generous of sacrificers, having foregone the external goods of leisure, money, and family life in favor of his pious service to the god (*Ap.* 23b–c, 31b–c), a service that—with his trial and conviction—includes the sacrifice of his very life.

It should be clear, though, that with the all-wise deities of Socrates we have few specific or *materially rewarding* deals to strike. Beyond the sincere, general imprecation that one be aided in pursuing virtue, there are few requests or sacrifices (if any) that all-wise deities can be *counted on* to respond to (since *we* can never know if any specific request would be virtue-aiding, and since the gods have no need of material things). Surely *this* implication of Socrates' moral theory cuts straight at the root of some of the popular traditional motivations underlying many cult practices.[205]

202. Dodds (4), 141.

203. Listed and discussed in B. Jackson: *Eud.* 275d; *Phd.* 117c; *Sym.* 220d; *Phdr.* 237a–b, 257a–b, 278b, 279b–c; *Rep.* 327a–b, 432c, 545d–e; *Phlb.* 25b, 61b–c.

204. On this view, then, Socrates' associate Aristippus may have been just going the Master one step better when he said that it was ridiculous to make requests of the gods, since they already know what ought to be sent (this is a paraphrase of Aristippus fr. 227 from Guthrie [6], 177; cf. *Mem.* 1.3.2 where Socrates is said to hold that we ought to pray for no specific thing, since the gods already know what is good for us).

205. E.g., the sort of motivation Socrates captures in his ironic characterization of Euthy-

Socrates' position also applies not only to the gods of the state and the sacrifices of the major religious festivals but to the lesser deities of everyday cult, those beings regarded by most Athenians as more intimately involved in their own lives and more directly helpful than the high gods of the state. But if Socrates rejects the enmities and lies of the gods *tout court*, and the efficacy of particular and improperly motivated requests, then he may well seem to some such-minded jurors even more threatening, irrespective of the probability that disbelief in Heracles "the helper" could not legitimately be used to convict someone of the official charge of nonrecognition.[206] For Heracles—most jurors would claim—would not be Heracles if he had not been conceived *via* the seduction of Alcmena by Zeus (arousing the jealousy of Hera) and could not be counted on (at least generally) to grant a suppliant's particular desperate imprecation. In addition, help from Heracles meant above all help against the unseen, nonhuman (and so less easily dealt with) forces bearing down on one, and for most Greeks this meant help against oppression from *other deities*. Take away the enmity of the gods, the dark powers of the dead, and the stories of Heracles' victories over monsters, and you take away the need for and the efficacy of *this* Heracles. But again, even more worrisome still to some pious sensibilities, there is no point and no hope in invoking a Heracles—bound by the chains of Socratic justice—against life's *particular* vicissitudes (after all, according to Socrates the vicissitudes just might be virtue-producing goods in disguise), especially if one requests a Socratically unjust response (e.g., the harm of enemies). To expand on this worry, consider the Socratic assessment of that central feature of Greek religion, curse imprecation.

As indicated earlier, most Athenians in the time of Socrates took it as a fact of life that curse imprecations were an effective means—in both the private and public sphere—of causing others harm; harms such as loss of material goods, pain, illness, and destruction of human life (cf. *Laws* 933c–e).[207] Now causing others these kinds of harms (harms that are not necessarily harms to the soul) *might* be acceptable in at least some in-

---

phro's last account of piety as a kind of cosmic barter (*Eu.* 14e); and see Plato's contempt for this view of piety in the *Laws*, e.g., 885b ff.

206. Yunis, 48–49.

207. See L. Watson, chap. 1, esp. 1.7, which notes that it was a piece of conventional wisdom that curses, private or public, were inevitably fulfilled; cf., e.g., Aes. *Choe.* 692, *Sept.* 655, *Prom. Vinc.* 910–911; and Hes. *Erga* 242 ff. The practice of cursing had a long prehistory in Greece, showing up prominently in Homer (e.g., *Il.* 9.453–457, 566–572 [cf. *R.* 393c–394b]; *Od.* 9.528–535), and was associated with major figures of the legendary age such as Oedipus, Pelops, and Theseus.

stances for a true Socratic.[208] Athenian law formally recognized curses as a way of promoting justice, Socrates seems to accept Athenian law and the idea that wrongdoers should "pay the penalty" (*Eu.* 8d–e), and we never see Socrates explicitly object to *polis*-authorized punishments per se, even though they were often characterized as cases of legal "harm to enemies" and even though he ends up facing punishment himself (see, however, Chap. 5.1, n. 77).[209] His distinguished military career is also evidence that causing physical harm to others is not out of the question for Socrates, so long as that is just and furthers the education of souls (*per Ap.* 25b–26a).[210] In fact, many curses seem *prima facie* Socratically acceptable in this way, since such maledictions were commonly thought to work by informing a god (esp. "Zeus who listens to curses" [So. *Phil.* 1183]) of some *injustice,* enrolling the god in one's cause (often employing material sacrifice); see, for example, the curse of Amyntor at *Iliad* 9.444–461.[211] But here, clearly, is a first incompatibility: Socrates' gods (esp. Zeus) have no need to be made aware of injustices since they already know everything (see Chapter 2.2.8, *Mem.* 1.1.19) and—being perfectly just—have no need to be enrolled in any just cause (and so have no use for material sacrifices accompanied by *that* sort of intention). Second, the justice most commonly appealed to is that of the negative *talio;* for example, "May those who killed me meet a like fate, O Zeus, god of guests,"[212] and—as we have seen— Socrates rejects the negative *talio* (preferring education to physical harms; see Chap. 5.1., n. 77). Moreover, it seems clear that the *talio* invoked in many curses is of that particularly objectionable sort which confuses personal revenge (motivated by a desire to humiliate and achieve emotional

208. Even Socrates engages in a bit of "cursing": he sometimes attests to the truth of his statements by swearing "by Zeus" (e.g., *R.* 370a7 [he invites Meletus to swear by Zeus at *Ap.* 26e3]), "by Hera" (e.g., *G.* 449d5), or "by the dog of Egypt" (viz., Anubis, whose Greek counterpart is Hermes); see, e.g., *Ap.* 22a1, *Lys.* 211e6, *Phd.* 98e5, and *G.* 482b5. Dodds (6), 262–263, argues that Socrates' oaths cannot be taken as having any deep religious significance.

209. See L. Watson, chap. 1 (esp. 1.7, 1.11), who notes, e.g., the provisional curse at the start of the assembly against potential deceivers (8), Plato's mention of "curses in accordance with the laws" at *Laws* 871b (21), and the curse by the Amphiktyones, which invokes Apollo and Athena Pronoia (threatening violators of a set of provisions with destruction of houses, families, and fertility [Aesch. *Contra Cts.* 110–111]) (19). On legal "harm to enemies," see Blundell, chap. 2, esp. 53–57.

210. Evidence of Socrates' career is provided by Guthrie (6), 59.

211. L. Watson, chap. 1. However, Watson also notes (1.3, 1.11–14) that it was believed that even without the assistance of a deity, simply the words of a curse could carry enough supernatural force to be effective (and independent of moral considerations).

212. L. Watson, 44; see her chap. 1.12 for further exposition on the prominence of the *lex talionis* in connection with cursing.

gratification) with justice conceived of as a rectification of debt and where the retribution envisaged includes harms, often gratuitous harms, to innocents (e.g., an enemy's children or an opponent's chariot driver).[213] Socrates, then, seems bound to take at least a skeptical if not an utterly outraged view of many conventionally "just" curses. The final incompatibility is more obvious: many curses were considered by even their makers to be cases of seeking an unfair advantage over an opponent, some aiming to procure Socratic harms (causing someone to be worse off in their soul by depriving them of their reason), and might be altogether unprovoked. Surely Socrates—for whom unjust actions pose harms for both agent and object (e.g., *Ap.* 30c–d)—must vehemently reject the collaboration of the gods in such imprecations (insisting instead that the gods will render such things useless; cf. Plato's mention of "those gods who give deliverance from curses" at *Laws* 854b).[214] Altogether, then, this central practice of Greek religion seems very difficult to square with Socratic moral theology. And even if Socrates were to remove his gods from serving as the emissaries of curse retaliation, he would still have to repudiate or severely qualify a valuable and time-honored practice of Greek religion.

Given all the above, it seems clear that if some of Socrates' jurors had been able to recognize the implications of his views for sacrificial cult, he would have been seen by them as threatening the stability of both state and household. The proper modern analogy here, however, is not Socrates

213. See Blundell, 50–51, 54–55, who notes that litigation was often treated as legalized revenge, and that the *talio* was thought to clash with other moral norms (e.g., wronging others as a favor to friends [Ar. *Rhet.* 1373a16 ff.]); L. Watson, chap. 1., notes the effects on innocents, the gratuitous and/or disproportionate infliction of pain some curses called for (e.g., death in exchange for damaging a tomb, one's entire lineage wiped out for breaking a contract [cf. Ar. *Thes.* 349 ff.; *Laws* 908e–909d]), and the efficacy of even unprovoked curses; see esp. 11–12, 32–36, and 41–42.

214. See, e.g., *R.* 364b–c, which testifies to the belief that certain "priests and soothsayers" can use their spells to constrain the gods to help a person harm his enemy unjustly (cf. *Laws* 933c–e); see also the complaint of Hippolytus that he is struck by an unjust curse (Eur. *Hipp.* 1347–1349). See L. Watson, chap. 1, esp. 1.3–4, 1.11–14, who cites curse tablets (*defixiones*) as the prime examples of unprovoked curses and notes their frequent use by litigants to impair the mental faculties of adversaries (42). Blundell, 50, notes that Gorgias mentions harming enemies as a plausible reason why one might act unjustly (*Pal.* 18; cf. *R.* 364c). Observe, too, how in Euripides' *Hippolytus* (887 ff.) Theseus is allowed to use one of the gift-curses from Poseidon to destroy his son on the basis of a false accusation. It is, finally, hard to believe that Socrates could endorse the idea—present in most provisional curses (L. Watson, 50)—that the violation of a condition spelled out in the curse would evoke the *anger* of the gods, since giving way to that emotion is associated by Socrates with lack of wisdom (*Prt.* 352a–352c; cf. *Ap.* 34b–d, *Eu.* 7b–c, and *Phd.* 113e–114b) and connected by him in the *Euthyphro* with Euthyphro's traditional quarreling, nonsocratic gods (7b) (see, e.g., *Il.* 4.20–50).

in a court packed with Bible-belters—they are far too intellectual and theologically infected to serve as a close analog. In their place we should substitute a court of pious Greek farmers who, in time of need, turn to the Blessed Virgin and/or their personal name-saints. Informed by an intellectualist critic that Mary was no virgin and that their name-saint performed no miracle "as the stories say," such individuals would be entirely within their rights to hold that this skeptic does not "recognize" the existence of their intercessors "under their description," a description that for them makes all the difference in the world. If a traditionalist were perceptive enough, then, he could have seen that Socrates' outlook *is* something of a threat to cult practice, for when everyday particularized, self-interested, retaliatory motives are the primary ones underwriting its performance— and this seems in fact to have often been the motivation behind various public and especially private sacrifices and dedications[215]—then what Socrates offers *is* a virtual repudiation of cult.

It appears, then, that Meletus might have improved somewhat on the number of jurors voting for Socrates' guilt if he had focused their attention directly on the implications for cult that Socrates' gods posed. Socrates, naturally, does not directly address this worry: he makes no explicit attempt to defend himself against the implications of the charge of nonrecognition that we have been entertaining.[216] So, we may wonder, if such a charge is plausible, isn't Socrates being derelict or disingenuous by failing to explicitly address that charge in his *apologia* (even despite Meletus's choice to interpret the initial charge of nonrecognition as one of atheism)?[217] I think not. Socrates is under no obligation to educate the jurors on the complete structure of his theology and conception of piety, and he surely has no need to go into those details that would inflame them against him in ways unrequired by or in violation of his moral duties, especially his duty to persuade them of the inaccuracy of *what he is actually charged with*. What Socrates does deny is that he is a Sophistic investigator of nature and an atheist, and this directly—if not with complete effectiveness—answers the official charge of atheism. In addition, by later affirming that he does believe in gods of some sort—both explicitly (*Ap.* 35d5–7) and implicitly through his constant reference to his god-ordered mission— Socrates shows that his innovations are not extremist, that is, not tanta-

215. Yunis, 49.

216. Cf. Brickhouse and Smith (8), chap. 6.2, who—observing this (and other factors)— argue that Socrates' revisionary views of the gods played no role in his prosecution and conviction.

217. Brickhouse and Smith (8), 182–187.

mount to complete atheism. Finally, on Socrates' own view (and as we shall see) the simple rejection of the gods' immoralities, enmities, and other anthropopsychicisms is not sufficient *by itself* to convict him of disbelief in the gods of the state as he conceives of those gods (or as they are conceived of in the minds of most jurors). After all, one influential side of the tradition had always insisted on the absolute justice and wisdom of the gods, and Socrates remains well within that aspect of it.

Socrates, then, is not being derelict or disingenuous in failing to point out how his conception of the gods (and philosophy) poses a threat to some traditional motivations for performing cult (thereby threatening "guilt" of the popular interpretation of the charge of disbelief in the gods of the state).[218] Rather, Socrates expresses exactly those beliefs necessary to his defense, despite the fact that some of them might have hinted to some of the more traditionally minded jurors his actual guilt of the charge of disbelief in the gods of the state (as they understood the charge); for example, that his gods care more for philosophical argumentation than for burnt offerings, that even their infliction of pain on us may be a good from the Socratic perspective. Socrates is under no obligation to convict himself of impiety as it may be construed by some (or even by the majority of his jurors), especially if he holds that he does recognize the *real* gods, the ones that Athens *should* (or really does) prefer to those that the many take to be connected to "the lies of the poets."[219] Whether and how he holds such a view is considered below.

218. Contra the implications of Brickhouse and Smith's replies to Vlastos (11) in the letters column of *TLS* (4), and now, (8), chap. 6.2. It is worth noting that Socrates can always be found guilty on *some* interpretations of the formal charges, and as Brickhouse and Smith themselves note, (2), 119, it is the *prosecutor's* interpretation of the charges which are the legally relevant ones. Socrates, then, *need only reply* to *that* specification of them, not to "any possible interpretation of the charges" (119). Not coming to grips with all those many others is not—as some like Brickhouse and Smith (8), 184–188, suggest—tantamount to *evasion* of relevant issues. So I think Socrates can both plead innocence of the legal charges—as he, Meletus, and most jurors construe them—while remaining guilty of the charge of nonrecognition of the Athenian gods in the eyes of those (few?) jurors who construe that charge as violated by someone who does not endorse the idea that these gods respond reliably to particular petitionary sacrifices, especially those *involving requests that run contrary to justice* (Socratically conceived) and who are "perceptive" enough to see that Socrates' theological position puts him in this camp. Note too that my view that *there was* a threat to cult in Socrates' position is not undermined by the argument that there is no evidence that anyone *saw* any such a threat or that the threat played no role in Socrates' trial (Brickhouse and Smith, [8], 188).

219. Brickhouse and Smith (8), 184–187, argue that Socrates' account of the origin of the formal charges in the first informal ones (20c4–24b2)—esp. given his explicit commitments to truth-telling (e.g., 18a5–6, 20d5–6)—means that he is a liar if he is conscious of the way in which his socratized gods threaten some of the motivations underlying the civic cult and

More important, though, Socrates does not address concerns about how his views undermine propitiatory religion because—as we have just seen— he simply does *not* undermine *all* motivation for religious ritual. Socrates' silence on his view of traditional cult and his own cult practices can, again, be explained by noting that time is running short in his defense (19a1–2, 37a6–7; cf. *Ap.* 37b) and that his jurors will have been well aware that cult observance is no guarantee of minimally correct belief.[220] Besides, if Socrates had cited his own cult observances, he would have deceptively suggested that contrary to his own conception of things such traditional *actions* actually *do* constitute good evidence of piety and theism, when clearly *they do not* for Socrates. Rather, for him piety—like any other virtue—is an internal matter pertaining to the soul, and no behavioral criteria are sufficient for fixing either its definition or its instantiation in the soul of another.[221] We might say, then, that Socrates both does and does not threaten the traditional cult.[222]

---

yet does not explicitly mention that there. I find this unpersuasive. Although it is true that Socrates never makes explicit his attitudes toward religious cult when he spells out the preju- dices that led to his trial, we can understand these as covered by the generalizations he uses to connect his alleged "investigation of the things aloft" with atheism at 18c, when he speaks of unspecified "slanders" connected with the allegations that he has "wisdom" at 23a, and when he notes the charge that he teaches about "the things aloft" at 23d (see n. 9). More- over, Socrates does cite the *Clouds* as a first accuser (19c), recalling for the jurors that its Socrates "spouts much drivel," drivel that included his accepting without a murmur Strep- siades' rejection of traditional sacrifice and prayer (425–426). Finally, I think it is (and prob- ably must remain) a live issue whether and to what extent the first accusers, the prosecutors, the jurors, and even Socrates himself—were able to consciously apprehend the threat to traditional cult motivations latent in Socrates' socratized gods. Just because this threat is not explicitly mentioned in the *Apology,* however, does not mean that it did not play a significant role in the minds of the various parties to the trial (in a way that keeps Socrates free of deceit and negligence).

220. Note, though, that Xenophon portrays Socrates as citing his public cult practice as a defense (*Apol.* 11–12). It's also worth observing that although Socrates may not have used all the time allotted for his defense speech, that is best explained by his having supporters (συ- νήγοροι) who spoke on his behalf (*Apol.* 22; D.L. 2.41; Brickhouse and Smith [12], 75–76). Socrates, knowing this in advance, may have counted on them to address those worries that might be held by a minority of jurors; e.g., the worry that Socrates is in some way or other an opponent of traditional religious practice.

221. Cf. B. Jackson, 34: "Plato never has a character pray in connection with a sacrifice. I would suggest that this separation of prayer from sacrifice . . . results from Plato's wish to avoid even the suggestion that in prayer one asks for payment for a service rendered." See also Irwin (4), 46–47, and McPherran (1), 126–129. This supports the view that what differ- entiates a pious act from a secularly just one is a matter of the intentionality of the person performing the act in question.

222. Note that not long after Socrates' death, it could be averred on the stage that "any- one who believes that he secures the god's favor by sacrifice . . . is in error. For a man must

Is there, though, evidence that Socrates was in fact thought by his contemporaries to threaten cult practice? Some have seen in Xenophon's zealous defense of Socrates on this point—claiming that he was "the most visible of men" in cult service to the gods (*Mem.* 1.2.64; cf. 1.1.2) and having Socrates himself testify that he often sacrificed at the public altars (*Apol.* 11–12; *Mem.* 1.1.1–2)—an indication that this was at least a serious concern, if not in fact the substance of the charges as they were understood.[223] But the silence of the *Apology* (and virtually the rest of the Platonic *corpus*) on the topic of Socratic sacrifice, and the difficulty of believing that someone so conspicuously virtuous in behavior and god-referring could be indicted for nonrecognition of the civic gods, suggests that Xenophon gives this testimony prominence primarily out of his own conventionalism and overly apologetic purposes. Hence, it is no indicator that it was not atheistic belief that was at the heart of the jury's concerns.[224] Nonetheless, it would be appropriate to combat atheism with testimony of religious practice—that would be *prima facie* evidence that the accused was not an atheist—and since it receives such an emphasis in Xenophon there must be something to it. It seems unlikely that he would offer as a defense a portrait of Socrates that no one could take seriously. Hence, and as we saw in section 3.2, it appears that the religious festivals and ancestral and household gods (cf. *Eud.* 302c4–303a3) that were such a large and prominent part of everyday Athenian life, and which carried no doctrinal baggage for Socrates (cf. *Phdr.* 229b1–230a7), would have been part of his life as well.[225]

Socrates' silence in Plato's works (esp. the *Apology*) on the topic of sacrifice and other issues that might be connected to the charge of nonrecognition, on the other hand, ought to be read as primarily a case of Socrates and his "biographer" sticking to the issues. The threat to cult for some Athenians posed by Socrates (given Socrates' characterization of the first accusations and the interpretation put on the later ones) is that posed by atheism. Someone who advocates the view that there are no gods, natu-

---

be useful by not seducing virgins or committing adultery or stealing and killing for money" (*Menander* fr. 683; cf. Isok. ii 20, for the claim that no offering or worship is superior to the effort to live a virtuous life; Xen. *Ages.* 11.2).

223. Burnet (3), notes on *Eu.* 3b3; *Ap.* 18c3, 24c1; Allen (1), 62; Chroust (3), 235 n. 119.

224. And see Hackforth (2), 58–79; Guthrie (3), 3:237 n. 2 ; Beckman, 55–56; Tate (1), 3–5, and (2), 3–6; and MacDowell (2), 202.

225. Reeve, 67. See Burkert (2), 216–275, and Parke (1).

rally, will be taken as denying to ritual most or all of its traditional meaning. Thus, by responding to the atheism charge, Socrates also addressed the fears of those who perceived a serious threat to cult practice in *that* charge. Moreover, since as we saw earlier (Chapter 2.2) Socratic piety turns out to be a service to the gods that requires philosophy of us, not burnt offerings (always or primarily), with his account of that service and his rebuttal of the atheism charge before his jurors, Socrates could judge his defense speech adequate and complete.

Nonetheless, it should be clear by this point that Socrates had in essence proposed important reformations of a linchpin of traditional religion: take away the conflicts of the myths and you defuse their psychological power, take away the expectations of particular *material* rewards and physical protections in cult, and you disconnect the religion of everyday life from its roots. And, even as it is today, the substitute of the often pain-producing Socratic *elenchos* and the search for universal moral standards offers little solace in the face of life's difficulties to those not centered on the development of their inner, intellectual lives. Socrates, then, raised the stakes for living a life of piety considerably by making its final measure the state of one's philosophically purified soul (with prayer and sacrifice more epiphenomena of this state than causative factors).[226] He thus represented a significant challenge to a crucial aspect of traditional Athenian life—and thus a dangerous threat to those unprepared to understand or change.[227]

---

226. Cf. Parker (1), 254, who notes that Greek religion "reflected and supported the general ethos of Greek culture. It discouraged individualism, a preoccupation with inner states *and the belief that intentions matter more than actions;* it emphasized the sense of belonging to a community and the need for due observance of social forms."

227. I must therefore agree with Kraut (2), who observes that Brickhouse and Smith (8), chap. 6.2, do not acknowledge how Socratic piety put traditional cult practices into doubt and do not explain adequately how their own understanding of Socratic piety—the knowledge of how to give aid to the gods in promoting wisdom in other human beings (178)—is compatible with the rituals of Greek religion. However, Kraut argues for this by maintaining that Socrates is "committed to saying that . . . rituals can bring no benefit unless they are guided by knowledge of what is good" (624) and this seems overstated. Surely we can imagine, for example, that Socrates would accept that a sincere prayer for help in doing Socratic philosophy by one for whom that sincerity is rightly expressed through material sacrifice might be rewarded without that request being guided by a knowledge or a wisdom more than human.

3.4.6 Socrates and the Gods of the State

In a very limited sense, then, it is true that the ethical transformation of the old gods wrought by Socrates was "tantamount to the destruction of the old gods, the creation of new ones," especially in the way he left religious ritual without *all* its former features and warrants.[228] But if that is accurate, how could it be possible for Socrates to affirm the existence of the gods of the state? Is it conceptually possible for Socrates to acknowledge *these gods* and at the same time reject the stories of conflict, deceit, and justice-indifferent *do ut des* cult and curse enforcement intimately connected up with them? I think we can answer in the affirmative. Observe first that Heraclitus had already shown the possibilities for theological, referential ambiguity several generations before in the gnomic utterance, "One thing, the only truly wise, does and does not consent to be called by the name of Zeus" (DK 32). For with this he seems to mean that God (as the Logos of the cosmos) resembles the Zeus of conventional religion in some respects (e.g., recall the popular stories of his justice and wisdom), but not in all those preserved in the tradition of anthropopsychic myth and cult.[229]

Socrates can apply this recognition of ambiguity to his own case by holding that the stories of conflict and justice-indifferent, material cult are—contrary to the view of the mistaken many—simply not an essential (or even accidental) feature of the real "gods of the state." To those who protest that they know full well of what gods they speak, Socrates can hold in typical fashion that they in fact do not fully understand themselves and what they believe (e.g., *G*. 482a–c). Rather, they harbor beliefs (e.g., those affirming the wisdom of the gods) that—if time only allowed— would permit him to elicit from them other beliefs that would elenctically demonstrate that they "do not agree with themselves," but rather with him, and so in fact do acknowledge the same gods as Socrates (cf. *G*. 275e ff.).[230] Thus, those who accuse Socrates of nonrecognition can be compared to later Christians who characterized disbelief in the miracles ascribed to Jesus as a lack of belief in the *existence* of Jesus. But here, as there, it is eminently possible to deny the essential connection such people make between certain characteristics and the existence of the being referred to. Socrates can simply hold that he believes in the *real* gods of the state—for

228. Vlastos (14), 166; cf. Connor, 56.
229. Kirk et al., 203.
230. For a thorough discussion of Socrates' view that we have a true self, possessing beliefs we may be unaware of, see Brickhouse and Smith (8), chap. 3, esp. 3.6.1.

example, the one that Athenians intend to refer to when they speak of "the power and wisdom of Zeus"—thus placing the burden of proof on those who accuse him of disbelief.

So far philosophical charity motivates this answer, but there are also two pieces of text that give a rather strong indication that the above is in fact Socrates' own understanding of his position. First, at 28a2–4 Socrates declares that he is "not unjust after the substance of Meletus's indict-ment." This is tantamount to an assertion that—despite his rejection of the myths of enmity—he is innocent not only of the interpretation of the first formal charge as one of global atheism but also of its popular, straightforward reading as one of nonrecognition of the gods of the state.

Next, at the very end of his defense speech, just where we should expect to see a final, firm affirmation of his innocence, Socrates informs the jury that if he were to say anything irrelevant and/or deceptive that would lead them to acquit him contrary to what the law demands—despite that being the correct thing to do—he would be convicting himself of impiety and unbelief in "the gods," and would also be guilty of enticing the jurors into guilt of impiety as well (34b–35d). He concludes:

> So do not deem that I . . . should practice such things before you which I hold to be neither noble nor just nor pious, and certainly, by Zeus, above all not when I am being prosecuted for impiety by Meletus here! For plainly, if I should persuade and force you by begging, after you have sworn an *oath,* I would be teaching you *to hold that there are not gods,* and in making my defense speech I would simply be accusing myself of *not believing in gods.* But that is *far* from being so. For *I do recognize* [νομίζω] *them . . . as none of my accusers do.* (35c7–d7)

In context, all that Socrates needs to say here to defend himself against Meletus's reformulated charge of atheism is to affirm that he believes that gods (of some sort) exist. And this he does quite vigorously, here as else-where, with the rhetorical effect of his denial that he teaches atheism and his remark that "I do recognize them" amounting to an assertion that, on his own view, gods do exist. But in this setting such remarks *also* rhetori-cally imply belief in the existence of the gods "about whom we've been speaking" (26b8–9)—that is, the gods of the Athenian *polis.* This implica-tion is also reinforced by Socrates' explicit mention of Zeus and the refer-ence to Zeus implicit in Socrates' reminder to the jurors of the connection between oathbreaking and impiety/atheism: Jurors at the time took an oath to judge according to the *nomoi* of Athens, and Socrates' audience will be fully aware that these *nomoi* sanction and support the civic religion and that it is *Zeus* (the Zeus of the civic religion) who is charged with punishing oathbreakers.[231] To encourage someone to break such an oath therefore would be to encourage disbelief in the gods sanctioned by the civic religion, and especially Zeus Polieus. So when Socrates says that he is "far" from attempting to do that, the obvious implication to be drawn by each juror—an implication so clear that Socrates, given his concern to tell only truths, could not allow to stand if he did not hold the implication himself—is that Socrates believes in Zeus Polieus and the civic gods.

But if this is an inference intended by Socrates, then why does he not come right out and assert in the clearest possible terms that he believes in the gods of the state, turning the very words of the initial indictment back on Meletus and his fellow prosecutors? Why also does Socrates consistently fail to *name* the gods he believes in, leaving anonymous even the god whose missionary he is (never calling him "Apollo" or by his cult names [e.g., Phoebus]) and never asserting that this god *is* the same as the Apollo recognized by the city?[232] Moreover, although Socrates does refer to one god, Zeus, by name, he always does so in a way that allows that reference to be explained as a colloquialism (e.g., *Eu.* 4e4; cf. Euthyphro at *Eu.* 4b3). If one focuses on just these points it might seem possible that Socrates is being disingenuous, hinting on the one hand that he believes in gods, gods he hopes that the jury will *wrongly* take to be theirs in every feature, while actually carefully avoiding the straightforward *deception* of declaring a belief in the Zeus and Apollo of Athens.

I think the proper response to these concerns can be found by paying close attention the last qualifying phrase in the passage above whose significance has gone unappreciated. Notice that although Socrates has thoroughly accomplished his aim of replying to the atheism charge in the above passage once he says "I do recognize them [the gods]," he doesn't stop there, but goes on to contrast his position with that of the opposition by claiming that he recognizes the gods in a way(s) superior to that of his accusers. Now Socrates cannot mean to assert that his accusers are insincere when they profess belief in the existence of either gods generically

---

231. The oath bound the jurors as both a matter of piety and the law to "hold no grudges and not be influenced, but . . . judge according to the laws" (see Andoc. *Myst.* 91, and MacDowell [1], 43–44).

232. See Burnyeat (2), 18; Reeve, 25, and n. 26; and West, 125.

understood or the gods of the state as *they* understand that phrase.[233] To all appearances, they have beliefs committing them to the existence of gods, gods such as the Athena of Athens. So the most plausible interpretation of Socrates' remark is to see it as claiming that his accusers do not believe consistently in (or act consistently in respect of) the *real* civic gods—"the gods of the state about whom we've been speaking"—gods that get accurately referred to only when references to their deceits, enmities, ignorance, and responses to justice-indifferent material cult are omitted from the meaning one intends by asserting "I recognize the gods of the state." It is such thoroughly moral gods that Socrates believes in, and all his beliefs and actions concerning them are seemingly consistent with one another; whereas Meletus—as shown by Socrates' interrogation—is prone to entertaining contradictory theological notions (e.g., he may hold like Euthyphro that they are wise but have enmities) and fails to pursue the truly pious task of doing philosophy. Hence, and in contrast to Socrates, it is Meletus who must be said to not really or adequately believe in the gods of Athens!

But finally, why does Socrates not spell all this out if he in fact has the conceptual resources to do so? The answer here must be quite speculative, but I believe, again, that Socrates would first point to the limitations of time placed on him (limitations he speaks of elsewhere). Given this constraint, he could do little more than make firm protestations of belief in the existence of the gods of the state. But to do this and go no further might risk violating his strict commitment to tell the truth, for given the interpretation of that phrase by some traditionalist jurors, such affirmations would foster the false belief in those same people that Socrates believes in the gods of the state as they conceive them; gods open to discord and the retribution of evil by evil, and who may be "bought off" contrary to Socratic justice by petitionary sacrifice. There is also insufficient time to provide the *sort* of defense Socrates prefers. For such a defense would have to be the elenctic one of revealing to each of his five hundred or so jurors that they harbor inconsistent theological beliefs that, when sorted out, would reveal that their gods are also his, namely, the real ones. This would be harder than might be thought, since—after all—how many jurors will own up to the idea that any of their petitions were ever unjust?[234]

---

233. And surely Socrates is not saying that he sacrifices more scrupulously than his prosecutors.

234. I take the discussion above to effectively rebut Brickhouse and Smith (4), chap. 6.2, who seem to think that the threat to cult posed by socratized gods requires Socrates to "stand outside the law" (184) by virtue of not believing in the gods of the state, and who think it

As I previously maintained, even if Socrates had the time to map out his referential distinction, he is under no obligation to help the jury wrongfully convict him of the formal charges, and surely *some* would have been inclined to do so once they were inflamed by his revelation that he disbelieves the myths of conflict, rejects and qualifies the priority of material cult, and disallows the efficacy of justice-indifferent petitions. In fact, Socrates is under a contrary obligation to prolong his philosophical mission (insofar as that is consistent with virtue) and to help his jurors arrive at a just *acquittal,* and that end would be undermined by making his theological reformations a point of emphasis. Socrates tells his jury with perfectly clear effect but without prejudicing his case that he believes *as his prosecution does not* that the civic gods exist; and just jurors will see that this is enough to clear him of the allegations of atheism. And if Meletus *had* tried to argue that Socrates was guilty of not believing in the gods of the state, we may be confident that Socrates would have shown how his view of them remains steadfast while Meletus's own belief, say, that Zeus is wise, must "move about" when placed against the credence he gives to the stories of Zeus's lies, enmities, ignorance, jealous rage, and responses to particularized, justice-indifferent sacrifice.[235]

In the end, of course, there is simply not enough evidence available to know which Athenians (and how many of them) were cognizant of Socrates' threat to popular cult, what degree of awareness of it they possessed, and what level of concern it would have generated for each. The simple answer I have tried to suggest above is that *some* of the jurors *may* have seen that Socrates' views bear on traditional cult in a way that is a threat to the motivations underlying *some* instances of traditional practice, that this realization *may* have prejudiced *some* of these jurors against him, and that Socrates himself probably saw that his view of sacrificial practice was at odds with these sorts of cases, but had reasons not to address this threat

---

possible that no one at Socrates' trial saw a distinction between "gods of the state" and "gods" (187). I have also tried to show that their alternative to this—that no one saw the distinction as significant and pertinent to the case (187)—is implausible. Again, just because Socrates must follow Meletus where he leads does not show that he, Meletus, and some jurors do not see a threat to Socrates on the issue of whether his socratized gods are the same as the gods of Athens.

235. Brickhouse and Smith (12), 126–127, and (8), 6.2, rely on *Phaedrus* 229e2–230a3, where Socrates says that he accepts the customary views about the gods, to argue that Socrates is simply innocent of the charge of nonrecognition of the gods of the state, despite his skepticism about the myths of conflict and immorality. But the "customary views" of the time *included* those very myths, and so the *Phaedrus* passage cannot be used as support for their view.

during the trial. Socrates is not, as some might have it, in a position where he must address simply every concern every juror may have about his philosophical views *or* be guilty of *lying* to the jurors.

But, again, and as we saw, there *was* a threat to cult in Socrates, even if few of the jurors detected it. Hence, Socrates was guilty as charged of non-recognition of the civic gods (1a) in a sense, the popular sense, of what it means to "not recognize the gods," if one tunes that charge finely enough so that it concerns the motivations for and expectations surrounding cult. Whether such formulations would have still produced a conviction is, of course, a puzzle for those skilled at the analysis of counterfactuals. Nevertheless, the conceptual changes Socrates instituted had theological ramifications whose effects not only impinged on Plato and the other Socratics, but through them, profoundly shaped antiquity and the history of Western religious thinking (see Chapter 5.2–3).

But there also remains a conservative side to Socrates that needs to be emphasized. First, of the actual charges Socrates is innocent in the ways we have seen. He is also in many ways a person quite willing to live within the established religious ways of the *polis,* not only in practice, but in belief as well. For part of the customary popular religion included an epistemic modesty in the face of the divine, a tradition with roots in Delphi and its cult of Apollo. As we shall see in further detail, Socrates viewed himself and his mission as essentially grounded in that tradition. Thus, although Socrates firmly rejects a few propositions concerning the civic gods, these denials do not amount to a thorough rejection of the gods themselves. Wise only in knowing that he lacks complete understanding (23a–b), Socrates will not dogmatically or actively dismiss those stories of the gods that are compatible with his few foundational propositions (e.g., that the gods are entirely wise), and will accept in a weak sense those that seem likely and have the backing of custom.[236] Thus, for example, Socrates accepts (perhaps weakly, without strong belief) the divinity of the moon and sun and the plurality of the gods, but does not pretend to the disgraceful ignorance (*Ap.* 29b1–2) of supposing that he *knows* such things to be so or how they are so. As he strolls with Phaedrus down to the banks of the Ilissus, the Platonic Socrates puts it this way:

---

236. He will, of course, readily accept those beliefs that turn out to have the backing of the *elenchos,* that have repeatedly survived the attempts of interlocutors to refute them (on which, see Chapter 4.2).

I should be quite in the fashion if I disbelieved . . . [the story of Boreas and Orithyia], as the men of science do. . . . I myself have no time for the business [of explaining them scientifically], and I'll tell you why, my friend. I can't as yet "know myself" as the inscription at Delphi enjoins, and so long as that ignorance remains it seems to me ridiculous to inquire into extraneous matters. Consequently I don't bother about such things, but accept the current beliefs about them, and direct my inquiries . . . to myself, to discover whether I am a more complex creature and more puffed up with pride than Typhon, or a simpler, gentler being whom heaven has blessed with a quiet, un-Typhonic nature. (*Phdr.* 229c–230a; trans. Hackforth)[237]

3.4.7 The Corruption of Youth

As mentioned earlier, the third formal charge, that Socrates "wrongs the youth by corrupting them," depends upon the other two. It is *teaching* the doctrines specified by the other two charges that constitutes the charge of corruption. Socrates' initial response to the charge is to interrogate Meletus by means of two arguments that attempt to display the implausibility of the charge in its own right, irrespective of what he is alleged to teach. The first (24c–25c) tries to show this by eliciting from Meletus the extremely unlikely claim that "all of Athens improves the youth while Socrates alone corrupts them." The second (25c–26a; cf. 37a) attempts to show that since no one wishes to be harmed (25d1–2), attempting to corrupt the youth is something that Socrates would never willingly do.[238] To establish the actual *falsehood* of the corruption charge, however, Socrates must show that the alleged content of his teaching as represented by the religious charges against him are substantially inaccurate, and we have seen something of this defense above—both against Meletus's "development" of the first charge into one of atheism and as a hypothetical reply to the original charges of nonrecognition and recognizing καινὰ δαιμόνια.

It seems likely that the corruption charge is in itself the most weighty of

237. Cf. Brickhouse and Smith (8), 188–189. Still, this passage should be read with a grain of salt: Socrates is a traditionalist, but not when those traditions run up against his elenctically arrived-at nontraditional results; see Chapter 4.1.

238. See, e.g., Brickhouse and Smith (12), 117–119, and Reeve, 87–93, for further discussion.

the charges leveled against Socrates.[239] This can be seen most clearly in Socrates' response to Euthyphro's description of himself as someone who spouts off about "divine things" to the Assembly: "In my opinion, the Athenians don't much mind anyone they think is clever, so long as he does not teach his wisdom. But if they think he makes others like himself, they are incensed" (*Eu.* 3c7–d2; cf. 3d6–9).

Here we are in effect told that the mere possession of unconventional beliefs that are only rarely communicated is generally a relatively safe thing, but to propagate them is an entirely different matter: *that* sort of thing will *incense* Socrates' fellow citizens. Can such activity sufficiently incense them to take legal action? We have every reason to think so. Besides the trial of Socrates itself, the concern over orthodox religious teaching exhibited by the decree of Diopeithes, the legislation introduced by the Thirty making "teaching the art of speech" illegal (*Mem.* 1.2.31), and the recollections of Aeschines that Socrates was executed because he was the *educator* of Critias (*Contra Tim.* 173) all testify to the seriousness with which Athenian law viewed unorthodox teachings.[240] The burning of the φροντιστήριον in the *Clouds* also gives some indication of how deadly passions could turn on the subject of suspect teaching.[241] A final sign of the formidable weight of the corruption charge is that Socrates adds a last and final defense against it toward the end of his speech, when from 33a through 34b he maintains his innocence of corruption by arguing that he is simply not a teacher of doctrines and by challenging Meletus to produce a single instance of corruption from among his associates.[242]

Socrates' protestations effectively maintain that he is no teacher in the damning sense by being a paid private instructor of unorthodox dogmatisms—a professional Sophist of some sort—but they cannot disabuse either his ancient jurors or his modern students of the conviction that Socra-

239. Vlastos (14), 293–297. Vlastos's contention, however, that Socrates' unconventional religious views *by themselves* would not have been sufficient to indict him is not well supported. Moreover, Vlastos, 296, is incorrect in holding that there was no reference made to his teaching in the formal indictment; see *Ap.* 26b2–6.

240. Vlastos (14), 295–297. Note too how *M.* 91c–92d presents one of Socrates' future prosecutors, Anytus, as incensed by the *corruption* that sophistic teachers engender.

241. Although the *Clouds is* a comedy—and so we may imagine the concluding scene to involve actors howling and slapping at their padded burning rumps—it is also *black* comedy of the sort that derives its humorous punch by relying on our recognition of an underlying darkness (e.g., as with scenes from J. Heller's *Catch-22*).

242. Thereby addressing whatever other senses of "corruption" may have been at work; e.g., that through his teaching Socrates encourages youths to treat their elders with disrespect, or to engage in shameful sexual activities.

tes is nonetheless a teacher in a very real sense.[243] Socrates may not directly promulgate specific doctrines—and he is clearly innocent of the revised charge of teaching atheism—but he is also just as clearly on a "mission from god" to exhort his fellow citizens to care for the virtue of their souls and to understand the depths of their ignorance by means of elenctic philosophy (cf. 30d–31c, 33c). But this makes it easy to imagine that Socrates is in a dangerous sense a teacher of new religious conceptions. As we have now seen in our examination of the *Euthyphro* and *Apology,* Socrates' philosophical activities do reaffirm aspects of the tradition—the gulf separating humanity from the gods in particular—but the activity itself is neither purely traditional nor purely and innocently aporetic. In view of the philosophical conception of piety Socrates "develops" in partnership with Euthyphro, for example, it is possible to imagine that Socrates has let stand unchallenged implications others around him have drawn for themselves from agreed-upon premises such as "the gods are wholly good," implications dangerous for some traditional motivations for performing cult (in particular, those seen earlier). Socrates has also all along been teaching (implicitly if not always explicitly) a radical, new understanding of piety, one that includes a nontraditional demand to transform the soul by means of philosophical self-examination, and this would have been easy enough—as Socrates himself tells us (23d)—to confuse with the sorts of teaching and methods of the new (and sometimes agnostic or atheistic) intellectuals (see Chapter 4.2).

3.4.8 Why Was Socrates Convicted?

Socrates' fellow Athenians managed to tolerate some forty years of his philosophical activity before they finally put him into the docket. Since there is no indication that his views underwent a radical change toward the end of his career, it seems better to search for additional explanations for Socrates' prosecution—and thus ultimately his conviction—in the changes that we know Athens experienced in the late fifth century that made religious deviancy much more dangerous than it had ever been during Socrates' long career.

Martin Ostwald has mapped out a compelling picture of these changes—the "Polarization of the 420s"—in his monumental work on

---

243. See Brickhouse and Smith (12), 197–200.

fifth-century Athens, and there is no need to repeat that story in detail here.[244] It is sufficient to note that the social and political atmosphere in Athens at the time of Socrates' trial was highly volatile. First, since mid-century there had been a severe decline of confidence in the truth and efficacy of the traditional religious assumptions (a glimpse of which is found in the *Clouds*). In addition, this decline seems intimately connected with what Dodds termed a "regression of popular religion," that is, a growing interest in magic and more primitive forms of worship as provided by the foreign cults that infiltrated Athens at the end of the fifth century.[245] This decline and regression apparently generated a conservative reaction, one marked by the decree of Diopeithes and (perhaps) by the prosecution of Anaxagoras.[246] This decline was also connected in the Athenian public mind with the sufferings of the terrible plague that touched virtually every family (c. 430), the hardships of its long war with Sparta and the humiliating defeat that followed, all this culminating in the terror imposed by the Thirty Tyrants (installed by Sparta in 404). The democracy was soon restored (403), but it is nonetheless evident that resentments over Athens's debasement still festered, and that in the search for its causes one popular target was the skeptical influence of the new intellectuals (both Sophists and *phusiologoi*).[247] These thinkers were perceived to be tied to the interests of the upper and educated classes, while the interests of the newly established democracy were just as clearly bound to the lower-class majority and their popular—thus centrally propitiatory—forms of religion.[248] During such a time, and given the general intolerance ancient societies showed toward deviancy in religious practice, it is understandable that many Athenians would imagine that their *polis* had come to grief out of a failure to preserve the values and practices that had once protected her

244. Ostwald, chap. 5, esp. 274–290; see also Brickhouse and Smith (12), 18–24; Connor, 51–56; and Dodds (4), chap. 4.

245. Dodds (4), chap. 4, esp. 192–195; see also Klonoski, 135–139.

246. On the decree, and other possible, similarly motivated prosecutions of intellectuals such as Protagoras, Stilpon of Megara, and Theodorus of Cyrene, see Burkert (2), 119–125; Dodds (4), 188–195; Dover (2), 40–41; Kerferd, 21–22; J. Mansfeld; MacDowell (2), 200; Momigliano (2), 565–266; Ostwald, 274–279; Reeve, 79–82; and I. F. Stone, 230–247. One of the more brazen examples of intellectual atheism from the period is the speech in the satyr play *Sisyphus* (attributed to Critias, but probably by Euripides), which characterizes religion as an invention by a "shrewd man" designed to inhibit secret wrongdoing through fear of all-knowing, all-powerful deities (Sextus E. *Ad. Math.* 9.54); see Ostwald, 281–283.

247. See Dodds (4), 189–192, and Nilsson (5), 265, and (5), 77–78.

248. Nilsson (5), 274–275.

and made her great.[249] Moreover, although belief in every aspect of the ancient pieties had begun to fade, the grounds were still there for a revival based on resentment and fear. Finally, whatever deviances were tolerated by the Thirty would, after their demise, be more likely to be seen as threats to the newly reestablished democracy.

Thus the belief that Athens had been the recipient of punishments that—in the end—had a divine origin would be easily incited. By failing to preserve the old piety undiminished—demonstrated in particular by the outrages of the mutilation of the Hermai (415) and the alleged profanations of the Eleusinian mysteries by Alcibiades (415; one of Socrates' associates)—and by tolerating religious deviance instead, Athens had called upon herself the divine retribution that scrupulous piety preserves states against.[250] The natural popular response would have been a heightened vigilance concerning religious conformity, and this seems borne out by the prosecution within a year or so of Socrates' own trial—and by a certain Meletus—of Andocides on a double charge of impiety related to the Eleusinian mysteries.[251] Again, the year of Socrates' trial was also the year Nicomachus was prosecuted on charges quite similar to those leveled at Socrates, namely, neglecting traditional practices and introducing new ones.[252] Given this atmosphere, a defendant's interpretation of "the gods of the state" and his or her "innovations" and attitudes toward the civic cult would have received strict scrutiny. Thus, I think we can be relatively sure that if a radical reformer of the ilk of Heraclitus (someone who explicitly ridicules the small hearth-worship of farmers) had been faced with the lot-picked jury of Socrates (hence, packed with traditionalists), he would have suffered the same verdict as Socrates, and surely by a wider margin of votes.[253]

This atmosphere would also have magnified the significance of a number of Socrates' eccentricities and politically charged attitudes, and—since "the common coin of political exchange at this time [was] the charge of religious deviancy"[254]—would have also helped to motivate the formal indictment on a charge of impiety irrespective of the prejudices of the first accusers and the actual warrant such accusations might normally provide.

249. Cohen (1), 215.
250. Nilsson (4), 78.
251. Andoc. *Myst.*, 81–89; see Mikalson (1), 114, and Connor, 51.
252. Lysias 30 (*Against Nichomachus*); see Connor, 52.
253. Dodds (4), 182.
254. Connor, 52.

Among the most worrisome of these "eccentricities" would be Socrates' links to the old enemy of Athens, Sparta, and thus to oligarchical tendencies: Aristophanes, for example, portrays the pupils of his "Socrates" as long-haired, unclean, laconizing toughs (*Nu.* 833–837; cf. *Av.* 281 ff.). Next, Socrates goes beyond the usual deference shown toward the Delphic Oracle by deriving his mission to hound respectable Athenians from its message, and this is an oracle with a pronounced preference for Sparta (Thuc. 1.118). Finally, Socrates' criticisms of popular leaders such as Pericles were reminiscent of the gossip tossed around by the laconizing boys of the gymnasium (*G.* 515b–517c; cf. *Meno* 93a–95a).[255]

More generally, and despite Socrates' resistance to the Thirty (*Ap.* 32c–d) and their reciprocal hostility toward him, it would have been known that he refused to leave Athens with the democratic exiles when the Thirty were installed. This, together with his penchant for embarrassing political figures in public, his explicit reluctance to engage in public partisan politics because of its dangers (*Ap.* 31d–32a), and his criticisms of democratic mechanisms as failing to follow the principle that it is the expert and not "the many" who ought to rule (*Mem.* 1.2.9, 3.9.10; *Cr.* 44d) would at least have helped to tilt some members of the jury against him.[256] In particular, Socrates' opposition to making appointments by means of the lottery (*Mem.* 1.2.9) would have had religious repercussions relevant to the formal charges, since it was generally thought that the lot made it possible for the knowledgeable gods, rather than fallible humans, to decide the matter at issue (*via* divine foreknowledge and power).[257]

In view of all the factors we have seen to be working against Socrates, his conviction seems overdetermined. On the interpretation I have argued for, though, a primary indictment-making, conviction-making factor is the allegation of atheism, aided and abetted by the hatred and envy (21c–e, 28a) Socrates' philosophical mission generated and his subsequent failure to offer a false and shameless defense (38d–39a; cf. 34b–35d, *G.* 522c–e). But since we have reason to be confident that Socrates is innocent of this particular allegation, and in view of the rhetorical power of his defense on

255. Note too Socrates' preference for the law of Sparta which mandated that capital court cases be allotted more than a single day (*Ap.* 37a–b).

256. I am persuaded by the arguments of Vlastos (4) and Brickhouse and Smith (12), 69–87, 170–184, and (8), chap. 5, however, which find Socrates to have preferred democracy over all other available forms of government. I am also somewhat convinced by Brickhouse and Smith (12), 69–87, and (8), chap. 5.4, that Socrates' reputation as the teacher of Alcibiades and Critias was not of *special* concern to the jurors.

257. Sourvinou-Inwood, 321.

this point, it is hard to believe that most of the jurors convicted him on those grounds (or those grounds alone). What other element(s), then, of all the many rumors and charges we have seen, might be cited as fundamental conviction-making factors?

As indicated in our earlier examination of the informal and formal charges, I think it likely that a quite damaging allegation was the charge that Socrates believed in and taught about "new divinities," where for most jurors this means above all his *daimonion*. While certain jurors might have been discerning enough to see or intuit the danger to traditionally motivated cult in Socrates' views of the gods—what I have identified as his gravest genuine threat to Athenian religion—the attention of the jurors who voted for conviction was most likely to have been drawn to his apparent introduction of a new dispensation without seeking the sanction of the *polis: that* will have seemed his most obvious and glaring violation of accepted norms.[258] Naturally, given the constellation of factors working against Socrates, jurors who believed him guilty of this may well have made further damning inferences concerning his teachings.[259]

It should be no surprise, then, that Socrates' defense was ultimately unsuccessful. In fact, what is surprising is how close it came to succeeding (failing by only a margin of thirty votes [36a5–6]). Our best interpretation of Socrates' *apologia*, I think, is that it is a sincere attempt at the most effective rebuttal of *all* the allegations ranged against him, though—as we

258. Thus, I am sympathetic with Reeve, 84 n. 14, 97, who holds (though for few apparent reasons) that it was primarily the *daimonion* that led to the charges against Socrates, and not the rejection of the gods' conflicts and immoralities. Although Socrates himself never names the *daimonion* as a source of the first accusations that led to the formal charges—as with the worries about cult—it may be alluded to when he speaks at 23a of unspecified slanders connected with the allegations that he has wisdom and when he notes at 23d–e the allegation of teaching about "the things aloft." Note too that Socrates does say at 31d that Meletus "wrote about" the *daimonion* in the indictment. In fact, since it is clear that the *daimonion was* the source for the formulation of one of the formal charges, it seems likely that Meletus would try to use a formulation that *does* pick up a preexisting prejudice and that the *daimonion*—as the source for the charge's formulation—was, then, a source of pretrial prejudice. Brickhouse and Smith (8), chap. 6.2.3, agree that Plato and Xenophon identify the charge of innovation as motivated by the *daimonion* and assert that "where the ancients agree, we see no reason not to believe them," but also hold *per* 19b1–2 that Meletus was led to bring his charges by the first accusations (183). Hence, I should think they'd have to agree that Meletus saw the *daimonion* as covered by the first accusation that Socrates teaches about "the things aloft" (23d–e).

259. Perhaps connecting these in turn with his apparent laconizing ways; e.g., they may have inferred that his insistence on the priority of justice and philosophizing over lavish sacrifice (cf. *Mem.* 1.3.3) marked him out as a friend of Athens's old, austere enemy, Sparta; see Connor, 53–56.

have seen—not the most thorough he might have provided had he (possibly) not been warned against preparing a defense in advance (*Mem.* 4.8.5–6) and/or had he had more of the time he saw necessary for a complete response (37a–b). Thus, we can understand why Socrates does not follow up every possible insinuation, which, from our standpoint, is in need of rebuttal (not explaining, for example, *why*—as he well might have in the fashion of Xenophon [*Apol.* 11–13]—the *daimonion* is not an unapproved foreign import). In the end, the prejudices and charges against Socrates proved so numerous and broad-ranging that he was in effect—as was so common in Athenian trials—put on trial for the conduct of his entire life. That conduct, commanded by a divinity and exemplifying the new piety Socrates had forged, proved all too prone to misrepresentation before an undiscerning crowd. And from the outside that new piety looked to be nothing more than the sort of old familiar impiety that Socrates himself would have condemned.

4

Socratic Reason and Socratic Revelation

4.1 Dreams, Divinations, and the *Daimonion*

Readers of even a resolutely secular bent should not have been entirely put off by the Socrates of the preceding chapters. Although he is not from their perspective as theologically "forward-thinking" as some Sophists, this Socrates nevertheless takes a large step in the direction of sophistic humanism through his rejection of naive voluntarism, divine immorality and enmity, and those other anthropopsychisms that support the full set of traditional *do ut des* motivations for practicing cult. In fact, and as I will elaborate further, Socrates' revisions of Greek religion were more sophisticated, and—in the long run—more philosophically fruitful, than the simple, uncompromising atheism with which Meletus had tried to associate him.

Nevertheless, when we turn to the epistemological aspects of Socratic theology we encounter what appears to be a quite unreformed, unreflective—even embarrassingly superstitious—holdover from conventional Greek religion: Socrates, for all his rationalism, appears to give clear and uncritical credence to the alleged god-given messages found in dreams, divinations, and other such traditionally accepted incursions by divinity.[1] For

---

1. During Socrates' lifetime, divination (μαντική) was widely employed by both states and individuals, and appeared in roughly three forms (in order of prestige): (1) divination by

example, we have seen him claim that his philosophical mission to the Athenians "has been commanded [προστέτακται] of me . . . by the god through oracles [μαντείων] and through dreams [ἐκ μαντείων καὶ ἐξ ἐνυπνίων] and by every other means in which a divinity has ever commanded [προσέταξε] anyone to do anything" (Ap. 33c4–7; cf. 30a5). In Xenophon (e.g., Mem. 1.1.5–9), we even find Socrates sending his students to oracles and seers for advice. Finally, given the conscientious trust Socrates displays in the well-known and frequent warnings of his supernatural voice (the *daimonion*), he may begin to appear even more superstitious than the average Athenian(!): Not at all the sort of behavior we expect from the paradigm of the rationally self-examined life. After all, if such enlightened contemporaries as Pericles and Thucydides could stand aloof from popular superstition,[2] and if even traditionally minded playwrights (Aristophanes; e.g., Av. 521, 959–988; Eq. 1080–1085; V. 380; Nu. 332) could poke cruel fun at seers and "oracle-mongers," how could Socrates not do so as well?[3]

But to make matters more complicated, we must also recognize that Socrates owes his reputation in intellectual history almost entirely to his powerful, rational, probing intellect. In Socrates' encounters with various interlocutors, he constantly affirms (in word and deed) that we ought to be persuaded only by the best *reason* (λόγος), where it is natural to take this as referring to the "secular ratiocination" provided by his characteristic elenctic method. As *Crito* 46b4–6 puts it:

> C Not now for the first time, but always, I [Socrates] am the sort of man who is persuaded by nothing in me except the reason [τῷ λόγῳ] that appears to me to be the best when I reason [λογιζομένῳ] about the matter. (Cf. 48d8–e5)[4]

But in our most reliable re-creations of Socratic thought, the early Platonic dialogues, the *elenchos* fails to secure any complete Socratic definitions of

---

lots (κλῆροι) (cleromancy); (2) interpretation of signs (σημεῖα) such as thunder, the direction of flights of birds, and the reading of sacrificial entrails; (3) the production and interpretation of oral oracles by a seer (μάντις) (with these being recorded, collected, and interpreted by "oracle-mongers" [χρησμολόγοι]). See, e.g., Zaidman and Pantel, 121–128.

2. Thanks to his association with Anaxagoras, Pericles "was made superior to the fearful amazement that superstition produces on those who are ignorant of the causes of events in the higher regions" (Plutarch *Life of Pericles* 6). For Thucydides, see 2.8.2 (also 2.21.3, 2.54.2, 5.26.4, 7.50.4, 8.1.1).

3. See N. Smith (1) on Aristophanes and these two classes of diviner.

4. My attention was first drawn to this passage by Vlastos.

the virtues, and Socrates confirms these results by disclaiming expert moral knowledge (e.g., *Ap.* 21b2–5). This attitude of rationalistic skepticism and the commitment to reason testified to by C thus seem very much in conflict with the presuppositions underlying Socrates' reliance on oracles, dreams, and the *daimonion*. As noted earlier (Chapter 1.1), Socrates never explains how he can be sure that he is not suffering from hallucinations, and on first inspection one might see little rational justification for his religiously based claims. Moreover, his acceptance of theological postulates and extrarational indicators appears to be at odds with the tough, argumentative stance he takes toward the religiously based claims of others (such as Euthyphro).

In what follows I offer an interpretation of the role extrarational sources of conviction play within the Socratic philosophical mission that will resolve these puzzles, reconciling the rationalistic, skeptical, and religious tendencies exemplified by our texts. By the end of this chapter it will be clear that on my account (at least) Socrates does not endorse a form of the intellectualist rejection of divination's efficacy,[5] but also does not merely take the operations of traditional divinatory practices at face value. Rather, he will be seen to accept the traditional notion that the gods really do provide humankind with signs (e.g., that the gods provide us with truths through oracles and dreams), while insisting that traditional, haphazard methods of oracular interpretation must give way to his sort of rational, elenctic methods for interpreting and testing such signs.[6]

5. For example, in the manner of the characters of Euripides, who challenge both the abilities and honesty of traditional seers (e.g., *Philoc.* fr. 795) and the existence of the gods who allegedly provide foreknowledge (*Bel.* fr. 286; *TW* 884–87; *Fr.* 480; Sextus *Ad. Math.* 9.54). See Ostwald, 279–290, for discussion.

6. Socrates, however, is not the first to "draw divination into the new field of rational human discourse" (J.-P. Vernant [1], 311), since in the story recounted by Herodotus (7.140–145), Themistocles was able to convince the Athenian Assembly by means of secular deliberation that the Pythia's ambiguous reference to "wooden walls" was a reference not to a previously existing thorn-hedge, but to a naval fleet. However, I will show that Socrates' rational approach to divination marks a substantial advancement over this case, which appears not to be a true case of impartial investigation into the real meaning of the god's sign. Rather, here the interpreter advanced an interpretation of a gnomic utterance whose primary virtue was that it would help further a course of action that the interpreter had *already* decided on independent grounds the gods *should* be recommending.

Although there was significant public worry in the fifth century concerning the efficacy of popular divination, we can imagine that some Athenians would have been offended by the idea that genuine divination requires the services of rational philosophy (which they might confuse with sophistry and natural science). Since other rational critics of divination do not

4.1.1 Reason, Revelation, and the *Euthyphro*

Socrates is frequently depicted as acting on the assumption that he has quite dependable (though perhaps fallible) access to the truth of a number of particular claims concerning the advisability of various courses of action on the basis of extrarational sources of information. He is, for example, convinced that his *daimonion,* being divine in nature, is a trustworthy guide that warns him away from harm and falsehoods (e.g., *Ap.* 31d1–4, 40a2–c3). The warnings given by this sign are practical and particular, and Socrates clearly regards them as useful and good. It is fair to say that he thinks that he *knows* in some sense that its "advice" is sound.[7] Socrates is, as we saw, also convinced that it is "true" (ἀληθῆ, [*Ap.* 33c8]) that he must philosophize even at the cost of his life because of a command given by divinations and in dreams (*Ap.* 33c4–8;[8] see also *Cr.* 44a5–b4 and *Phd.* 60d8–61b8, where Socrates takes divinely given dream messages seriously). Finally, Socrates is convinced that his philosophical mission is divinely sanctioned and of supreme moral worth in virtue of the claim of the Delphic Oracle that "no one is wiser" than he (*Ap.* 20e3–23c1, 33c4–7). He is so sure that he understands what pious service it is that the god wishes him to perform, that not even a sure threat of death could persuade him to abandon that mission (*Ap.* 28d6–29d5). Thus, he *knows* that he is obligated to philosophize, for as he puts it, his jury should be aware that it is a "truth" (ἀληθείᾳ, [*Ap.* 28d6]) and should "know well" (ἐυ ἴστε, [30a5]) that he philosophizes under a divine mandate.

Nonetheless, Socrates is primarily a vigorously argumentative denizen of the marketplace, seeming to derive and/or warrant his actions and moral convictions—e.g., that it is better to suffer injustice than to do it (*Cr.*

---

appear to have been prosecuted for their doubts, however, I do not find a significant source of pre-trial prejudice in Socrates' critique of traditional divination.

7. Again, I presume that the correct understanding of virtue that Socrates seeks and is depicted as having failed to achieve is a general theoretical understanding of *why* each virtuous thing is virtuous. Failure to achieve this sort of knowledge does not ipso facto preclude a pretheoretic knowledge of *particular* instances falling under an unanalyzed concept (thus Socrates can consistently affirm his ignorance of virtue but also claim to *know* that "it is disgraceful to do wrong" [*Ap.* 29b6–7]). Hence, e.g., Socrates can be as certain as is humanly possible that his mission is virtuous without having a complete and certain account of either his mission or the attending ethical concepts; see Chapter 2.2 and Brickhouse and Smith (14) and (4), chaps. 2 and 4.5.

8. The inclusive claim of this particular passage allows us to assume that the positive signs commanding Socrates to philosophize were understood by Socrates to be further supported by the failure of his *daimonion* to issue its customary warning (cf. *Ap.* 41d3–5).

49c10–d5; G. 509c6–7)—by subjecting them (and their negations) to the scrutiny of elenctic examination (e.g., G. 508c–509a; but, again, see Chap. 1, n. 14). What, then, is the relation between these two sources of conviction, "elenctic testing" and "extrarational signification?" Xenophon, at least, suggests that Socrates thought that these were two distinct avenues of inquiry, each appropriate to somewhat disparate subject matters (Mem. 1.1.6–9).⁹ According to Xenophon's Socrates, for example, it is *irrational* to suppose that every future event is open to reliable, nondivinatory rational prediction; hence, he advises us that

> M   . . . what the gods have granted us to do by help of learning, we must learn; what is hidden from mortals we should try to find out from the gods by divination. (Mem. 1.1.9; trans. Marchant)

Socrates, in other words, finds it advisable to be guided by rational considerations *whenever feasible,* but divination otherwise.¹⁰ But then this suggests a hypothesis for how we might initially reconcile the view that Socrates is persuaded by nothing but what passes the test of reason (text C), with his reliance upon divine monitions. He will insist upon elenctic testing for all beliefs for which that is appropriate and feasible, but he will also acknowledge that some beliefs are legitimately derived from extrarational sources (which then count as practical "reasons"). However, given Socrates' commitment to elenctic testing, and his view of the deities as themselves superlatively rational (Ap. 23a–b), even these beliefs will be the subjects of elenctic interpretation and testing ("reasoned about" per C).

The tentative adoption of this hypothesis will allow us, first of all, to address a grave difficulty lurking within the *Euthyphro,* a moral problem of the sort relished by those who fear that by taking the religiously oriented passages of our texts seriously we are left with a Socrates-turned-religious-fanatic. At the conclusion of the *Euthyphro,* as Socrates in typical ironic form bids Euthyphro stay for one more round of instruction, Euthyphro is told that

> E   . . . we must begin again from the beginning and ask what the pious is. . . . For if you did not know the pious and the impious clearly,

9. Again, although Xenophon's testimony is made suspect by his apologetic exuberance, here (it will be seen) it is paralleled by other sources, and so can be used to generate the sort of hypothesis I advance below. On this issue, see D. Morrison.

10. Socratic divination appears limited to certain dreams, the *daimonion,* and the reports of the Delphic Oracle; but see Xen. Apol. 12–13.

you surely would never have undertaken to prosecute an elderly man, your father, for murder on behalf of a hired man. Rather, as to the gods, you would have dreaded the risk that you would not do it correctly, and as to human beings, you would have been ashamed. (15c11–d8)

Socrates' criticism of Euthyphro here echoes his earlier awe at the moral *risk* Euthyphro was running that initiated his questioning on the topic of piety (4a2–e8), is consistent with the goal of that search for a Socratic definition of "what the pious is," and conforms to the Socratic endorsement of the division of the virtue of justice into two parts, piety and secular justice (*Eu.* 11e4–12d10).[11] Hence, the general moral principle invoked in text E is Socrates' own.

To formulate that principle requires a careful interpretation of E. It appears at first glance that Socrates is asserting that without a general conceptual understanding of piety—that is, without grasping and being able to use as a moral yardstick the definition of the one paradigmatic *eidos* by which all pious things are pious (6d9–e6)—one ought not to attempt actions whose performance poses a significant danger of impiety and injustice (and so harm) (cf. 4e4–8 and 15e5–16a4). This initial reading is also supported by its incorporation of the familiar Socratic doctrines that (1) consistently virtuous action requires knowledge of virtue, and (2) that one ought to avoid doing evil at all costs.[12] Thus, we seem bidden by text E to endorse the principle that

A   . . . those actions that may be plausibly construed to pose a significant danger of immorality—despite there being positive counter-

11. See Chapter 2.2 and McPherran (14), 284–287; note also that 4a11–b2 and 4e4–8 seem to embody the same principle encompassed by text E. Recently H. Benson (4) has made a powerful case for the view that E and those passages related to it provide evidence of Socrates' commitment to a strong version of the principle of the "priority of definition," where only if one knows the definition of some quality F-ness can one know that some instance of F-ness is such; cf. Beversluis (2), Geach, and G. Santas. Here and elsewhere I assume that this is too a strong a version of the principle, whose more precise expression is that only if one knows the definition of some quality F-ness does one possess the divine wisdom on F-ness that makes one an expert on F-ness (such that one can *always* recognize F-instances and understand why they are such); a position most recently and extensively defended by Brickhouse and Smith (8), chap. 2.3; cf. Beversluis (1), Lesher, Nehamas (2), and Vlastos (13). Hence, I shall be assuming that most people can recognize instances of F-ness without possessing expert knowledge of F-ness.

12. See, e.g., *Cr.* 47a–49e, *La.* 194d, and *Pr.* 361b; cf. *G.* 460b, 479b–e, and 507a–513c and Brickhouse and Smith (8), chap. 2.1.6.

vailing reasons for pursuing them—ought to be refrained from in the absence of complete theoretic understanding of the relevant moral concepts involved.

This interpretation of the principle evoked in text E is also suggested by the parallel Plato must intend for us to draw between the case of Euthyphro's father and Socrates (cf. Chapter 2.1): Socrates is also elderly (*Eu.* 3a2–4), and "goes to each Athenian like a *father,* persuading each to care for virtue" (*Ap.* 31b3–5), yet now finds himself, like Euthyphro's father, rashly indicted by a younger man on the grounds of piety (*Eu.* 5a9–b5). Hence, and *per* A, Meletus and the citizens of Athens, having had their ignorance of virtues such as piety repeatedly brought home to them by Socrates, ought to retract their writ of impiety against him, just as Euthyphro ought to abandon his suit (despite his countervailing reasons; e.g., the importance of pursuing murderers impartially and of removing the religious pollution they engender [4b–e, cf. 5d–6a]).[13] In neither instance do the prosecutors understand what piety is, and since moral harm is incurred through unjust action (*Cr.* 47a–49e), the moral risk posed by a mistaken conviction means that neither set of prosecutors can prudently or morally use the concept of piety as the basis of their respective lawsuits (see *Ap.* 30d–e).

Such is the moral of the most obvious analogy in the *Euthyphro.* But, as I argued earlier (Chapter 2.1), the parallel between Socrates and Euthyphro's father is not the only one intended here. Euthyphro also makes a number of remarks to the effect that he *and* Socrates share an interest in and understanding of theological matters vastly superior to that of the many, and that this has had the result of making the Athenians hostile to them both (*Eu.* 3b–e). Euthyphro sees Socrates as a kindred spirit not only because of the laughter and envy they have excited, but because Socrates, like himself (3c2, 3e3; cf. *Crat.* 396d2–397a1), is something of a diviner (μάντις; cf., e.g., *Phd.* 85b4–6). While Euthyphro predicts future events for the benefit of the Assembly, Socrates is himself the privileged recipient of a predictive "divine sign" that warns him away from unbeneficial courses of action (3b–c).[14]

---

13. Again, on Euthyphro and his prosecution, see, e.g., W. D. Furley.

14. Note that a traditional μάντις, a ritual specialist in interpreting a divine sign, would not—like Socrates—be looking to decide what action should be refrained from, but what positive action *should* be done.

Although the ironic humor of Euthyphro's comparisons (and Socrates' proposal to become Euthyphro's student in crackpot theology [5a–c]) is lost on few readers, it has been little noticed how they also form one of the dialogue's subtexts, one that prompts us to see just how dangerously close to Euthyphro's position Socrates is.[15] For one lesson of the Socrates-Euthyphro parallel seems to be that—given Socrates' own quite religious outlook—Euthyphro need not, after all, scurry off at the end of the dialogue to his "pressing engagements" (15e3–4). Rather, he could respond by claiming that Socrates cannot consistently affirm the previous general principle A, his frequent claims of moral ignorance, and nonetheless assert with confidence that his religious mission to the Athenians is a great good (e.g., *Ap.* 30d5–31c3). That mission, after all, is composed of numerous actions, many of which have involved some risk of physical and moral harm to himself and others; e.g., the danger that those who eavesdrop on elenctic conversations will have their restraining moral beliefs removed without their being replaced with positive ethical doctrine (cf. *R.* 538d–e). So if Socrates is as ignorant of theoretical moral knowledge as he claims, how then can he consistently pursue his mission and not—as he warns Euthyphro—"dread the risk he would not do it correctly" (15d6–8)?

Given Socrates' reliance on extrarational indicators, as well as text M's admonition, it seems likely that Socrates would respond to this challenge by qualifying A in view of his own access to those sources. Moral risk-assessment, after all, involves an appraisal of *future* possibilities and outcomes, something especially resistant to reasoned calculation in the here and now (*Mem.* 1.1.6–7). Thus, in refining our interpretation of text E we shall want to say that individual actions posing a significant moral risk may be justifiably performed in the *absence* of the complete knowledge of the concept under which the action falls in at least those cases where extrarational guidance is at hand.[16]

But then, as it stands, this course of revision is dangerously incomplete, insofar as all sorts of morally blameworthy actions might be suggested by

15. Again, I see Euthyphro's literary function as twofold: (1) he serves as a nontraditionalist, hubristic patient for Socrates' therapeutic *elenchos*, and (2) as a dark doppelgänger of Socrates, a lesson in what Socrates is *not*. See Chap. 2, n. 23.

16. Cf. Brickhouse and Smith (8), chaps. 2 and 6.3–4; (7), 127–130; and (12), 88–108. Another argument for the qualification of A is that it prohibits a whole range of morally risky actions that ought normally to be pursued, since not even Socrates possesses the complete expert moral knowledge specified by A.

extrarational promptings. For example, it opens up to Euthyphro the ever-so-satisfying possibility of replying *tu quoque* that—oddly enough—he too has been commanded in divinations and in dreams "and by every other means in which a divinity has ever commanded anyone to do anything" to prosecute his own father. He conceives of himself, after all, to be—like Socrates—an expert diviner in the interpretation of such signs, so such a response is easily conceivable. Fortunately, there is an obvious riposte to this suggested by text M, and provided by the hypothesis that allowed us to reconcile Socrates' acceptance of the extrarational with text C; namely, that for Socrates reason plays a necessary role in both the interpretation and confirmation of extrarational indicators. Whenever possible, such signs must—in a sense I shall spell out—be rationally inspected and must pass that inspection.[17] Principle A, as an interpretation of text E, therefore, must be recast in light of this.

Before doing so, however, notice also that A is insufficiently specific concerning what it is for something to pose a "significant danger of immorality." A is useless as a practical guide to action without this being spelled out in some way. Given Socrates' apparent shock at Euthyphro's prosecution of his father (contrary to the tradition of filial piety [*Eu.* 4a11–b2, 4e4–8]) and his generally conservative retention of the *content* of traditional morality (and see the pragmatic remarks Plato attributes to Socrates in the *Phaedrus* [229c6–230a7] to the effect that he generally follows tradition in religious matters), I think that he would advise our using the traditional moral framework to pin down the sense of immorality employed in A; e.g., he will take theft and patricide to be endoxic cases of prima facie immorality. Naturally, since Socrates is also a severe critic of many aspects of the traditional outlook, especially its conceptual basis, those elenctically grounded tenets constituting Socrates' moral theory will have an overriding status for Socrates. Compelling grounds for acting *against* the canons of traditional piety and justice would then have to be founded on either (1) extrarational sources of information whose meaning can be deciphered plainly and consistently (e.g., by observing their repetition in various contexts and media and by elenctic testing) or (2) a demonstrably superior concept of piety or justice. So I suggest that Socrates would want to endorse the following emended version of A as an interpretation of the general principle invoked in text E:

---

17. Something the gods have "granted us to do by help of learning" *per* M.

A'   Actions traditionally held to be evil and/or impious ought to be refrained from in the absence of compelling divinatory or "secularly" rational evidence to the contrary. Such evidence must allow one's moral beliefs to be consistent, so far as this can be determined though elenctic testing (where possessing a complete understanding of the moral concepts involved would constitute the best rational exemptive evidence possible).

Revised in this way, A' now allows Socrates to charge Euthyphro (and Meletus) with its violation without being left open to a similar charge. In bringing suit against his father, Euthyphro violates traditional attitudes of filial piety and justice, and then fails under elenctic examination to escape the charge that what he believes he ought to do is inconsistent with all the various other things he is convinced of. Finally, his purported mantic abilities manifestly fail to give him any "revelations" whose meaning he could plainly decipher or rationally defend (and, again, note how his predictive powers fail at 3e4–6). It is also open to Socrates to point out that since Euthyphro's Homeric, Hesiodic gods are reputed to be notorious liars—unlike Socrates' own honest gods—they can never be the source of reliable, worthwhile information.[18]

Socrates, on the other hand, has engaged in few or no activities that actually violate the traditional code, and (on his own account) has certainly never violated the essential dictates of traditional piety (especially once these are rightly understood).[19] True, he has run *some* moral risk in pursuing his life of elenctic-examination, but his belief in its overriding moral worth has survived a lifetime of elenctic-testing. He has, in particular, labored at great length to derive and confirm elenctically his understanding of the Delphic Oracle's pronouncement (originating from an honest god [*Ap.* 21b5–8]), revealing a divine command to philosophize (*Ap.* 20e3–23c1, 29b9–31c3) and has received varied and consistent extrarational indications that back up his interpretation (*Ap.* 33c4–8; that are, in turn, subject to elenctic testing). So interpreted, the command to philosophize becomes—on the ground that commands of good and virtuous gods

18. See Klonoski, who argues that Plato uses the figure of Euthyphro to represent the popular regressive interests in magic and foreign religious imports (e.g., Asclepius, Cybele, and Bendis) that marked the end of the fifth century in Athens.

19. See Chapter 2.1 and McPherran (14), 297–309. The attribution of principle A' to Socrates is also supported by his advocacy of antihubristic "human wisdom," since to engage in activities that tradition has deemed immoral would seem to presume just the sort of superior moral wisdom that Socrates disavows.

ought to be obeyed—an unmitigated obligation of piety for Socrates, whose neglect would be impious and unjust. Finally, Socrates has "secular" justification and confirmation of this *via* his conception of the virtues for believing that his mission to the Athenians is a great good (cf. *Ap.* 30a, 30d–31a).[20]

The preceding account, then, preserves both Socrates' attachment to elenctic testing and his reliance on supernatural guidance. As principle A′ and text M suggest, Socrates does not wish to take divination and assorted practices as a *replacement* for rational calculation; rather, they serve as an important "supplement and . . . stimulus to rational thought, not a surrogate for it."[21] I want now to confirm and extend this interpretation by attempting to discover whether Socrates, in his reliance on the extrarational, in fact conforms to A′.[22] Also requiring our attention are issues concerning the epistemic status of divine admonitions; in particular, the extent to which they constrain Socrates' allegiance to rational decision-making procedures.

4.1.2 Socratic Reason and the *Daimonion*

There are two basic varieties of Socratic, extrarational indicators found in our texts: (1) private, "internal" psychological phenomena such as the *daimonion* and divinely given dreams, and (2) external, publicly observable oracles and divinatory signs, such as the report of the Delphic Oracle. For my purposes here, I will confine myself to Socrates' treatment of internal phenomena only, and chiefly the *daimonion,* since that account extends, with minor modifications, to dreams and external phenomena as well.

Socrates' *daimonion* is an internal, private admonitory sign (σημεῖον)[23] and voice (φωνή)[24] caused to appear within the horizon of consciousness by a god(s) or a divine δαίμων/*daimôn*.[25] It has occurred to few or none

20. For an analysis of Socrates' interpretation of the oracular pronouncement as revealing a divine command to philosophize, and his "secular" arguments that we all have a similar obligation, see section 2 and McPherran (9).

21. Dodds (7), 198 n. 36.

22. That he sees himself as obligated to *interpret* divinatory signs is indicated (again) by his efforts to understand the Delphic Oracle's report.

23. *Ap.* 40b1, c3–4; *Eud.* 272e4; *Phdr.* 242b9; *R.* 496c4; *Mem.* 1.1.3–5.

24. *Ap.* 31d1–3; cf. *Phdr.* 242c2 and Xen. *Apol.* 12.

25. See *Ap.* 40b1 together with 26b2–28a1. See also *Ap.* 31c8–d4, 40a4–6, 40c3–4,

before Socrates (*R.* 496c3–5) and has been his companion since childhood (*Ap.* 31d2–4; *Thg.* 128d3).[26] The *daimonion*'s intervention in his affairs, on matters both great and small (*Ap.* 40a4–6), is something well known (*Ap.* 31c7–d1; *Eu.* 3b5–7), and is understood to operate generally (or always) by giving him a sign that—without prior notice—warns him *not* to pursue a course of action that he is in the process of initiating (*Ap.* 31d3–4; cf. *Phdr.* 242b8–c3, *Thg.* 128d4–6).[27] Although (apparently) the divinity in charge of the sign cannot be induced to make it appear on demand, it is regarded as unfailingly correct in whatever it indicates (*Mem.* 1.1.4–5), just as we would expect the gift of an unfailingly good divinity to be.[28] Sometimes the *daimonion*'s generosity even extends to warning Socrates of the inadvisability of the actions intended by others,[29] but in no case does it provide him with general, theoretical claims constitutive of the expert moral knowledge he seeks and disavows having obtained. Neither does it provide him with a ready-made explanation of its opposition. Rather, it yields, I shall argue, instances of what we might call nonexpert moral knowledge of the inadvisability of pursuing particular actions; e.g., the knowledge that it would not be beneficial to let a certain student resume study with him (see, e.g., Xen. *Symp.* 8.5, *Tht.* 150e1 ff.). Finally, these divine signs always concern *future* harmful—or more broadly, unbeneficial—outcomes, and especially those whose reasonable prediction

---

41d6; *Eu.* 3b5–7; *Thg.* 128d1–131a7; Xen. *Mem.* 1.1.2–4, 4.8.1; *Apol.* 4–5, 8, 12–13; and *Symp.* 8.5. Interest in the nature of Socrates' *daimonion* has been nonstop, extending from Xenophon and Plato, through Cicero (*On Divination* 1.54.122–124) and Apuleius (*On the God of Socrates*), to present times. Recent accounts of the *daimonion* include those by E. D. Baumann, 256–265; Beckman, 76–77; Brickhouse and Smith (12), 34–36, 105–108, 237–262; (8), chap. 6.3; E. Frank; P. Friedländer, 32–36; H. Gundert; Guthrie (6), 82–85; Y. Iwata; H. Jackson; R. E. MacNaghten; H. Maier; W. Norvin; C. Phillipson, 88–98; Reeve, 68–69; and E. Zeller, 89 ff. Reeve's recent account concludes on the basis of *Ap.* 26b2–28a1 that the source of the *daimonion* must be the *child* of a god (rather than a god) (68–69), but this claim contradicts his implication that Socrates understands the *daimonion* to come from Apollo (26 n. 27). In fact, what evidence there is (see esp. *Ap.* 27c10–28a1, 40b1) suggests that although Socrates is uncertain about the nature and identity of the divinity behind this sign Apollo is a prime candidate in his eyes.

26. I cite the *Theages* here and below, although none of my main claims hinge on its authenticity. On this, see, e.g., Guthrie (3), 5:392–394.

27. But positive advice to *do* things is attested to by, e.g., *Mem.* 1.1.4, 4.3.12, and 4.8.1, and by *Apol.* 12.

28. McPherran (14), 303–304. In fact, Socrates' trust in the *daimonion*'s accuracy is testified to precisely by his unhesitating location of its source in "the divine," rather than opting for a more cautious specification that would identify the sign as simply a hunch or rational intuition; see nn. 51, 64, and 65 below.

29. *Mem.* 1.1.4; Xen. *Apol.* 13; *Thg.* 128d–131a.

lies beyond the power of human reason (*Ap.* 31d; *Mem.* 1.1.6–9, 4.3.12). It is, in short, a species of the faculty of divination (ἡ μαντικὴ τέχνη), true to Socrates' description of it as his "customary divination" (*Ap.* 40a4) and himself as a μάντις (*Phd.* 85b4–6; cf. *Phdr.* 242b3–4). But Socrates is no run-of-the-mill diviner. As we saw, his elenctic treatment of Euthyphro, his remarks at the end of the *Euthyphro* (text E), his divinely ordered duty to philosophize, and his actual practice (e.g., his interpretation and testing at *Ap.* 21b–23b; cf. 40a2–c3) all suggest that he takes it to be obligatory to subject occurrences of the *daimonion* or other such signs to rational confirmation (and perhaps interpretation) whenever possible. Consider a few examples of the *daimonion*.

A key instance of Socratic reliance on and rational confirmation of a daemonic warning occurs at *Apology* 31c4–32a3, where Socrates notes his obedience to the *daimonion*'s resistance to his entering public partisan politics (cf. *R.* 496b–c). Now those who see Socrates as finding no more than subjective reassurance through the *daimonion* will fasten on Socrates' use of a possibly tentative "seems" (δοκεῖ [*Ap.* 31d6]) to introduce his rational explanation for this warning.[30] But in fact this must be read as *understated conviction*, given Socrates' admonition to the jury that follows that they should "know well" (ἐὺ ἴστε [31d6]) the truth of his explanation for the *daimonion*'s opposition on each occasion he was about to undertake some political act; namely, that an active life of public politics would have brought him a premature death, thus curtailing his vastly beneficial mission to the Athenians.[31] This account is also introduced in the manner of one wholly convinced of not only that explanation, but of the extrarationally indicated truth that prompted that explanation; namely, that the *daimonion* opposes now (31d5)—and has in the past as well (31d7–9)—his every attempt at "going to do" (μέλλω [31d4]) politics. Hence, this is one argument that the *daimonion* is a source of particular knowledge claims (e.g., "This political act I intend will be unbeneficial") and that *per* A′ Socrates sees an obligation to construct a coherent, rational account for such claims when they warn him away from actions traditionally thought

30. E.g., Vlastos (14), 225, 230–232.
31. Socrates' use of δοκεῖν and its cognates is not necessarily epistemologically deflationary, but rather, often marks only aristocratic understatement. In the *Apology* alone there are numerous uses of δοκεῖν indicating strong belief or knowledge; e.g., at 21e4–5 it "seems" (ἐδόκει) to Socrates that the business of the god is most important and at 28d8–10 it "seems" (δοκεῖ) to him that one must obey the commands of a superior come what may. Finally, it is the way things "seem" (δοκοῦντα [*Cr.* 54d6]) to Socrates in the *Crito* that keep him from fleeing Athens (cf. 43d2).

to be obligatory (viz., public partisan politics; cf., e.g., Thuc. *History* 2.40).[32]

A perspicuous (albeit less momentous) case of daemonic activity is found at *Euthydemus* 272e1–273a3. There we find that Socrates had formed the intention to leave his seat in the palaestra, but just as he was getting up he experienced his "usual sign" and so returned to his seat. Here, with his recognition of the divine voice as such, and together with whatever interpretation the content of its admonition may have required, Socrates appears to have *no doubt* that its warning is utterly reliable. However, the wisdom of remaining in that particular position and location may only begin to be understood *later*. For only well after the fact of Socrates' obedience is it possible to account for its opposition by producing an explanatory *reason* for the sagacity of the daemonic advice; namely, that in obeying it Socrates was given the opportunity to educate and be entertained by his late-arriving interlocutors. Hence, Socrates puts great trust in the *daimonion,* although *how* or *why* it is that the result of his obedience will be good-producing—like many future events—is opaque to reasoned calculation (*Mem.* 4.3.12, 1.1.8–9). And there are similar cases of daemonic warnings where the precise nature of what is warned against is left open and no further explanation is attempted, and where Socrates nonetheless exhibits supreme confidence in the *daimonion* (e.g., *Tht.* 150e1ff.). But this is in no way *irrational,* for, as Socrates puts it, the "worth of the sign may be tested" (*Ap.* 33c7–8; *Thg.* 129d4–5); that is, it may be rationally confirmed in its wisdom and so given the greatest credence, on both an inductive and deductive basis. Inductively, since (1) in Socrates' long experience of it, it has never been shown to be unreliable (Xen. *Apol.* 13; cf. *Ap.* 40a2–c3), and (2) the reliability of its alarms has been confirmed by the good results that flow from heeding it and the tragedies that ensue for others when its warnings are ignored (*Thg.* 128d–131a); deductively, since (3) the *daimonion* is taken by Socrates to be a

---

32. *Pace* Reeve, 69. Another case of daemonic reliance where an interpretation quickly follows upon the heels of the *daimonion,* and where it both clarifies and gives rational backing to its warning, is *Phaedrus* 242b8–243a3. There the *daimonion* warns Socrates away from crossing the river Ilissus, and its interference is accompanied by the phenomenon of a voice declaring that Socrates has committed a sin at this spot that must be expiated (however humorous and ironical this may be, it hints at other similar, sincere cases). Socrates then claims to have a modest skill, sufficient for his purposes, at divinatory interpretation—we all have this rational power in virtue of our νοῦς he implies (cf. 244c2 ff.; *Alc. I* 127e6 ff.)—and this allows him to connect his own rationally arrived at misgivings with the daemonic intervention; viz., that his previous speech offended divine *Erôs.*

divine gift (a warning not to perform some act-token), and the gods give us nothing but good (*Eu.* 14e9–15a2), would never deceive us (*Ap.* 21b6–7; cf. *R.* 381e–382c), and are superlatively wise (*Ap.* 23a–b; *HMa.* 289b). Although, for Socrates, unaided ratiocination may make some accurate predictions of future events, it is unable to do so with reliability (*Mem.* 4.3.12). Thus, it is eminently rational for him to place his trust in the predictive capacities of his rationally warranted daemonic alternative, and even irrational to ignore or override it (*Mem.* 1.1.8–9).

Finally, at *Apology* 40a2–c3, Socrates takes some pains to show that the *reason* for the failure of the *daimonion* to oppose every small act constituting his participation in his trial is that the outcome of the proceedings, and hence his death, are for the best (cf. *Ap.* 41d3–7; cf. *Mem.* 1.1.5, 4.8.5–6, *Apol.* 4–5). Here Socrates insists that the *silence* of his voice counts as a "wonderful," *great proof* (μέγα τεκμήριον [40c1]) of the goodness of the final outcome of his trial, something he would claim to know, since he says that it is this evidence *ex silentio* that makes it "clear" (δῆλόν [*Ap.* 41d4]) that it is better for him to be dead.[33] But if the daemonic *silence* can be used to infer a conclusion that is accorded this degree of assurance, the *daimonion* itself must be regarded by Socrates as something that will oppose him on every, or almost every, occasion that is *not* for the best, and which can thus serve as a source for inferences of a highly reassuring and dependable sort.[34]

In sum, for Socrates the extrarational is a valuable aid in arriving at particular judgments of action and is in principle (if not always at the moment of decision) in harmony with the dictates of morality and secular reason; e.g., Socrates has discovered eudaimonistic warrants for pursuing philosophy, even in the absence of a daemonic or oracular command.[35] These extrarational sources constitute a supplement to our merely human, rationally derived account of things; but nevertheless, our effective use of

33. Δῆλόν carries with it a suggestion of certainty and the most secure sort of knowledge; see Liddell and Scott (1966, s.v. "δῆλος"); Reeve, 183. The "great indication" itself might be given the following inferential structure: (1) The *daimonion* has often and repeatedly opposed Socrates when he was about to do something wrong (in cases great and small); (2) but in this particular case, the *daimonion* did not communicate with Socrates in the course of his doing many things connected with the pursuit of his legal case; (3) hence, Socrates is about to do something good. See Brickhouse and Smith (12), 238–257, who discuss the problematic details of this inference (e.g., there are no guarantees that the *daimonion always* opposes wrong-making actions) and similar arguments from daemonic silence; cf. Reeve, 181.

34. For other ancient references to the *daimonion*, see Plutarch *De gen. Soc.* 580c–582c, 588c–e, 589f, and 590a.

35. See section 4.2 and McPherran (9), 545–548.

and proper confidence in such signs generally requires the application of a rational assessment that both interprets and tests them. Socrates, then, is simply unusual in having an additional, and extremely reliable, extrarational source to put to that same rational test, viz., the *daimonion*. Thus the *daimonion* gives us particular warrant to attribute principle A' to Socrates, since its reliability is—even prior to its onset—a matter of rationally established fact, and because in no case do we find Socrates relying *solely* upon its guidance *in situations manifestly morally risky*. Rather, in those cases where moral risk is plain (e.g., his avoidance of politics), he appears to follow up the daemonic warning (or its continued absence) with an attempt to provide elenctically testable and corroborating reasons for the wisdom of its opposition.[36]

4.1.3 Some Objections

Several objections have been raised by Gregory Vlastos in response to those such as myself who wish to credit the extrarational with a genuine epistemological role in Socratic thought.[37] In particular, he inclines to interpret this view as tantamount to the claim that Socrates endorses "two distinct systems of justified belief," where the *daimonion* is thus "a source of moral knowledge apart from reason and superior to it."[38] And this, he contends, is at odds with the clear evidence of our texts. But note first that this objection overlooks the possibility that one can assign epistemic significance to the extrarational *without* also endorsing two systems of justified

36. Where there is no manifest moral risk (e.g., *Eud.* 272e1–273a3), Socrates exhibits no interest in explaining the opposition of the *daimonion*. I do not mean to suggest here that it is clear that Socrates submits the *daimonion*'s warning to an elenctic test where moral risk is plain *before* he responds with initial obedience. He *may* do this, but no text demands it. It does appear, though, that *per* A' he sees a need to account for its opposition in such situations before settling in on a long-term course of obedience. The preceding analysis is buttressed by *Alcibiades I* 105d–106a, where Socrates conjoins the *daimonion*'s warning against his taking Alcibiades on as a pupil with the *explanation* that during that time of opposition Alcibiades lacked the high political ambitions he subsequently acquired. I take it that *Alcibiades I*, even if not by Plato, is a possible source of genuine Socratic practice (see Guthrie [6], 79), though nothing hangs on that possibility here.

37. Vlastos (14), 223–232; cf. McPherran (14), 300–304. Vlastos's criticisms also pertain to Brickhouse and Smith (12), 107, 241, and passim. In addition, see Vlastos's review of Brickhouse and Smith (12), (20), the letters of response by Brickhouse and Smith (4), Vlastos's replies (6), my interjection (11), and Brickhouse and Smith's latest contribution (8), chap. 6.3–4.

38. Vlastos (14), 224; cf. McPherran (14), 300–301.

belief. For again, as I have it, extrarational phenomena (especially the *daimonion*) are seen by Socrates as a source for the *construction* of particular moral knowledge claims that are themselves rationally grounded, if not wholly rational in origin. So Vlastos and I agree that Socratic revelation will always appear in the docket of Socratic reason (*per A′*), and thus I do not endorse the view that Socrates has two distinct systems of rationally justified belief. Instead, on my view, Socrates sees there to be two distinct sources of information that he is privilege to—divination and secular reason—but employs only one method of justification, viz., elenctic grounding. Where Vlastos and I part company, then, is in my insistence that despite the pride of place Socrates grants to "secular" ratiocination, he also holds that extrarational signs make significant contributions to his knowledge and belief-states. On this account, the reign of secular reason will be *constrained* in many cases by the pure preinterpretive content of those signs.

But now for Vlastos's contentions. First, on his account it appears incorrect to consider the *daimonion* to be anything more than a voice whose minimal presentational content serves to prompt Socrates in the vaguest of ways to identify particular courses of action as unbeneficial. Contrary to my sketch, Vlastos's *daimonion* is no extralogical channel of *information,* but only an alarm that sets reason to its task: it simply *occasions* Socrates' employment of an interpretive *elenchos* that yields an elenctically warranted, practical (fallible) certainty that an action will be unbeneficial, and it does this without communicating to Socrates anything of cognitive value.[39] So the *daimonion* for Vlastos is no more than a kind of subjective presentation—a hunch—whose content *in no way* determines the belief it occasions.

There are several considerations that can be produced in favor of Vlastos's view. First, since Socrates subscribes to the common Greek opinion that the wisdom of the gods is infinitely more secure and complete than is ours, and since on my view he conceives of the *daimonion* and dreams as sources of information, these sources might then appear to constitute avenues of information *superior* to that provided by the *elenchos*. But—goes this objection—Socrates never claims certainty for such divine monitions. Rather, Socrates views them most tentatively.[40] For example, in

39. Practical, as opposed to logical certainty, is the sort one attaches to the claim of a life-long friend that the wine she has just served you is not poisoned (a notion suggested in correspondence by Vlastos).
40. Vlastos (8), 223–224; cf. (14), chap. 6. And, after all, a daemonic warning may leave

the *Phaedo* (60d8–61b8) we find that Socrates has often had a dream "urging" (ἐπικελεύειν [61a2]) and "commanding" him (προστάττοι [61a6]) to make music and that formerly he had *assumed* (ὑπελάμβανον) that this meant he should pursue philosophy, "since philosophy is the highest music" (61a3–4; this passage may refer to the dream command of *Ap.* 33c4–8). However, it has now occurred to him that the dream *may* mean that he is to make music in the popular sense, and so "just in case" *that* is the meaning of the dream command it has now *seemed* (ἔδοξε) to him "safer not to depart [from life] before fulfilling a sacred duty by composing verses in obedience to the dream" (61a8–b1).[41]

From this and other similar cases (e.g., *Cr.* 44a5–b4), it might be inferred that Socrates here and in general sees *all* extrarational "signs from the god" as susceptible to interpretation in such a way that the meaning of the sign is wholly determined by the use of unfettered critical reason.[42] And this would mean that although Socrates "preserves the venerable view that mantic experience is divinely caused," he has utterly "disarmed the irrationalist potential of the belief in supernatural gods communicating with human beings by supernatural signs," by robbing mantic experience of any claims that *might* conflict with the "exclusive authority of reason" for determining questions both practical and theoretical (*per* a strong reading of text C).[43] Thus, on this account, Socrates' extrarational indicators are no more than supernatural "pats of assurance on the back in the dark." Such pats are opaque in meaning, but Socrates—with a kind of partisan optimism—chooses to put the best face on things by taking them as encouragement for what he does even without the promptings of such pats.

Next, Vlastos finds support in the observation that the *daimonion* is a species of divination by linking *all* divination with the Socratic understanding of divine possession developed in the *Ion* and alluded to in the *Apology:* "I soon perceived that *it is not through knowledge* that poets produce their poems but through a sort of inborn gift and in a state of inspiration (ἐνθουσιάζοντες), like the diviners and soothsayers, who also speak many

---

many important gaps of information in Socrates' understanding about the wrong-making features of an act: Socrates may not know precisely (a) in which aspect(s) of it, if any, the wrongness lies; (b) which aspect(s) of the environment of this act, if any, contribute to its wrongness; (c) what it is about both the act and the environment that make it wrong (Brickhouse and Smith [12], 253, and [8], chap. 6.3).

41. Vlastos (18), 224–225.
42. Vlastos (18), 228–229.
43. Vlastos (18), 229.

admirable things but *know nothing of the things about which they speak*" (*Ap.* 22b8–c3; trans. and emphasis Vlastos).

On this theory, the god is *inside* an inspired poet, where such possession shoves aside the poet's rational faculties. When possessed of the god the poet is "out of his mind" (ἔκφρων), intelligence or understanding (νοῦς) is no longer "in" or "present" to him or her (*Ion* 533c9 ff.). This may indeed allow poets to *say* many admirable and true things, but they have no knowledge of that of which they speak. The above passage from the *Apology* and the text of the *Ion* (cf. *Meno* 99b–100c) make it clear that it is *because* poets are *like* diviners that they cannot know that of which they speak; and hence, this analysis is also true of diviners in Socrates' view. Thus, insofar as this analysis applies to Socrates' own divinatory experiences, it might seem that Socrates must regard his own mental state during the occurrence of the *daimonion* and other divine monitions to be one wherein there is no knowledge, no understanding. On these grounds it might be thought that extrarational interventions cannot be counted as sources of information, and certainly not knowledge, since the conscious mind is at the moment of intervention in no position to understand or grasp any part of the meaning of that intervention. The responsibility for making sense of what has occurred, then, is entirely that of reason restored. Since Socratic rational examination proceeds elenctically, any resultant beliefs will be standard instances of elenctically justified beliefs merely *occasioned* by the uninformative "blast" of the *daimonion* or other divinely caused inner event.[44] So on this view, when Socrates says something like "the *daimonion* opposes my leaving" (*per Eud.* 272e1–273a3), he is telescoping into one description three events: (1) the daemonic incursion, where Socrates's mind/soul (νοῦς/ψυχή; *nous/psuchê*)[45] leaves him in such a way that his consciousness is no longer under his control or observation, followed by (2) a memory of that state and the daemonic sign as was observed by the residue of irrational consciousness, that then (3) is followed immediately by the rational interpretation "that was the *daimonion*, something *caused* by the divine," with subsequent further interpretation, such as "such a thing means 'No,' and that means 'Don't leave this general location,'" and whatever further explanations and confirmations of its intervention may follow. The net result of this and the preceding, then, is an argument contending that extrarational signs do not constitute for Socra-

---

44. Vlastos (18), 225–229.
45. For an account of Socrates' theory of the soul, see Chapter 5.1.

tes a separate channel of information, but rather, are susceptible to interpretation in such a way that their meaning is *wholly* determined by the use of "unfettered critical reason." Thus Socrates simply treats blasts from the extrarational as subjective encouragements for what he does for secular reasons *even without such extrarational promptings.*

4.1.4 Some Replies

As I see it, this position has Socrates "accepting the supernatural" in little more than name only. I shall now contend that although it is correct to suppose that for Socrates the informational content of the *daimonion* is generally minimal, he also sees it as charged with sufficient epistemic significance to challenge the "exclusive authority of secular reason." If this is right, then Socrates accepts the supernatural to a significantly greater extent than Vlastos's reductionist account will allow.[46]

First, it is clear that the *daimonion* ought not to be treated as being on a par with dreams. Dreams, after all (even seemingly god-given prophetic ones), are not unique to Socrates, whereas the *daimonion* apparently is. Second, since Socrates will admit that many dreams are false (cf. *Tht.* 157e–158d) and that he does not take any one god-given dream to provide secure information, dreams should—for Socrates—be set apart from the *daimonion,* whose individual occurrences *are* taken by him to be an unerring source of trustworthy guidance (cf. *Od.* 19.560–561 for the ancient recognition that dreams are open to multiple interpretations). Finally, even in the case of Socrates' admonitory dreams it is incorrect to hold that they are susceptible to the "utterly unconstrained" interpretive powers of critical reason. Socrates, for instance, does not think of interpreting his *Phaedo*-dream as a command to make pots, go fishing, or flee Athens (cf. *Cr.* 44a5–b5). Rather, such dreams seem to have a determinant content for Socrates that *constrain* his interpretation to several possible meanings (a content that, however, as a "sign of the god," must be true [*Ap.* 21b6–7; *R.* 382e–383a; cf. *Laws* 800a]). But since in at least some cases Socrates can never be certain that *all* possible interpretations of a dream sign

---

46. That may not make him as radical a "great religious radical of history" as Vlastos sees the evidence as warranting (11), but—arguably—it does give us a less anachronistic Socrates; one who more closely means what he says when, on trial for his life, he speaks of the role divination and the *daimonion* played in the long mission to the Athenians that eventually put him into the docket.

have been exhausted, the one meaning or set of meanings attributed to some divinely given dream cannot be trusted with complete confidence— something else that *distinguishes* dreams from the *daimonion.*

Of course, as with instances of the *daimonion,* Socrates regards some dreams as containing a kernel of assured truth. But unlike dreams, the *daimonion* appears to consist of an intrinsic core of *singular* and determinant meaning that is *not* open to question; namely, that Socrates (or another) is engaged (or is about to engage) in an unbeneficial course of action. The *daimonion* is also portrayed as a source of practical certainty, whereas dreams call for rigorous elenctic testing and, for the reasons just given, always retain a degree of uncertainty. Hence, a theory of Socratic dream interpretation cannot be assumed to encompass the *daimonion* as well. Note also that since Socrates' *daimonion* is apparently unique to him, the level of epistemic assurance it provides (e.g., that Socrates' mission is divinely sanctioned) is not one that can be legitimately assumed by others such as Euthyphro in accounting for their actions. Thus, all someone like Euthyphro could appeal to for extrarational warrant in pursuing some action are *other* sorts of divination. But in such cases their lack of determinateness would invite (*per* principle A') rigorous philosophical interpretation and testing, and we can well imagine that any jussive appeals to divination that Euthyphro might produce in defense of his prosecution of his father would not survive such Socratic scrutiny.

Just as the *daimonion* may not be treated as being strictly analogous to dreams, neither may it be assimilated with confidence to Socrates' analysis of "inspired" poets and diviners. Such people are possessed by a *daimôn* or god, but by contrast, Socrates never treats the *daimonion* as a phenomenon of this sort.[47] Rather, the adjectival character of τὸ δαιμόνιον differentiates it from a straightforward substantive use of δαίμων or θεός, and Socrates stresses that it is a "voice" or "sign" that comes *from* either a δαίμων or a god.[48] *Apology* 27b3–c10 implicitly supports this point: Socrates has been indicted because of his references to the *daimonion;* that is, on the basis of his belief in novel divine *matters,* and he argues that on that very basis he must therefore believe in divine *beings* (cf. *Ap.* 31d1–2, *Eu.* 3b5–9, Xen. *Mem.* 1.1.2 and *Apol.* 12). But such a demonstration would

47. Seen by Vlastos (14), n. 40.
48. See section 4.1.2 above and, e.g., *Mem.* 1.1.4. Δαιμόνιον τι (e.g., *Ap.* 31c8–d1) is elliptically substantival, and so could refer to a divine creature, but the argument following shows that this is not intended by Socrates; rather, the "something divine" he refers to is the *sign* given by the god. See Burnet (3), 96.

be pointless if he had taken the *daimonion* to be a divine being in the first place. Finally, it is entirely in keeping with Socrates' epistemic modesty that he should avoid any firm specification of its nature. Hence, we ought not to analyze daemonic events as *Ion*-type instances of possession—of having a divinity within one—and thus they are not susceptible (at least in a straightforward way) to the *Ion's* analysis of traditional divination. Rather, the *daimonion* seems to involve the *other* sort of psychological disassociation recognized by late—and so possibly early—antiquity, where "subjects' consciousness persists side by side" with the intrusive divine power.[49] In any case, if the *daimonion was* seen as being of the other replacement variety, then given Socrates' and Plato's general disparagement of divine inspiration as a source of intellectual and moral guidance, we should expect Plato to have tried to explain how Socrates' reliance on the *daimonion* (as a species of *Ion*-type inspiration) fared against that criticism. But we find no such attempted explanation in our texts: that silence, and Plato's suggestion that the *daimonion* is unique to Socrates (unlike traditional divinatory possession), therefore tell quite loudly against taking the *daimonion* to involve a theophantic replacement of consciousness.

Finally, I want to question whether the *sort* of divination discussed in the *Ion* can be appropriately compared with the sort of divination provided by the *daimonion*. The *Ion* suggests that for Socrates divination traditionally conceived is not at present any more a craft (τέχνη) than is poetry or poetic interpretation. It is not by knowledge or skill in a craft that a poet, rhapsode, or traditional μάντις says "many lovely things" (534b3 ff.). Rather, these are the products of a "divine gift" (θεία μοίρα [534c1, 536d3]), a "divine possession" akin to Bacchic frenzy, where "the God himself is the one who speaks" (534d3 ff.) through the mouth of one deprived of all reason (νοῦς) (533c9 ff; cf. *Meno* 99c–d, *Phdr.* 263d). Hence, the best judge and interpreter of the sayings of such diviners will clearly not be those diviners themselves: they, as much as the poets, require a sane authority who is not ἔκφρων (cf. *Tim.* 71e2–72b5, *Laws* 719c1 ff.). Naturally, it would be desirable for such authorities to be the postinspiration interpreters of the sayings that emerge from their own mouths (538e–539c), but it is apparent that as Socrates sees it, there are few or no such diviners at present.[50]

49. Dodds (5), 54; cf. (1), 297. What this state is like for Socrates is hard to say, but contrary to the implications of Vlastos (14), 225–229, it is never described as a mindless or impaired condition.

50. I do, however, agree with Brickhouse and Smith (3) (cf. [8], 196) that the *Ion* (538d7–

Socrates, however, clearly does regard *himself* as possessing some skill as a diviner, given that he has his own *daimonion* (and his own dreams), a skill not constituting a τέχνη, but one provided by νοῦς that is "good enough for his own purposes" (cf. *Phdr.* 242c3–6). Hence, it would seem that the sort of *daimonion*-divination practiced by Socrates—a proper sort that includes a rational evaluation of the daemonic message—ought *not* to be identified with the ἔκφρων-variety of traditional μαντική where there is an irrational state of mind due to the influx of a divine power or being. And again, neither should it be assimilated to the case of divinely caused dreams, which *are* ἔκφρων-type irrational states, which thus accounts for Socrates' treating them as having an epistemic status inferior to that of the *daimonion*.

On my view, then, the consciousness and rationality of Socrates are wholly present during the daemonic event, an event Socrates regards as having great practical significance. But even if this is incorrect, Vlastos's own account still leaves room for Socrates to regard the *daimonion* as providing information that—subsequent to its postinspiration interpretation (supposing that is necessary)—is of reliable, practical import and that is still *not* open to utterly *unconstrained* interpretation. For if Socrates takes the daemonic experience, whatever its content, to be tantamount to a loud "No"—meaning "Stop what you're doing (or intending to do)"—he cannot plausibly interpret that, in the context of getting up from his seat in the palaestra, to mean "keep on getting up and leave." Rather, Socrates may be utterly confident that he ought not to get up.[51] Nonetheless, we need to inquire further into the content of this event and what that event yields. Naturally, any account of this is bound to suffer from the obscurity of the subject and the recalcitrance of our texts. But it seems possible to provide some minimal interpretive story, and the most plausible one, I believe, is at odds with the previously outlined position that drains the

---

e3; cf. *St.* 260d11–e2, 290c4–6) has Socrates crediting diviners with a certain kind of menial craft knowledge; namely, the knowledge of how to put themselves into a position to receive a god's revelations (so that they are not—as Vlastos [14], 170, has it—complete know-nothings).

51. Since Vlastos accepts the analysis of the *Ion* and *Apology* (22b9–c3) ([18], 225–229, and [14], chap. 6), where it is held that those inspired *do* utter "many fine and true things," he ought also to accept that the *daimonion* provides Socrates with *truths*, not hunches or subjective reassurance. Moreover, in light of his view that the *daimonion* at the very least *occasions* Socrates' employment of an interpretive *elenchos*, Vlastos cannot also plausibly maintain that Socrates would have come to the same conclusions that he does (e.g., at *Ap.* 31c3–d6, 40a2–c3, and *Eud.* 272e1–273a3) even without the promptings of the *daimonion*.

daimonion of all determinate, intrinsic informational content, leaving Socratic secular reason unchallenged by Socratic revelation.[52]

That view, I think, is too extreme a reading of our texts. True, Socrates would not wish to call the assurance he receives from a daemonic alarm the knowledge he elsewhere denies possessing (e.g., *Ap.* 21b4–5). But we ought not to think that he disavows *all* moral knowledge, since, first, he acknowledges having some share of what he calls "human wisdom." This "small bit" of wisdom (*Ap.* 21d6) is Socrates' knowledge that—unlike politicians, poets, craftsmen, and Sophists who falsely believe they have knowledge of virtue—he does not possess such knowledge. The sort of knowledge he lacks is a knowledge "*more* than human," an expert moral τέχνη-knowledge that as such can explain *how* a course of action is wrong by making appeal to a complete definition of the relevant concepts of virtue. As a kind of expert knowledge it must be infallible and certain (*Eud.* 280a7–8; *R.* 340d7–e1), it must not require luck in obtaining or retaining it, and it must be teachable. In short, *this* is the sort of knowledge Socrates constantly seeks and, failing thus far in that search, continually disavows possessing.[53]

Nevertheless, in addition to Socrates' "one bit of human wisdom," he also possesses particular moral convictions that, since implicitly shared by everyone, do not make him *wiser* than anyone and so do not constitute a τέχνη of virtue (e.g., that it is wrong to disobey a moral superior's orders [*Ap.* 29b6–7; cf. *Ap.* 30c6–8, 37a5–6, 37b3–4, 41d3–5, *Cr.* 47d7–48a7]). However it is that such items of "non-expert moral knowledge" are known by Socrates, he disavows possessing the explanatory account of their truth that constitutes expert moral knowledge (*G.* 509a4–7), they are not luck-resistant, and they cannot be taught. Hence, such items are not cases of expert knowledge. Further, since it is uncertain whether some future *elenchos* might not overturn these items, they cannot be considered

---

52. Readers should also consult the similar account of the *daimonion*'s nature and relationship to secular reason provided by Brickhouse and Smith (8), section 6.3 (an account also developed in response to Vlastos's [14], chap. 6, and [18]).

Also, it will be shown below that although I agree with Vlastos (18), 227–228, and n. 64, that what the *daimonion* provides *in and of itself* is not, in its primary sense, *revelation* ("disclosure of knowledge"; *O.E.D.*, s.v. "revelation"), since it may require a non–divinely guided interpretation to grasp its full meaning, it nonetheless provides a god-given "disclosure of something previously not realized" (cf. *O.E.D.*) that clamps a *constraint* on the products of elenctic interpretation.

53. Brickhouse and Smith (8), 33 n. 11, rightly note that Socrates does not merely say that he *thinks* or *believes* that he lacks real wisdom; rather he says that he *knows* (ἔγνωκεν) it.

infallible (*elenchos*-proof) but are instead elenctically warranted by their past survival of elenctic refutation. But the very survival of such propositions justifies our calling them items of knowledge, albeit a knowledge that is incomplete, nonexplanatory, non-luck-resistant, and nonteachable. And although such items may contribute on a piecemeal basis to expert moral knowledge, each item by itself does not constitute the theoretical understanding presupposed by expert moral knowledge.[54] Where then does daemonically derived knowledge fit into this scheme?

As noted above, the *daimonion* leaves so many gaps in Socrates' understanding of its warning that no one warning can constitute expert moral knowledge: (1) daemonic events do not contain within themselves explanations of their judgments, and hence, offer no criteria or grounds for judging other actions; (2) they are somewhat agent-independent by being "divine dispensations" (θεία μοίρα [*Thg.* 128d2; cf. *M.* 100b2–3]), requiring the beneficence of the divinity whose sign the *daimonion* is; and (3) they are not teachable, since they depend on the volition of a divine being and are internal mental experiences that cannot be implanted in others. Even a long series of such events would be insufficient to generate the sort of general and practically applicable moral theory Socrates is in search of.[55] Nonetheless, the *daimonion* is for Socrates a *source* for the construction of knowledge-claims; namely, foreknowledge *that* an intended course of action will lead to unbeneficial results, knowledge that is therefore always broadly moral in character: it is thus a source of nonexpert moral knowledge.

The fact that daemonic warnings yield a kind of knowledge and are not mere subjective hunches is indicated by Socrates' full confidence that the *daimonion* is always caused by a divinity that would never purposefully mislead him; i.e., it would never warn him away from an action that was not wrong, harmful, or unbeneficial (cf. *Mem.* 1.1.5; *Thg.* 128d1 ff.). This confidence is attested to by there being no instance in our texts of Socrates ignoring a daemonic alarm, and thus no case of Socrates actively attempting to ground the *daimonion* inductively through a process of disconfirmation. He simply assumes that as the gift of a perfectly moral god the alarm

---

54. The preceding analysis derives from Reeve, 33–62, and P. Woodruff (2), 60–84. Brickhouse and Smith (4), chap. 2, offer an excellent and compatible account, according to which the "divine wisdom" Socrates disavows possessing comprises not only what is termed here "expert moral knowledge," but includes nonpropositional features: "the ability to do the right things at the right times in one's field of expertise" and control over one's inclinations toward what's harmful (38).

55. Brickhouse and Smith (12), 245–253; (8), chap. 6.3.4.

could never in itself be deceptive. So then, does this daemonically derived knowledge amount to a nonexpert moral knowledge that is *certain*? That is, does Socrates hold the view that he knows with certainty, with infallible justification, that an act-token he was warned away from would lead to unbeneficial results?

The answer to this requires a careful distinction: it appears that occurrences of the *daimonion* are, for Socrates, cases where there *is* a psychic state carrying a perceptual tag identifying it with certainty as what he has come through experience to classify as a divinely caused warning (*Ap.* 31c8–d1, 40b1). Socrates simply never asks, "How can I know if that is the *daimonion*?" or "How do I know it comes from a god?" Hence, it seems that the judgment *that* a daemonic event is occurring *is* taken by him as certain.[56] Nonetheless, the interpretation Socrates gives to the *content* of a daemonic warning (supposing Socrates engages in this), the judgment *that* the course of action warned against would in fact prove unbeneficial, and his justification for heeding its warning must all be achieved through fallible, rational means, and for Socrates such interpretations and warrants must then always be open to further elenctic testing. I suggest then that this is how we should understand the *daimonion*: (1) after some prior deliberation (or without), Socrates forms the intention to perform some action-token x (e.g., leaving for the marketplace), and then (2) prior to or while engaged in x, Socrates receives a daemonic message similar to "No, don't do x," which he takes as certainly deriving from an all-wise authority. From that, (3) he infers that "doing x would be unbeneficial," something he would claim to know. But that claim, since it rests on Socrates' experientially warranted presupposition that daemonic warnings and his interpretation of them are always accurate, is taken by him to be only a practical, thus fallible, certainty. It is more certain, nonetheless, than the results of practical ratiocination in the here and now because of its superior inductive warrant (e.g., Socrates' recognition of the *daimonion* and the truth of its warning have apparently *never* gone awry in a lifetime's experience of it), a warrant that has convinced Socrates of its divine origin (this now adding to the justification for heeding it; cf. *M.*

---

56. Note that *Phdr.* 242b–d has Socrates *seeming* (ἔδοξα) to hear a voice, but *that* the *daimonion* is occurring is not doubted in the slightest. As Reeve, 69, notes, all the evidence suggests that Socrates never applies on-the-spot, independent rational tests to determine whether a daemonic sign is the genuine item (or a true report). Those put off by this should bear in mind the ancient tradition that saw no implausibility in a divinity offering revelation proper to mortals (e.g., the case of Parmenides).

99c7–9). So Vlastos is right in thinking that on such a view and in *this respect* the *daimonion* is superior to the practical judgments of "secular" elenctic reason. But this is Socratically acceptable, since the *daimonion* is also clearly *inferior* to the *elenchos* on several counts; e.g., it cannot be called upon at will, and cannot be implanted in others. It may also fail to provide an entirely useful, practical certainty. The preceding daemonic claim, for example, may fail to specify the precise *atomic* action-token or tokens to which it refers (is it his act of *leaving* or his *arrival* at the marketplace that's problematic?), and to get that reference and to explain its opposition some rational, reflective work is required. Even if continual daemonic occurrences begin to give Socrates warrant for holding some general moral claim, the warrant will in that case be inductive at best.[57]

Furthermore, interpretation admits of degrees: One can go farther and farther afield on the basis of a sign, given other relevant considerations, and the farther one goes, the less reliable the interpretation. Given a fixed amount of informational content, then, an epistemologically modest interpretation of some daemonic alarm would yield for Socrates a judgment that some act will be unbeneficial that, because *interpreted*, is *not* infallible. Nonetheless, this result may still be as certain as is humanly possible, given the vast amount of warrant Socrates has from the past reliability of his past interpretations of daemonic warnings (and its status as a *divine* sign), and this justifies our calling it a species of knowledge.

4.1.5 Some Further Worries and Replies

At this point, those sympathetic to Vlastos's position may bring a final set of objections to bear: first, it may be contended that the practical certainty Socrates credits to the *daimonion* derives all its jussive force from his daemonically-prior beliefs that the *daimonion* is unerring and divine and

---

57. Cf. Brickhouse and Smith (12), 245–253; (8), chap. 6.3, who point out in detail the problems that would prevent Socrates from using the *daimonion* as a substitute for philosophical activity. Reeve, 69, argues on the basis of textual silence that Socrates never has to *interpret* the daemonic "voice," but takes it as providing a precise specification of the action it warns against. It is true that we never see Socrates express doubt concerning the meaning of a daemonic sign, but his silence on this matter is not a particularly compelling one. I simply take into account here what I find a significant possibility; namely, that since the *daimonion* is called a sign, it perhaps required on some occasions some interpretive work to identify the particular action it warned against.

that the gods never lie. Since it is these beliefs that ground Socrates' confidence in the daemonic warning, and since these are elenctically warranted, Socrates' confidence in the *daimonion* can be no greater than his confidence in secular ratiocination.[58] Hence, there can at least be no cases for Socrates where a daemonic warning could take precedence over his prior reflective reasons for pursuing some course of action.

But clearly, this result doesn't follow. Whereas on my account Socrates' confidence in the *daimonion is* founded in part on its "secular" rational warrant, it can still override an opposed set of reasons, just as we commonly find one set of rationally warranted considerations overriding another equally rational but temporally prior set. We should also ask why we ought to think that Socrates holds that *all* beliefs are elenctically warranted and fallible to the same degree. There are several propositions that Socrates relies on and seems absolutely confident of, and we never see them subjected to the *elenchos;* e.g., the "entailment of virtue by wisdom," and the principle that "the form is everywhere the same" (*Eu.* 6d9–e6). This complete, unreserved confidence may be characterized as practical certainty of the *greatest* sort; that is, in some cases the certainty Socrates attaches to some propositions is such that they go *untested* and, thus, is *greater* than the certainty he displays in other elenctically warranted propositions. Hence, the same would seem to be true of the propositions that the gods never lie, and that they are supremely wise. Moreover, the argument here is not merely one from silence, but stands on the fact that Socrates is willing to *override* his prior elenctic reasons for pursuing some course of action *simply* by virtue of the daemonic warning; e.g., in the case of his being warned away from politics.

But in response, this last claim—that Socrates' trust in the *daimonion* is greater than he can or would put in the products of non-divinely occasioned ratiocination—can be disputed on the grounds that there are no texts where a daemonic warning unambiguously trumps prior ratiocination, since none of them explicitly portray Socrates as receiving and obeying daemonic opposition to a course of action that was the clear result of prior *rational deliberation.* In the case of *Euthydemus* 272e1–273a3, for example, we can imagine that Socrates simply had a prereflective impulse to get up and leave, rather than some deliberative plan of action. Hence, returning to text C, it will be held that this passage by contrast makes it quite clear that Socrates will always and only accept that proposition best

---

58. Cf. Vlastos (14), 229–232; Reeve, 70–73.

supported by deliberative ratiocination, and hence, that secular reason always trumps divination for Socrates.

I must say that the texts are not as clear on this matter as we should like. But first, I (again) fail to see why text C must be read in a manner that interprets "reason" and "reasoning" as *secular* "reason" and *secular* "reasoning."[59] Rather, given the prior rationally established reliability of the *daimonion,* it would seem that an occurrence of the *daimonion* would count in a perfectly straightforward way *as a reason* for not doing some act. Thus, if during or after a process of practical, rational deliberation the *daimonion* should burst in with a "No," it is eminently compatible with text C that the *daimonion* should trump those deliberations. After all, if one had very frequently in the past always obeyed the promptings of an internal warning that one believes to come from all-wise gods, and this had always been judged to have resulted in the best outcome, then one has the very best of reasons for letting this internal warning overrule one's "merely human" judgment. And clearly, in such a case what is overruled is but one episode of practical reason's engagement on one issue, not "reason itself."

Now it is true that there is no text where reasoned deliberation is explicitly overridden by the *daimonion,* but we at least do find evidence that the *daimonion* has often intervened when Socrates was "about to do something wrong," even in small matters (*Ap.* 40a3–6). Hence, there surely must have been some occasions when Socrates had arrived through deliberation at plan-of-action *x* and then refrained from it simply for the *reason* that the *daimonion* warned him against *x.* And why would Socrates say at *Apology* 40a3–6 that the failure of the *daimonion* to oppose him is "wondrous" if he had not already been going through the reasons for going through with his trial and had not in the past had the experience of arriving through ratiocination at some course of action only to have it *opposed* by the *daimonion?*[60] Finally, note that Socrates' account of how the *daimonion* has always turned him away "from what he was about to do" (*Ap.* 31d3–4) is made in the context of his explaining the *daimonion*'s opposition to his entering politics (31c7–d5). Here it seems highly implausible to think that Socrates would not have deliberated ("reasoned about it," *per* C) in this or some previous cases (e.g., prior to taking steps toward addressing the Assembly [*Ap.* 31c5]). And it is clearly unreasonable to

59. Cf. Vlastos (11).
60. A point suggested to me by N. Smith.

suppose, for example, that Socrates is so impulsive that he engaged in no prior deliberation, and so had no good reasons, for his vocal opposition to the trial of the ten generals (*Ap.* 32a4–c3). But since there was deliberation there, then surely there were instances of deliberation (and not just blind impulses) in favor of public political activity on some of those occasions which were subsequently interrupted by the *daimonion*.[61] Hence, for Socrates the *daimonion* trumps ratiocination in the sphere of practical activity.

Finally, we should ask how much content the *daimonion* provides before any interpretation takes over. Is it really next to nothing, as Vlastos's remarks seem to suggest? Given Socrates' frequent description of the *daimonion* as a voice, I would not think so.[62] This is especially true if it happens that those sources where the *daimonion* warns Socrates of the inadvisability of the actions of *others* are reliable (viz., the *Theages,* and also, e.g., *Mem.* 1.1.4). *Theages* 128e6, for example, appears to record an immediate report of the *daimonion,* consisting in the prescriptive phrase, "No, you [Charmides] must not train," and this is obviously not a mere "twinge." Socrates and Charmides interpret this report in context as meaning that he, Charmides, ought not to train *for the Nemean races,* and both explicitly recognize that the future harm warned against is left open to rational speculation. Nonetheless, I see no reason not to suppose that Socrates considered himself to know with practical certainty that "harm will ensue from Charmides going on to train in some way," simply on the basis of the *daimonion*'s immediate report. For what degree of informational content in the psychic event of the warning itself—prior to interpretive work—is it necessary to postulate in this case? A simple "twinge" or an internal voice merely saying "No!" would generally seem insufficiently informative for rational interpretation to yield the level of reliability Socrates credits to the daemonic warning. True, Socrates could compare a daemonic "No" with his set of current intentions and with the external circumstances he finds himself in and rule out the application of the "No" to those that are common and have been occurring for some time without daemonic opposition. Hence, he can rule out the possibility that the "No"

61. See Brickhouse and Smith (4) and (8), chap. 6.3.2; and Vlastos (11) and (6).

62. Of course, we do not have reliable access to the psychic states of *living* individuals, let alone those of Socrates. Thus, when Socrates tells us that the *daimonion* warned him not to leave his seat (*Eud.* 272e2–273a3), it is unclear whether the *daimonion* is a mere "electric shock" or a full-fledged voice-in-the-head saying "Don't attempt to get up from this bench for the next full hour." Nonetheless, texts such as the following indicate that the *daimonion* has more phenomenological content than a mere twinge.

means "Stop breathing" or "Stop philosophizing." He may thus safely suppose that the "No" applies to the new elements of his situation. But without greater content, the act-token the *daimonion* warns against will be indeterminate between the many new possibilities before him, and he is in no position to decide whether the daemonic "No" applies to his own or another's current set of intentions.

Whether or not this speculative account of the *daimonion*'s content is on track, the discussion preceding it has shown that it is inaccurate to suppose that Socrates has "nullified the threat" an acceptance of divination poses to the "exclusive authority of reason" by making the determination of the *meaning* of a sign a function of reason alone.[63] For as we have seen, the intrinsic informational content of a sign *constrains* the interpretive scope of reason to a choice of interpretations. And again, it appears that most instances of the daemonic alarm (however small their cognitive content) *are* instances of a conflict between "reason and revelation," although they are not explicitly portrayed as such (to expect otherwise is anachronistic). That is, generally when we find Socrates "held back" by a daemonic warning we must suppose that he had some *reason* to formulate or initiate the forbidden action to begin with; e.g., going into politics. But in these instances his reasons for proceeding are deemed insufficiently compelling by Socrates *simply* on the basis of the daemonic opposition[64] (and it is implausible to suppose that Socrates insincerely cites the *daimonion* as a cover for conclusions rationally arrived at).[65] Hence, secular reason does not have

---

63. Vlastos (14), 229.

64. And thus (again), Vlastos's characterization of the *daimonion* simply doesn't do justice to the commonsense supposition that Socrates has rational warrants for courses of action that, with the onset of the *daimonion,* get immediately overridden. In such cases there are no fancy reflections, no elenctic wrangling, no hesitation of any sort, just instantaneous recognition and obedience (seen by Reeve, 69). And how could this be coherent if Socrates had thought that the *daimonion* was "cognitively worthless," "only a hunch," or a mere "twinge" of feeling? Of course, there may be an inference here (from, say, the *daimonion*'s "Don't sit" to Socrates' belief "Sitting will lead to harm"), where the inference relies on the *daimonion*'s past dependability and on the belief that it, as a divine sign, is always true, and so we cannot say that Socrates has sufficient warrant for action until the inference is complete. But such an inference requires Socrates to take the daemonic presentational content to be much more than just a hunch, since in many cases there is nothing in the immediate environment for elenctic reason to "latch onto" to transform the hunch into something more substantive (e.g., at *Eud.* 272e1–273a3).

65. Nussbaum (2), 234–235, notices that (1) the *daimonion* sometimes plays a *confirmatory* role, "backing up" rationally arrived at results. However, she also holds that it is suspiciously like the *elenchos* by being (1) dissuasive rather than admonitory, (2) a "divine thing" halfway between animal instinct and godlike certain wisdom, and (3) peculiar to Soc-

complete and free interpretive rein in the case of the *daimonion*. Such conflicts for Socrates, after all, are not between his secular, elenctic reasons for *and against* performing some act *x*. Rather, these latter dissuasive reasons are held by the gods who—being good—mitigate his dangerous ignorance by sending him, not reasons, but a "sign." And in the absence of reasons approximating those had by the gods against doing *x*, reasons that we might elenctically inspect, only someone *irrational* would ignore the warning the gods send, preferring instead their own mortal judgment (see *Ap.* 23a5–7).

In sum, I think we ought to understand the *daimonion* to be a unique source of information for Socrates, information that yields instances of knowledge of the advisability of particular courses of action. In particular, it warrants his overwhelming confidence in the virtue of his philosophical

---

rates. Hence, she supposes that "the *daimonion* . . . is no standard tutelary deity at all, but an ironic way of alluding to the supreme authority of dissuasive reason and elenctic argument. . . . reason itself is being made the new god" (234).

We should resist all this, however. First, (1') the *daimonion* is not merely capable of doing confirmatory work, but can—as in the case of Socrates's "going to do" politics—"trump" the results of secular elenctic ratiocination; moreover, the *elenchos* is—arguably—not always dissuasive but is (or at least can be) used inductively to support positive doctrine (but see Chap. 1, n. 14). Next (2'), Nussbaum's second point (2) rests on the plausibility of supposing that Socrates identifies the *daimonion* as a sort of intermediary δαίμων. But we have seen above that this is an error, since Socrates identifies the *daimonion* as the *voice* of a divine being (probably Apollo). Finally, (3') contra (3), unlike the *daimonion*, the *elenchos* is a tool open to use by others, and whereas one must *voluntarily* employ it, the *daimonion* is an involuntary, unpredictable, unteachable, and "divinatory" event.

Nussbaum suggests in correspondence that Socrates understands his citations of the *daimonion* to be surreptitious references to his own secular powers of reason dolled-up in the language of the superstitious many: Reason, that is, understood as a form of intuition—a "hunch" produced by unconscious inference. But here again the weight of unrelenting and undisguised religious references in our texts and their integration in the philosophical thinking of Socrates argues that—to the contrary—Socrates really does take the cause of the *daimonion* to be a god—or possibly a δαίμων—in the traditional sense of those terms (cf. *Ap.* 27b3–28a1). This proposal also runs up against the characterization of the *daimonion* found in texts such as *Euthydemus* 272e–273a, where it is implausible to suppose that Socrates is able or supposes that he is able to unconsciously infer the unbeneficial result apparently warned against by the *daimonion*. In this case, after all, there appears to be no evidence at all available to Socrates of the future event he is daemonically warned against—namely, that leaving would mean missing the arrival of interlocutors and the wild educational free-for-all that follows. Finally, the proof texts against this proposal are *Lysis* 218c4–8 and 215c4–5 (see also *Euth.* 279c5–6; *Crat.* 411b; *Phdr.* 242b8–243a3), where Socrates recounts an experience of having a "rational hunch" but makes no mention at all of the *daimonion;* something we would expect if "*daimonion*" is Socrates' name for rational hunches; cf. Friedländer, 33.

mission and constantly aids him in its pursuit.[66] Nonetheless, neither divination nor elenctic testing are *in general* taken to be foundational by Socrates, but rather, are mutually justifying; that is, if his divinatory evidence is called into question, he is ready to subject it to elenctic testing; if the moral worth of elenctic testing is called into question, he may appeal to divination.

However, in different *particular* circumstances, one or the other—reason or "revelation"—will be the court of last appeal in the event of an apparent conflict between the two. A close study of our texts suggests that all extrarational signs *other* than those of the *daimonion* (e.g., dreams and oracular reports) have, for Socrates, an equivocal core meaning, and so require significant interpretation before their import can be adequately understood and relied upon. Moreover, *per* principle A', any action that might be prompted by an interpretation that conflicts with traditional norms must, for Socrates, receive and survive elenctic testing *before* that course of action may be pursued. Such nondaemonic sources will commonly allow for multiple interpretations, may be misreported, and so forth, in which case it will count against any one interpretation that it *does* conflict with established norms. Thus, except for the *daimonion,* Socratic reason is epistemologically prior to Socratic "revelation."[67]

But the *daimonion,* then, is an exception to this: (1) the *daimonion* may be instantly obeyed with no further rational checks so long as that action threatens to violate no traditional norms; and again, (2) if the *daimonion* should indicate a course of action at odds with established norms, that reading of it should be subjected to elenctic testing; but (3) in this case, and unlike all other extrarational sources of information, if interpretation or testing of the *daimonion* is procedurally impossible, the daemonic advice—having previously proven itself time and time again in the court of elenctic reason—will take precedence over all other considerations. So in this one case, daemonic revelation may supersede the dictates of both convention and the immediate results of secular practical reason.

Thus there is left some "threat" from the extrarational: there *can* be a conflict "between Socrates's unconditional readiness to follow critical [secular] reason" and his commitment to obey divine injunctions.[68] If, for ex-

66. E.g., in its role as extrarational "admissions officer" to prospective students; e.g., *Tht.* 150e1 ff.; *Alc. I* 105d–106a, 127e; and Xen. *Symp.* 8.5.

67. *Pace* Brickhouse and Smith (7), 127–130, and (12), 107, who see divinations in general as providing Socrates with *certainty.*

68. Vlastos (14), 229; my bracketed term.

ample, the *daimonion* should warn Socrates away from saving the lives of his children, something enjoined upon him by reason and tradition, and there is no way *at that point* to further interpret or test the warning, what then? Socrates simply appears never to have had to confront *this* sort of horrible, Abrahamic choice (he may think the gods would never allow such a situation to arise); but given my previous remarks—and his choice to risk his *own* life, anyway, at the behest of an extrarationally revealed command—I expect that the response would have been essentially the same as Abraham's.[69] Nonetheless, his is *not* the outlook of the sort of religious extremist feared by some commentators. Socrates is no fifth-century fundamentalist *Theogony*-thumper, since, on my account, he requires that the extrarational submit itself to the court of secular rationality.

Socrates, then, conceives of both the *elenchos* and divination as having provided him with moral guidance. And as he sees it, we are all so doubly-blessed with the rational faculties and gifts of extrarational (but non-daemonic) information necessary for living a life that has some measure of well-being. Here and elsewhere, however, as we reflect on the *daimonion* and the life of Socrates, we may find ourselves agreeing with Xenophon that "with you, Socrates, they [the gods] seem to be even more friendly than with other men" (*Mem.* 4.3.12).[70]

4.2 The Delphic Oracle and the Duty to Philosophize

We have seen that the Socrates of the *Apology* claims to philosophize in accordance with a duty so overriding that he will accept even death rather

---

69. Note that Reeve, 73, claims that Socrates "is not Kierkegaard's Abraham. He is a man of philosophy not of faith." This is surely true (in some sense), and in a way compatible with my account here, since I ground Socrates' confidence in the *daimonion* in reason (esp. its inductively established reliability) and not by an irrational "leap." However, Reeve's claim does seem to be at odds with his own analysis of the *daimonion* (68–73), according to which Socrates takes daemonic prohibitions to be certain, obeying them "without independently justifying them," and using them "to establish truths he could not establish in any other way" (70; cf. 181–183). For further criticism of Reeve's account of Socrates' use of extrarational guides, see McPherran (6) and N. Smith (2), 401–402.

70. Again (see Chapter 3.4.6), it seems perfectly compatible with Socrates' moral theory and theology that he should believe that the gods aid his mission to the Athenians by providing him with a daemonic guide to correct action; esp. as an extrarational "admissions officer" to prospective students (see n. 66).

than abandon his mission to the Athenians (29c5–d5; 28e5–6, 30a–b). As he characterizes it, the source of this obligation appears straightforward: Socrates has been ordered (προστέτακται) to do philosophy by a god (33c4–8; 23b, 28d6; 29a3, 30a–b, 37e–38a), and since one ought always to obey the command of a god at all costs (it is always impious [and so unjust] to refuse),[71] Socrates is obligated to philosophize regardless of any bodily danger (29d; cf. *R.* 368b–c). But religious appearances are not always (or perhaps ever) what they seem. So how then did Socrates become cognizant of this command and on what grounds could he display such confidence in it? These are questions I shall try to answer here.

Next, observe that Socrates also believes that he is divinely mandated to urge others to philosophize (e.g., 29d–e, 30a–b, 38a; cf. *G.* 526e). From that seems to follow the Socratic dictum that "the unexamined life is not worth living *for a human being*" (38a5–6),[72] meaning that people other than Socrates are under some sort of a uniquely *human* obligation to philosophize by elenctically examining themselves and others. Nonetheless, the existence of a Socratic duty to urge others to do philosophy does not allow a direct inference that Socrates believed that all others—like himself—have a duty to do philosophy.[73] After all, in his concern for everyone's welfare (31a), the god may have ordered Socrates to go to great lengths to urge others to philosophize precisely because others do not actually have his sort of duty—or inclination—to engage in it. For their own good people might require the special prodding to philosophize (in a limited and conventionally prudent fashion) that Socrates provides in obe-

---

71. Since Socrates' gods are by far our intellectual and moral superiors, and since—on Socratic principles—to know the good is to be good, whatever they command must be just and virtuous; hence, it is wrong not to obey the commands of such superiors (see Chapter 2.2; and, e.g., *Ap.* 29b6–7, 29d3–4; *Ch.* 176b–c; *La.* 184e8–9; and *Phd.* 61e5 ff.). Again, this amounts to an acceptance of what is only a *non-naive* kind of voluntarism (contra Nehamas [2], 305–306, who maintains that there is *no* trace of voluntarism in Socrates).

Throughout this section I use the terms "duty" and "obligation," but in a nontechnical fashion, since there are no "Kantian duties" in the thought of Socrates. So I want to make clear that when I attribute to Socrates the belief in a "general duty" or "obligation" to do philosophy, I mean only to claim that Socrates believed that most people of the age of reason ought—prima facie—to do philosophy, that doing philosophy will benefit them and ought generally to be preferred over all other activities, and that philosophizing is virtuous; but, nonetheless, that on certain occasions one ought to refrain from philosophizing.

72. Here the source of his obligation seems equally straightforward: one ought to obey the commands of a god at all costs, and so because Socrates has been commanded by a god to urge others to philosophize (e.g., *Ap.* 30a–b), Socrates ought to urge others to philosophize.

73. Moreover, it is not at all obvious in the *Apology* that the god has commanded everyone—or even most people—to philosophize.

dience to the god: just as a parent might have a paternalistic duty of assistance to urge his children to do *x*, where they themselves do not possess the parent's *duty* to do *x*.[74] Hence, the ascription to Socrates of a belief in a general obligation to philosophize is in need of justification.

This ascription is also in need of clarification. We need especially to ask about the nature, extent, and limits of a Socratic obligation to do philosophy. Does it require, for example, that a half-wit give up his menial occupation—adopting the poverty of a Socrates—in order to employ the *elenchos* in an ineffective and/or counterproductive fashion? Or perhaps the sort of philosophizing Socrates urges on others differs in kind from the elenctically based sort Socrates himself practices: A less intellectually demanding type of rational reflection perhaps.[75] And, again, how exactly did Socrates discover this general, religiously mandated obligation to philosophize and to what extent did his method of discovery conform to the previous account of his reliance on extrarational sources?

In the following, I respond to these questions by providing an interpretation that explains and connects Socrates' particular god-ordered mission to do philosophy with the more general demands of piety as Socrates conceived them (and with a further articulation of the idea previously seen in Chapter 2.2 that Socrates supposes that others besides himself possess a prima facie religious obligation to do philosophy).

4.2.1 Piety, Prudence, and the Delphic Oracle

The text of the *Apology* makes it crystal-clear that Socrates regarded his philosophical activity as divinely enjoined upon him through a variety of extrarational channels. We have already seen the *locus classicus* for this thesis, *Apology* 33c4–7, where Socrates is portrayed as having been commanded to philosophize through the medium of "oracles and dreams and in every other way in which a divinity has ever commanded anyone to do anything," an order that Socrates—just prior to this passage—compares to the orders of a military commander (28b–29b). However, much earlier in his defense—as Socrates endeavors to explain how the slanders of the

74. In fact, *Ap.* 31b uses just this sort of analogy: Socrates goes to individuals as a father or older brother might, persuading them to care for virtue (i.e., to care for the improvement of their souls and, thus, to do philosophy).

75. G. Vlastos brought this possibility to my attention.

first accusers developed out of his having a certain kind of "wisdom" (20d–e)—he connects the origin of that "wisdom" and his philosophical service to Athens with one oracle in particular, the Delphic Oracle (the Pythia) (20c–23c).[76] It is through that Oracle, he says, that he learned that the god who speaks through the Pythia (20e7; namely, Apollo)[77] had stationed (τάττοντος) him in Athens, obliging (δεῖν) him to philosophize and examine himself and others (28e4–6), and because of this, his activity now "aids the God" (23b7) "according to the God" [κατὰ τὸν θεόν] (22a4, 23b5). Thus, Socrates finds the Oracle's pronouncement to mark a turning point in his life and to somehow underwrite a philosophical mission to the Athenians.[78]

Much to the puzzlement and/or disbelief of most modern commentators, however, the report of the Oracle appears to be utterly nonprescriptive, and hence, no source of obligation at all.[79] Delphi's response to the question of Chaerephon, who asked if anyone was wiser than Socrates, was—after all—simply that "no one is wiser [σοφώτερον]" (Ap. 21a5–7), and

76. On the Oracle and its functions, see J. Fontenrose, esp. 34–35, and Parke and Wormell, esp. 17–45. E. Strycker doubts that the Oracle was of paramount importance in Socrates' life, but his arguments are unpersuasive; see arguments in favor of its importance in Brickhouse and Smith (12), 88–91, (8), chap. 6.4; Reeve, 28–32; and M. Stokes (2). Plato himself exhibits the greatest admiration for Delphi (R. 427b1–c4). I see no reason to agree with J. Daniel and R. Polansky, 83–85, that the Oracle only served to confirm for Socrates the necessity of his mission and did not contribute to that mission's "origin" in some sense (Brickhouse and Smith [6], 663 n. 13).

77. See Reeve, 25 n. 26.

78. According to Stokes (2), 73, Ap. 33c demotes the Oracle story, making it just one of several indications of what the god wants of Socrates. But I think that the text and its dramatic structure make it plain that the Oracle continues to be central, with the mention of "indications" at 33c serving primarily to confirm Socrates' interpretation of the Oracular pronouncement as inaugurating his "mission"; cf. Reeve, 24.

79. See, e.g., Bury (2), 580; A.-H. Chroust (3), 31–32; A. Doering, 57; E. Dupréel, 45; O. Gigon, 99; T. Gomperz, 2:104–108; Hackforth (2), 89–91; Montuori (2), 57–143, esp. 133 ff.; Parke and Wormell, 1:401–403; and Stokes (2). For a history of this problem, see Brickhouse and Smith (6), 657–658 nn. 1–4, and now Stokes (2), 29–33. Reeve, 25, notes that the oracular response also says nothing about elenctic examination, or elenctic examination on ethical issues. Stokes (2), 30–31, rejects accounts like mine (see below), which appeal to Socrates' prior commitment to the virtue of piety (P6 in Chapter 2.2) on the grounds that this forces Plato's audience to read the Apology backward (i.e., read the Oracle story in light of its later sections, which reveal the Socratic pious obligation to do philosophy) and requires them to have prior knowledge of the Euthyphro. But this is not a weighty objection, for as Stokes himself suggests (50; cf. 62–68), Socrates and his jurors would all assume well before the trial that the gods enjoin just behavior of humans; and since they will have also already thought that piety is a form of justice, then they will in fact have the essentials of P6 on hand in order to make rough sense of Socrates' account of how he felt compelled to make sense of what Apollo had said.

this seems only descriptive, not prescriptive.[80] Moreover, it would appear that Socrates had already for some time been pursuing a life of philosophy, believing it to be something beneficial that he ought to do, and so the pronouncement of the Oracle will not have been what *initiated* his philosophical career.[81] Given all this, it is understandable that some have found Socrates' derivation of his alleged divine obligation as analogous to pulling a rabbit from a hat: A rabbit concealed within the hat by the magician himself.[82] In particular, those persuaded by Vlastos and the other skeptics of the previous section might think that since Socrates says of his analysis of the Oracle that he "supposed and assumed" [ᾠήθην τε καὶ ὑπέλαβον] God had commanded him to philosophize (*Ap.* 28e5; as with the dream of *Phaedo* 60d8–61b8), that this "derivation" is really a prime example of Socrates' utterly free use of rational interpretation to make up whatever plausible story his *prior* philosophical beliefs would warrant; a story of obligation that he then slips into the top hat of the god.[83] Hence, Socrates' talk of having been divinely ordered to philosophize is not nearly so much a *description* as an ironic public-relations ploy made in "the language of popular morality" for the sake of his jury.[84] After all, would Socrates really set out, as he says, to "*refute*" (ἐλέγξων [21c1]) the oracular pronouncement in order to uncover its meaning if he seriously took it to be a message from a *god*, a god who never lies (21b5–7)?[85] And given then that Socrates

---

80. Cf. Xen. *Apol.* 14, which—while omitting Chaerephon's question—presents a negative form of the response (namely, in response to Chaerephon's inquiry, "Apollo answered that no man was more free than I, or more just, or more prudent"); D.L. 2.37–38 also supports Plato's version. On the probable and widespread assumption that Xenophon had Plato's version in mind when composing his own Socratic *apologia*, his account would be a natural expansion of Plato's (Brickhouse and Smith [12], 89 n. 71). However, P. Vander Waerdt (2) has recently argued that Xenophon has *revised* much of Plato's version "in the service of his own quite different interpretation of Socrates's philosophical mission" (29). As he sees it, Xenophon's main purpose with his *Apology* is to remedy the impression Plato's version fosters that Socrates conducted his defense imprudently. Xenophon's oracle story fits into this strategy by providing Socrates with a basic reply to all the formal charges that he can then go on to elaborate; cf. Stokes (2), 56–58.

81. Cf. Brickhouse and Smith (6), 663–664, and Kraut (2), 271 n. 43.

82. Vlastos (8), 229–230, (14), chap. 6, esp. 171; Nehamas (2), 305–306.

83. Reeve, 66, 71, also seems inclined to this view of things.

84. Versenyi (1), 112; cf. 123; also see the sympathetic views on this score of Burnet (4), 107; Hackforth (2), 101–104; I. G. Kidd (2), 482; A. E. Taylor (1), 160; and Vlastos (18). Again, for example, Nehamas (2), 306, claims that there is "not a trace of voluntarism in Socrates's 'obedience' to the god; on the contrary, he only does, as he always did, what he thinks is, *on independent grounds,* the best thing" (my emphasis; cf. Reeve, 63).

85. Burnet's criticism (4), 92, 172; also, Hackforth (2), 88–104; Ryle, 1966; H. Teloh (2), 111; T. G. West, 106; Nehamas (2), 305–306.

is prepared to seriously doubt the truth of a divine sign, *no* such sign could be sincerely supposed by him to ground his belief in the obligations and methods of his mission. It might thus even begin to appear that the god is *cut off* from direct communication with mortals, since the interpretation of a divine sign will depend on the initial beliefs present in the interpreter prior to the divinity's attempt to communicate. And from that one could conclude that the gods are powerless to provide Socrates with those antecedent beliefs of his that enable him to *read into* the divine signs the obligation to philosophize he seems to have found there. Socrates on this view simply *supposes* and *assumes* that it is a divinely mandated task that he has been assigned; he *hypothesizes* that he is to do for the gods what they do not (or cannot) do: improve souls (his and those of his fellow Athenians).[86]

Diametrically opposed to this view is one that maintains that Socrates can in fact be *certain* of the god's command and the moral correctness of his mission simply by virtue of the various signs he takes himself to have received from the god(s)—especially his discovery of the meaning of the Oracle's pronouncement:

> The certainty of Socrates's belief in the enormous moral significance of his mission is logically independent of whatever beliefs he may have about the nature of virtue. . . . Since he is certain that divinations, properly construed, provide truth, and because he is certain that the God has made his wishes known to him through various divinations, Socrates has what he at least considers excellent reason to be convinced that . . . [his] activities . . . are virtuous.[87]

My own position is found between these two accounts, although it is closer to this latter one than it is to the former.[88] I shall contend that Socrates discovers genuine informational content in the pronouncement of the Oracle, a content that seriously constrains his attempts at rational interpretation, but that the epistemic reliability of the result falls below the level of infallibility or logical certainty. I shall also offer a close reading of the *Apology* which shows that while the pronouncement of the Oracle did not in fact *launch* Socrates' philosophical career, it did mark a crucial turning point in it by initiating a course of reflection that led him to the

---

86. Vlastos (18), 231–232; (14), chap. 6, 173–174.
87. Brickhouse and Smith (7), 128; cf. (12), 107, and (8), chap. 6.4.
88. Cf. Reeve, 63.

realization that he—more than anyone and even at the cost of his life—is obligated to elenctically examine others (and himself).[89]

In examining the story of the Oracle, we may distinguish three periods in the philosophical life of Socrates: (1) his intellectual activity prior to Chaerephon's visit, (2) his subsequent investigation of the meaning of the oracular pronouncement, and (3) his philosophical activity following the discovery of its meaning.[90]

1. What philosophy was Socrates doing prior to Chaerephon's visit to Delphi? We saw that there is evidence that he "investigated nature" in his youth (Chapter 3.1–2; cf. Chapter 5.2), and we should in any case imagine him to have been intellectually vigorous and, thus, curious and knowledgeable about a wide variety of topics.[91] Moreover, in the course of his philosophical activities it seems likely that Socrates would have displayed a degree of intellectual ability sufficient to have incited Chaerephon to visit the Oracle with his question.[92] And on the hypothesis that Delphi was

89. Reeve, 71 n. 83, claims that I am mistaken in this account of the unique extent of Socrates' obligation, since according to Socrates (*Ap.* 28d6–10) *everyone* must do the just thing, never the unjust (cf. *Cr.* 48b–49d), and "not take into account death or anything else compared to what is shameful" (*Ap.* 28d9–10), where philosophy is a just thing to do. Although my original formulation on this matter (McPherran [9], 542) was less than transparent, the rest of that paper (and this section) makes it clear that my interpretation acknowledges that Socrates *does* hold that we all have an unconditional prima facie duty to do philosophy (hence, even at the cost of our lives); but that (just as Reeve's interpretation has it, 70–72) Socrates discovers through the mediation of the Oracle that he is less constrained than most people by the factors that can mitigate the extent of this obligation. Hence, on both our accounts Socrates discovers *via* the Oracle that the scope and sacrifice required of him in the practice of philosophy is much greater than for others.

90. The reasons for taking the story of the Oracle seriously have been clearly and persuasively laid out by Brickhouse and Smith (6) and (12), 87–100. Various dates for Chaerephon's visit have been proposed (see Brickhouse and Smith [6], n. 11), but most scholars now date it c. 430 (while acknowledging the paucity of good evidence); see J. Ferguson (1); Guthrie (6), 85–86; Parke and Wormell, 1:401–403; E. de Strycker (2), 40–41; and esp. Stokes (2), 48, 52–54. At any rate, *Ap.* 28d–e is a good indication that the visit occurred after the battle of Potidaea (430).

91. As Stokes (2), 68, notes, though, Socrates cannot have imagined himself wise on various topics, since that would make nonsense of his later being puzzled by the report of the Oracle. Stokes is in error, though, to think that Socrates couldn't have gained a reputation for elenctic refutation early on, since there is no need to think that Socrates only began to employ the *elenchos* subsequent to Chaerephon's visit to the oracle.

92. On this point, see Brickhouse and Smith (6), 662–663; Guthrie (6), 86; Kraut, 271 n. 43; and A. E. Taylor (2), 78. Of course, and as Stokes (2), 29, 68–69, notes, it may not have

relying on evidence in making its response to Chaerephon, it also seems likely that this show of talent would also have to be something with enough merit from Delphi's point of view to warrant the Oracle's claiming that "no one is wiser," and yet also of the sort that would help to explain Socrates' *puzzlement* at the Oracle's response.[93]

Now, given the skill at elenctic examination Socrates testifies to possessing subsequent to Chaerephon's report (21b–23a), it is reasonable to suppose that Socrates had been wielding the *elenchos* on topics of ethical import for a good deal of time prior to his setting about to "refute" the Oracle.[94] In fact, Socrates must have been quite proficient at *elenchos*-wielding, sufficiently proficient that Chaerephon (at any rate) came to think of him as being *wise;* so wise in fact that he was prompted to travel to Delphi to take the measure of that wisdom from the god himself.[95] After all, Socrates nowhere says that he began to wield the *elenchos* only *after* the re-

---

taken much to set Chaerephon off, since—apparently by way of explanation for his heading off to Delphi—Socrates characterizes him as having an overenthusiastic, impetuous temperament (*Ap.* 21a3; *Ch.* 153a–b).

93. See, too, e.g., Brickhouse and Smith (12), 94–95; Burnet (4), 74–75, 90–91; Kraut (2), 271 n. 43; A. E. Taylor (2), 78–79; and Vlastos (13), 26–29. Support for this hypothesis is also generally found in the idea that the priest's interpretations of the Pythia's utterances would have been slanted by their interests and knowledge; see Parke and Wormell, 1:30–41. But note too that the Oracle was keenly interested in telling suppliants what they wanted to hear; see Fontenrose, 7–8, 11–57, 233–239. Some have observed that besides a written response based on an interpretation of the Pythia's remarks, there was also the much less expensive oracle by lot ("the two beans"). Using this, they argue that since Chaerephon was poor, this was the more likely method, and hence, that the Oracle cannot be supposed to have relied on evidence of Socratic wisdom (Parke [4], 249–250; [2], 72–88, 112–113; Parke and Wormell, 1:17–45; see Reeve's discussion, 28–30). However, Fontenrose, 219–223, and Stokes (2), 58–60, present arguments against assuming Delphi's use of the lot. My account is essentially unaffected by this problem, since what matters here is not Delphi's method, but Socrates' response to the report brought by Chaerephon.

94. Stokes (2), 53–54, argues convincingly that the opening scene of the *Laches* (187d–188a) presents evidence that Socrates "engaged in elenctic practice soon after he *ceased to be a boy*" (viz., soon after the age of 18–20). Note, too, that the *Parmenides* portrays a youthful Socrates (approx. 20) who has already acquired great philosophical ability. The *Symposium* continues this idea, showing us a Socrates in his early thirties who already possesses a reputation for wisdom and philosophical ability.

95. Brickhouse and Smith (12), 94–95; Kraut, 271 n. 43. Chaerephon could have come to the conclusion that Socrates possessed some sort of wisdom in the same naive way some of his fellow Athenians had (23a1–5)—by watching Socrates elenctically refute those with a reputation for wisdom (note that Chaerephon had known Socrates from youth [20e8–21a1]); cf. Reeve, 32. Again, the evidence of the *Phaedo* (97b–99a) and Aristotle (*Met.* 987b1–4, 1078b19–20) suggests that Socrates was always centrally concerned with ethics, thus his alleged wisdom would likely have been of the ethical sort; see Chapters 3.1–2 and 5.2.

port of the Oracle; rather, he implies that it was the report that initiated his "mission," the point at which he began to *systematically* examine people with a reputation for wisdom (21b9–23b4). Also, Socrates' characterization of his puzzlement upon learning of the oracular response indicates that he *already* thought that he was without wisdom (21b4–5), and the best explanation for this piece of self-understanding is that he had come to it by means of the primary tool of self-examination: the *elenchos* (or its prototype) (*Ap.* 28e5–6, 29c6–d1).[96]

But despite Socrates' own inevitable awareness of his impressive philosophical talents, he found Chaerephon's account of Delphi's response a stunning paradox, leaving him to ask: "What is the god saying, what riddle is he uttering [τί ποτε αἰνίττεται]?" (21b3–4). The oracular report "No one is wiser"—as Socrates read its surface meaning—appears to credit some wisdom to him, a wisdom that makes him wiser than all humans (21b–c).[97] But Socrates believed that his previous *elenchos*-wielding had given him no wisdom at all in the sense he usually ascribes to "wisdom" (21b4–5). That is, his elenctic activities had not produced the positive answers that contribute to possession of real *wisdom* of the "greatest things," a wisdom laid claim to by some politicians, poets, and artisans (22c9–e1); in particular, it had not produced complete Socratic definitions of the virtues (those vainly sought after in the aporetic dialogues). Rather, his activities had only revealed to him that he lacked all such wisdom, while others seemed to have a portion.

But *that*, then, would appear to be precisely why *Delphi* praises him; namely, that he had, prior to Chaerephon's visit, been discovering the very same antihubristic truths constitutive of the wisdom appropriate to humans that Delphi itself had always insisted upon; namely, that humans are far inferior to the gods in power and wisdom, that god is the "measure" of truth, not humanity, and so forth.[98] Especially important is that Socrates

96. Reeve, 31–32; de Strycker (2), 46; Vlastos (8), 31–32.

97. At 21b (cf. 21c2) Socrates says that the god implies that he is the *wisest* (σοφώτατος) of men, yet the Oracle had only said that "no one is wiser." As I see it, the explanation for this inferential leap is that Socrates is introducing into his interpretation of the Oracle a revelation that only came later, after he had elenctically tested many "experts"; namely, that he of all humans is wisest by best realizing his own ignorance of expert moral knowledge. Also, as *Ap.* 23b1–4 indicates, the category "wisest of humans" is open to others besides Socrates. To be "wisest" then is to be a member of the class of humans who, like Socrates, know that in truth their wisdom is worth nothing in relation to real wisdom (*Ap.* 23b1–4).

98. This connection between Socrates and the antihubristic message of Delphi is well drawn by Reeve, 28–32; cf. the less satisfactory suppositions that it was Socrates' scientific accomplishments (testified to by the *Clouds*) that recommended him to Delphi (Burnet [4],

would already seem to have been coming to *know* that he does not possess the sort of wisdom the gods possess: "divine wisdom" (*Ap.* 20e1, 23a5–6), in particular, the sort of expert moral knowledge he has been seeking and failing to find.[99]

The Oracle at Delphi and its god had long been understood as underwriting the virtue of humility and self-effacing restraint—and insisting on the vice of *hubris*—in the face of divine wisdom. On the walls of the temple at Delphi there were inscriptions to just that effect (e.g., "Know thyself" [γνῶθι σαυτόν], meaning, "know that you are but a human, not a god"; "Hate hubris" [ὕβριμ μείσει]; and so forth).[100] There are also many stories somewhat parallel with that of Socrates where persons noteworthy for their wisdom or other accomplishments request that Delphi declare the identity of "him who is the wisest" (or most pious, and so forth), in the full expectation that they themselves will be named. But instead, the Oracle endorses some poor and obscure person living a life of humble contentment; the message obviously being that a person living a life free of *hubris* and pretension has a life much more in accord with the pious spirit of Delphi than any self-important man of the world.[101] Delphi's Apollo must, therefore, similarly call Socrates "wise," for *he*—just as the god—has also

---

74–75, 90–91); or rather, his elenctic ability (Vlastos [13], 26–29); or his philosophical doctrines (Brickhouse and Smith [12], 94–95). On the Greek concept of hubris and its religious import, see Dover (3), 54–55, 110–111; MacDowell (2), 129–132; and Nilsson (4), 52–59.

99. See Reeve, 25–26, and Vander Waerdt (2), on why Socrates came to focus exclusively on *ethical* inquiry.

100. Also "Nothing in excess" (μηδὲν ἄγαν), "Curb thy spirit" (θυμοῦ κράτει), "Observe the limit" (πέρας ἐπιτέλει), "Bow before the divine" (προσκύνει τὸ θεῖον), "Fear authority" (τὸ κρατοῦμ φοβοῦ), and "Glory not in strength" (ἐπὶ ῥώμῃ μὴ καυχῶ). See Guthrie (2), 183–204; Parke and Wormell, 378–392; and Reeve, 30. According to Plutarch (*Ad. Col.* 1118c), it was the Delphic inscription "Know thyself" that set Socrates off on his inquiries.

101. E.g., the person whose sacrifices most please the god is not the wealthy Magnesian who sacrifices a hecatomb to Apollo, but the poor and obscure farmer, Clearachus of Methydrium; see other such stories collected in Parke and Wormell, 378–392, and reported by Reeve, 31; cf. Nilsson (5), 197–199, and Stokes (2), 60. Stokes (2), 60–62, presents an interesting account of how the *Apology*'s Oracle story systematically reverses in various details the "standard" Oracle tale. It goes too far, however, to use this as he does to conclude that the *Apology*'s story is purely or primarily fictional, since literary elaboration of an actual event with actual significance is compatible with this phenomenon. Cf. other similar moves by Montuori (2), 57–146; Armleder; and Fontenrose, 34. It is disturbing, as Stokes (2), 55 (cf. 62), notes, that we don't hear more about the Oracle story from Plato and others. At the bare minimum, however, it is the sort of literary device (or pious fiction of the Socratic circle) that presupposes Socrates actually possessed the sort of religious motivations I have ascribed to him (cf. Stokes [2], 67).

been vigorously insisting on the "human wisdom" (ἀνθρωπίνη σοφία [23a7, 20d8]) of acknowledging the great epistemological and metaphysical chasm separating humanity from the gods; a chasm rarely bridged and only by the intentional *descent* of a divinity and never through human attempts at *ascent*.[102] Socrates would have us labor to perfect ourselves, but with no hope (as things now stand with our nature) of *our* ever crossing this divide.[103] Given this explanation for Delphi's praise of Socrates, it is evident that Socrates was satisfying the general religious obligation to serve the gods (*via* philosophizing) that we derived from the *Euthyphro* (Chapter 2.2) even prior to Chaerephon's trip:

> P6   Piety is that part of justice that is a service [ὑπηρετική] of human beings to the gods, assisting the gods in their work, a work that produces some good result (on the analogy of a slave/assistant assisting his master/craftsman).[104]

Socrates' philosophizing meets the demands of P6 on the grounds that it serves the likely desire of the gods that human happiness should be promoted; it furthers this end by producing a valuable awareness of human limitations ("human wisdom") in himself and others and by grounding his moral beliefs *via* elenctic examination. As we shall see, given that it is Socrates' commitment to something like P6 that makes sense of his interpretation of the Oracle as providing a special religious mandate for his philosophical activity, we ought to suppose that Socrates was aware of his belief in P6 well before the visit of Chaerephon to Delphi. Nonetheless, since he was puzzled by the Oracle's declaration of his wisdom, it would seem that he had yet to recognize fully the true worth of the antihubristic,

102. Moreover, Socrates is especially worthy of Delphi's praise because he was explicitly acting out of piety (principle P6 in Chapter 2.2), as evidenced by the fact that he undertakes his interpretation of Chaerephon's report not out of idle curiosity or superstitious prudence, but because he believes that "the business of the god is of the highest importance" (*Ap.* 21e4–5) (Brickhouse and Smith [12], 95). As Reeve, 25–26, argues: "Who but a religious person . . . would puzzle over one of his [Apollo's] oracles . . . and persist in that activity even when it made him poor and unpopular?"

103. Something that very much distinguishes the religion of Socrates from that of his pupil, Plato; see Chapter 5.3; McPherran (2); and Vlastos (13), 94–95.

104. Because, as I will argue, Socrates' firmly held religious justification for doing philosophy (*Ap.* 39b) is founded on this principle, I would contend that Socrates would claim to know P6 (although it would be a "fallible" claim to knowledge: something similar to Vlastos's "knowledge/e" [13], 48–58, or the nonexpert knowledge sketched out above). For evidence of a Socratic commitment to the master-slave/superior-inferior metaphor, see, e.g., *Phd.* 62d–63d, *Ion* 53e, *Parm.* 134d–e, *Alc. 1* 122a, *Mem.* 1.4.9–12, and Chapter 2.2 herein.

deflationary results he was achieving through his elenctic activities and, thus, was not yet in a position to understand the full extent of the demands P6 enjoins upon him with respect to philosophical activity.[105]

For Socrates to discover a motivation to philosophize in P6, however, he would have to have had the prior belief that his philosophical practice is productive of virtuous happiness (thus subsequently realizing that this serves the desires of the gods). But since we all desire this good,[106] Socrates will therefore have had a secular, eudaimonistic motivation prior to Chaerephon's visit for his pursuit of philosophy. We even see evidence that Socrates recognized this distinction between "divine" and "secular" warrant for pursuing courses of action when he distinguishes between being "stationed by a [divine] ruler" and "stationed by oneself" at *Apology* 28d–e, and between "obeying god" and "doing what is a great good for a human being" at *Apology* 37e–38a.[107]

One such secular warrant derived from explicitly Socratic tenets that might well have been discovered or endorsed by Socrates prior to Chaerephon's visit is this:

S   (1)   Anyone ought to do what is right and never what is wrong, taking nothing else into account (e.g., *Ap.* 28b, 28d, 29b; *Cr.* 48c–d, 49b).[108]

105. Cf. Kraut, 271 n. 43.

106. E.g., *Ap.* 28b5–9, d6–10; *Cr.* 48c6–d5; cf. G. 499e; see also Brickhouse and Smith (8), chap. 3, and Vlastos (14), chap. 8.

107. Stokes (2) sometimes seems to miss this distinction, supposing that it was the Oracle *alone* that gave his mission its meaning (68–70) and that there is thus something puzzling about Socrates trying not only to test *for himself* (as part of his "trying to refute the apparent meaning of the oracular response") someone's claim to wisdom but—once the claimant's ignorance was detected—to go on to try to demonstrate this *to the claimant* (*per Ap.* 21b–d)(41–42). On my account this puzzle dissolves: even prior to the oracular response Socrates had grounds for thinking that elenctic examination of others and the revelation of ignorance it brings are good things for a human being, and that we ought to do what's good (see, e.g., *Ap.* 29d–30b, G. 470c, and below). Moreover, it is reasonable to suppose that first-time hearers/readers of Socrates' *apologia* would have supplied a similar motive: it would have been conceded by many that you often do another (and yourself) a good turn to bring his/her ignorance to their attention. Finally, and as Stokes indicates, elenctic examination by its very nature makes it rather difficult to keep its revelation of ignorance away from the awareness of an interlocutor ([2], 49). There is no need then to read 21c as *burying* the difference between detection and demonstration so as to "stop awkward questions arising" ([2], 42).

108. (1) is true, since everyone wants above all to avoid harm and possess instead the ευδαίμων life (e.g., *Ap.* 25d, *Cr.* 48b, *Eud.* 281d–e; cf. G. 499e), and that requires doing what is right (*Ap.* 28b, 28d, 30a–b; *Cr.* 48b, 48c–d; cf. G. 507d–e, 469b–c); cf. Brickhouse and Smith (8), chap. 3, and Vlastos (14), chap. 8.

(2) To do right and avoid wrong consistently requires knowledge (or elenctically tested beliefs for more consistent virtuous behavior) concerning what is right (*Ap.* 29d–30a) and an awareness of one's lack of moral knowledge (so as to avoid the wrong; see principle A' in Chapter 4.1).[109]

(3) Knowledge (or elenctically tested beliefs) concerning what is right and (especially) an awareness of one's lack of moral knowledge are obtainable primarily by means of the practice of philosophy.[110]

(4) Therefore, anyone (prima facie) ought to practice philosophy (as much as is consistent with virtue).[111]

This argument has logical force.[112] There is also ample evidence that Socrates believed its conclusion as well its premises and found that conclusion to be additionally warranted by "secular" considerations connected with our general well-being. For example, Socrates claims that "it is the greatest good for a human being to discuss virtue every day and the other things about which you hear me conversing and examining both myself and others, for the unexamined life is not worth living for a human being" (*Ap.* 38a2–6). In other words, all human beings (and as opposed to non-humans) profit from engaging in elenctic moral inquiry (if only by coming to see how deficient they are in true wisdom [*Ch.* 166c7–d2])(see also *Ap.* 22d–e, *G.* 470c).[113] Next, Socrates insists that thanks to his elenctic service

109. Cf. Brickhouse and Smith (8), chap. 2.1.6, and Irwin (4), 90–94. Note that since knowledge of the virtues appears to Socrates to be unobtainable in this life (and perhaps the next; see *Ap.* 40e4–41b7), the value of the *elenchos* lies in its ability to secure Socratic moral beliefs (e.g., that it is better to suffer injustice than to do it) and to deflate hubristic claims to knowledge. The latter is especially valuable because (1) the inclination to hubris and ignorance is perennial, and because (2) one must believe oneself in need of knowledge in order to be sufficiently motivated to search for it (see, e.g., *Meno* 84a–d).

110. Cf. *Ap.* 29d–30b, *Cr.* 46b–48d, and *Ch.* 157a–b; cf. *G.* 457c–458b, 506a ff., and 527b–e; also Irwin (4), 90–94. Here I say "primarily" because of Socrates' reliance on extrarational sources of truth (e.g., *Ap.* 33c4–7) and "especially" because of the problems connected with ascribing a constructive role to the *elenchos,* see Chap. 1, n. 14.

111. Cf. the accounts of Vlastos (14), chap. 6, (18), and (8); and the comments of Reeve, 177–179.

112. Especially if we supply the premise that we ought to do those things that provide the necessary conditions for our doing what is right, and the provision that such things may be done only if their performance is consistent with the principles of virtue.

113. As Stokes (2), 50, perceptively observes, *Ap.* 22c–d argues that since Socrates thought he was better off knowing his own ignorance, he would have thought that subjecting others to the *elenchos* and its revelations is to confer a benefit on them. Stokes later (63–67)

to the Athenians, they enjoy the greatest good (30a5–7) and that whereas the Olympic victor makes them merely *seem* happy, he makes them *be* happy (36d9–e1).[114] *Apology* 39d3–8, in turn, asserts that those many Athenians deserving moral criticism will not escape such examination by putting Socrates to death: "This way of escape is neither possible nor creditable. The best and easiest way is not to stop the mouths of others, but to make yourselves as good as you can."

Again, at both 29e–30b and 36c we are told that Socrates urges everyone to care above all for the well-being of their souls. Since, then, one ought to make one's soul as good as possible, we are allowed to infer that the moral improvement philosophical activity makes possible renders that activity an obligation for all of us (since we are all of us morally imperfect). In the *Gorgias* we find that Socrates exhorts "all other human beings" to perfect their souls, pursuing the truth by means of philosophy (507d–e, 526d–e, 527b–c; cf. *Pr.* 348c5–7), and that "if anyone proves evil in any way, he should be chastised" (527b; cf. *Ap.* 25e–26a): Presumably by means of a Socratic interrogation (at least), and through the examination by others besides Socrates who are qualified to do so (should there prove to be any). Finally, Socrates imagines that it would be an inconceivable happiness for him to test and examine people in the next life (should there be one) (*Ap.* 41b5–c7).

Although many of these assessments of the value of the *elenchos* occur well after his account of the Oracle, they nonetheless support the idea that secular considerations such as those spelled out in S, and not the Oracle, initially provided Socrates with a sufficient motive for philosophizing. Hence, there are independent, self-interested, eudaimonistic reasons for wielding the *elenchos;* viz., it keeps one from the path of hubris and rash

---

constructs a secular explanation for Socrates' sense of mission based on the idea that it would be unjust to withhold the benefits of the *elenchos* from the Athenians, but does not show how this could account for the *extent* of obligation Socrates perceives *himself* alone as under (a perception, I argue, that explains the special place of the Oracle's revelation in Socrates' sense of mission).

114. This suggests another derivation of an obligation to pursue philosophy: in view of Socrates' arguments for remaining and not fleeing Athens in the *Crito* we may expect him to argue that since he and all other Athenians have derived benefit from the institutions of the *polis,* they owe it benefits in return . . . and the greatest benefit to it would be to improve the souls of its citizens *via* elenctic philosophy (cf. Chapter 2.2 on *Eu.* 14e–15a) (Stokes [2], 63–66). Note, however (and contra Stokes [2], 65), that this will not generate the degree of determination and obligation we see instanced by Socrates; that, we will see, is what the Oracle helps to reveal.

moral decision-making (*per* A′) and secures our moral beliefs.[115] Nonetheless, Socrates saw the Oracle as revealing to him some sort of special obligation to philosophize κατὰ τὸν θεόν (*Ap.* 22a4, 23b5) distinct from that provided by secular considerations (28e, 21e–22a, 30a). The likely explanation for this, I contend, is that prior to hearing of the oracular pronouncement, Socrates had yet to (1) realize the full importance of the anti-hubristic effects of the *elenchos,* (2) see himself as specially qualified to elenctically examine all and sundry and, thus, did not yet (3) conceive of himself as obligated to pursue philosophy ceaselessly and even at the expense of those external goods that may make incidental contributions to general human happiness (e.g., money and leisure [*Ap.* 23b, 30a–32a]). He saw his duty at this point—we might say—as significantly qualified by ordinary prudential considerations and so he had yet to conceive of himself as he later did, namely, as free of the normal prudential restrictions that limit the obligation we all possess to pursue philosophy. For although Socrates has secular reasons (S) available to him for the view that everyone ought to pursue philosophy, it should be recognized that this obligation is qualified by considerations having to do with what it is that justifies doing philosophy in the first place: the development of human happiness and virtue. Hence, our duty to engage in it is mitigated by those circumstances where engaging in it would be contrary to justice and the production of happiness. As we shall see, for many people—but not for Socrates, his peers, and his true pupils—this will place significant limits on the actual opportunities for satisfying their obligation to philosophize: not so many, however, that those who flee Socratic examination are absolved from moral condemnation.

On the preceding account of our secular philosophical obligation, any individual possessed of inordinate intellectual abilities and moral integrity will be inordinately obligated to philosophize actively; and were such a person to in fact realize the degree of moral deficiency (esp. moral hubris)

---

115. With this outline of the prudential reasons for doing philosophy I lean toward agreement with Irwin (4), 91, who holds that Socrates values philosophy solely for its results (*pace* Kraut [2], 271 n. 43). The *elenchos,* for Socrates, is a means to a good end (virtue and recognition of ignorance), but nothing chosen for the sake of a final good is a good in itself (*Ly.* 219c–d, 220a–b; cf. *G.* 472c–d, 500c). See also Reeve, 177–179, esp. n. 84, who claims that the value of the *elenchos* derives (instrumentally) from its unique power to keep us from hubris and blameworthy ignorance. Against all this must be weighed Socrates' claim at the end of the *Apology* that an afterlife of *elenchos*-wielding among the famous dead (with no mention of expert-knowledge-gaining or hubris-reduction) would be an "inconceivable happiness" (ἀμήχανον εὐδαιμονίας [41c3–4]).

alleged to be present in the Athenian *polis*—as (I will show) Socrates is later made to realize by the Oracle—he would be morally negligent not to practice the *elenchos* assiduously, "stationing himself" to his task (*Ap.* 28d) even at the risk of death. Such an individual would pursue philosophy for prudential reasons of self-improvement and to ensure right moral action (*per* S), but also because piety (*per* P6) demands it. This obligation, then, is fully independent of the method of discovery of the present moral lack in oneself and others that may bring it into play: it may be by oracle, by insight, or by failing the test of Socratic examination.[116]

2. The manner in which the Socrates of the *Apology* arrived at an understanding of himself, Athens's moral deficiency, and his own obligation to philosophize must be located in his interpretation of the oracular pronouncement. Again, we should suppose that Socrates was committed to a number of beliefs concerning the nature of piety even prior to the pronouncement of the Oracle; in particular, that he was persuaded of the truth of something like principle P6.[117] Given that Socrates believed P6, we may then view the origin of Socrates' supererogatory understanding of his obligation to philosophize in this way: first, the report of the god that no one is wiser than Socrates was initially something Socrates found mysterious and paradoxical, for—given the deflationary results of his previous investigations—he was not conscious of being wise *in any way* (*Ap.* 21b4–5). Nonetheless, another theological commitment of his is that the god's claim cannot be false, "for that would not be lawful [θέμις] for the god" (*Ap.* 21b5–7). On what grounds can Socrates claim to know this? The Homeric, Hesiodic gods are notorious liars, after all, and even discounting

116. The mention of *Ap.* 28d above suggests that Socrates is capable of the previous sort of understanding of things: by suggesting that the order he has received from the god to do philosophy in Athens is comparable to the order from a general stationing him to a military post (28d–e), Socrates tacitly grants the possibility that a person might (1) initially post himself and do battle on his own initiative, (2) then be told by a general "no one's better," (3) be puzzled by that report, (4) set out to comprehend it by engaging in combat with leading warriors, (5) do so by experiencing endless successes, and finally (6)—*via* the prior belief that generals should be obeyed and that every citizen should fight to the extent that he produces good results—this person would naturally end up with the view that he has been "ordered" to fight ceaselessly and without regard to personal sacrifices (*per* 29c–d, 31a–c); cf. Stokes (2), 70.

117. The following derivation of Socrates' obligation to philosophize from the oracular pronouncement owes much to Brickhouse and Smith (6), 664; cf. Reeve, 21–32. In brief, they argue that Socrates has a sense of obligation to the god which derives from antecedently held beliefs about the requirements of piety that are not based on a direct command of the Oracle.

that kind of divinity, most ancients (and ancient eudaimonists) and moderns would still maintain that good beings might lie in order to achieve some noble end. However, as we've seen, Socrates takes it as one of his tasks to "launder" the Homeric gods: his gods are perfectly good, a goodness entailed by their boundless knowledge and wisdom. Hence, that goodness is also so vast, that conjoined with their power, they have no need to deceive (R. 381e–382c).[118]

In any case, though, grant that Socrates at this point in his interpretive sojourn holds that the god who speaks through the Pythia has said something both true and paradoxical. It would then be natural for him to reason that since anything a superior might say to an inferior under his command could conceal a demand for some sort of service on the inferior's part, and since (according to P6) piety requires that we serve the gods, it is part of his pious obligation to discover the meaning of the god's claim. Naturally, for his method of discovery, of interpretation, Socrates turns to his customary elenctic method, attempting to refute (ἐλέγξων) the *apparent meaning* of the oracular pronouncement taken at face value, not—as a literal reading of the text (and some commentators) would have it—the Oracle or the god (21b9–c2).[119] After all, how could one hope to refute that which cannot be false? Furthermore, it was not uncommon to think that the Oracle might speak in an obscure or incomplete fashion, and that any sensible person ought—if only for strictly prudential reasons—to look past any obvious meaning for whatever truer meaning might be concealed underneath (cf., e.g., *Ch.* 164e; Herodotus 1.91–92).[120] This interpretive

---

118. At *Eu.* 9c1 Socrates tells Euthyphro that the gods will listen to him, *if* he "speaks well" (εὖ λέγειν), and this usually means "speaks the truth" in Plato (e.g., *R.* 338b), indicating that for Socrates the wisdom of the gods implies a love of truth on their part. The above again indicates why it is incorrect to entertain the supposition we saw earlier (Chapter 2.2) that the gods of Socrates are *powerless* to improve souls. If they are perfectly knowledgeable and powerful—and especially if they are the creators of souls—then it is *possible* for them to create morally perfect souls that are in no need of the purification elenctic testing brings. Hence, it is *possible* for antecedent beliefs such as P6 and the belief that the gods are perfectly knowledgeable to be implanted in the soul.

119. The text says that Socrates went to those reputed to be wise, since there *if anywhere* he might "refute the divination [ἐλέγξων τὸ μαντεῖον]" by showing the Oracle (ἀποφανῶν τῷ χρησμῷ) that "'this man is wiser than I, but you declared that I was [wiser].'" Stokes (2), 34–37, raises interesting grammatical questions relevant to Socrates' intentions, but in the end concludes that the text does not support the view that his procedure expresses doubts regarding the god's veracity.

120. Any Greek would have thought it especially well advised to unpack the meaning of an oracle that makes personal reference to oneself in view of the Oracle's reputed past dealings with figures such as Croesus and Oedipus (Stokes [2], 32, 46–47; cf. Guthrie [6], 87,

activity is said to have occupied Socrates for a length of time, and that helps us to see that although Socrates says that he "supposed and assumed" that the god had stationed him in Athens (28e), that phrase does not warrant the view that his interpretation of the Oracle is due to the free, unconstrained play of reason: If Socrates were free to simply *make up* the meaning he settles on, there would be no reason for him to have been *baffled* by the Oracle for a long time (*per Ap.* 21b).[121]

So, then, Socrates proceeds to elicit the true meaning of the pronouncement "No one is wiser" by the constant elenctic interrogation of those whose claims would falsify the Oracle if true, namely, those with a reputation for possessing the sort of wisdom he understands the Oracle to be referring to: the expert moral knowledge claimed by the politicians, poets, and artisans (*Ap.* 21a–b; 22a). What Socrates discovers in case after case is that the kind of knowledge presumed by these individuals, "knowledge of the greatest things" (*Ap.* 22d7; viz., expert moral knowledge) is in fact quite beyond them. As Socrates began his elenctic interpretation of the Oracle *via* the elenctic examination of these individuals, he then gradually came to realize the meaning of the oracular phrase, a meaning that reflexively confirms the reliability of the Oracle: namely, that he *is* the wisest of the Athenians in comparison with such self-proclaimed "experts" by grasping something that they do not, namely, "that he is in truth worth nothing with respect to wisdom" (23a–b).[122]

3. Having uncovered this underlying meaning of the oracular pronouncement—that he possesses the "human wisdom" of understanding the

---

and Reeve, 23). A. D. Nock, 2:536–540, provides evidence that it was generally assumed that whatever the Pythia said must be fulfilled and that one should use one's reason to interpret the meaning of her pronouncement. However, see Stokes (2), 33, 58–62. Fontenrose argues persuasively that the Pythia's reputation for obscurity is merely legendary (as in the Herodotus reference above) and that historically she spoke "clearly, coherently, and directly" (10). For all that, it's her *reputation* that counts here.

121. Contra Vlastos's view (14), 172. Socrates also refers to his interpretive investigation as "Herculean labors" performed "on behalf of the god" (22a), and this is further testimony that—far from showing irreverence by attempting to "refute" the apparent meaning of the Oracle—it instead demonstrates the intensity of his pious commitment to always put "the god's business" first (Brickhouse and Smith [6], n. 15). Additionally, Socrates' actual procedure in this section of the *Apology* blocks the objection of those like Vlastos who hold that genuine Socratic interpretation would make the gods powerless to improve souls, on the grounds that the required antecedent beliefs of interpretation cannot be provided by the gods to those such as Socrates who *doubt* their signs, for neither here nor anywhere else does Socrates doubt the *truth* underlying what he takes to be a divinely given sign.

122. Cf. Kraut (2), 271.

depths of his own ignorance—however, why doesn't Socrates simply leave other self-deceived individuals alone? After all, why continue to pursue a course of action that causes him to be hated and, thus, plagued by pain and fear (22e)? The answer, Socrates says, is that he *had to* go on κατὰ τὸν θεόν (23b5) to examine all those with a reputation for wisdom, "*considering what the Oracle was saying*," and given that "it seemed to be necessary to regard the business of the god as most important" (22c). How important is this business? More important, says Socrates, than even the task of securing the standard human goods of leisure, family life, and money. Others whose happiness is contributed to by the pursuit of such things must also consider this business of utmost importance, but it seems that their inferior skill at *elenchos*-wielding significantly qualifies their obligation to do philosophy (23b–c, 31b–c; and see below). Socrates, on the other hand, now conceives of himself as a unique gift of the god, specially qualified to awaken the Athenians elenctically (30d–31b). Apparently, Socrates reflected on the true meaning of the oracular pronouncement and in it found an obligation to examine elenctically all human beings (especially those who conceive of themselves as possessing expert moral knowledge) without regard to everyday prudential, qualifying factors. What path did these reflections follow?

Something like this, I hypothesize: at this post-Oracle stage of his career Socrates has examined and deflated many instances of self-proclaimed wisdom and now has good inductive warrant for his developing view that he is unique in his appreciation of his understanding that he lacks wisdom (expert moral knowledge). Naturally, however, he would want to consider any case of alleged wisdom that came to his attention, since there is no way for him to be certain that there are no genuinely wise human beings somewhere on the face of the earth, and so—as he says at 21e–22a—he wishes to go to *all* those reputed to be wise so that his interpretation of what the Oracle means will remain unrefuted. This unfinished—and unfinishable—"labor," nevertheless, can be understood without postulating an obligation to do philosophy on Socrates' part.[123]

However, in virtue of his ability to deflate epistemic presumption Socrates has at this point elicited from the pronouncement of the Oracle an item of knowledge: his understanding that he lacks knowledge of virtue. Moreover, and as the Oracle has informed him, this knowledge constitutes a form of *wisdom* (human wisdom), a wisdom endorsed by the god

---

123. Stokes (2), 42–47.

Apollo.[124] Prior to the report of the Oracle, then, Socrates had not fully realized the value of the antihubristic results of the *elenchos* and thus the *elenchos* itself, and had yet to hear the corresponding oracular message that he alone of all the Athenians had best instantiated this god-valued activity. Moreover, the now-interpreted report of the Oracle is also tantamount to the claim that all other Athenians are not only lacking in the knowledge of virtue Socrates has uncovered but also in the god-valued awareness of that lack. All these results, then, allow Socrates to recognize the much greater extent to which he is obligated to philosophize in accord with the demands of principle P6. He, more than anyone, is obligated to philosophize without regard to standard prudential considerations, since— as the god has now informed him—he of all the Athenians has achieved the highest level of self-understanding, knowledge, and skill requisite to performing this labor in satisfaction of our general pious obligation.[125] He, of all the Athenians, is in the best position to serve the gods' desire that the hubris of the Athenians be removed. He too is the only person to have this prescriptive interpretation of the Oracle confirmed by the *daimonion* and backed up via other dreams and divinations (*Ap.* 33c4–7).[126]

There is also a further and less general argument made plain in the text (22e–23c): Socrates claims that he now continues to philosophize because as a result of the testing initiated by the Oracle he has come to the realization that he is being used by the god as a paradigm[127] to deliver the message that any person "is wisest, who, like Socrates has become cognizant that in respect of wisdom he is in truth worth nothing" (23b2–4).

Socrates' argument at this point seems predicated on the view expressed, again, by principle P6, that he is obligated to serve the gods. Here the service is revealed to be twofold. One service to the gods is to uphold the pious view that they never utter falsehoods (21b5–7). Since the god has

---

124. See Reeve, 33–37, on "human wisdom."

125. We should probably say here that for Socrates philosophy-as-elenctic-examination is the best method for the attainment of virtue and happiness "in the present situation"—that is, given the present state of moral ignorance in Athens—thus leaving open the possibility that another form of philosophizing might replace the use of the *elenchos*, should its propaedeutic function result in a general advance toward the knowledge of virtue.

126. I take it here that "oracles . . . and every other way in which a divinity has ever ordered anyone to do anything" at 33c4–7 must be intended by Socrates to include the *daimonion* (where perhaps, *per* the argument of 40a2–c3, it is the silence of the *daimonion*— not its active prescription—that indicates his duty).

127. Stokes (2), 44–50, argues convincingly that παράδειγμα at 23b1 is not being used in a merely instantiating sense (so that Socrates provides but one example of human wisdom), but in a recommending, paradigmatic sense (viz., "if you want to be wise, be like Socrates").

said of Socrates something that would be falsified by anyone else's turning out to have more wisdom than the minuscule portion Socrates possesses, whenever anyone claims to possess greater wisdom than that, it is then Socrates' duty to reveal the falsity of their claim elenctically. Second, since it is the god's wish to use Socrates as the paradigmatic vehicle for the delivery of the message of our ignorance of divine wisdom by claiming that no one is wiser than Socrates, then it would seem that part of Socrates' pious service in accord with P6 is to aid the god in this task. However, the message that we are all (like Socrates) ignorant of real wisdom would be rejected out-of-hand by those who believe they have expert moral knowledge, were that message to be directly asserted (recall the example of Euthyphro, if you will). Hence, its delivery must take the form of an *ad hominem* demonstration: specifically, through an elenctic refutation of the relevant knowledge claims. Thus when Socrates finds a person who pretends to moral expertise, he "come(s) to the god's aid" (23b7); that is, he serves the god Apollo in accord with the demands of piety encapsulated in principle P6 by delivering the antihubristic message of the god concerning our ignorance *per demonstrandum*.[128]

With this analysis we can see why Socrates' derivation of his duty to do philosophy from the oracular pronouncement has proved so puzzling. The prescriptive element was *not* what the Oracle provided. Rather, that element lay implicit in Socrates's antecedent commitment to obey divine commands and to the truth of principle P6.[129] What the Oracle provided was a enigmatic descriptive component that—given Socrates' commitments—*prompted* him to go on to discover the factual conditions it referred to (that his discoveries of ignorance were endorsed by the god and that the Athenians lack antihubristic human wisdom), which brought the obligations of P6 into full play (just as, e.g., I may have a duty of charity, but this duty becomes action-guiding for me only insofar as I am made cognizant of opportunities for exercising that obligation). Put another way, what the Oracle provided was "information" that—subsequent to much interpretive work—enabled Socrates to fix the scope and degree of the

128. As pointed out by Reeve, 27–28, once Socrates achieves a satisfactory interpretation of the truth of the oracle, his elenctic activities do not become useless; rather, they are valuable insofar as they continue to promote the value placed by Apollo on the importance of recognizing and avoiding hubris. This interpretation is backed up by *Phd.* 85b, where Socrates claims to be a fellow servant of Apollo (along with Apollo's prophetic swans). Cf. Stokes (2), 44–50.

129. Contra such interpreters as Grote (2), 284–287; Phillipson, 293–296; and Friedländer, 2:162.

effort and sacrifice piety required of him. For although for both pious and prudential reasons everyone ought to philosophize (even at the risk of death, since one ought simply to follow the best course [28d; *Cr.* 48b–d]), this obligation—we shall see—is qualified differently for different individuals. The Oracle, then, reveals to Socrates that in his case, the obligation to philosophize is free of virtually all the mitigating factors present in the case of other people.[130] Freedom from these, however, meant becoming the sort of refutational busybody around whom slanders begin to multiply (*per* 20d–21a).

4.2.2 Reason, Revelation, and the Delphic Oracle

Given this account of Socrates' derivation of his understanding of the nature of his mission, what does it reveal about Socratic attitudes toward the extrarational? In particular, was Socrates' use of reason "completely unfettered" by the extrarational—did he put the whole rabbit in the hat, and is it therefore a wholly elenctic rabbit?—or is oracular divination so reliable and independent a source of information for Socrates that it yields certainty?

The analysis I have provided shows, I believe, that both alternatives are unjustifiable extremes. Although on my account it is true that Socrates interprets the oracular pronouncement against the backdrop of his preexisting beliefs concerning piety and his preexisting secular warrant for doing philosophy, as I argued in section 4.1 these are the sorts of rational constraints Socrates requires all of us to employ with respect to the extrarational. This is true especially when A′ is called into play by one's taking the extrarational to offer behavior-guiding advice that impinges on the tenets of traditional morality. But, again, it would be wrong to infer from this that for Socrates the extrarational poses no *potential* conflict with

130. Thus, on my interpretation, Reeve is quite incorrect to suggest that *only* Socrates has a religious reason for living the examined life (72). Rather, principle P6 implicitly commends philosophy as a pious practice for all (see Chapter 2.2). It is still, for example, just as much our prima facie duty to demonstrate to others that the god did not lie when it declared Socrates wise as it is Socrates' duty. Reeve's own account (72) seems to contradict itself: as he has it, only Socrates is religiously obligated to be an elenctic missionary, but what grounds his obligation is the strong commendation of its antihubristic results by the god Apollo (interpreted as a kind of disguised imperative [27]), and that *would* seem to make elenctic philosophy a religious requirement for all. Cf. Vlastos (18), 231–238, and (14), chap. 6, 173–178.

reason, or that reason is "utterly unconstrained" by the extrarational. It is apparent to Socrates, for instance, that the *daimonion* has stopped him from philosophizing in certain ways—e.g., in the way concomitant to a life of politics (31c–e)—and therefore it should be perfectly conceivable to him that it might stop him from philosophizing-at-all-costs, or philosophizing altogether, and this despite all the purely secular, rational warrant he has on hand for pursuing philosophy. Furthermore (and again), Socrates reports being puzzled for *a long time* by the answer of the Oracle (21b7), and that is something that we would *not* expect if reason had an utterly free hand at interpretation. Also, it is hard to see how "no one is wiser" could be thought by Socrates to be open to utterly unconstrained interpretation (as, say, revealing a command to commit injustices).

Finally, it is evident that although Socrates had plenty of rational, secular warrant for supposing he had a duty to philosophize prior to, during, and after Chaerephon's visit to Delphi, it appears that it was the oracular pronouncement—together with the extrarational input that later followed (33c)—that allowed him to recognize the lack of mitigating limitations on that duty as applied to his own person. For it is only *after* he elenctically examines all those self-professed moral experts in the course of trying to refute the surface reading of the oracular claim taken as true that Socrates comes to a recognition of the true worth of his recognition of his own ignorance (and the true worth of the method that revealed this), the extent of moral deficiency in Athens, and his talent for *elenchos*-wielding. Thus it is the extrarational impetus provided by the Oracle that prompts him to realize that since one ought to philosophize to the extent to which that furthers the good, that he, *Socrates,* is inordinately obligated to philosophize by virtue of these revelations.[131]

Is, then, this confidence based on a judgment taken to be *certain,* as others (e.g., Brickhouse and Smith, nn. 67, 87 above) might suggest? I think not, since first of all, and as we have seen, there are epistemologically deflationary markers in this section of the text (e.g., "supposed and assumed" [28e5]). In particular, note that at 23a–b he carefully says that "*probably* the god . . . means this by the oracle," and "He *seems* to [be] making me an example."[132] Next, consider Brickhouse and Smith's

131. Thus, although Socrates' secular and religious reasons are not wholly independent, it is the Oracle that explains the extraordinary *extent* of Socrates' particular philosophical obligations; cf. Vlastos (14), chap. 6, 173–178, and Reeve, 72.

132. Stokes (2), 48.

own account. "Divinations," for Socrates, they say, *"properly construed, provide [certain] truth."*[133] I agree that Socrates takes the oracular pronouncement in its pre-interpretive form to be extremely reliable, but even Socrates would have to allow for the possibility of human error in the chain of message-transmission stretching from the god through the Pythia and Chaerephon to himself. And as I've previously argued, the reliability of its "proper construal"—its post-interpretive meaning—is a function of the method of interpretation employed. If Socrates had used a Ouija board for interpretive purposes we should not give it any weight at all, even if it had spelled out, "Do philosophy ceaselessly. Best of luck, Apollo." But Socrates didn't use a Ouija board. Rather, he used a rather more reliable inductive method: he accumulated *many* cases where self-professed experts were unable to pass the test of the *elenchos,* and that indicated to Socrates that probably *all* such human experts were not wise, something he didn't know previously, and that hence his wisdom partially consisted in knowing this. That by itself gives him inductive probability at best, then, for his belief that "no one is wiser than Socrates." For, again, there may be genuine human experts he has yet to encounter. Socrates may even have mistakenly judged some interlocutors to have been refuted who were not (and who were unable or unwilling to point out that Socrates' seeming refutation was no refutation at all). Of course, once Socrates begins to use this inductive generalization to derive his duty to philosophize, the probability of the accuracy of his interpretation begins climbing to the high level of probability that he sees it as having, since the resulting judgment "the god wishes me to do philosophy" is confirmed by his previous and ongoing rational, secular warrants for philosophizing.

This level of high probability is in general all Socrates can expect of himself and others when dealing with the interpretation of external extra-rational phenomena (e.g., the dreams of others, the flights of birds, the utterances of an oracle, and the sayings of an inspired prophet). But there is one key difference between these individual cases and that of the oracular pronouncement: Socrates claims not only a secular rational warrant for doing philosophy (*per* S) that corroborates his interpretation, but (*per Ap.* 33c4–7) also those warrants provided by an abundance of other extrarational indications of various kinds (voices, dreams, the *daimonion,* and so on). These all must be imagined to constrain rational interpretation in var-

---

133. Brickhouse and Smith (7), 128; cf. (8), 195, and (12), chap. 5.5.

ious ways; hence, when every subsequent interpretation of extrarational signs corroborates the initial interpretation of the oracular pronouncement and the prior rational warrant for philosophizing across the span of many years, Socrates is in a uniquely secure position. He has a body of evidence extremely large in instances and broad in source. Nonetheless, it is not enough to give him certainty.[134]

In sum, I think that in the above account of the place of the Oracle in Socrates' life we have found an instance of what some call the "*elenchos* of interpretation*," a relation of rational examination to the extrarational, where interpretation is nonetheless constrained by what is taken to be true (since divine) informational content.[135] But I've also shown that such an examination of extrarational material can play a confirmatory role of conclusions arrived at rationally; for example, in the way that Socrates' examination of his *Phaedo* dream confirms his secular reasons for philosophizing. Once such confirmation has been received, one may in conformity to A′ "rely on the extrarational." In the case of the Oracle, the reliance is upon a piece of extrarational input rationally interpreted that reveals the existence of heretofore unrealized conditions that bring into play a long-standing obligation of piety. One may in turn find the converse procedure at work at *Apology* 31d–32a (and *Phaedrus* 242b–c). In this passage the command of Socrates' divine voice is first followed by obedience and then by a rational account that explains the moral correctness of the divine injunction, which then in turn confirms the wisdom of Socrates' initial obedience.

134. This agrees with Reeve's denial of certainty to Socrates' interpretation of the Oracle (71); however, he misses the *confirmation* that interpretation receives from the *daimonion* (33c4–7) when he says that "the next elenctic examination may show . . . [his interpretation] . . . to be mistaken." Such extrarational confirmations (which Reeve acknowledges are unchecked by further rational interpretation or justification [69]) make Socrates' interpretation of the Oracle much less open to revision than a "standard" elenctically justified belief. Stokes (2), 72–74, argues that to buttress the warrant the Oracle provided by citing the "oracles" (μαντείων) of 33c5 encounters various problems; primarily (1) the use of the plural, and (2) the late placement of the passage. I see no problem with (1), though, since it would be a natural way for Socrates to refer to the constant confirmatory role play by his "customary oracle" (μαντική [40a4]), the *daimonion*; (2) simply shows the *apologia* to mimic realistic oral discourse, where it would be natural to focus first on the event that inaugurated one's interpretive quest, and only later mention whatever confirmatory "signs" one encountered along the way (which then do not *pace* Stokes [2] "demote" the Oracle [73]). Stokes complains (73) that we are not told how to test these signs, despite Socrates' claim that they are "easy to test" (33c8), but for all we know Socrates just means that his dreams, etc., are easily asked about and would be found weighty by any good dream-respecting Athenian.

135. See Woodruff (1), 83–84; cf. Stokes (2), 37–41.

4.2.3 The Extent of the Duty to Philosophize

In the previous section I have relied on the results of Chapter 2.2 to show that, as Socrates conceived of it, philosophical activity is a pious obligation for all insofar as it is a service that aids the gods in at least some portion of their work.[136] In addition to those religious considerations, we saw that an argument (S) for a "secular" obligation to do philosophy could be constructed from explicitly Socratic principles. Those considerations led us to infer that the moral improvement philosophical activity makes possible renders that activity an obligation for all who are morally imperfect. We also saw that in the *Gorgias* Socrates exhorts "all other human beings" to pursue philosophy, submitting (presumably) to elenctic interrogation at the hands of Socrates (at least), and those of others who are qualified to do so, should there prove to be any.[137]

This last qualification raises an important question. To this point I have assumed that the philosophizing Socrates is urging on his fellow Athenians is to be conducted after the Socratic model: an activity pursued through the relatively autonomous use of the *elenchos,* which aims at freeing people of their pretensions to wisdom (*Ap.* 23b, e, 28e, 38a) and their overly zealous care for material things (29e–30b), directed at the perfection of the soul (29e) through its possession of the most precious good there is— virtue (30a–b, 31b). Is there any justification for this assumption, or is it possible that Socrates believes that *our* philosophical practice—as distinct from his—should consist primarily in submitting ourselves to Socrates (the sole master of the *elenchos*) for belief-testing, a testing requiring only the exercise of a less intellectually demanding sort of "rational reflection" on our parts? I think there is both conceptual and textual evidence that supports the former assumption over this latter proposal, although there is not as much—nor is it as explicit—as I would like:

1. There is no textual evidence in favor of attributing a conscious distinction between *elenchos*-wielding and "rational reflection" to Socrates. Moreover, it seems that much serious rational reflection often involves an

---

136. The claim of pious service upon us is substantial: our aid to the gods, for example, is said to be more important than what the many think of us (*Ap.* 21e).

137. Given *Ap.* 20e and 31a (cf. *G.* 521d), it seems unlikely that Socrates (or Plato) would grant that there are any *elenchos*-wielders in Athens as qualified as Socrates, but that need not completely absolve others from the duty to philosophize actively.

elenctic style of inference and the sort of one-step refutations produced by the use of counterexamples.

2. Socrates may be a genius of the first order, but he would be foolishly arrogant to think that he alone possesses the necessary intellectual requirements for utilizing elenctic procedures with at least some measure of success; e.g., some noted Sophists could successfully employ it. It would also be very odd indeed for someone with Plato's dialectical skills to credit his teacher—in the very act of reconstructing that teacher's many ἔλεγχοι— with the belief that no one else possesses the intelligence demanded for producing successful elenctic encounters.

In reply to these first points, it might be said that *intellectual* skill—in our contemporary sense of, say, an ability in logic—is not what Socrates would appeal to in order to justify a limitation on our use of the *elenchos*. Rather, it might be our comparative moral inferiority that would lead him to restrict our use of the *elenchos*, which, as Socrates' own life illustrates, is a tool fraught with danger even for the wisest of Athenians. However plausible this line of thought might be, though, I do not think it is a Socratic line, as the following textual considerations indicate:

3. At *Gorgias* 487e–488a Socrates says that we should all inquire how to live. So here and elsewhere I should think that Socrates would be guilty of misleading us if *he* firmly believes—but does not make clear to us (as he does not)—that we are not supposed to attempt the inquiry he urges on us in the same manner in which he inquires.

4. At *Gorgias* 447c–448c Chaerephon is invited to question Gorgias (and then Polus takes his place), and the style of questioning is clearly elenctic in nature; again, at 458a Socrates imagines himself being elenctically examined by *another*.

5. At *Apology* 23c–d Socrates clearly states that the young who follow him *imitate* him by *examining* (ἐξετάζειν) others, and the implication is that they succeed in some measure to refute others elenctically (see also *R.* 539a–e).

6. As Vlastos has claimed, in Socrates' characterization of what he would be giving up if he stopped philosophizing—"search nor philosophize" (*Ap.* 29c8)—the "nor" is epexegetic; and at 41b5–6 "to philosophize" is ren-

dered "to examine" (ἐξετάζειν; where this is a common reference to the *elenchos;* cf. *Ap.* 28e5–6).[138] Thus since we should all be contentiously eager to know the things the aforementioned search promises (*Ap.* 30a–b; cf. *G.* 505e), it seems to follow that we must all try to philosophize and so all try to wield the *elenchos.*

7. At *Apology* 31b2–5, Socrates claims that "I always do *your* business [i.e., what you should be doing] . . . persuading you [often by means of the *elenchos*] to care for virtue" (my emphasis).

8. At *Apology* 37e5–38a5 we find Socrates contrasting his god-ordered obligation to philosophize with another consideration in favor of a general obligation to philosophize:

> For if I say that this [to cease to philosophize in Athens] is to dis-obey the god and that because of this it is impossible to keep quiet, you will not be persuaded by me, on the ground that I am being ironic. *And on the other hand* . . . this even happens to be a very great good *for a human being* [i.e., for lots of people]—to make speeches every day about virtue and all the other things about which you hear me conversing and examining both myself and *others* [my emphasis].

In other words, doing what Socrates does—exhorting and elenctically ex-amining himself and others ("making speeches")—is a very great good (i.e., it should be preferred to many other sorts of activities) for a great number of people. Since we all ought to pursue the good, we all ought to examine ourselves and others elenctically.

9. At *Apology* 39d it is forecast that people other than Socrates will soon refute his prosecutors (i.e., elenctically examine [ἐλέγχοντες]).

10. At *Euthydemus* 282a Socrates declares that "every man shall *in every way* [thus, elenctically] try to become as wise as possible," insofar as he desires happiness (my emphasis).

11. At *Charmides* 166c–d (passim) Socrates claims that by wielding the *elenchos* he tests his own beliefs; thus, when he enjoins us to test ours, it is

138. Vlastos (8), 31–32.

natural to suppose that he is recommending that we perform a similar testing (of ourselves and others).

12. Socrates even advises the jurors who voted to condemn him to trouble his own sons "in the *very same way* I pained you [i.e., elenctically]" (41e2–3; my emphasis), should they prove uncaring of virtue, and that such a "troubling" would be just treatment (42a1).[139]

Given all this, then, it looks as though Socrates believes that everyone ought to examine both themselves and others, and that they ought to do so in the way in which Socrates "examines"; that is, everyone ought to philosophize in the elenctic fashion, both through interior dialogue and through the examination of others. But to what extent did he think that he and others ought to practice philosophy? What goods, in other words, ought to be sacrificed in the pursuit of philosophical activity? Should one, for instance, pursue philosophy at great personal sacrifice even if one is an inept philosopher? If one does not pursue philosophy with a relentlessness worthy of Socrates, does that render one impious by virtue of a violation of principle P6? What if a person is already willing to concede their ignorance of virtue and affirms the truth of the principles that the *elenchos* leads to? Is such a person still obligated to do philosophy? Finally, if one has received an oracular "command" to do philosophy, is one's duty to pursue it of the same extent as Socrates' reputed duty?

First, it is hard to believe that Socrates would advise literally every human being (and so, e.g., children and idiots) and regardless of probable outcomes to engage in philosophy in what I will term the "active mode"; namely, the manner of philosophizing that Socrates most commonly exemplifies (where one submits others to elenctic interrogation; this, in contrast to the "passive mode," where one engages in philosophy by serving as the interlocutor to an *elenchos*-wielder).[140] More than anything else Socrates desires to promote virtuous action and happiness,[141] and if philosophiz-

---

139. In their comments on Vlastos (16), Brickhouse and Smith (14) have argued on the basis of several of the passages I have cited above that "though Socrates may be safely assumed to be its [the *elenchos*'s] greatest master, any adequate account of the elenchus must permit its being sensibly commended to any of us inclined sincerely to employ it" (195); now see Brickhouse and Smith (8), chap. 1.

140. I think this is true despite the fact that Socrates generally welcomes all comers to elenctic discussion. Anyone he meets at any given time (*Ap.* 29d), as well as young and old, citizen, foreigner, or slave (*Ap.* 30a; *Meno* 82a ff.). See Vlastos (8), 34–35, and my Chap. 1, n. 13.

141. See Irwin (4), 91.

ing—normally the means to those ends—were to undermine this some-how, then the obligation to engage in it would be to that degree vitiated. Socrates, for instance, does not advise everyone to despise financial gain or to ignore it completely in favor of elenctic dispute. Rather, he only advises people not to think *more* of financial gain than of well-being (*Ap.* 36c, 29e–30a) and the knowledge that is needed for the virtuous use of such material goods (*Ap.* 30b; *Eud.* 282a). Socrates may hold that the wisdom secured by philosophy ensures our happiness (e.g., *Eud.* 281e–282d), and that one ought not to take account of bodily danger but only what is just (e.g., *Ap.* 28b, d; *Cr.* 48c–d), but this does not entail that philosophical practice guarantees the acquisition of wisdom or that it cannot on occasion come into conflict with what is just or that certain external goods are not necessary for the happiness of at least some sorts of people. In the *Crito* (47d–e) and the *Gorgias* (505a), for example, Socrates suggests that the possession of a healthy body is a necessary condition for anyone's leading a truly satisfactory life.[142] Hence, at the point that one's philosophical practice seriously threatened the loss of such a good without promising a net gain in goodness and virtue for oneself and others, one could justly neglect philosophy.

Next, Socrates insists (*Ap.* 33a, 36c) that his own philosophical activity is to be construed as being in some sense a "private" mission, and that if some of Socrates' students imitate him by elenctically examining others,

---

142. Irwin (4), 93. In a subsequent essay (8), Irwin has argued for an adaptive, Stoic account of Socratic wisdom. On this view, wisdom secures happiness irrespective of prevailing external conditions. Given the passages I have cited which conflict with this (noted by Irwin), I am disinclined to accept his view. Rather, I am more persuaded by Vlastos (3), that for Socrates there are a class of "subordinate constituents of the good: non-moral goods. . . . [W]e shall be happier with than without them" (201). It is quite conceivable that for some individuals the continued practice of philosophy might present the possibility of a loss of such goods with no countervailing possibility of a gain in wisdom: here the greater happiness is secured by refraining from philosophizing. A much stronger argument for my view that goods necessary for our greater happiness could be undermined by our philosophizing is provided by Brickhouse and Smith (11) and (12), chap. 4.2; cf. (8), chap. 4. They argue for a Socratic distinction between virtue, considered as a condition of the soul, and virtuous activity. On that basis they then attempt to show that Socrates believed in the necessity of the former for happiness, but the sufficiency of only the latter (thus rejecting the "Sufficiency of Virtue for Happiness Thesis" [held by Irwin (4), 100, and Vlastos (3), 192–196]; cf. Brickhouse and Smith [12], 163–166, and [8], chap. 4). Accordingly, since a severely damaged body may prevent one from performing the virtuous actions necessary for "living well," a person may be harmed bodily to such a degree that he is better off dead rather than alive (regardless of his philosophical powers). With this, it is then easy to imagine situations in which the threat of this sort of harm (without the promise of a countervailing production of goodness elsewhere) will qualify a person's obligation to philosophize.

they do so of their own volition (αὐτόματοι [*Ap.* 23c3–5]).[143] I take this to mean that when Socrates admonishes others to do philosophy (*Ap.* 29d, 30a–b, 38a), he is not thereby setting himself as a standard for us whereby if we fail to pursue philosophy in the active mode regardless of other normally prudential factors (e.g., bodily danger) we are morally culpable.[144] Given this and the above, then, I want tentatively to credit Socrates with an instrumentalist qualification of both our pious and secular obligations to do philosophy; that is:

IP   Philosophy ought to be practiced to the extent to which that practice may be supposed to result in moral improvement for everyone concerned.

This attribution is additionally warranted by the fact that both the pious and secular obligations established by P6 and S for engaging in elenctic activity were themselves established by appeals to instrumentalist considerations. What renders philosophical activity pious is its performance with the intent to serve the gods by furthering people's well-being, and what renders philosophical practice an obligatory practice without reference to the gods is that it—once again—aims at that same end (see Chapter 2.2).

In the *Apology* (31c–32a, 36b–c) we find that Socrates himself limits the scope of his philosophical activity for consequentialistic reasons. There he justifies his failure to engage in public political activity—an activity that in his case would involve philosophical practice, and in an area that might reasonably be supposed to be ideal for his god-ordered work—on the grounds that doing so would leave him prematurely dead and so unable to accomplish the good that he might otherwise accomplish in a private practice. As he says at 36c2–3, he did not enter into matters where he stood to be of no *benefit* to anyone, either himself or others. Indeed, it would seem that to engage in the *elenchos* without due regard for whether or not the consequences would be beneficial would be to act intemperately, and intemperance is not a good (*Ch.* 175e). Thus the examination philosophy provides is not to be conducted without an eye to consequences; rather, since such examination is worthwhile only insofar as it is productive of

143. This term may well imply the unbidden doing of an act.
144. It is true that *Apology* 38a is a blanket exhortation to philosophize. There it looks as though Socrates is saying that everyone should spend at least a good part of their day doing what he does in the agora. Nonetheless, Socrates nowhere explicitly demands of others the same selfless devotion to philosophy that he demands of himself, and even then, he moderates his own mission with an eye to long-term consequences (*Ap.* 31c–32a, 36b–c).

virtuous humility, correct moral beliefs, and happiness (or at least useful perplexity), one ought to philosophize (or not) only when doing so (or not) maximizes these outcomes.[145]

The *Theaetetus*, finally, contains what might be the record of a genuine Socratic practice that supports the view that Socrates did not understand the obligation to philosophize to be a perfect (unqualifiable) duty. In the course of comparing himself to a midwife (148e–151d), Socrates observes that a number of students have left him sooner than they should have, and that to some of those—presumably because of their intemperate nature and "lack of understanding"—he has refused further philosophical intercourse with himself (on the advice of the "divine voice" [150d–151a]).[146] Here it looks as though such students ought not to philosophize, even with the assistance of the paradigm practitioner of philosophy, because it has been estimated that there will be no profit in it for anyone (cf. 151b; *Thg.* 129e ff.; *Alc. 1* 105d ff., 127e). Again, those whose minds are (in contrast to the previous pupils) unable to have even a few conceptions of their own have no need of Socrates, and so he finds them intellectual partners who will better profit them (*Tht.* 151b). But here, one of the alternative partners Socrates has in mind—Prodicus—will surely not engage the pupil in Socratic *elenchos* and self-discovery. Rather, the implication at this point seems to be that, as Myles Burnyeat has so aptly put it, "an empty mind

---

145. Irwin (4), 91. See also G. Anastaplo, 18–20, who argues that the Socratic examination of one's life requires the examination of the lives of others, since all share in the one life of the community: an understanding of one's life requires an understanding of its setting. Examining a number of others (and not just a select few, who might play into one's vanities) also seems a prerequisite of self-examination because of its therapeutic protection against the natural human tendency toward hubris and self-deception. These two reasons for pursuing the *elenchos* with a great number of people constitute a brief reply to Reeve, 72, who holds that the explanation for the greater scope of Socrates' activity is primarily based on religious, not secular, reasons. Cf. Vlastos (14), chap. 6, 176–178, and (18), 235–237, who holds that only a religious reason for doing philosophy can explain Socrates' other-regarding mission (in contrast to what he alleges are only self-regarding secular motives for pursuing philosophy). My position here, in contrast, is that while both the religious (*via* P6) and secular (*via* S) prima facie obligations to do philosophy are of equal scope and strength, the Oracle had prodded Socrates into understanding that the usual qualifications attaching to both warrants for philosophizing do not apply in his case.

146. I find the episode Socratic, since the practice of rejecting students is paralleled elsewhere (*Mem.* 1.1.4; *Thg.* 128d8ff.; *Alc. 1* 105d5–106a1), and because there are birthing metaphors and some possible allusions to the midwife image in the *Clouds* (e.g., 137, 633 ff.; see D. Sider. However, I am persuaded by Burnyeat's arguments, (1), 7–16, that the midwife metaphor may be a Platonic invention, and naturally, I want to concede that the late date of the composition of the *Theaetetus* significantly undermines its value as a source of reliable information on the views of the Socrates of the early dialogues.

which has no conceptions of its own (cf. 148e) is fitted only to be sown with another's seed."[147] But this is nonphilosophical "instruction" of the sort that Socrates explicitly disavows, and which is to be distinguished from philosophical examination. For instance, at *Apology* 19d–20a, Socrates denies that he provided the sort of education men such as Prodicus offer, and that he has been no one's teacher (*Ap.* 33a–c; i.e., he has practiced elenctic philosophy with them, but he has not provided set doctrines). Thus, this indicates that Socrates believed that some individuals are better off if they do not philosophize and are therefore—by virtue of the consequences—excused from the duty to do so.

The attribution of the consequentialistic principle (IP) to the historical Socrates also has corroboration independent of the Platonic *corpus*. In Xenophon's *Memorabilia,* for instance, Socrates praises men who possess enough self-knowledge to know that "by refraining from attempting what they do not understand they make no mistake and avoid failure" (4.2.25–26). This would seem to apply equally to all activities, even to engaging actively in elenctic philosophizing. Again, *Memorabilia* 4.7.1–10 indicates that Socrates took pains to make his students "independent in doing the work *that they were fitted for*" (4.7.1; my emphasis) and urged prudence in intellectual work; e.g., he limited the study of mathematics to what was useful (4.7.8).

4.2.4 The Duties to Philosophize

Given all the above, I think we can confidently ascribe to Socrates the principle (IP) that although philosophical activity is, in the main, an obligation of piety and eudaimonistic self-interest, since such obligations are warranted by a system of ends, the obligation to philosophize may be instrumentally overridden. Socrates assuredly believes that we all ought to do what is just without regard to death or other physical harms per se, but then clearly, if doing philosophy should happen to be contrary to justice in some circumstance, one ought not to philosophize. This principle, then, in conjunction with our previous observations, allows us to derive the following account of the differing particular qualified obligations to do philosophy borne by differing sorts of individuals on the basis of their moral need and philosophical talents, as those factors bear on their potential for pro-

147. Burnyeat (1), 9.

ducing *eudaimonia* through philosophical activity. Unfortunately, this account must remain somewhat speculative in its details because of the lack of corroborating text and a clear Socratic specification of the nature of *eudaimonia*.

1. Most individuals (of the age of reason), ranging from those possessing very limited intellectual gifts to those who are masters of elenctic dispute—and regardless of moral development—will be obligated to pursue philosophy in the passive mode by serving as interlocutors in elenctic discussion whenever (within reason) so engaged by an effective *elenchos*-wielder. Indeed, it would seem obligatory to seek out an expert craftsman in moral training—or at least an effective *elenchos*-wielder (e.g., Socrates)—if one is to gain in well-being from such an encounter (*Cr.* 47c–48a; *La.* 184e–185e, 201a–b).[148] Since "Socrates is the wisest" of the Athenians, and is yet ignorant of what virtue is (*Ap.* 22c–d), this will mean that virtually all humans are obligated to seek elenctic treatment (and take any resulting refutations to heart). Moreover, the experience of being so refuted by the *elenchos* is even of greater benefit to oneself than actively refuting another (by virtue of the great value of remaining free of hubris [*Charm.* 166c7–d4; cf. *G.* 458a]).

The *elenchos*-wielder himself must, in addition, be honest in the sense that his or her intention must be to establish truth, belief-consistency, or moral improvement. There is no obligation to undergo the elenctic examination of an ill-intentioned Sophist unless (oddly enough) there promises to be a net gain in virtue for all. Given IP, exceptions to the obligation to undergo elenctic examination will exist for those who are unable to profit from such examination because they lack sufficient intellectual powers (e.g., the power to recognize contradictions), and especially for those who, in addition to this, modestly admit their own lack of moral knowledge and nonetheless both concede Socratic principles of virtue and consistently act (fortuitously) in accord with those principles.[149] Socrates does not himself, for instance, relentlessly impose the *elenchos* on those who do not make

---

148. As Socrates has it, there is no worse evil for a man than a false opinion on the subject of the proper care for the soul (*Cr.* 47a–49e; cf. *Phd.* 115e; *G.* 458a): even the perplexity brought on by the *elenchos* or a Socratic confession of ignorance is thus an important gain (*Ap.* 23a–b). Hence, we should seek out the "charmer" who will help us attain either truth or perplexity (*Ch.* 175d–176c). See Kraut (2), 235 ff.

149. Should such consistent action even be possible; see premise (2) of argument S. I am imagining here that this possibility would not require the doing of philosophy in even the passive mode.

illegitimate inferences from particular knowledge claims to general knowledge claims concerning the moral virtues (the "greatest things" [*Ap*. 22c–e]). Elenctic examination is generally reserved by Socrates (in his own case) for those who implicitly contradict the Oracle by asserting confident moral knowledge claims (e.g., the "experts" of *Ap*. 22a–d), which, if true, would be constitutive of real, divine wisdom. Since he does not seem to demand of himself that he impose the *elenchos* on others of the above sort, then he would not seem to demand of us that we do so (cf. *Mem*. 4.2.25 ff.), or that such subjects themselves must undergo it.[150]

Individuals of the above sort may at least satisfy the demands of piety connected to P6 by performing virtuous acts with the intention of pleasing and serving the gods and other self-effacing acts of piety (such as those which constitute correct Socratic sacrifice).[151] Aside from such rare exceptions, submitting to effective *elenchos*—engaging in philosophy in the passive mode—is pious in accord with P6 and is an obligation for virtually everyone because doing so will lead to moral improvement in those who require it (virtually everyone). As for those rare individuals who do not require improvement or who at least concede Socratic principles of virtue and their own ignorance—should there even be any—doing philosophy passively serves as a check on the development of unjustifiable confidence in one's epistemic state and on the reliability of previously accepted beliefs. On the other hand, those who lack an epistemic humility proportionate to the actual state of their knowledge (e.g., Euthyphro), and who stand in the greatest need of moral development, would be those most obligated to

150. Given Socrates' blanket claim that the unexamined life is not worth living (*Ap*. 38a), I will have to say that Socrates would find the present class of individuals a very small one at best. This Socratic principle admits of exceptions because, as Irwin notes, (4), 91, "self-examination [for Socrates] is worth while [solely] because of the importance of correct beliefs about morals," and "when [moral] knowledge is found, the elenchos should no longer be an essential method of moral instruction" (97). In these cases I am discussing, there is no concern that the *elenchos* is to be valued apart from its results (because, say, "the right way of holding beliefs is good in itself apart from its results" [97]), since people who are intellectually deficient cannot "rationally and autonomously" employ the *elenchos* in a defense of their views.

151. See Chapters 2.2 and 3.4. There is but one instance—a dubious one at that—of Socratic religious sacrifice in the Platonic corpus (*Phd*. 118a). Nonetheless, there are numerous passages in Xenophon's *Memorabilia* (1.1.2, 1.1.19, 1.3.64, 4.3.16–17, 4.6.4–6) that testify to Socrates' orthopraxy. Again, although Xenophon may well have exaggerated the extent of that orthopraxy, he seems to confirm a degree of traditional practice independently testified to in Plato (e.g., *Eud*. 302c, *Phdr*. 229e, *Phd*. 117c). In accord with my interpretation of piety (P6), secularly just acts will also be pious acts if performed with the intent to please and serve the gods.

serve as interlocutors to effective *elenchos*-wielders. After all, if all evil is the result of ignorance, the greater one's ignorance the more likely it is that one will be (and do) evil.[152]

As for third parties to an elenctic discussion, it would seem as though they are free to listen in or not, depending solely on interest (*Ap.* 33a). The actual practice of philosophy (active or passive) involves for Socrates a degree of intellectual engagement that does not seem ordinarily possible for third parties. They are not, for instance, required to state honestly what they believe.[153] Nonetheless, it seems clear that Socrates believes that everyone ought to be interested in the subject he examines people on— moral improvement—and our texts show some support for the view that bystanders to an elenctic discussion are obligated to listen in, since they will be helped merely by paying attention to such discussions. For instance, Socrates claims that "you [jurors] will even be helped by listening [to Socrates's *apologia*]" (*Ap.* 30c4), and in the *Gorgias* he is willing to give a *speech* on virtue rather than abandon the audience (505e–509e).[154]

2. The obligation to engage actively in *elenchos*-wielding would seem to be in direct proportion to the likelihood of moral development for interlocu-

---

152. Given the attention he shows to the case of Euthyphro (in both the *Euthyphro* and elsewhere [*R.* 377e ff.; *Laws* 886b ff.]), Plato appears to take Euthyphro as a paradigm case of hubris and its dangers: As Socrates indicates (*Eu.* 4a–b, 4e, 15d–e), the gap between his arrogant claims of knowledge and the actual state of his knowledge was so wide that he was prepared to prosecute his own father on the basis of those false claims (*Eu.* 3e–5a).

153. See, e.g., *Eu.* 9d7–8, *Cr.* 49c11–d1, and *Prt.* 331c4–d1; cf. *G.* 458a1–b1, 500b5–c1; *R.* 349a4–8; and Vlastos (8), 35–38.

154. Of course, Socrates may well be thinking here that he is a uniquely qualified individual, and that we need not pay attention to just any *elenchos*-wielder who happens to be in town. He may think that he is the only competent *elenchos*-monger around. This possibility raises a problem that crucially affects our duty to undergo the *elenchos:* is our obligation to undergo elenctic examination an obligation to undergo (1) only the *elenchos* given by Socrates, (2) only good *elenchos*, or (3) any *elenchos* whatsoever? If my account is close to the truth, then Socrates will reject the idea (1) that we are under no obligation to philosophize once he is dead, as well as (3), since we ought to positively avoid some elenctic encounters (where false beliefs will be encouraged by incompetent or ill-intentioned *elenchos*-wielders). So although it is then clear that our obligation is to seek out (2) only good *elenchos*, our problem will then be to identify it. But if I am in great moral ignorance, how shall I recognize good *elenchos* and good *elenchos*-wielders and so differentiate the philosophers from the sophists and fools? (Socrates may have had a greater faith in the power of divine guidance than we dreamed.) Perhaps Socrates would have simply advised the pursuit of all elenctic encounters that appear to pose no significant danger, trusting in what few true beliefs even a Thrasymachus will possess and in the power of the soul to profit more from the possession of true beliefs and their testing than it suffers from the possession of those that are false.

tor, audience, and *elenchos*-wielder, which must in turn be calculated on the basis of a number of interrelated factors, primarily the intellectual ability of the *elenchos*-wielder in question to employ the *elenchos* effectively (e.g., demonstrate the inconsistency of inconsistent moral beliefs), and the moral status of the *elenchos*-wielder. This first factor is relevant since inconsistent and false moral beliefs will only be encouraged in everyone by failures of the *elenchos* to reveal the inconsistency and falsity of such beliefs (cf. *Phd.* 115e, *G.* 458a). To instill inconsistent and/or false beliefs is to harm others, and this must never be done (*Cr.* 47e–48a, 49b–c). Hence, a person who is unable to wield the *elenchos* effectively is excused, say, from attempting the public examination of a clever Sophist advocating immorality; indeed, he or she positively ought to avoid doing so. However, when the danger is less grave, it would seem permissible—though not obligatory—for those less skilled in the *elenchos* to employ it.[155] On the other hand, one skilled in the *elenchos* ought to examine himself and others as much as is consistent with an overall increase in moral virtue, even if death is a risk (*Ap.* 28b). Because of the stiff intellectual requirements involved in the successful employment of the *elenchos* and the standard distribution of such skills across human communities, those obliged to wield it will be of fewer numbers, it would seem, than those obligated to suffer it.[156]

Another important factor bearing on our obligation to philosophize actively is the moral status of the *elenchos*-wielder. A Sophist of the immoralist variety, for instance, ought not to wield the *elenchos* in an attempt to convince others of what is patently an immoralist thesis (e.g., that it is morally acceptable to do what is unjust), for this poses a real danger of harm to others. In a case like this, in fact, Socrates would probably deny that such an attempt would be an instance of philosophical practice as he

155. For instance, it is apparently permissible for the jurors who found Socrates guilty to "trouble" his sons with elenctic examination (*Ap.* 41e).

156. Despite this limitation on the number of people obligated to philosophize actively, one still gets the overall impression from the early dialogues that Socrates generally sees little need to restrict access to the philosophical enterprise, especially in the passive mode. He appears to think that philosophizing in even a limited fashion is a good for virtually all people. Clearly, Plato came to restrict philosophy to the well-qualified few because he perceived some danger in this attitude, thinking—it seems—that Socrates was overly generous in his estimation of the power of rational persuasion and the intellectual and moral potential of ordinary people (see, e.g., *R.* 494a, 519d, 537e–539e [esp. 538d–e]). For an excellent discussion of the very different attitude the mature Plato exhibits toward unrestricted access to (and so a general obligation concerning) philosophizing and the *elenchos* (e.g., in the *Republic*), see Nussbaum (1), esp. 81–88.

understands it, since this would not be a search for either truth or moral virtue. On the other hand, a virtuous person with elenctic skill ought to examine himself and others in preference to all other (external) goods.

4.2.5 Socrates' Duty to Philosophize

In light of the preceding discussion, I want now to reconsider the case of Socrates. On my account of Socratic piety and philosophical obligation, any individual possessed of inordinate intellectual abilities and moral integrity will be inordinately obligated to philosophize actively; and were such a person to in fact realize the degree of moral deficiency alleged to be present in the Athenian *polis*—as Socrates has been made to realize by the Oracle—that person would be morally negligent not to practice the *elenchos* aslsiduously, "stationing" himself or herself to the task (*Ap.* 28d) even at the risk of death. Such an individual would pursue philosophy for prudential reasons of self-improvement and to ensure right action (S), but also because piety (P6) demands it, since it is a likely desire of the gods (esp. Apollo) that all humans should possess the human wisdom of knowing the full extent of their ignorance of virtue and thus obtain some measure of *eudaimonia*.[157]

On this account, Socrates must be seen as someone with an inordinate degree of self-confidence and relative certainty concerning his own intellectual talents and moral worth. For given Socrates' endorsement of IP, his interpretation of the Oracle's pronouncement as a command to do philosophy ceaselessly and regardless of material and bodily consequences must result from a judgment that he, Socrates, is uniquely qualified as the person who best stands to net the greatest gain in good for himself and others currently residing in Athens.[158] In fact, and in confirmation of my thesis

157. On this view of piety, then, it is primarily the desire of the gods for our well-being that is the source of our altruistic pursuit of philosophy in the active mode. It is for this reason above all that we should try to refute others (for prudentially, we might only seek to be refuted ourselves). Nonetheless, refuting others in fulfillment of our pious service will benefit us as well, for the gods are not indifferent to the welfare of good men (*Ap.* 41c–d; *Eu.* 14a; *Mem.* 1.4.5–19). See my Chapters 2.2, 3.2, and 5.2 for evidence that Socrates would attribute a desire for our happiness to the gods.

158. On my account, Socrates' refusal to propose exile as a punishment (*Ap.* 37c–38a) results from a judgment that since he must philosophize no matter where he goes, death, or pointless wandering at best, will be his fate (*Ap.* 37d–e). Additionally, his death may further

that the duty to do philosophy is consequentially variant, this is just how Socrates is portrayed (*Ap.* 30c–32a, 36b–e). He is said to be a rare gift of the gods (*Ap.* 30a, 30d–e), a great benefactor of the city (*Ap.* 36d).[159] Furthermore, Socrates' obligation to pursue philosophy actively is portrayed in the *Apology* as being of far greater extent than that which is borne by others. He has neglected his affairs, both public and private, and his family (23b, 31b), he has done it without the rewards of enjoyment, money (23c, 31b–c), and leisure (23b), and it has been a seemingly inhuman and unreasonable (31b1–2, 31b7) vocation in just that way: an obligation over and above the obligations of others that would be wrong to ignore or moderate (39d, 37e). He alone, finally, seems to be the one Athenian assigned with the task of exhorting others to philosophize, even at the risk of death. Whether or not we agree with the self-assessment on which he based this account of the extent of his own duty—and his ultimately optimistic judgment about the philosophical potential of his fellow human beings—it proves difficult not to wish that he was right.

But such sentiments aside, it will be noted that the preceding account has made use of the Socratic view that the practice of philosophy enjoined on us is connected with the improvement of what Socrates continually refers to as "the soul." This raises issues addressed in the next chapter; namely, whether Socrates possessed a positive doctrine of the soul, and if so, what the implications of that view are for his moral theory, theology, and eschatology.

---

his divine work. Thus, he should not propose exile. Other alternative punishments that would diminish his capacity for the virtuous activity of philosophizing would for that reason make his life not worth living and are thus to be rejected (see Brickhouse and Smith [12] and [8], chap. 6.5; and now, Calef [3]).

159. As the *Gorgias* has it, it is in fact only Socrates—of all the Athenians—who practices true statesmanship (521d).

5
Socratic Religion

5.1 The Soul and Its Fate

According to Socrates, the philosophical activity in which he engages and which he has been divinely commanded to urge on all and sundry has as its primary goal the care and tendance of the ψυχή, the soul (τῆς ψυχῆς ἐπιμελεῖσθαι [*Ap.* 29e1–e3; Xen. *Mem.* 1.2.4–5]; θεραπεία ψυχῆς [*Pr.* 312b8–c1; *La.* 185e4]). Thus, he goes about asking: "My good friend . . . are you not ashamed of caring for money and how to get as much of it as you can, and for honor and reputation, and not caring about or taking thought for wisdom and truth and for your ψυχή, and how to make it as good as possible?" (*Ap.* 29d7–e2). Again, Socrates exhorts "young and old alike" "not to care for your bodies or for money sooner than, or as much as, for your ψυχή, and how to make it as good as you can" (*Ap.* 30a7–b2; trans. after Burnet).[1] It is safe to presume that since the ψυχή is the focal point of Socrates' philosophical mission he must have had at least some minimal account of what it is (after all, it's the odd man who urges others to care for something he knows not what). So what, then, did Socrates understand the ψυχή to be?

This question is an important one, and no exact consensus on its answer has emerged. But there is now wide scholarly agreement that we can at least be sure of part of the answer, namely, that Socrates was committed to—or at least weakly "accepted"—the view that the soul is such that its

1. Burnet (6), 243.

postmortem fate is not annihilation, but continued existence in another realm.[2] In what follows, I shall contend that this attribution is not warranted by the evidence, and that if we must credit some sort of eschatological stance to Socrates, a variety of considerations—especially the *Apology*'s argument for death's goodness (40c–41d)—show that a qualified agnosticism is our best bet. This result contributes in a variety of ways to our understanding of Socrates' moral theory and his rational reformation of traditional Greek religion; in particular, it helps to illustrate once more how the religious dimension of Socratic philosophy rests on a unique amalgam of skeptical restraint and religious commitment. Before considering the evidence for a Socratic belief in immortality, it will prove useful to develop first a brief account of Socrates' conception of the soul.

5.1.1 Socrates on the Soul

As the previously cited passages from the *Apology* and elsewhere make clear, the ψυχή is above all for Socrates the subject/agent of moral judgment, choice, and action—that in which vice and virtue reside (e.g., *Cr.* 47d–48a). But more than this, the soul is also the *entire, real self*, the "I" of consciousness and personality, and the part of us that engages in intellectual activity. The *Protagoras,* for instance, shows Socrates raising the question of what the consequences are of entrusting the care of *one's soul* to the Sophists, where this is said to be the same as putting *oneself* into their hands (312c, 313a–314b).[3] And since according to Socrates the soul is the seat of all the virtues, and the virtues are forms of knowledge (314a–

2. N. Smith has suggested in correspondence that some will argue that *Phaedrus* 229c–230a shows that Socrates merely accepts the customary view on immortality and is not disposed to look for contrary evidence, since that is not in his line of philosophical interest and since such acceptance nowhere conflicts with his moral theory. But while the distinction between committed belief and the less intense epistemic state of mere acceptance may have merit, it will be seen that there is no one customary view on immortality sufficiently dominant in fifth-century Athens for Socrates simply to acquiesce to.

3. Note too that in Socrates' paraphrase of *Apology* 29d9–e2 at 36c5–7 the subject of mental and moral well-being is referred to by means of a personal pronoun (ἑαυτοῦ); cf. *La.* 185e–186a; *Pr.* 312c, 313a–e (ψυχή: a2, a7, b2; σαυτόν: b5, c2); and Beckman, 20–21. Although, as I shall argue, the *Gorgias* is not a reliable source of Socratic thought on the soul, note that at 486e, for example, its Socrates employs "my soul believes" for "I believe" (Vlastos [12], n. 28, and [14], 55). It also seems likely that Socrates retained the traditional view of the soul as a "life-force"; cf. Xen. *Apol.* 30, *Mem.* 4.1.4, and *Crat.* 399d–400a.

b), it is thus the part of us that engages in discursive reasoning. It is, in short, our mind, our νοῦς.⁴

Throughout the early Socratic dialogues this view is linked to the idea that the ψυχή is not identical with the body, but rules over it from "within." The *Charmides*, for example, distinguishes fair souls from fair bodies (154d–e; cf. 156e–157d, 160a–b; *Mem.* 2.6.32, 4.1.2), and locates the virtue of temperance in the soul (175e).⁵ In the same way, the *Crito* (47d–48a), *Laches* (190b; cf. 185e, 192c), and *Protagoras* (312c; cf. 313a–314b, 351a–b) portray the soul as a distinct governing agent lodged in a body. To "care" for it is to endeavor to make it as good and happy as possible by cultivating its virtue and guarding it from vice (e.g., *Cr.* 47c–49b), a task best accomplished through correct intellectual training, elenctic testing, and virtuous action.⁶ In addition, since the soul is the locus of what makes life worth living, virtue is to be valued more than physical health (*Cr.* 48b; *Ap.* 28d–e, 30a–b) and the soul must be deemed more valuable than the body.⁷ Finally, while some have argued that Socrates conceives of the soul as a nonseparable aspect of a person's living body, rather than a distinct element "housed" in a body, this seems clearly incor-

4. See, e.g., *Ch.* 157a–d, 160a–b; *Pr.* 313c–314b; *HMi.* 372e–373a; and *Mem.* 1.2.53, 1.4.8–9, and esp. 13–14, where the soul is described as engaging in various cognitive activities (e.g., remembering, reasoning). Also, at *HMa.* 296d8 Socrates speaks of what "our ψυχή wished to say"; cf. *Mx.* 235a–c. Aristophanes as well testifies to the unusual intellectual and moral role of the ψυχή in Socratic thought when he has Strepsiades derisively describe Socrates' students as "*wise souls* [ψυχαί]" (*Nu.* 94; cf. 414–415, *Av.* 1555). Note, however, that when Socrates entertains the possibility that death is a migration of the soul to another place (*Ap.* 40c–41c), his picture of the disembodied ψυχή in Hades is not that of a purified Orphic-Platonic soul contemplating invisible, bodiless Forms. Rather, it is something that moves about establishing contact with other individuals and continues to have somewhat ordinary perceptual experiences (thus retaining aspects of the Homeric notion of the soul as a "shade").

5. At *Charmides* 155d–157c, Socrates recounts the view of a physician-follower of the "God-King" Zalmoxis of Thrace, who held that just as one needs to cure the entire body to cure the head, so one must cure the soul to cure the body, since "all good and evil, whether in the body *or the whole person,* originates . . . in the soul" (156e6–8). This passage suggests that Socrates entertained a more complex relationship between body and soul than simple nonidentity (with the soul "inhabiting" the body), one wherein the soul is the principle of organization for the whole person conceived of as a psychosomatic unity. But Socrates never actually endorses this theory in the text, and so it would be rash to attribute it to him (*pace* Beckman, 21–22). Cf. D. Claus, 170–172.

6. See, e.g., Vlastos (3) and (20), and Brickhouse and Smith (10) and (11); see also their (8), chaps. 3 and 4, on the place of virtuous action in Socratic moral theory.

7. *Cr.* 47e–48a; *Eud.* 279a–281e; *Pr.* 313a–b; *HMi.* 372d–373a; cf. *G.* 477a–e, 511c–512b, and *Alc. I* 131a–c; and see Brickhouse and Smith (5), 159, and (8), 206–207.

rect in light of the preceding passages.[8] Such a view is also incompatible with Socrates' conviction that it is genuinely possible that death results in a separation of the soul from its body followed by a migration to another "place," a migration that leaves no part of the soul behind (*Ap.* 40c–41d; cf. *Cr.* 54b–c, *G.* 523a–527e).[9]

Socrates' conception of the ψυχή as an "ego-soul"—a center for self-consciousness, sensation, rational thought and choice—might suggest that he locates the origin of all the passions and appetites there. But while the soul, as the locus of all conscious experience, must also be the location of *felt* appetitive and emotional experience, there is reason to think that for Socrates the appetites themselves (at least the "bodily appetites" such as thirst) are properties of the body, not the soul (cf. *Phd.* 81b). Socrates, after all, appears to hold that vicious conduct motivated by appetite is a purely intellectual failing due to ignorance of virtue (e.g., *Pr.* 352b–e, *Mem.* 3.9.5, *EN* 1144b, *EE* 1216b), and were he to also think that the noncognitive appetites are a constitutive part of the soul, that would suggest that he endorses a complex psychology wherein the soul has "parts." But it is Plato, not Socrates, who is generally understood to have developed this sort of psychology with his tripartite model of the soul: a model apparently developed in reaction to the sort of Socratic intellectualism just mentioned, since it accepts the existence of incontinent, nonignorant vicious conduct (ἀκρασία) by granting the irrational factors of appetite and passion an autonomous motivational role *within* the ψυχή (*R.* 435a–444e). This consideration (and some textual evidence) strongly suggests that Socrates located many such nonrational factors in the body rather than the soul, thereby undermining the potency of their challenge to reason's rule.[10]

Beyond this modestly spare account Socrates goes not much further, if at all. True to his disavowal of "divine wisdom" (*Ap.* 20d–e; cf. 19c–d) and his focus on the moral dimension of things (to the relative neglect of epis-

---

8. See, e.g., Beckman, 19–23.

9. Note also that *Memorabilia* 1.4.8–10 has Socrates asserting the nonsomatic nature of the mind/soul; cf. *Phd.* 115b1–116a1, where Socrates holds that to call his body (rather than his soul) "Socrates" is false.

10. Contrast *Pr.* 352a–360d with *R.* 442a–c, for example; see Vlastos (12), n. 65, and (14), 86–91, and esp. *Mem.* 1.2.23–24, 1.3.14–15, where Socrates locates carnal pleasures, passions, and appetites in the body. Also, since Socrates imagines that his soul might enjoy a lively, pleasant, conversational association with the dead (*Ap.* 41a–c), it would seem that various emotions have their source in the soul, whereas there is no need or reason for bodily appetites such as thirst to "carry over."

temology and metaphysics), he is unwilling to expound a more detailed metaphysics of the ψυχή.[11] He gives concise testimony to this at *Crito* 47e8–48a1 by speaking of the soul as "that in us, *whatever it may be*, that has to do with justice and injustice" (cf. *Sym.* 218a3).[12] It is sufficient for Socrates—a moral philosopher pure and simple—that the soul should be both the agent and the object of his ethical inquiries, the locus of our conscious experience, and a thing nonidentical to the organism that gives it agency in the material world.

I shall not attempt to canvass here the historical influences on Socrates' view of the ψυχή. But Burnet seems to me right when he says that the originality of Socrates' contribution lay in his combining the Ionian view of it as the seat of consciousness with the Orphic-Pythagorean doctrine of the purification of the ψυχή.[13] For these latter schools of thought—and unlike the Homeric view of the soul as a powerless shade—the soul is a persisting individual thing, independent of the body (whose death it can survive), a fallen divinity in the tomb of the body, requiring moral purging and care (Herod. 2.123; Eurip. *Hipp.* 1006; cf. Pindar O. 2.68–70, fr. 131b), all eminently Socratic requirements (although it appears that for both Orphics and Pythagoreans the soul did not incorporate the normal personality). Pythagoras, like Socrates, is also supposed to have urged self-examination on his disciples (D.L. 8.22) and was a devotee of Apollo (Orpheus's reputed father).[14] Finally, it seems likely that Socrates would have been influenced by Democritus, Gorgias, and the early sophistic and medical writers, who took an interest in the moral value of the ψυχή, its correlation with the body (σῶμα), and psychosomatic soul-therapy. So although Socrates' use of ψυχή was highly original, it was not entirely without precedent.[15] Socrates' greatest contribution is surely his continual

11. Vlastos (14), 47–48. Note too that unlike Plato, Socrates never addresses the question of whether the soul is immaterial or not in the early dialogues ([14], 55; cf., however, *Mem.* 1.4.8–9).

12. Vlastos (12), 94, and (14), 55.

13. Burnet (6), 257.

14. For further discussion of the development of the Bacchic, Orphic, and Pythagorean conceptions of the soul, see Burkert (2), 296–301, and (3), 133–135, 162–165; W. Jaeger (3), 88–106; and E. Rohde 2:1–37 (and for evidence that Socrates would have been knowledgeable about these developments, see below).

15. Thus Guthrie (6), 149, hesitates to endorse Burnet (6), 245, that no one before Socrates had ever said "that there is something in us that is capable of attaining wisdom, that this same thing is capable of attaining goodness and righteousness, and that it was called 'soul' [ψυχή]."

insistence on the importance of the ψυχή and his systematic integration of it into his moral psychology.[16]

5.1.2 Death and Immortality in the *Apology*

It is a natural temptation to suppose that Socrates' distinction of human ego-ψυχαί from the bodies that possess them, together with his view that the soul is a precious gift of perfectly moral gods who ensure that no harm comes to the good person,[17] led him to adopt the view that the most likely postmortem fate of the soul is continued conscious existence. It has also appeared to some that Socrates reveals a positive faith in immortality in the *Crito* (54a–c) when he has the Laws speak confidently of the life-to-come in Hades.[18] Finally, the concluding myth of the *Gorgias* (522c–527e) seems to clinch the case, for there Socrates confidently declares that death is a separation of soul from body followed by a trial before divine judges, judges who reward just souls with an eternally pleasant afterlife in the Isles of the Blessed and sentence unjust ones to punishments in Tartarus.[19] Not surprisingly, then, these considerations have led virtually all scholars to conclude that Socrates believes that the soul has a life beyond the grave.[20]

16. See Claus, esp. chap. 5, and Guthrie (6), 147–153; cf. Vlastos (12), 93–95, and (14), 53–56, esp. n. 37, and E. A. Havelock (2), 197–201.

17. E.g., *Mem.* 1.4.13–14, *Ap.* 41c9–d2, *Eu.* 14e11–15a2, and *R.* 379b; see Chapter 2.2 and McPherran (14), 302–309; Vlastos (14), 162–166.

18. Vlastos (12), 94, and (14), 55. Again, however, this passage may indicate only a non-committal "acceptance" of immortality. Note that although *Menexenus* 243e–244b shows Socrates urging an audience to offer sacrifices and prayers in order that two parties of war dead might be reconciled, the speech is supposedly not by Socrates but by Aspasia, the dramatic date of the speech is twelve or thirteen years *after* Socrates' death, and its style suggest that Plato intends to parody contemporary oratory, not deliver doctrine; see Guthrie (3), 4:312–323.

19. Vlastos (12), 94, and (14), 55. Socrates displays his conviction that this account is true no fewer than four times (523a1–3, 524a8–b1, 526d3–4, 527a5–b2).

20. E.g., Burnet (6), 257; Guthrie (6), 160–162; A. E. Taylor (4), 31; Vlastos (12), 94–95, and (14), 54–55; and now most recently, Brickhouse and Smith (5) and (8), chap. 6.5. Taylor is even moved by the above to claim that "it requires a singularly dull and tasteless reader not to see that his [Socrates'] own sympathies are with the hope of a blessed immortality" (31). But—dull and tasteless though it may be—we may expect a philosopher of Socrates' rigor to have distinguished between sympathy and reasoned judgment. Although Vlastos, Guthrie, and Taylor want to make immortality an article of unargued *faith* for Socrates, this is somewhat at odds with Vlastos's own view, (14), 157–178, that Socrates is a consummate rationalist, willing to commit himself to the truth of only those propositions that he can ground

Notwithstanding Socrates' *hopes* on this issue, however, the evidence is at best equivocal between Socratic agnosticism and Socratic commitment, with the smart money riding on the former.

If any dialogue gives us warrant for attributing a view to Socrates, it is the *Apology,* and there at least we find evidence of agnosticism.[21] First, at 29a4–b6 Socrates asserts that to fear death is to presume a knowledge of the nature of death that we humans simply do not have; in particular, someone who fears death assumes that they possess the "wisdom" that death is always a bad thing (presumably a piece of the "divine wisdom"— the expert moral knowledge—he earlier disavowed [20d–e, 23a–b]). But it is presumptuous to fear death as "a fate worse than life" then; rather, for all we humans know, death could be the greatest of blessings (although this too is something we do not know with certainty; cf. 37b5–7).[22] Socrates is wiser than others on this matter not by having certain and complete knowledge about the events following death, but by realizing better than anyone his profound lack of such knowledge. Death is therefore not to be feared, for we lack certain and complete knowledge of what it is, and because in comparison to what we *can* be sure is of importance—how to do what is right and avoid injustice—death, whatever it may be, is of distinctly secondary importance (29b, 32d; cf. 35a–b; *Cr.* 48b, 53a–54b; cf. *G.* 522d–e). And again, given our ignorance, we have to agree that death might be not only "nothing to fear" but "the greatest of all goods" (29a8).

This passage assures us, then, that at the very least Socrates does not profess *expert knowledge* about the nature and value of death.[23] However,

---

through reasoned reflection (*per* his interpretation of *Cr.* 46b4–6). M. Morgan (2), chap. 1, is—to his credit—more restrained. On his account, Socrates' affiliation with imported, ecstatic rituals and cults (e.g., that of Zalmoxis) led *Plato* to think of Socrates as committed to the soul's immortality (31), but that all we can say with any confidence is that Socrates "seriously entertained—and perhaps also adopted" a belief in the immortality of the soul (30). Beckman, 19–23, then, is the exception to all this: he argues that Socrates takes the soul to be only an aspect of the body and thus must think that it stands a good chance of perishing. As a result, his Socrates is an agnostic on the issue of immortality. While I reject this particular line of argument, I agree with Beckman that *Apology* 40c–41d is evidence of Socratic agnosticism (cf. J. Adam [2], 344–346, as well, who appears to take this line).

21. Contra Burnet (6), 257, who holds that the *Apology*'s insistence on the soul's need for care (and its identity with waking consciousness) allows us to infer as a "necessary corollary" that Socrates held the soul to be immortal.

22. Brickhouse and Smith (5), 156, and (8), 202.

23. Once again, we ought not to think that Socrates disavows *all* knowledge. As a human, he possesses some garden-variety nonmoral knowledge and as a veteran of the *elenchos* has gained a "small bit" of "human wisdom" (*Ap.* 21d6): the knowledge that—unlike those who

there is a curious and little-discussed problem in Socrates' analysis of fear: While fear of death (*not* fear of dying; cf. *G.* 522e) does presuppose a commitment to the view that death is bad, that commitment needn't take the form of a claim to expert knowledge.[24] I would think Socrates would have to concede this, given his later argumentative attempt to disabuse the jury of the fear of death on the grounds that death is a *good* thing and not bad (40c–41d). Hence, Socrates must agree that someone might fear death simply because they have what they take to be a rationally grounded commitment (short of a claim of expert knowledge) to the badness of death. There is a simple and plausible solution to this puzzle, however: it is reasonable to suppose that in the previous passage Socrates is speaking of the *kind* of fear *most* people exhibit toward death. So when he claims that "people fear it [death] *as if they knew it were the greatest of evils*" (*Ap.* 29a8–b1) he is saying that *most* people fear it with the sort of intensity and conviction that depends upon their ranking it as not just an evil of some sort or other, but as the greatest of them all, something that typically involves the confident assumption of a determinate account of *how* death is evil (i.e., expert knowledge of the "things in Hades"). Socrates' remark that he lacks sufficient (ἱκανῶς [29b5]) knowledge of the events following death also supports this reading: what Socrates disclaims is knowledge of the sort *sufficient* for generating intense fear, that is, expert knowledge that death is bad. Hence, Socrates may allow that moderate fear of death that takes it to be some kind of evil *could* be based on a proposition held with a lack of complete conviction and without a complete account of the "things in Hades," but that this just isn't the case for the great majority of those to whom he speaks. Nonetheless, and as we shall see next, Socrates would find even this limited sort of presumption unwarranted since he thinks that it is unreasonable to fear death and think death bad, for in-

---

believe they have knowledge of virtue—he does not possess such knowledge (and that human knowledge is not worth much and that only the god is wise [23a–b]). See Brickhouse and Smith (12), chap. 2; McPherran (15), 364–365, and chap. 4.1.5; Reeve, 33–62; and Woodruff (2).

24. D. Roochnik, 212–220, holds that Socrates' analysis of the fear of death is inaccurate because such fear is simply a response to the pure, *unknown* possibilities that death poses. But this strikes me as a non sequitur: Socrates would presumably respond that such an account of intense fear of death still involves the presumption that one *knows* that one of death's unknown possible outcomes is extremely bad (just as I might intensely fear becoming unemployed not simply because of its unknown possibilities, but because I presume to know that one genuine possibility it poses is quite bad).

stead, reason dictates the belief that death is a good for all (possibly so great a good [29a8] that everyone is better off dead).

Subsequent to his conviction and condemnation, Socrates closes his defense speech with a "friendly chat" (39e1–40a2) designed to console the jurors who voted for his acquittal by persuading them that his death will be a good thing.[25] Socrates offers them two reasons for the truth of this claim: first, he recounts the "great proof" of the goodness of *his* death provided by the repeated failure of his *daimonion* to interfere in the trial-proceedings (*Ap.* 40a–c, 41d); and then, he confirms this "proof" by producing a general argument for the proposition that death is no evil *for anyone* (40c–41d).[26] It is now commonly agreed that these assurances are not in conflict with Socrates' previous disclaimer of knowledge of the "things in Hades" (29a–b), since neither the daemonic "proof" nor Socrates' argument presuppose or purport to establish any expert knowledge claims. As he will next argue (40c–41d), *either* a substantive life-after-death *or* annihilation can be the good fate indicated by the *daimonion*'s silence.[27] Moreover, the "great proof" is only directly relevant to the postmortem fate of *Socrates,* indicating to him that *he* is "about to do something good." Although this conclusion might appear to credit Socrates

---

25. M. Miller suggests in correspondence that Socrates' previous uncompromising declaration of agnosticism (28e–30b) is a more sincere expression than what now follows, delivered as it is before an audience of undecided jurors in whom he wishes to generate self-examination and *aporia*. As he sees it, the argumentative standards are loosened when Socrates now turns to console the "friendly jurors" with some "story-telling" (διαμυθολογῆσαι [39e5]). Although I do think Socrates is being quite sincere at 28e–30b, I don't see any need to suppose that things then "loosen up," especially in view of Socrates' interest in not harming souls with falsehoods or half-truths. Also, there's no reason to suppose that Plato is using "story-telling" to indicate anything less than what is rigorous (cf. *G.* 523a–527e, where the "story" is said to be *true* [523a, 524ab, 526d, 527a–b] and rationally defensible [527a–b]).

26. Brickhouse and Smith (1) and (12), 237–257, offer an exhaustive discussion of the "great proof." For my purposes I shall simply follow their account in thinking that what Socrates takes the silence of the *daimonion* to provide is "excellent inductive reason for supposing that the net result of all his actions [composing his trial] is no evil," and is thus a good ([13], 247). As I see it, since Socrates holds that the level of assurance provided by the *daimonion*'s silence alone makes the goodness of his death a practical certainty, the confirmation of this provided by the argument that follows explains why it is that Socrates can hold his death to be good with such utter conviction at 41d4 (again, δῆλον carries with it a suggestion of certainty and the most secure sort of knowledge). For a detailed account of how Socrates conceives the relation between extrarational signs (esp. the *daimonion*) and discursive rationality, see Chapter 4.1 and McPherran (15).

27. Brickhouse and Smith (5), (8), chap. 6.5; E. Ehnmark, 105–122; R. Hoerber (1), 92; and G. Rudebusch, 35–45, all save Socrates from this threatened inconsistency in roughly this same way.

with the sort of wisdom and expert knowledge he disclaims, it does not, since it is not *general* nor does it specify in any detail *how* it is that his death—or death in general—is a good thing. Again, while for most people *intense* fear of their death implies their presumption of a confident knowledge *that* death is evil and *how* it is evil, Socrates' own confidence that his particular death will be good and his consequent lack of intense fear of it doesn't imply a positive or complete knowledge of *how* death is good. This is in part why at the very end of the *Apology* Socrates can say that it is "unclear" (ἄδηλον) whether it is the live jurors or the soon-to-be-dead Socrates who will enjoy a better fate (*Ap.* 42a3–5), and yet still claim that it is "clear" (δῆλον)—that is, that he has nonexpert knowledge—that *his* death is good.

Despite his lack of wisdom on the fate of the soul, Socrates treats the silence of his *daimonion* as evidence that not only is being dead now good *for him* (since it releases him from his "troubles" [41d3–5; cf. *Cr.* 53c–54b]), but that death is good *for everyone*.[28] This "great proof," naturally, is not "great" enough to offer much consolation to jurors skeptical of the *daimonion*'s authenticity, and so Socrates now offers the jurors "much hope" (πολλὴ ἐλπίς [40c4]; cf. 41c8) concerning death by demonstrating that his explanation of the *daimonion*'s silence admits of independent, rational confirmation. Construed as an attempt at formal argumentation, Socrates' reflections take the form of a constructive dilemma: (1) Being dead is either (a) like "being nothing" (μηδὲν εἶ ναι [40c6]), with no perception (μηδὲ αἴσθησιν; [40c6], cf. 40d1) of anything; or (b) it is like a journey, "a change and migration of the soul from here to another place" (40c7–9). (2) If death is (a) the first alternative of annihilation, then death is like an eternity of dreamless sleep without perception, and as such, would be a "wonderful gain" (θαυμάσιον κέρδος [40d1–2]; cf. 40e2–3). For in comparison with the other experiences of our lives, a dreamless sleep would be counted better and more pleasant than virtually any of those, even by the Great King of Persia, who presumably must find nearly all of his waking experiences quite pleasant (40d2–e4). (3) If, on the other hand, death causes the soul to undergo something like (b) a "change and migration," and *if* various unspecified "things that are said" (τὰ λεγόμενα [40e5–6]) are true, then (c) one will arrive in Hades and associate with its

28. This is implied by Socrates' remark that "probably what has happened to me has turned out good, and there is no way that those of us are right who suppose that being dead is bad" (40b7–c1), and by his then going on to argue for the view that death is good (40c4–e1).

inhabitants, which include great judges, poets, and heroes.[29] As Socrates sees it, to meet and converse with such individuals—and especially to engage them in elenctic cross-examination—would be an "inconceivable happiness (ἀμήχανον εὐδαιμονιας [41c3–4]). (4) Thus, Socrates concludes, death is not bad, but good (cf. *Phd.* 84e–85b).

5.1.3 Some Objections and Replies

Not too surprisingly, Socrates' reflections—construed as an attempt at rigorous argument—have been found wanting by a number of commentators.[30] First, it has been held that the alternative of annihilation (a) cannot be seriously intended, since what makes dreamless sleep pleasant are the perceptions that one has upon waking (and without perception there can be no pleasure).[31] However, the reply to this is straightforward: Socrates surely does not think that for death-as-annihilation to be good it must involve any sort of positive sensation, but rather, probably holds that by comparison with the events that fill most of our lives, death—*modeled* after dreamless sleep—is relatively untroubled and, thus, is a "wonderful gain" in a relative sense (for virtually all of us).[32] It is also typical of Socra-

29. Namely, judges such as Minos, Rhadamanthys, Aeacus, and Triptolemus; poets such as Orpheus, Musaeus, Hesiod, and Homer; unjustly persecuted figures such as Palamedes and Ajax, and heroes like Agamemnon, Odysseus, and Sisyphus. For a discussion of Socrates' list of names, see G. Anastoplo, 8–29, 233–246.

30. E.g., P. J. Armleder, 46; Reeve, 182; and Roochnik. For more charitable accounts, see Brickhouse and Smith (12), 257–267, (1), and especially their revised account in (8), chap. 6.5; Ehnmark; Hoerber (2); and especially Rudebusch.

31. Roochnik, 214–215. M. Miller has noted in correspondence the *strangeness* that Socrates—the hero of the self-examined life—should appeal to the opinion of the nonphilosophical Great King and praise the *cessation* of consciousness (while going on in the next breath to call an afterlife of elenctic examination an "inconceivable happiness"). While acknowledging the strangeness Miller points to, though, I think we should note that it is really the lived *experience* and not the opinion of the Great King that Socrates appeals to (and surely Socrates is right to use the King as an example of someone who—unlike most of the jurors—really has experienced the positive extremes of most pleasures). Note, too, that those to whom Socrates holds out the pleasures of annihilation are in all likelihood not going to decrease the frequency or intensity of their experiences of inner conflict by much (even if they convert to the Socratic mode of life) before they die. Hence, the cessation of inner conflict *via* annihilation could mark a real gain in a Socratically acceptable sense.

32. Brickhouse and Smith (12), 258–259. Rudebusch, 37–40, has also offered a promising account, according to which Socrates sees a distinction between "sensate" and "modal" pleasures, where only the former sort require a consciously aware subject feeling a sensation. But

tic argument to treat opposites such as pain and pleasure as exhaustive alternatives, so that annihilation, which is without pain, must be counted as a pleasure. And although (as Socrates recognizes [40d–e]) others may not share his positive assessment of permanent unconsciousness, that does not make his view senseless.[33] On the contrary: it is quite in the gloomy spirit of much popular, ancient Greek sentiment,[34] and agrees perfectly with the Apollonian tradition endorsed by Socrates which holds that for mortals to expect the immortality enjoyed by the gods is sheer impious presumption (cf. *Ap.* 23a).[35]

The next objection is more telling: Socrates has appeared to some to be assuming without any justification that he has exhausted all the postmortem possibilities with his two alternatives when in fact there are any number of unpleasant eschatological possibilities that might be imagined even

---

a modal pleasure—like a night's undisturbed sleep or complete absorption in an activity—is still a valuable thing, and if death is *like* such a pleasure then it too may be said to be good.

See now Calef (3), who attempts to show that death-as-annihilation is counted a "blessing," "a great advantage," and "pleasant" by Socrates, since the best and most pleasant life is the virtuous one. Because continued life for Socrates requires an escape from Athens, something that would diminish his virtue and seriously impede his leading an examined life, even annihilation then is a "pleasure," since it saves Socrates' soul from corruption (see *Cr.* 47a–54e).

33. Of course, one might still speculate that although Socrates apparently thinks that annihilation—insofar as it means the end of pain—is good, he must then think that those responsible for putting us into this painful situation—the gods—are not so good after all. See my speculative solution to this Socratic "Problem of Evil" below at n. 96.

34. E.g., *Il.* 17.446–447, 24.525–533; Lysias 6.20; and Herodotus 1.31.

35. It was often held that immortality is the jealously guarded prerogative of the gods alone, a view preserved in the formula "Earth to earth and air to air" in Euripides' *Suppliants* 533 and the epitaph of those who fell at Potidaea (*I.G.* 1.945 [*C.I.A.* 1.442]); cf. Burnet (6), 248–249. As Guthrie (2), 176, puts it, the belief in immortality "seemed a barbarous tenet to most of the Greeks, whom we know to have been brought up in the tradition of the aristocratic gods of Homer, with whom any infringement on their privileged position as the Immortals was a deadly sin and a courting of destruction." Note too the connection between Sleep and Death in Homer (*Il.* 14.231, 16.672, 16.682). Brickhouse and Smith (5), n. 11, point out that a number of ancient sources counted total extinction to be a probable (or quite possible) outcome of death; e.g., *Phd.* 69e–70a, Hyperides 6.43, Democritus fr. 297 (Diels), and Xenophon *Cyr.* 8.7.19–23. Rudebusch, 40, observes that Pindar *Pyth.* 8 suggests that death is our natural state, life the anomaly. For surveys on Greek attitudes and practices concerning death, see Mikalson (1), chaps. 7 and 10, and esp. p. 80; Dietrich; Garland (1); and Zaidman and Pantel, 72–79. Recent discoveries concerning the popularity and rites of those who promise a life beyond the grave such as Dionysus and Orpheus (e.g., the Hipponion and Pellina tablets [see, e.g., F. Graf, S. Cole]) do not do much to undercut this assessment. The Elusinian Mysteries, as well, gave *promises* of a better fate than that faced by noninitiates, but no more than that; says Burkert (1), 29: "There was no dogmatic faith in overcoming death in mysteries."

if death *is* a migration to a place of some sort (e.g., a place where vultures nibble your liver à la Tityos [*Od.* 11.575–581] or where you roll rocks forever at the side of Sisyphus [*Od.* 11.593–600]). So as Homer suggests (*Od.* 11.476, 488–491), perhaps even a life spent here as a slave is preferable to one spent in Hades.[36] This "fallacy" is so obvious, however, that one ought to hesitate to credit it to Socrates. In fact, a careful reading of the text shows that this objection confuses Socrates's *initial* and vague formulation of his second alternative (b) as some sort of "change of place" (40c7–9) with his later elaboration of that change in (3) using certain τὰ λεγόμενα (40e4–41c8). At the outset of the argument Socrates does not claim that death can *only* be annihilation or an eternal life of conversation with the famous dead. Rather, as George Rudebusch has shown, the alternatives presented as being exhaustive are (a) annihilation and (b) "change of place," and these do indeed seem comprehensive.[37] Like any reflective person, Socrates will have observed the correlation between bodily impairment and impairment of consciousness (exemplified, for example, by blows to the head and by the consumption of strong drink), and so it seems probable that he made the natural inference from this correlation to the supposition that the ultimate degree of physical harm might well result in the ultimate degree of mental impairment: permanent and complete cessation of consciousness tantamount to "being nothing." But if death is *not* like this, then the soul does not utterly perish, and since the body obviously does, the soul must undergo a "change of place" in some sense of that phrase.[38]

We ought then to see Socrates' argument as demonstrative and aimed at establishing the probable—not certain—truth of death's goodness by employing premises that represent what Socrates takes to be the two most likely, hopeful, and commonly accepted alternatives available to comfort the friendly jurors.[39] Note especially that in Socrates' more optimistic ac-

---

36. As Roochnik, 214, so nicely puts it, "Perhaps the dead Socrates will discover that he would rather be a simpleton on noisy earth than a philosopher king in dim Hades." See Brickhouse and Smith (12), 257, and Reeve, 182.

37. Rudebusch, 37–40.

38. Rudebusch, 37–40, argues that if death is not annihilation, the soul must go "somewhere," if only in the sense that it is cut off from its former community (as would be the case with, say, instantaneous reincarnation).

39. Brickhouse and Smith (12), 259 n. 61, and (5), 156–157, focusing on Socrates' offer of "much hope" (*Ap.* 40c4) to the jurors, have suggested that Socrates' argument is non-demonstrative and designed more to reassure rather than convince. But Rudebusch, 35, points out in reply that reassurance requires some degree of conviction, and then provides an interpretation that gives Socrates a formally valid deduction. In their recent (8), chap. 6.5,

count of the second alternative of migration (3), he is careful to locate the source of its details in popular stories (40c7, 40e5–6, 41c7; cf. *Mx.* 235c, *R.* 330d–331a) and scrupulously withholds his assent to their exact *truth* (41c6–7). Thus, Socrates should be understood as offering the jurors consolation and "much hope" (40c4)—indeed, even reasons for confident belief—that death is good, but without providing a definitive account of what follows death. In any case, none of this militates against his being an agnostic on the immortality of the soul.

Socrates elaborates the second alternative of migration by appeal to "the things said" (τὰ λεγόμενα [40c7–9]) (3c). *If* death is migration and not annihilation, then Socrates is convinced that at least the gist of these tales will prove true.[40] Here Socrates invokes and endorses some of the more optimistic story-elements concerning the afterlife available in fifth-century Athens and neglects the more pessimistic accounts found in Homer. On this latter picture of migration, what leaves a person at death is the ψυχή, but a ψυχή conceived of non-Socratically as a kind of ghostly image (εἴδωλον), bearing no sensations, thoughts, or vital energy.[41] After drinking sacrificial blood these ψυχαί may recollect themselves and speak, but otherwise flutter about like shadows or gibbering bats in a cave.[42] So Socrates hearkens instead to the tradition of the Elysian Fields, realm of Rhadamanthus, wherein Menelaus has the "easiest life" in a delightful climate, lovely Helen by his side (*Od.* 4.561–569). True to his theology of all-good gods and his social-class-busting account of the virtues, however, he generously extends this quite exceptional fate to *all* the dead (not just the wronged or special dead), adding as well the purely Socratic hope of con-

---

Brickhouse and Smith are persuaded that their earlier accounts underestimated the argument's logical force ([8], 203 n. 47), and offer a reformulated account.

40. This account is vague in its details and provides no reason for thinking that Socrates is fabricating out of whole cloth a fully original or unorthodox religious hypothesis; cf. Ehnmark, 116. Note the similarity of Socrates' migration story to the one at the end of the *Phaedo* (cf. esp. 115d and 117c). Ehnmark, 120–122, takes the *Apology*'s migration story as probably historical and indicative of a Socratic inclination to immortality of the soul. But contra Ehnmark, there is nothing inconsistent with accepting what is said there as a true account of what death would be like if it were a migration, and also supposing that Socrates thought it just as likely that death marks the soul's passage into nothingness.

41. Items that properly belong to the body and so perish with it; cf. Il. 23.72 and Od. 11.83, 11.476, 20.355, and 24.14; also see Il. 5.449 and Od. 4.796. For further descriptions of Hades as a place of the "stupid dead," see E. Vermule, 23–27, and J. Bremmer, 78–82.

42. Od. 10.495, 11.207, 24.6–9. See Burkert (2), 194–199. L. Watson, 29, notes that there are cases of curses where a dying person threatens to inflict vengeance *after* their death (e.g., by becoming an avenging Fury); cf. R. 330d–331a, for one popular tale of punishment in the hereafter.

tinuing his divinely commissioned task of elenctic examination by testing the great and famous dead. And fortunately *there,* he notes, *elenchos*-wielding cannot be a capital offense (41c).[43] If this is death's outcome, Socrates asks, what greater good could there be? (*Ap.* 40e4–7).[44]

Socrates, however, never explicitly grounds the probable truth of even the general substance of this hypothetical account of migration. How can he so generously suppose that if death is migration that it delivers us to a happy shore and not to the halls of some dank Homeric hell? By this point the best explanation is clear: Socrates' confidence in the general accuracy of his portrait of migration is best explained as deriving, again, from his unshakable conviction that the gods are completely good (this also grounds his later claim that the fortunes of the good person "are not a matter of indifference to the gods" [*Ap.* 41d1–2]).[45] Although this principle will not generate every one of the clearly speculative details of Socrates' version of Hades following *Apology* 40e4–7,[46] given his view that elenctic examination is a divinely enjoined activity and the greatest good imaginable for all,[47] divine goodness would seem a reasonable guarantee that *if*

---

43. For accounts of the many Greek views of the afterlife, see Adkins (4), 138–139; Dover (3), 243–246, 261–267; Mikalson (1), 74–82; and E. Rohde, 236–242, 539–544. It is impossible to say whether Socrates' story draws on doctrines positing a substantial life after death that were in the air at the time (e.g., Dionysian or Orphic). Even then, it remains unclear how many adherents such views found, and among those, just how many mustered confident belief. Cole, 292, for example, finds it surprising that there are no Dionysiac grave inscriptions that promise solace in the idea that "although the body lies in the earth or dust, the soul is among the blessed, in the heavens, or among the stars."

44. *Ap.* 41c9–d2 ("There is nothing bad for a *good* man, whether living or dead, and the gods are not without care for *his* troubles") and the fact that here Socrates is addressing only those jurors who performed their duty virtuously (39e1–40a3, 41c8) might be taken to suggest that only those more good than bad are guaranteed migration, with annihilation the fate of others (corrupt souls being unable to survive the "transition" out of the body). Nonetheless, it is clear that Socrates assumes that if any soul migrates then all souls do. Note, too, that this suggestion runs somewhat counter to Socrates' view that he will encounter those who "suppose they are wise but are not in Hades" (41b). Finally, since Socrates holds that all humans are morally imperfect, that everyone can benefit from elenctic examination, and that the gods are truly good, it seems likely that he thinks that if death is migration then all the dead migrate to and associate in "the other place" so as to make possible the further elenctic improvement of their souls. Thus, since death is good *simpliciter,* it is good even for the bad (*per* the implication of 40b7–c1).

45. Again, see, e.g., *Eu.* 6a–d, 14e–15a; *Ap.* 21b, 30a–31b; *G.* 508a; *R.* 379b; *Phd.* 62d–63c; *Mem.* 1.4.1–19, 4.3.1–18; McPherran (14), 297–309; and Vlastos (14), 162–166.

46. Note that Socrates makes only conditional claims regarding the afterlife at 40e7–41c7; e.g., "*if* one meets Orpheus, Musaeus, Hesiod, and Homer there, it will be worth dying many times" (41a6–8); see Rudebusch, 42–44.

47. E.g., *Ap.* 20e–23c, 28d–29a, 29c–d, 30a–31b, 33c, 38a, 41b5, and 41c3–4.

death is a journey of the soul to another "place" where all the dead are gathered that Socrates will enjoy further continued consciousness, self-identity, and whatever else is required for the beneficial pleasures of continued elenctic practice (cf. *Phd.* 63b–c).[48]

Notwithstanding these considerations, it has been suggested that Socrates' portrait of Hades does not provide a *general* reason for being reconciled to death, but rather, poses a permanent vacation-holiday only for Socrates and other devotees of moral improvement.[49] After all, how many of the "friendly jurors" would judge death to be all that good if it meant an eternity spent in the elenctic clutches of Socrates? Moreover, while *Socrates* may have nothing to fear from the virtuous judges he installs in the hereafter (*Ap.* 41a3–4), some of his less virtuous jurors might. But for Socrates such considerations are quite beside the point, the point being that he has given reasons that *ought to* comfort every juror. On his view, it is simply never just to inflict harm, and so from perfectly just gods and judges one may confidently expect perfectly nonharmful judgments (no matter how painful they might seem). And as for the "threat" of eternal elenctic testing: this is precisely what everyone ought to look forward to— as a matter of implicit belief *does* look forward to—inasmuch as everyone aims at the good and happy life.[50] The experience of elenctic examination, both as patient and practitioner, may not always be found to be a pleasurable one (in a non-Socratic sense of "pleasure"), but the improvement to the soul it provides ought always to be preferred to what *seems* pleasurable. Socrates will concede that we cannot know with certainty that such elenctic scrutiny is the fate of the dead, but since the gods are good, he can be confident that if death is a migration then whatever awaits us at the end of that journey must be at least as good as what he takes to be the greatest of imaginable goods.[51]

It is no surprise that Socrates' sympathies appear to rest with his ad-

48. Rudebusch, 40–44. Socrates' dilemma has a parallel in a funeral oration by Hyperides for the dead heroes of the Athenian revolt of 323 (6.43), but the parallel is not surprising because Hyperides may well have been a student of Socrates' student Isocrates. It is worth pointing out in support of the above argument from divine goodness that Hyperides also goes beyond Socrates' dilemma by claiming that "if men have perception in the house of Hades and if they are cared for by the daimonic [element], *as we suspect they are,* then it is reasonable to assume that *those who defended the abused honor of the gods find the greatest care from the daimonic* [element]" (trans. Mikalson; my emphasis).

49. Brickhouse and Smith (12), 261–262.

50. See Chapter 4.2; McPherran (9), 542–549; and Reeve, chap. 3.10.

51. Rudebusch, 40–44, makes this same point—and in a similar fashion—by appealing to the goodness of Socrates' gods.

umbration of the second alternative, offering as it does the "inconceivable happiness" of elenchos-wielding among the wise and not-so-wise dead (e.g., note that he spends more time on this possibility). But does he also think it the *more likely* alternative as well, and is it that belief that underwrites his evident tranquillity in the face of death? Some have thought so, since the sources of Socrates' τὰ λεγόμενα are poets, and poets—says Socrates—can say many fine and true things when possessed by a god.[52] Some of these stories also provide just the sort of optimistic picture of the afterlife implied by Socrates' philanthropic gods, and they have a certain degree of endoxic status. All this, taken in conjunction with the previously mentioned passages of the *Crito* and *Gorgias*, constitutes a formidable case for the view that Socrates ranked migration as more probable than annihilation.

Despite the apparent weight of this case, however, we ought to withhold assent. Although Socrates does not make a point of it, the first alternative of eternal annihilation is at least as equally well grounded in τὰ λεγόμενα and popular belief as is his version of migration.[53] Hence, although Socrates often accepts (without firm commitment) customary belief and mythological tales *per Phaedrus* 229c–230a, on this issue there appears to be no one settled customary view for him to simply "accept."[54] And in any case, Socrates' own account of the migration alternative is clearly not the view popularized by Homer, and is—in all likelihood—not the view of a

---

52. *Ap.* 22a8–c8; *Ion* 533c9–535a2; Brickhouse and Smith (5), 157–158, and (8), 204–205.

53. Again, see, e.g., Euripides *Suppliants* 531–536, 1140; *Helen* 1014–1016; *I.G.* 1.945; and Hyperides 6.43. Philosophers also acknowledged this possibility: Democritus, Socrates' contemporary, held dissolution of the soul to be the most likely outcome of death (*On Tranquillity* Stob. ii [*Ecl. Eth.*] 52, 40; see also, e.g., *Phd.* 69e–70b. *Phaedrus* 229c6–230a2 may suggest that Socrates is willing to accept common beliefs and mythological tales when there is no countervailing evidence and when they do not conflict with the elenctically tested tenets of his moral theory, and this aids the case that Socrates holds that his *two* alternatives are the most likely of all possible fates. Although the *Phaedrus* is a later dialogue, this portion of it coheres with the early dialogues; see Brickhouse and Smith (5), n. 10, and (8), n. 53. There is, unfortunately, no piece of testimony where Socrates comments explicitly on Athenian funerary practices. *Phaedo* 115a–116a simply shows Socrates anticipating the standard three-act affair: (1) the washing and laying out of the body by female kin; (2) the funeral cortège, which conveyed the corpse to the graveyard; and (3) the burial of either the body or the cremated remains. Socrates leaves this last issue up to Crito.

54. To quote Mikalson (1), 74: "The Athenian's views concerning the afterlife show more variety and uncertainty than their views on any other religious topic" (see also 74–82). Note too Cebes's testimony to popular uncertainty on the fate of the dead at *Phd.* 69e–70b; cf. Cephalus's report at *R.* 330d–331b.

majority of Athenians.[55] Socrates also knows full well that poets (and "the many") are not always inspired, even when they all agree (cf. *Ion* 534d–535a). Additionally, it would seem that Socratic agnosticism on the fate of the soul at least *ought to* have prevailed over Socratic optimism, since there appears to be little empirical or conceptual evidence to which Socrates could appeal that would allow him or his audience to give precedence to either of his alternatives, especially the more attractive one of migration. Neither are we told of any extrarational warrants for taking sides on the matter: something we would expect to hear about had there been any, in view of Socrates' evident interest in comforting the jurors and given his bold use of the *silence* of his *daimonion* on the issue of death's goodness. Xenophon's silence on this issue also carries weight in favor of Socratic agnosticism, for his Socrates is on all topics pertaining to the soul *other than* immortality positively chatty, and—significantly—Xenophon has no problem crediting a belief in immortality to his other ideal figure, Cyrus (*Cyr.* 8.17–22).[56]

Finally, there is no compelling reason to think that Socrates' commitment to the existence of good, philanthropic gods and to the principle that "there is nothing bad for a good person, whether living or dead" (41c9–d2) led him to endorse immortality. Socrates contends that the soul is harmed *only* by vice—that not living, but living virtuously is what counts (*Ap.* 28d–29b, 30c–d, 31c–32d; *Cr.* 47e–48b; *Eud.* 288e–289b; cf. *G.* 511b–512d)—and since death-as-annihilation appears to foster neither vice nor virtue (nor ignorance) but simply removes the subject of experience from harboring them, even this sort of death is no harm (in the Socratic sense) to the soul.[57] Socrates recognizes that many of his jurors will hold otherwise, thinking that extinction is a terrible and evil fate (30d), but in doing so they presume contrary to Socratic principles that the extension of life per se has an absolute positive value and that being killed is a great evil. Socrates is quite clear on this point, however; it is not killing that is bad, but killing unjustly (30d).[58]

---

55. See N. J. Richardson, 50–66, and Mikalson (1), 80–82.

56. Adam (2), 345; Vlastos (14), 103 n. 84. See, e.g., *Mem.* 1.2.1–5, 19, 23–24, 53; 1.3.5, 14–15; 1.4.8–17; 2.1.20–23; 2.6.30, 32, 36; 3.10.1–8; 3.11.10; 4.1.2, 4; 4.3.14; *Apol.* 7, 18; *Symp.* 1.9; 2.24; 4.2; 8.8–15, 36, 41, 43.

57. Even Xenophon's Socrates, who characterizes the soul as the "precious gift" of generous gods (*Mem.* 1.4.13–14), does not assert that it outlasts the body (the gods' other "precious"—but clearly perishable—gift).

58. I think that the thesis of Brickhouse and Smith (5), 156–162, and (8), chap. 6.5, that Socrates holds not only that death is a good thing but that everyone is *better off* dead than

The textual evidence that Socrates nonetheless considered migration the more likely alternative also does not clinch the case. *Crito* 54a–c is dubious evidence, since there the personified Laws of Athens, not Socrates in his own voice, assume the soul's migration. Although these imaginary representatives of Athens may be recommending a practical decision—even a political philosophy—with which Socrates partially or completely agrees, they cannot be supposed to be identical with the *actual* laws and legal system of Athens or to fully represent popular opinion, and their reference to postmortem judgments and their "brothers" in Hades need not be anything more than a device by which Socrates (or Plato) legitimizes them as the genuine civic voice of Athens.⁵⁹ Note too that in making their arguments (46b–50a) they invoke not the Socratic perspective on justice, but that of "the many."⁶⁰ Socrates also clearly envisions that the Laws are capable of making errors (by commanding unjust behavior [50c1–6, 51e7]), and so he need not be convinced of anything he puts into the

---

alive (even the good person) is a bit exaggerated, since this requires a Socratic belief in immortality (see esp. [5], 162; [8], 211–212). This is so, because the healthy good are only clearly better off dead on *either* alternative if their lives are such that death-as-annihilation is better than life. But if death *is* annihilation then not *every* such person is *always and in every case* better off dead. After all, Socrates would seem to agree that a virtuous, happy, useful person living a self-examined life is better off existing alive than not. N. Smith now argues in correspondence that since (1) Socrates was a good man and "no evil comes to a good man" (*Ap.* 41c9–d10), and since (2) Socrates will be better off dead, that (3) even death-as-annihilation is better than life for the good man. But this, I think, neglects the special circumstances Socrates finds himself in: it is his "present troubles" (41d3–5) that tip the scales in Socrates' particular case, troubles that make even annihilation better than continued life. Of course, on either alternative—annihilation or migration—the incurably evil and those with severely ravaged bodies are better off dead (e.g., *Cr.* 47e3–5; cf. *G.* 512a2–5). Vicious souls are better off in death, since presumably once free of the body they will no longer be able to harm themselves or others. Further, if at death bad souls migrate, then those souls capable of improvement may be redeemed (cf. *G.* 525c, *R.* 380a–b).

59. Legitimizing them, that is, by providing them with a more specific version of the divine backing Athenians vaguely attributed to their actual legal system. Although it is clear that the Laws do—on the one hand—speak for the real laws of Athens (see 51d, 52a, 52b, 53a–54b), punishment in the afterlife was not a sanction cited in the actual laws. See Kraut (2), 40, 66, 81–82, and Mikalson (1), 27, 78. Also, the speech of the Laws is clearly a fictional "tale" (μῦθος), and what they say is qualified by a "perhaps" (ἴσως) at 51c6. Hence, although Brickhouse and Smith (8), 211 n. 63, are correct that "if Socrates is not expressing his own view here, he is attributing a view of the afterlife to the laws which is . . . unwarranted by the actual laws," I see no problem in that for my reading of the *Crito*.

60. G. Young. The idea that a violation of Athenian law might evoke the *anger* of the gods (54c) is clearly a traditional idea, one with which "the many" might be expected to be sympathetic (see Chapter 3.4.6); moreover, this seems a non-Socratic notion, since giving way to that emotion is associated by Socrates with lack of wisdom (*Prt.* 352a–352c; cf. *Ap.* 34b–d, *Eu.* 7b–c, *Phd.* 113e–114b; cf. Chap. 3, n. 214).

mouth of the Laws. Finally, it seems unlikely that Socrates would take it on the "authority" of the Laws that the soul migrates, given his earlier concession in this text that he lacks a clear sense of what the soul *is* (47e8; cf. *Sym*. 218a3).[61] Socrates *seems* to hear (δοκῶ ἀκούειν [54d2–3]) that the Laws receive deceased lawbreakers badly, but what his own entire view on the matter is seems difficult to ascertain.[62]

Socrates' positive endorsement of the eschatological myth at the end of the *Gorgias* (523a–527e) is the best textual evidence that in his own view migration is the most likely fate of the soul, but even here skepticism is warranted.[63] First, we have independent reasons for thinking that the *Apology* is a more reliable source of evidence than the *Gorgias* for Socrates' views, and so where they diverge, the testimony of the *Apology* is to be preferred.[64] On this issue they do diverge, and in such a way that if one takes the end of the *Gorgias* to represent Socrates' own commitments on immortality, then one is saddled with an improbably deceptive and irrational Socrates in the *Apology*. This is so, because Socrates presents his two competing postmortem alternatives in the *Apology* free of any assessment of their relative likelihood, and in context this has the rhetorical effect of suggesting that in his view both are to be accorded equal proba-

---

61. Also, the purpose of suggesting a postmortem life for the soul at this point in the *Crito* is to emphasize that disobedience to the Laws in this world will result in unfavorable treatment by the "brothers" of the Laws in Hades, but postmortem punishment is—arguably—a Platonic theme, not a Socratic one. It is worth noting also that the Laws never express any typically Socratic concern for the justice or health of anyone's soul (noted by Weiss [1]). Note also the view of S. Yonezawa, who contends that Socrates' views in the *Crito* are so at odds on several fundamental points with those found in the *Apology* that we should conclude that the *Crito* is, together with the *Gorgias* and *Phaedo,* much more a middle dialogue than a companion piece to the *Apology*; see also H. Thesleff, 20–26.

62. Four scholars have also offered powerful arguments for the view that the Laws do not represent Socrates' deepest convictions and that Socrates may develop them in order to provide himself with a philosophically competent *protagonist* (or to reconcile Crito to his imminent death); see H. Brown, G. Young, M. Miller (1), and Weiss (1). If this is right, Brickhouse and Smith (8), 211 n. 63, are incorrect when they object to my thesis by holding that "Plato's readers . . . may reasonably assume that all of the other [non-afterlife] pronouncements by the Laws are accepted by Socrates." Although they worry that Socrates must be seen as misleading Crito if he is not using the Laws as his mouthpiece, Weiss presents a good case for the view that Socrates' own moral principles and the exigencies of the situation (esp. Crito's lack of philosophical ability and his sympathy with "the many"; see, e.g., 44d, 48c), require Socrates to use a rhetorical strategy to bring Crito around to his own view that he should not leave Athens; cf. Young.

63. See Brickhouse and Smith (5), 158, and (8), 205–206, who rely almost exclusively on this passage to make their case for a Socratic commitment to immortality.

64. See Chap. 2, n. 75.

bility. After all, were Socrates to have judged the probabilities to be *unequal*—despite the difficulties involved in making such an assessment—we would expect to hear something about the matter, given that at least most of the jurors he wishes to console would find greater comfort than his actual argument provides were he to reveal that in his judgment (and for what reasons he might have) his account of migration is the more likely alternative of the two he presents. Also, if Socrates were to leave the impression of equal probability in place while believing the contrary on a matter of such grave moral import, he would be in danger of violating the various legal and moral commitments that oblige him—at least in the context of the *Apology*—to tell the truth, to foster care for the soul, and to "hold nothing back" from his jurors (cf. *Ap.* 24a).[65] Finally, if Socrates nonetheless harbored the unexpressed judgment that migration is more likely than annihilation in the *Apology,* but is only forthcoming about it in the *Gorgias,* we must suppose that Socrates endorsed a quite startling metaphysical supposition that Plato is willing to portray him as having *declared* but nowhere *proved.*[66] But that scenario is rather at odds with Socrates' well-known dedication to rational justification.[67] When it comes time for Plato to spell out *his* reasons for believing in the immortality of the soul in the *Phaedo, Republic,* and *Phaedrus,* he is perfectly candid on the topic, and so it seems improbable that he would withhold Socrates' reasons from us (or not know of them).[68] I suggest then that we take the

65. Even though Socrates' argument comes *after* his defense proper, Socrates says that he will *display* his views of things "as to friends" (40a1), indicating that his commitment to nondeception remains in force, although strictly speaking, the promise to "hold nothing back" may well not extend to his "tale" (διαμυθολογῆσαι [39e5]). Does this imply that Socrates misled Crito by employing a myth of migration (*Cr.* 54a–c) without counterbalancing it with the annihilation alternative? I don't think so, since Crito would have heard Socrates' closing speech in the *Apology* (see *Ap.* 33d9, 38b6) and so would know that Socrates holds annihilation to be a viable alternative to judgment in Hades.

66. Vlastos (12), 94, and (14), 55; cf. Brickhouse and Smith (5), 161, and (8), 209–211. Only in Plato's middle dialogues does "Socrates" offer rational proofs of immortality.

67. Someone might object here that Socrates also does not attempt to prove other propositions that he is firmly committed to—such as the complete goodness and wisdom of the gods—but in such cases I think Socrates would see a difference between such "analytic" claims (e.g., that gods are wise) and other "empirical" claims (e.g., that the soul migrates). Naturally, those who hold that Socrates merely "accepts" without firm commitment the immortality of the soul cannot appeal to this line of objection. They also cannot appeal to the testimony of the *Gorgias,* since there Socrates repeatedly displays a firm commitment to the *truth* of his myth's eschatology (see n. 19).

68. Vlastos (14), 53–54, argues that *Plato's* theory of the immortal, transmigrating soul with prenatal cognitive powers makes its first appearance at *M.* 81a–b.

Gorgias's myth of migration to represent a Platonic addendum rather than a Socratic eschatology.[69]

There are other, less indirect reasons for adopting this view as well. The most obvious worry is that the *Phaedo* and *Republic* have eschatological epilogues similar to the *Gorgias*'s that also postulate immortality of the soul, and yet both are middle dialogues representing Platonic, not Socratic, thought. Although it is true that the *Gorgias* myth differs from the other two accounts (and the *Phaedrus*'s) by remaining silent on the possibility of reincarnation, its Socrates seems to accept a number of elements distinctive of Platonic eschatology and its Orphic and Pythagorean sources (e.g., that "life is death and death is life," that the body is a tomb, and that the dead suffer punishment [*G.* 492e–494a; cf. *Phd.* 61e–62c, 81d, 82e, 92a, 114b; *Crat.* 400c; *Tim.* 44b]), and hence suggests a Platonic—not Socratic— account of the soul.[70] The *Gorgias* is also linked with the *Phaedo* and *Republic* by the fact that all three dialogues portray Socrates' companions—companions who ought to be familiar with his views—as skeptical and/or shocked by his professions of faith in immortality (*G.* 523a, *Phd.* 70a–b, *R.* 608d), a literary technique readily explicable as a signal that here we encounter not Socrates, but "Socrates the mouthpiece of middle-dialogue metaphysics."[71] The *Gorgias*'s view that the soul (and not the body) contains good-independent appetites that are restrained in those that are virtuous and harmonious (491d–e; 503d–507e) does not parallel the intellectualist moral psychology of the early dialogues (which identifies virtue with knowledge)—and the Socratic account of the soul developed above—so much as anticipate that of the *Republic* (e.g., *R.* 439e–440b).[72]

69. Brickhouse and Smith (8), 210, n. 62, object to my view on the grounds that "Plato himself seems to have accepted a Pythagorean form of reincarnation, but no trace of this can be found in the *Gorgias, Crito,* or *Apology*. In McPherran's view, the *Gorgias* does not accurately reflect either Socrates's or Plato's own mature view of death and the afterlife." To this the clear reply is that given my view of Plato's philosophical development and his dramatic purposes (Chapter 1.2), we shouldn't expect to find Plato's Pythagoreanism in either the *Apology* or *Crito*. As for the *Gorgias*, there may well be Pythagorean traces in place (*G.* 492e–494a; see below), and in any case, I—like many others—find it unsurprising that a "transitional dialogue" (see Chap. 1.2, n. 4) would not fully capture Plato's (developing) middle-dialogue views on immortality.

70. See Dodds (6), 296–299, 375; Guthrie (3), 4:305–307; and Vlastos (14), 55–56; but note I. Linforth. According to Claus, 175–180, the *Gorgias* marks a decisive turning point in Plato's writing on the topic of the ψυχή.

71. As Burnet (6), 257, observed, ". . . it is not a little remarkable that, both in the *Phaedo* [70a1 ff.] and the *Republic* [608d3], Plato represents the closest intimates of Socrates as startled by his profession of belief in immortality."

72. See, e.g., Irwin (3), 123–124; 143, note on 468ab; 218, note on 505bc; and 221, note

Finally, unlike the Socrates of the *Gorgias,* the *Apology*'s Socrates says nothing about postmortem punishments, despite the fact that such possibilities were well recognized by the Athenians of that period.[73]

This last contrast is worth pursuing. The Socrates of the *Apology* insists that he doesn't care about death as a consequence of his actions *in any way at all,* but that his *whole care* is to avoid injustice (28b5–9, 32d1–3). Here and elsewhere there is no significant trace of extrinsic, afterlife-regarding motivations for pursuing the virtuous life, and prolonging one's life is only important insofar as it contributes to one's happiness and the good (*Ap.* 28d–29b, 31c–32c; and esp. *Eud.* 288e–289b).[74] Furthermore, there is nothing to indicate that the judges of the *Apology*'s afterlife pass judgment on the deceased on the basis of their former lives.[75] The *Gorgias*'s Socrates, on the other hand, introduces the *Phaedo-Republic* theme of postmortem rewards and punishments as a way of providing additional, extrinsic motivations for virtuous behavior during the course of our earthly existence.[76] Note in particular "Socrates'" pronouncement that sensible people *fear* not dying, but evildoing, and this they fear because of the pain and agony imposed on evildoers in the afterlife (522e1–6). Endorsing this endoxic belief, "Socrates" indicates that he motivates himself and others to pursue virtue *not only* by reflection on the necessary conditions of obtaining happiness (*eudaimonia*) in this life, but by the additional consideration of how one might secure the best fate after death, especially

---

on 507b; J.C.B. Gosling and C.C.W. Taylor, 61–62; and the paragraph following. A problem with this line of thought, however (observed by Irwin, notes on 468ab and 507b), is that it imputes to Socrates two contradictory accounts of motivation within the space of a single dialogue, since at the outset of the *Gorgias* Socrates assumes that *all* desires are good-dependent (so that one can do what one *thinks* is best without doing what one really desires [467c1–468e5]). On this problem, and how it might be possible to interpret Socrates' talk of "restraining the appetites of the soul" (491d–e, 505b) in a way consistent with the early dialogue account of motivation, see Brickhouse and Smith (8), chap. 3.5.5.

73. Cf. *R.* 330d–331a and Richardson, 57–60. For further accounts of postmortem judgment contemporaneous with Socrates, see Dover (3), 263–268, and Mikalson (1), 78–82.

74. Note also that although the Socrates of the *Memorabilia* (4.4.20–25) holds that the gods enforce various unwritten laws of morality with punishments, those punishments are not dished out in the afterlife (but, rather, are built into these laws by the gods as natural outcomes of violation; e.g., ingratitude is "punished" by loss of friends).

75. Or at least enforce such judgments, since—as N. Smith has pointed out in correspondence and in (4), 206 n. 56—they are probably not placed there just to judge beauty contests. So what do they judge? Well, in Homer, at least, Minos only settles *lawsuits* among the dead (*Od.* 11.568 ff.). My earlier criticisms of using the *Crito* as a source for Socrates' views of the afterlife apply also to using it to establish that Socrates endorsed punishments in the afterlife (contra Brickhouse and Smith [4], 206 n. 56).

76. *Phd.* 107c–d; *R.* 380b, 612a–621d; thus doing so for the first time.

by avoiding the frightful sufferings of both curable and incurable wrong-doers (524a–527a, esp. 525b). This sharply displays, I think, the shift in moral psychology from the Socratic intellectualism of the early dialogues to Plato's more complex account, where we find a willingness to use pain and pleasure as nonintellectual inducements to virtuous behavior in the case of those as yet unready to pursue virtue for its own sake.[77] It is also going to take an interpretive stretch to show how the *Gorgias*'s endorse-ment of the rationality of the fear of death (i.e., the *fear* of punishment after death) might be made compatible with the *Apology*'s analysis and rejection of the fear of death (29a4–b6). Hence, we ought to find the myth of the *Gorgias* testimony only to the Platonic, not Socratic, account of the soul's afterlife.[78]

77. See esp. *R.* 380a–b, 445a, 591a–b, and *Laws* 731b–d, 735d–e, 862b–863a, 880d–881b, 957e. It is not possible to rule out a Socratic acceptance of certain physical punish-ments, since Socrates does seem to accept that those who do injustice must "pay the penalty" (*Eu.* 8d–e) (his military career also argues that Socrates can sanction the infliction of physical harms; on Socrates' career, see Guthrie [6], 59). But observe how Socrates' argument at *Ap.* 24d–26a suggests a line of thought on what the "penalty" should be. Since no one wants to be harmed, and since those who are harmed do harms to others, no one harms fellow citizens voluntarily (knowingly); hence, those who do harm to others should be taught (διδάσκειν) and admonished (νουθετεῖν), not *punished* (κολάζειν) (suggesting that any physical penalties should be of the moderate sort that "teach" correct moral belief). It also seems significant that the Socrates of the early, nontransitional dialogues never endorses a standard Greek punishment: whipping (cf. *Laws* 764b, 890c, 949c). Punishment-by-beating is sanctioned at *Cr.* 51a–b—but by the Laws, not Socrates—and at *Pr.* 325c–d—but by "the many," not Socrates.

In a recent article, R. F. Stalley, 14–19, notes that both he and T. J. Saunders (163) see "a psychological emphasis in the *Gorgias,* the *Republic,* and the *Laws,* which we do not find in the *Protagoras*" (16), a dialogue that features an intellectualist Socrates who thinks "virtue is teachable not because it consists in a set of character traits which may be acquired by training but because it is knowledge" (18). The *Gorgias* (esp. 476a–480d), in particular, employs the notion that wickedness is a disease requiring treatment (even "whipping"), an idea connected to the complex tripartite psychology of the *Republic* (and *Laws*). It is in this later work that Plato combines both Socratic and Presocratic (Protagorean?) "character-training" insights: Socratic intellectualism *is* correct—justice in the soul does require knowledge of virtue—but that alone is insufficient, for the desires and emotions of the soul must also be "trained."

78. The account of the *Gorgias,* then, is "an expanded, transformed version of Socrates' speculations at the end of the *Apology*" (Beckman, 27). Admittedly, charges of middle-Plato contamination of the early dialogues often serve as cheap interpretive ploys, but here the weight of evidence—and the reasons for understanding the *Gorgias* to be a "transitional" dialogue (e.g., its moral pyschology, its concluding eschatological myth, its loquacious Socra-tes, etc.)—justifies the claim. Note that Brickhouse and Smith (12), 12–13, express great skepticism of any claim concerning the views represented in the *Apology* whose only or best defense must be made by appealing to a transitional dialogue like the *Gorgias*—a work

The upshot of all this is straightforward: the received view that Socrates endorsed the soul's immortality ought to be abandoned and should give way to suspension of judgment on the matter. But if bets must be placed, then I suggest that the primacy of the *Apology,* the rhetorical implications of its eschatological dilemma and Socrates' general epistemological modesty on metaphysical issues ought to incline us slightly toward the view that Socrates was himself an agnostic on the topic of immortality.[79] In taking this advice, I have shown at least how we are able to leave Socrates with not just a groundless wish, but the rational warrant provided by his two most likely alternatives for taking an optimistic attitude concerning the hereafter.[80] It was surely his fervent hope that there was yet a world to come where he might continue to enjoy the "inconceivable happiness" of pursuing his elenctic mission, and with his most talented audience yet. But more than hope he does not venture—at least in the *Apology*—lest he presume the "most blameworthy ignorance" of supposing that he has sufficient rational grounds for preferring his happy story of migration to its somewhat more somber alternative. Instead, Socrates recommends that we turn our attention to what we can be sure *is* of importance: the improvement of our souls in the not-so-Elysian here and now.[81]

"taint[ed]" by its middle-period concluding myth and other later-Plato "colorations or even corruptions" that may be lurking (13). Nevertheless, in their (5), 158–162, it is the *Gorgias* itself that serves as their best evidence for crediting the *Apology*'s Socrates with a faith in immortality.

79. Again, the fact that despite all the many views concerning the soul ascribed to Socrates in Xenophon's *testimonia* there is no mention of the soul's immortality strongly suggests that Socrates was agnostic on the issue.

80. If even dreamless sleep would be a gain for Socrates, and the alternative of migration an even greater one, it might appear as though he has sufficient motivation for committing suicide. But it must remembered that since these two alternatives are only thought likely, not exhaustive, death may be worse than any life led here; hence, our best course (generally) is to pursue happiness in this present life. Suicide would also be opposed by Socrates, it would seem, on the grounds that we all have a pious duty to render service to the gods and because we are the property of the gods (*Phd.* 61d–63b; see Chapter 2.2 and McPherran [14], 287–292, 297–309).

81. I venture that Socrates would find congenial Confucius's remark that "if we do not yet know about life, how can we know about death?" (*Analects* 11:11). Xenophon's Socrates is "even more earth-bound" than the Socrates of Plato's early dialogues, never even hinting that we might enjoy communion with the divinities of a "higher realm" (Vlastos [14], 103, 79–80; cf. *Mem.* 1.1.1; 4.7.4–7).

5.2 Cosmology, Moral Theology, and the Gods of Socrates

As we have seen, the bedrock of Socratic religion is the "Socratic reformation": That moral cleansing of the Homeric deities which frees them of those various unsavory characteristics that make them less than perfect exemplars for us imperfect mortals. As a result, Socrates' gods are thoroughly good beings, and toward humanity they have an entirely benevolent and caring attitude (*Ap.* 41c9–d2, *Eu.* 14e–15a, *G.* 508a).[82] The evidence also suggests that Socrates affirmed the superlative wisdom, knowledge, and power of the gods.[83] None of this "reformation" moral theology, however, directly implicates Socrates in the kind of innovative teleological cosmology and theodicy Xenophon ascribes to him in the *Memorabilia* (1.4.1–19; 4.3.1–18; cf. Sextus *Ad. Math.* 9.92–94). There, among other things, we find Socrates arguing for the existence of an omniscient, omnipresent God: the Maker of an orderly and beautiful universe—one especially suited to satisfying our human needs and wants—a Maker who also now governs it in a fashion analogous to how *our* minds govern *our* bodies (1.4.2–18; cf. 4.3.3–8).[84]

Many scholars—most recently Gregory Vlastos—deny that Socrates was in fact a "dabbler in teleological cosmology" as suggested by Xenophon (since "given his [Socrates'] obsessive concentration on ethics, a *natural theology* he could not have produced").[85] Constrained by the limits of this study, I can only offer a brief account and assessment of Xenophon's teleological argument. Initially I concentrate on its philosophical merit without raising worries about its origins. However, I then argue that there are better reasons than not for giving modest credence to Xenophon's ascription.[86]

---

82. See, e.g., *Ap.* 41c–d; *Eu.* 14e–15a; *G.* 508a; *R.* 377e–383c, and *Mem.* 4.4.25.

83. *Ap.* 21b, 23a–c, 42a; see also Chapter 2.2.

84. See, e.g., the accounts of Adam (2), 346–350; and Burkert (2), 319. Jaeger (3), 169, makes the interesting observation that earlier thinkers simply took the existence of the Divine as fact; and thus when faced with the conflicting representations of the folk religion, they saw the real problem as one of identifying the true form of the Divine; cf. *Mem.* 4.3.13. The arguments preserved in Xenophon, says Jaeger, mark a fundamental shift: "The problem of the form of the Divine lapses into the background as insoluble, and the existence of the Divine as such becomes the real matter to be proved."

85. Vlastos (14), 162; cf. Vlastos (8), 2, and G. Striker, 90–91. Adam (2), 349, and Guthrie (6), 155, are two scholars who do accept Xenophon's attribution.

86. Cf. Morrison, 16.

5.2.1 Socrates' Proof of God's Existence

The primary teleological argument contained in the *Memorabilia* holds that since individual beings in the universe are either the products of intelligent design (γνώμη) or mere dumb luck (τύχη), and since human beings are clearly products of intelligent design, we then ought to be persuaded that there exists a vastly knowledgeable and powerful God, a God who is (moreover) a "loving and wise Maker [δημιουργός]" (1.4.2–7; cf. 4.3.1–18). Several additional considerations are offered in support of this. First, invisible, massless human minds (mind [νοῦς] = soul [ψυχή]) reside in and give order and purposive direction to the human bodies that possess them. But since our bodies have a share of all the elements (such as earth and water) composing the infinitely many ordered bodies that constitute the universe, it would be most unlikely that the universe—possessing a vastly greater portion of those elements—should then lack that one element, mind, which *we* possess. Indeed, it would not only be unlikely, but an unbelievably "lucky chance" (εὐτύχημα) that *our* bodies alone of all bodies would somehow "snap up" minds, and quite unlikely that the universe could manifest its orderly activity without possessing a similar purposeful Intelligence of its own (1.4.8; cf. *Phlb.* 29a–30e).[87] In reply to the objection that this alleged cosmic Intelligence is not directly perceivable, Socrates points out that we also do not observe our own invisible souls (or those of others, he might have added) (1.4.9; 4.3.13–14; cf. *Cyr.* 8.7.17). If visibility were a requirement for attributing a purposeful, directing intelligence to things, then we should have to say that *we* (and others) do nothing by design but everything by chance. Next, in reply to the piety-undermining objection that the Demiurge might be so great (μεγαλοπρεπέστερον) that it is *indifferent* to our needs and our attempts to meet them through religious propitiation,[88] Socrates offers a series of reflections designed to reveal the philanthropic, human-serving design of the cosmos and, thus, the providential love of its Maker (1.4.10–19; cf. 4.3.2–14). An addendum to this holds that the age-old belief in the gods' ability to aid or thwart us—a belief held by the most thoughtful people and the wisest, most enduring nations—would by now have been revealed

87. According to Jaeger (3), 246 n. 91, both this section of the *Memorabilia* and the corresponding section of the *Philebus* derive from a common source(s). I will argue below that this source may well be Socrates himself.
88. And hence, not a "loving" being, but a noninterventionist deity of the Epicurean sort or the kind of natural divine force favored by the *phusiologoi*.

as a fraud if it were false (1.4.15–17). Rather, the better explanation is that this belief is one implanted (ἐμφύειν) in us by the δημιουργός (*Mem.* 1.4.16; cf. 1.4.7).

Bypassing a consideration of these admittedly underwhelming supporting considerations, the primary argument of the text (*Mem.* 1.4.2–7)—with a bit of interpretive polishing—can be given this formal structure:

1. Everything that is clearly purposeful (ὠφέλια; a beneficial adaptation of means to ends) is the product of intelligent design (γνώμη; i.e., art [τέχνη]) (and not mere dumb luck [τύχη]).
2. Human beings (and other features of the universe, living and nonliving [1.4.8]) exhibit "signs of forethought" (προνοητικῶς) (1.4.6); e.g., eyes have protective eyelids and lashes, teeth are adapted to cutting, and the anus is far removed from the nostrils.[89]
3. Things that exhibit "signs of forethought" are clearly purposeful.
4. Thus, human beings are the product of intelligent design.
5. The existence of products of intelligent design implies the existence of an intelligent designer-creator (one possessing the intelligence and power necessary for producing its products; cf. 1.4.2–4).
6. Thus, an intelligent designer-creator of the cosmos exists.

All things considered, this is a fairly impressive piece of philosophy to find in Xenophon—or any fourth-century text for that matter—since the argument is no mere prototype but close to being a full-fledged version of the classic Argument from Design.[90] Although the gist of the argument and

89. The term πρόνοια is first attested in Herodotus (3.108), who discovers the "providence of the divine" in the fact that creatures which pose a danger to us humans and which are unfit as sources of nourishment (e.g., lions) have small litters, while their prey and ours (e.g., rabbits) have large ones (Adam [2], 349; Burkert [2], 319).

Jaeger (3), 168–169, notes that the interpretation of nature at this point in Xenophon is entirely technological—eyelashes are sieves, eyebrows cornices, intestines a system of conduits—something that he takes as evidence for the argument's source being Diogenes of Apollonia; cf. Xen. *Symp.* 5.5–8 and Aris. *Thesm.* 14, 18. Be that as it may, Socrates seems himself to be committed to a technological account of the cosmos, taking it for granted in the *Euthyphro* that the gods are divine craftspeople, who—like shipwrights or housebuilders—use their skill to produce some product (13d–14a). Since it would be natural for him to think that *the* product (or one major product) of the gods is the cosmos, it seems eminently plausible that Socrates endorsed this teleological argument.

90. This inference was adopted by the Stoics as their main theological proof and made a crucial contribution to their thinking about natural law (note, e.g., the clear influence on Cicero's *de Natura Deorum* ii; cf. Sextus E. *Ad. Math.* 9.88–104, esp. 9.101). See J. De-Filippo and P. Mitsis for a full, excellent discussion of this. They employ arguments quite

the view it supports is—even if genuinely Socratic—probably not fully original with Socrates, the thesis that he actually endorsed it and added some refinements to it is at least consistent with his philosophical stature.[91] And despite the many trenchant criticisms that the argument has generated (too well known to require a full cataloging here), subsequent versions up to the present moment have added little to its overall strategy and structure.[92]

Naturally, in view of our present understanding of physical law and evolutionary mechanisms it will seem puzzling to many of us that the truth of (1) and the simple dichotomy between intelligent design and luck it embodies should seem so obvious to Socrates, but it is not an utterly foolish proposition to hold, especially from the ancient pre-Newtonian perspective, which took the categories exploited by (1) for granted. In *Physics* II, Books 4–6, Aristotle, for example, works within the opposed categories of chance and purpose, where no inanimate thing can *do* anything by chance (197b1–13). Something might happen *to* an object (or something might generate an object) by chance—the existence of the heavens might be due to chance in some sense—but nevertheless nature and purposive mind are the prior causes of the entire universe (198a5–13). The same distinction is, arguably, implicit even within our own talk of physical *law* (law legislated by whom?) and evolutionary *mechanisms* (designed and built by whom?). Indeed, once we purge such talk of its teleological implications concerning the inner natures and "powers" of things—aligning it

---

similar to my own, supporting the view that Socrates did not dismiss natural philosophy *tout court*, but used it "to establish the existence of the divine and a link between piety and happiness" (259).

91. It should, of course, be noted that I am crediting to Socrates a piece of "natural theology." Is it anachronistic to do this or to describe his argument in such terms? I do not think so (cf. Burkert [2], 320, who sees this sort of argument as marking a break with Homeric theology by instituting a new synthesis of "the natural and the divine"). Although we never see Socrates make the sort of distinction between "natural" theology and "revealed" theology the natural theologians of the seventeenth and eighteenth centuries employed, the basic difference between the two appears to be recognized by Socrates *in practice*. For although on the one hand we see here (and elsewhere) an attempt to develop and justify a conception of divinity through the unaided use of "secular reason," we have seen that Socrates also retains an important role in his philosophizing for the extrarational incursions by the divine recognized by ancient religious tradition. These sources are properly termed "extrarational"—and in a sense comparable to modern talk of "revelation"—because Socrates commonly sees them as standing in need of elenctic interpretation and confirmation (e.g., observe his secular justification for the *daimonion*'s continual opposition to his going into public partisan politics at *Ap.* 31c4–32a3). For further elaboration and justification, see Chapter 4.1.

92. As a quick glance at even A. Plantinga's sophisticated account will confirm (95–111). See also Swinburne, chaps. 8 and 10.

instead with modern Humean notions that "natural laws" are an imposition of external frameworks and a shorthand for statistical prediction—our explanatory choices seem reduced once again to the opposition between conscious design and a kind of luck (e.g., evolution-as-chance).[93]

Socrates does, however, show himself to be a bolder theologian than many modern teleological philosophers. The actual conclusion he encourages and accepts in the text goes beyond (6)'s mere assertion of existence by characterizing the Demiurge as "wise and loving" (1.4.7).[94] This appellation, naturally, does not strictly follow from the argument, but Socrates offers support for it later on when he responds to Aristodemus's postulation of an indifferent Demiurge. Again, says Socrates, we appear to have been not only designed, but designed to the *greatest advantage* over other living creatures. First, we exhibit a superior adaptation of means to ends in our *physical* being; e.g., our upright stance, our versatile hands, our capacity for speech, our nonseasonal sexual abilities, and the fitness of our bodies for housing the kind of soul we have been given (1.4.11–12, 13–14; cf. 4.3.11). In addition, the rest of the material Universe also exhibits an intelligent and solicitous design insofar as it appears especially constructed with the requirements of human happiness in mind, for it offers light, seasons, and food crops adapted to those seasons. Even the motions of the sun and earth seem providentially coordinated to serve the needs imposed by our (necessary?) human frailty (and presumably those needs imposed on animals) (4.3.2–14). Furthermore, when our reason is unable to discern the future adequately, the gods send portents to our aid (1.4.15, 18; cf. 4.3.12).[95] So generous does Socrates' theodicy become in the fourth book's account—and so seemingly neglectful of earthquakes, tyrants, and plague—that he even claims that *everything* in the Universe is "fair and good" (4.3.13; cf. 1.4.13). Caught up in this swell of teleological

93. See, e.g., L. Betty.
94. The attribute of "loving" marks a new and startling development, for the traditional attitude held that being a human-lover is beneath the dignity of Zeus (Burkert [2], 274).
95. Vlastos (14), 162 n. 26, argues that this endorsement of portents (*terata*) shows that the argument's natural theodicy is an *ad hoc* apologetic addendum offered by Xenophon in the interests of traditional piety (the sort he wants to credit to Socrates), since it represents a breach of the natural order that is foreign to the cosmologists' faith in the unexceptionableness of that order. The latter part of this claim may be true, but the argument's theodicy may nonetheless still represent a Socratic, nonmechanistic theory of divinity which includes daemonic intervention (e.g., as with his *daimonion*) as part of the operations of the divine Intelligence which oversees the cosmos (note that at 4.3.12 Socrates' *daimonion* is characterized by Euthydemus as an instance of divination).

gratitude, Euthydemus himself exclaims that he begins to doubt whether the gods have any work *other than* that of serving humanity (4.3.9)![96]

But for Socrates the grandest, most telling sign of the Maker's philanthropy is the existence of the invisible, nonphysical human soul (1.4.13–14; 4.3.11–12, 14). This is the best (κράτιστος) sort of soul in our domain of existence, since it has the capacity for perception, memory, governance of the body, enjoyment of good things, theoretical and practical inference, and knowledge (e.g., knowledge of the gods, of how to relieve sickness, and of how to enact laws). In all this, and because of its many other powers and its fitness for residing in the kind of body it has been placed in, we can see that more than any other thing in the Universe the human soul "partakes of the divine" (τοῦ θείου μετέχει [4.3.14; cf. 1.4.13–14; *Alc. I.* 133c]).[97]

Based on the preceding—and utilizing other scattered references throughout books 1.4 and 4.3 of the *Memorabilia*—we can say this much about Socrates' cosmic Maker-god. First, given the analogical relationship between It and the human soul (e.g., both are invisible)—Socrates' conception of It appears to be an extrapolation from his own understanding of the human soul.[98] This explains why he is confident that his Maker-god has many, if not most, human mental characteristics raised to the level of virtual or actual perfection. We are told, for example, that this deity has

96. Here as elsewhere in the Socratic testimonia, we never see Socrates grapple directly with the "Problem of Evil" generated by his moral theology of how his good and wise god(s) is (are) to be reconciled with the existence of natural disasters and moral evil (due to human ignorance). Note too, for example, how the Socrates of the *Symposium* (201d–e) simply takes it for granted that Athens' plague was postponed ten years through sacrifice (to gods, gods who might then have called the whole mess off). However, his view that piety involves serving the gods by improving our souls *via* philosophical examination, and his seeming view that we are—*qua* human beings—constrained from fully possessing the knowledge of virtue constitutive of "divine wisdom" (e.g., *Ap.* 20d–e, 23a) suggest that he might have held something akin to the traditional "soul-building" response to the problem. On this account, there really are no natural evils (e.g., ocean storms, diseases, and death itself are not in themselves evil, but are either good or bad for any one person by relation to the moral status and development of that person's soul; cf., e.g., *G.* 511c–512e), and moral evils are a consequence of our having imperfect—but improvable—human souls, an imperfection that is a necessary condition of nondivine human beings having been created in the first place (which is a good thing).

97. Xenophon's passages thus run together various species of teleological argument that modern theists now commonly distinguish; namely, the classic teleological argument (i.e., that sort which argues for God's existence from a general pattern of order), arguments from consciousness and beauty, and the Argument from Providence. See, e.g., Swinburne, chaps. 8, 9, and 10.

98. The connection between universal and human soul goes back at least to Anaximenes.

complete knowledge of the present, possessing sight, hearing, and general awareness of all things at once, even our every misdeed (1.1.19, 1.4.19), by being present everywhere (1.4.17–18).⁹⁹ The Deity also has knowledge of the past, thanks to Its possession of an all-encompassing divine memory, and It has sufficient knowledge of the future to allow It to send us reliable portents of the things to come (cf. Xen. *Symp.* 4.47–49). Vast power, as well, must be ascribed to this Being: power sufficient to allow It to implement Its cosmic plans (*Symp.* 4.48). Finally, given its extrapolated characterization, it is not surprising to find that this Deity has desires and affective states. Xenophon's Socrates, for example, takes the human-serving design of the cosmos as evidence of the Deity's *care* and *love*. This God is also capable of pleasure, since Socrates recommends that we honor and venerate It and other gods on the grounds of prudence, given that these Deities confer benefits on those who *please* them with obedience and honor (4.3.17).¹⁰⁰

The relation between this omniscient, omnipresent Deity and the other gods is left entirely obscure. Socrates speaks at one moment of that singular Deity as responsible for our creation and aid, and in the next breath depicts the plural gods as doing the same (e.g., 1.4.10–11, 13–14, 18). Next, he distinguishes this one Deity *from* the other gods by characterizing It as that particular god who "coordinates and holds together the entire cosmos" (4.3.13) but also treats that Deity as fulfilling *all* the functions of the gods. To reconcile such oddities with what evidence there is that Socrates would affirm a belief in Delphic Apollo and plural Greek gods (see, e.g., *Ap.* 29d, 35d), we might imagine the Maker-god to be a supreme Deity overseeing a community of lesser deities in the manner of Xenophanes' "greatest one god" (DK 21 B23), or we can follow Guthrie, who holds that Socrates shared the then not-uncommon view of the gods as manifestations of a singular supreme Spirit.¹⁰¹

99. A characteristic generally at variance with the traditional conception of divinity (Mikalson [1], 39).

100. It has been generally held that the text's application of its teleological arguments to the issue of the proper attitude to traditional sacrifice and the civic cult (1.4.2, 11; 4.3.2., 12.15–18) is either Xenophon's or Socrates's own addition (Jaeger [3], 168; Theiler, 49 ff.).

101. Guthrie (6), 156; Zaidman and Pantel, 176 ("As the Greeks saw it, the divine simply manifested itself in multiply diverse aspects"). Guthrie also notes that an indifferent use of "the god" (ὁ θεός), "the gods" (οἱ θεοί), and "the divine" (τὸ θεῖον) is "characteristic of the age." As Glenn Rawson has pointed out to me, Socrates' own flexible usage may be due to his view that the gods, being all wise, are consequently "of one mind" in all respects (and so, e.g., will be equally pleased by the same thing, will all be served when one is, and so forth), and thus the distinction between plural gods may be hard for Socrates to make out. But still,

5.2.2 Some Objections Considered

It is now high time, however, to throw some cold water on this theistic revel. For among other things, the ambitious and optimistic teleological reasoning Xenophon credits to Socrates is nowhere clearly paralleled in the early dialogues, and so it may seem—and has seemed to several noted commentators—to be a piece of non-Socratic argumentation foisted on Socrates by Xenophon as part of his apologetic agenda.[102] Besides this argument from silence, however, such scholars also find positive support in various texts for denying the plausibility of Xenophon's ascription.[103] First, according to Aristotle, Socrates spent his philosophical energies by "occupying himself with ethical questions, and not at all with *nature as a whole* [τῆς ὅλης φύσεως]" (*Met.* 987b1–2; cf. Euseb. *PE* xv.62.7 ff.). Second, in the *Apology* Socrates says that he has "no expertise, much or little" on and "no share [οὐδὲν μέτεστιν] in" the natural science of the *phusiologoi*

Socrates' usage may be irrelevant to his real concerns, or may be insignificant in a way analogous to someone's indifferent use of "philosophers," "the philosopher," and "the department of philosophy" (in the case of a very harmonious collection of like-minded philosophers). There is—in any case—little reason to think that the sort of theology that might be suggested by these passages would have provided sufficient grounds by itself (i.e., without drawing out its implications for cult practice) to have clearly rendered Socrates guilty of the formal religious charges he faced in court (viz., nonrecognition of the civic gods and the introduction of new ones); see, e.g., Brickhouse and Smith (12), 124–128. It is perhaps worth noting that Socrates' "flexibility" on the issue of the number, identity, and hierarchy of the gods warranted by his teleological argument nicely anticipates and accommodates the Humean sort of objection to it; namely, that the teleological argument implies a "design-team" of deities just as much as it might imply a monotheistic Maker; see Hume, 36, and Swinburne, 141–142.

102. As seen, for example, at *Mem.* 4.2.2, 18. Jaeger (3), 167 and notes, is surely correct when he implies that the argument Xenophon attributes to Socrates does not originate with Xenophon. Jaeger, 170, is also probably right in thinking that the argument is not entirely original with Socrates, noting for example "Socrates'" claims in the *Philebus* (28d–e, 30d) that this sort of argument is due to "earlier thinkers" (in the plural). Notice too that the argument shows up from an independent source in, among others, Aristotle (*De part. an.* 2.15.658b14) and Euripides (*Suppl.* 201–213); cf. Theiler, 38, 50. Nonetheless, Jaeger, 167, leaves it open that Xenophon may have been reporting something Socrates had adopted on the basis of prior reading and discussion (see also Vlastos (20), 115 n. 84). Vlastos (14), 162 n. 26, modifies his earlier position of 1952 by accepting Jaeger's 1947 thesis that the primary source for the argument Xenophon attributes to Socrates is Diogenes of Apollonia. Theiler, 168, however, notes that the anthropocentric theodicy of the argument is foreign to Diogenes, who offers no hint that the imposition of measures on celestial motions was made for human benefit (DK B3).

103. The arguments that follow below derive from Vlastos (18), 213–237; cf. Vlastos (14), chap. 6.

(19a8–d7; cf. 18b–23e; *Phd.* 96a–99d). And third, Xenophon even appears to contradict his teleological ascriptions when he says of Socrates: "Nor did he discourse, like most others, about the nature of the universe, investigating what the experts call 'cosmos' and through what necessary causes each of the celestial occurrences are generated. Those who did so he showed up as idiots" (*Mem.* 1.1.11; trans. Vlastos).[104]

Here we have a dispute worth settling, for if these objections and the textual interpretations they rely on can be overcome, other considerations may be allowed to justify the claim that the teleological sections of the *Memorabilia* are acceptable pieces of Socratic testimony. Moreover, if that can be accomplished, Socrates may then be recognized as being a more important figure in the history of theology than has usually been thought and a primary influence on Plato's introduction of the Demiurge into his own philosophy.[105] Finally, a Socratic commitment to the sort of teleological outlook outlined above has important implications for our understanding of the religious dimensions of his thought in general and his rational reformation of Greek religion in particular.

To begin with, then, I want to argue that the preceding text from Xenophon offers no real aid to our anti-teleologists. For not only is it at variance with Xenophon's own lengthy teleological attributions, but a careful reading of it in context indicates that here Xenophon is simply distancing Socrates from those nature philosophers who employ the notion of mechanistic, necessary causation to explain natural phenomena such as wind. Hence, Xenophon does not imply the existence of a Socratic prohibition covering literally *all* discussion of the cosmos. Rather, he appears to be saying there that unlike "most others" who discuss the cosmos, Socrates did not involve himself in detailed, *mechanistic* (hence, *nonteleological*) theorizing about the universe. Moreover, just a few lines later (1.1.16), and while reinforcing the very same point made by the passage, Xenophon claims that Socrates' conversation "was always of human things" and yet offers as the first example of this Socrates' question "What is pious and impious?" But Socrates steers discussion of that same question in the *Euthyphro* in such a way as to make clear that he supposes any competent investigation of it will need to address issues concerning the nature of the gods and their role in the order of things; for example, such issues as the

---

104. Note too that *Phdr.* 229c–230a suggests that Socrates has no time for—or great interest in—the investigation of matters not directly connected with his main concern: securing a greater portion of self-knowledge and knowledge of virtue for his fellow Athenians.

105. Cf. Graham (2).

nature of their "chief work" (χεφάλαιον ἔργον) in the cosmos (*Eu.* 13d–14c) and how it is that we might benefit the gods (*Eu.* 14e–15a).[106] The *Apology,* as well, portrays a Socrates who is not at all reluctant to discuss topics that make reference to the nonhuman sphere: in particular, those having to do with the divinity who has stationed him in Athens (e.g., Socrates is willing to assert—and surely to defend elenctically—that it is not lawful [θέμις] for Apollo to lie [*Ap.* 21b], and that it is Apollo and not he who is truly wise [*Ap.* 23a]).[107]

Xenophon should thus be understood to mean that Socrates' conversations were always of "human things" in the *broad sense,* where such discussions may at times involve an examination of the gods and their works and signs and whatever else may bear upon the virtuous conduct of a human life.[108] And note that this is precisely the sort of practical interest which initially motivates the Socrates of Xenophon's teleological report; namely, Socrates' concern for Aristodemus's lack of respect for prayer and sacrifice (1.4.2). What Xenophon's remark presumably *does* rule out for Socrates is active investigation into or professions of expertise on the physical structure and causes of natural phenomena: spending time away from the most important "human" issues of moral philosophy to ask, for example, whether the sun is a god or merely a hot stone (cf. *Ap.* 26d). This, then, also indicates why Socrates' disavowal of scientific knowledge of the cosmos in the *Apology* (19a8–d7) is also no threat to his engaging in teleological reasoning; namely, his disavowal applies strictly to the sort of theorizing that terminates in accounts invoking naturally necessary, non-teleological, physicalistic causes of things (cf. *Phd.* 98b–99c; Sextus *Ad. Math* 7.190; Apul. *De Deo Socr.* prol. II, p.2, 11 ff.).

This brings us to Aristotle's testimony. To use it to discount Xenophon's attributions one needs to suppose not only Aristotle's accuracy but that Socrates drew a distinction between the moral domain ("ethical ques-

---

106. Note, too, how in the Euthyphro (5a–c) Socrates professes to take an interest in "divine things." Of course, the "competent investigation" of such topics for Socrates will not be conducted in the hope of achieving complete and certain knowledge about the subject of investigation, but rather, will simply aim at the most complete knowledge that is humanly obtainable.

107. Note too that if passage (3) is interpreted as evidence for Socratic hostility to all teleological speculation, then not only is it at variance with Xenophon's own lengthy teleological attributions, but it is also at odds with *Apology* 19c. Although there Socrates denies the informal accusation of being a *phusiologos,* he nonetheless hastens to add that he does not disparage such wisdom (were anyone to have it).

108. Cf. D.L. 2.45; Morrison, 16.

tions") and the entire natural domain ("nature as a whole" [τῆς ὅλης φύ-σεως]) according to which teleological reasoning about the cosmos must always fall into the latter category. But this second supposition is quite foreign to Socratic thought, and hence, the last bulwark of the case against Xenophon's teleological attribution falls.

First, although Socrates in his maturity may have avoided inquiry into "nature *as a whole*" (i.e., including its modes of physical operation), focusing instead on the moral dimension of things, we have seen that he is nonetheless willing to engage in *moral theology* by treating as universal the methodological and moral principles of his philosophizing, bringing the gods and their activities under the purview of a single conception of justice (see esp. *Eu.* 6c–16a).[109] Hence, Aristotle's report is compatible with Socrates' taking an interest in the *moral* dimension of the cosmos while ignoring its mechanistic details, and thus neglecting "nature as a *whole*," that is, in the sense of neglecting to account for *all* of Nature's aspects. Indeed, it even seems likely that Aristotle would himself have contrasted a teleological argument of the kind found in Xenophon with the sort of "physical causation" argument he himself preferred (and saw as more fundamental; viz., one concerning the "first part" of nature which is substance [hence, the First Mover argument of *Met.*, Bk. 12]), and would view the former argument as "ethical" in comparison to the latter physicalistic sort.

Next, and more important, note that Xenophon's Socrates treats his teleological argument as a part of a larger *moral* argument; that is, he takes his argument to establish not just that the universe is a product of divine design, but that its design is *human-serving* and, hence, must be the product of a Maker operating out of the best of philanthropic intentions. And from this moral consideration, in turn, Socrates is able to contend that such providential care creates a *moral obligation* on our parts to honor the divine and to refrain from impiety and vice, even when in solitude (1.4.10, 18–19 [cf. 1.4.2]; 4.3.2, 14–17; and see the arguments of the *Crito* for our having a moral obligation to the state).[110] It is admittedly a bit troublesome that at 4.3.16 we find Socrates only recommending to Euthydemus that he honor the gods by means of sacrificial propitiation (thus also honoring their directives that they be so honored); we would expect Socrates to also (or instead) advise Euthydemus to honor the gods

---

109. Something Vlastos (14), chap. 6, acknowledges as well. Note too that the Greeks tended not to distinguish what we term "moral value" from value in general.
110. Cf. Gulley, 190.

as he, Socrates, does by improving his soul through the practice of elenctic philosophy.[111]

As we saw in Chapter 3, this concern involves a variety of complex issues. But for our purposes it can be adequately met by paying heed to a number of mitigating factors. First, Xenophon's great interest in presenting Socrates as traditionally pious despite his philosophical reshaping of Greek religious tradition (e.g., note the pietistic overkill of *Mem.* 1.1.2). Second, Plato's possible motives for underplaying Socrates' retention of popular religious attitudes. Third, the reasons (both textual and conceptual) we have seen for thinking that Socrates *did* hold that traditional sacrifice—*if* properly motivated as an attempt to honor and not bribe the gods—was an acceptable mode of pious service. Fourth, the possibility of interpreting Socrates' reference to "sacrifice" in the above passage as inclusive of the sort of sacrifice that philosophical activity represented for him (note too that only generic "service" and not traditional rites are recommended in the main teleological section [1.4.18]). Finally, fifth, it needs to be remembered that the reference to sacrifice here occurs in a quite nontraditional context of radical theodicy.

Be all this as it may, in view of my previous arguments Aristotle's testimony seems utterly compatible with the sort of teleological inference about the cosmos we find represented in Xenophon, since it concerns— strictly speaking—an "ethical question": the existence of the gods, their nature and moral character, and our moral obligations toward them. And although Xenophon may be the one who makes Socrates' grand-scale teleological inference explicit, the existence of such an inferential tendency in Socrates is corroborated by Platonic testimony. First, it is obvious that the moral theory of the early dialogues is thoroughly teleological, presupposing that to understand anything one must understand that thing's purpose or function. It is, after all, altogether typical of Plato's Socrates (and Xenophon's) to reason in an analogical/teleological fashion by means of craft analogies (*G.* 491a; *Mem.* 1.2.37). We even see a willingness to use such craft analogies in respect of the divine when, in the *Euthyphro*, Socrates "aids" Euthyphro to see that if piety is the part of justice that *tends* the gods, it must then improve them (12e–13d), and when he fosters the notion that the gods are divine *craftsmen* with a specific *ergon* (13d–14c) from whom we receive all good things (15a). But the *kind* of teleological reasoning found in Xenophon is surely little more than that; it is simply

111. See McPherran (14), 297–309, and (9), 541–560, and Vlastos (14), 174–178.

reasoning that *compares* crafted artifacts that possess known imposed useful purposes (e.g., doors) to similar things (e.g., eyelids) that, by analogy, then also seem to have similar, intelligently imposed useful purposes, finally extending this kind of analogical reasoning to the cosmos.[112] Indeed, it seems clear that the craftsperson-gods of the *Euthyphro* have the kind of forethought (πρόνοια) about their projects that Xenophon's Socrates attributes to the δημιουργός, and who—in the same way—give us good things out of *love* for us, and a *care* that we do well (cf. *Ap.* 41d).[113]

The best evidence for a Socratic willingness to argue in a teleological mode that is at once moral *and* cosmological is found in the *Gorgias* at 507e–508a.[114] Here Socrates explicitly argues that the happiness of an individual or an entire community of individuals requires the appetite-restraining, harmonious order provided by temperance and justice (recalling

112. Cf. E. Caird, 65–66, and Graham (2). It is important to remember that Socrates is a eudaimonist, and eudaimonist moral theories are not only compatible with a "friendly," virtuous, ordered, purposeful cosmos but "work best" in the context of—if actually do not presuppose—such a cosmos. A virtuous, ordered cosmos, in turn, "works best"—if actually does not presuppose—a virtuous, end-setting and function-overseeing deity. Evidence for this first claim can be found in another eudaimonist, Aristotle. In his *Politics* (i 1) we are told that the state is a natural growth, existing for the sake of the good human life, grounded in human nature's aim at the sort of self-sufficiency the state promotes. Nature has generously provided us with the abilities that make the formation of such communities possible, in particular, the power of speech and our moral qualities (esp. justice). Without such "generosity" on nature's part, then, and those other stable, ordered conditions necessary for human flourishing provided by nature, *eudaimonia* would be impossible. We could even use Aristotle's own argument that the state is prior by nature to the individual (since a socially isolated individual is not self-sufficient) (*Pol.* 1252b12–1253a39) to argue that an ordered cosmos is prior by nature to the state, since no state can be self-sufficient or even function without there existing a well-organized cosmos. And, after all, nature does *nothing*—not, presumably, even manifest its own order—without there being a purpose to it (1252b1–5, 1253a7–10; *De caelo* 271a33). Evidence for a virtuous, ordered cosmos is plentiful in thinkers before and after Socrates. Plato, at any rate, takes it as natural that an ordered cosmos is ordered by intelligence, and that any intelligence must exist by being present in some kind of soul (*Tim.* 27d–30b; cf. *Sophist* 249a). On my view, then, Adam (2), 347, sums things up nicely (in an understated way) when he says, "One who consistently preached the rule of Reason in the individual and the state [viz., Socrates], might well conceive of God as the Reason that rules the world."

113. The implication of *Eu.* 3d and following according to Morris, 311–313.

114. Although it is controversial whether the *Gorgias* is an "early" or "transitional" dialogue, most commentators treat it (at least everything prior to the end myth [523a–527e]) as a legitimate source for ascertaining the views of the historical Socrates; see, e.g., Vlastos (14), 46. As Irwin (3), 226, notes, although G. 507e–508a suggests an interest in the Pythagorean conception of a κόσμος controlled by mathematical proportions, that interest "may be no more Platonic than Socratic, and no more in Pythagoreanism than in Presocratic theory in general" (see, e.g., Heraclitus, DK 22 B 114). Given the previous section's skepticism in respect of the *Gorgias*, however, I must emphasize that nothing essential to my thesis here is riding on my citation of the *Gorgias*.

503d–e; cf. *EN* v 1, viii 1, viii 9). But, we are told, the *entire universe* is a community composed of gods and humans and thus, as such, it too is governed by the virtues of temperance and justice. It is precisely for this reason that the wise call the universe a "world order" and not a "disorder."[115] It seems but a short step from this line of thinking to an inference that the cosmic moral order is one that has been imposed by a Maker-god, one who then also ensures (in line with *Eu.* 14e–15a) that the objects constituting the universe are themselves ordered with an eye to their own well-being, an order we can find exemplified in such things as the human body.[116] In this way, we can even see how the teleological argument preserved by Xenophon is in a sense a *political* argument: the existence of well-ordered human communities argues for the existence of what is a necessary condition of such order, namely, a divine lawgiver, a being who provides the foundations for conventional legislation by laying down principles of natural justice and by providing human beings with the requisite powers of reason and communication (see esp. *Mem.* 4.3.12 and 4.4.19–25; cf. 1.4.12; Heraclitus, DK B 114; and Sophocles *OT* 863–872).

Finally, and in light of all this, we should *expect* Socrates to have attempted the sort of teleological argument Xenophon credits to him, on the grounds that—as a committed theist and servant of Apollo—he would have seen a need to respond in a positive, philosophical fashion to the corrosive atheism of certain Sophists (such as Diagoras of Melos) and the growing number of religiously indifferent youth of the type represented by Aristodemus (*Mem.* 1.4.2).[117] Hence, Socrates does not reject all reasoning about the cosmos, but—as *Phaedo* 96a–99c (and later) suggests—only the epistemologically presumptive (*Mem.* 1.1.11–13) and *mechanistic* sort, the sort propounded by the *phusiologoi*. He rejects not *all* reasoning about the *subject* of their discussions (the cosmos), that is, but the *kind* of account they attempt to provide of it that will explain how—but not why (*per* a teleological account)—it is as it is.[118]

---

115. And hence, not only will it be impossible for a disorderly, intemperate human to be a friend to his fellow humans, but he or she will also be incapable of friendship with the gods, since such a person is incapable of living well in community.

116. Again, it seems natural to associate a eudaimonistic theory of human conduct with a teleological view of the universe; a universe, that is, whose natural purpose organically includes—and so helps promote—the natural end-purpose of human life; see n. 112.

117. Nilsson (5), 275–276.

118. It may be wondered how Socrates' endorsement of a teleological inference to the claim that "a Maker-god exists" can be rendered compatible with his disavowal of knowledge. Again, without getting mired in offering a complete, global resolution of the problems

5.2.3 Some External Corroboration

Still, given Xenophon's evident taste for apologetic overkill and Plato's virtual silence on Socratic teleological theology in the early dialogues (excepting *G.* 507e–508a), Xenophon's testimony requires a good measure of external corroboration before we can attribute his version of Socratic teleology to the historical Socrates with any adequate measure of scholarly comfort—or, at least, the degree of comfort we allow to those who derive the views of Socrates from the early dialogues of Plato. It seems to me that there are many items of suggestive evidence that when marshaled together tip the scales in favor of accepting Xenophon's ascription of teleological theology to Socrates:

1. First, there is a strong philosophical affinity between the Socrates of the early dialogues and the Xenophontic character of the teleological passages, especially since both consider the human soul to be uniquely precious (e.g., *Ap.* 30a–b, *Cr.* 47e–48b). The *Memorabilia*'s teleological argument also implies that we are under an obligation to care for that "precious gift," that gift to us which more than anything human "partakes of the divine" (1.4.13; 4.3.14)—namely, our soul—something Plato's Socrates also never tires of affirming (e.g., *Ap.* 29d–e, 30a–b; *Cr.* 47c–48b). Finally, we have every reason for believing that Xenophon's friendship with Socrates was long-lasting and complex and, thus, good reason for believing that Xenophon was in a position to accurately represent the gist of Socrates' philosophical conversations and some reason for thinking that what we find in the *Memorabilia* is true to the historical Socrates.

2. The somewhat nontraditional view of the gods taken by Xenophon's Socrates also parallels exactly the previously mentioned moral theology of Plato's Socrates wherein the gods are supremely wise and powerful and are responsible for only good and never evil (see, e.g., *Mem.* 4.4.25). Note in particular that the gods of Plato's Socrates—like the deity Xenophon credits to Socrates—have a *purpose,* a craft-like work that we assist them

---

generated by this disavowal, I think an initial solution can be had simply by noting once more how similar the argument's reasoning is to Socrates' usual pattern of moral argument for those theses that he does hold with great firmness (e.g., that it's always worse to do wrong than to suffer it) and which he holds without displaying any sense of there being a conflict between this and his epistemic modesty. These claims are theses that we can characterize as constituting noncertain, "non-expert knowledge," among which we can then place his acceptance of the existence of a designer-God.

in, and evidently also possess a desire to help and nurture us (e.g., *Ap.* 41d).[119]

3. Socrates is also linked with the thinking of Xenophanes by their mutual moral cleansing of the Homeric pantheon, and in Xenophanes' constructive theology we also find a singular, omniscient god, who, like the deity of the *Memorabilia* (1.4.17), rules over the cosmos (including other gods) like a mind in a body (DK 23, 24, 25, 26) (see Chapter 3.2.4).[120]

4. Socrates' disciple Antisthenes claimed to follow Socrates *in all things* (D.L. 6.2, 8; *Mem.* 3.11.17; Xen. *Symp.* 4.43–44) but also gave expression to one of the most avowedly monotheistic theologies of the time; saying, for example, that "according to *nomos* there are many gods, but in nature, or in reality, there is but one" (Philod. *De piet.* 7).[121] A Socratic sympathy for monotheism, in turn, makes it more plausible to connect Socrates with the quasi-monotheistic argument Xenophon attributes to him.

5. Plato is willing to put into Socrates' mouth in the *Philebus* (28c–30e) a teleological argument of remarkable similarity to the *Memorabilia*'s (cf., esp., *Mem.* 1.4.8 with *Phlb.* 30a). Although the lateness of this dialogue undercuts its testimonial weight, note that the Socrates of this text avers that *all* the wise (πάντες γὰρ σοφοί) and his own predecessors (οἱ πρόσθεν ἡμῶν)—hence the historical Socrates?—agree that the universe is given order by a cosmic Mind (28c; cf. *Laws* 897b ff.).

This, naturally, raises again the question of Plato's reluctance to attribute such an argument to the Socrates of the early dialogues. A satisfactory answer to this question seems impossible, but it is perhaps worth noting that Xenophon introduces the teleological section of his *Memorabilia* (1.4.1) by contrasting Socrates' belief-*removing* public activity of elenctically examining the self-professed wise—which, we are told, has

---

119. McPherran (14), 297–309; Vlastos (14), 174–178.

120. This is only suggestive evidence, however, since it may be that it is Xenophon who draws on Xenophanes to help construct an argument to attribute falsely to Socrates. However, as evidence that Socrates (or at least Plato) was well acquainted with the views of Xenophanes it's worth noting the striking similarity between Socrates' suggestion of state maintenance in the Prutaneion as his "penalty" (*Ap.* 36b–e) and Xenophanes' proposal of the same as what he deserves for his "services of wisdom" (DK B2).

121. For similar testimony, see Cic. *ND* 1.13.32, and others collected in Caizzi as frr. 39a–e and 40a–d; also see Guthrie (2), 247–249, 304–311.

seemed to some to be a fairly unsuccessful method of inculcating virtue—with his positive, belief-*inducing* daily discussions among his intimate friends. Here he characterizes Socrates' teleological argument as one such instance of a positive, private talk. Since Plato seems most interested in his early dialogues in portraying the elenctic, belief-removing Socrates and his seemingly fruitless struggle with various determined opponents, that interest might explain his neglect of the positive, belief-inducing teleological Socrates.[122]

Although we cannot, on the other hand, utterly rule out the possibility that Socrates' design argument is simply a fabrication of borrowings by Xenophon, it is worth noting that apart from the teleological sections of the *Memorabilia* there are no instances in Xenophon of such complex pieces of philosophy being attributed to Socrates that are not directly mirrored in Plato or that must be traced to a non-Socratic source.[123]

6. Next, while there are reasons for being skeptical about the authorship of *Alcibiades I*, its author has seen fit to put into the mouth of Socrates a view quite similar to that of the *Memorabilia*; namely, that the part of our soul concerned with knowledge and thought resembles God in those same respects (133c).

7. Finally, and most tellingly, according to the testimony of *Phaedo* 97b–98b and *Cratylus* 400a, Socrates was very much attracted to Anaxagoras's postulation of a cosmic, ordering Intelligence.[124] While both passages are from middle-period texts, this particular section of the *Phaedo* at least is avowedly biographical and stands apart from the middle-dialogue meta-

122. And although the *Apology* might seem just the sort of place where we ought to find Socrates offering an argument for the existence of God as a defense against both the formal and informal accusations of atheism, there are many reasons why he might neglect to outline it there. A primary one is that a teleological argument of the sort we've seen above would have sorely tempted Socrates's jurors to read it just as Vlastos (14), 162, read it; namely, as simply further confirmation that he is, after all, guilty of the informal accusation of being a speculator about the "things in the heavens" (*Ap.* 18b, 19b, 23d).

123. Note that although Xenophon introduces both of Socrates' conversations (with Aristodemus [1.4.2–19]; and with Euthydemus [4.3.2–18]) with the claim that he heard these discussions himself (1.4.2; 4.3.2), this is fairly worthless testimony, since he likewise claims to have heard Socrates speak the whole of the *Oeconomicus* (1.1); cf. *Mem.* 1.6.14; 2.4.1; 2.5.1.

124. Again, there is also the tradition that Socrates was a pupil of Archelaus, who had a doctrine of Mind and who was in turn the pupil of Anaxagoras (DK 60 A1–3, A5, A7). However, Woodbury (2), 299–309, has made a good case for withholding assent from this tradition.

physics hawked before and after it. Here we find Socrates advocating the clear superiority of teleological accounts of natural events to mechanical, materialistic ones and emphasizing his sympathy with the view that the directing force of Mind arranges these events toward the realization of a good final end. Socrates tells us that what he had hoped to find in the work of Anaxagoras was the sort of explanation that would help to answer both particular and general questions such as "Why is the earth round?" or "Why is everything as it is?" by assigning "causes" to general or particular things. These accounts, he had hoped, would inform us how a particular or general arrangement of things is for the overall best by reference to the ordering provided by an overseeing Intelligence. But the mode of explanation preferred by the Socrates of the *Phaedo* is just what the Socrates of the *Memorabilia* provides with his various accounts of how particular things—such as our eyelids—contribute to the overall good (viz., they protect our eyes and so help to facilitate our good vision, which presumably helps us to aid the gods in their cosmos-ordering work [1.4.6]). Hence, the common thread of teleological reasoning connecting Plato's Socrates with Xenophon's again supports the authenticity of Xenophon's teleological ascriptions.[125]

Taken all together, then, there seems sufficient warrant for treating the teleological arguments of the *Memorabilia* as re-creating a genuinely Socratic—or at the very least, possibly Socratic—line of reasoning. This conclusion, naturally, leaves open the question of how much of the argument and its associated claims are original with Socrates. I cannot hope to settle this difficult historical issue here, but—painted in very broad strokes—I find the following the most plausible account.

First, the previous items of evidence used to support Xenophon's attributions also strongly suggest that Socrates' teleological argument is not entirely original with him, but draws upon pre-Socratic thought. Xenophanes, and Anaxagoras in particular, ought to be credited with providing Socrates with the notion of a Mind that "arranges all things in order and causes all things" (*Phd.* 97c; DK 59, B12), although neither thinker appears to have developed this thought into a full-blown teleological account

125. Note also again that although Aristophanes' *Clouds* offers a portrait of Socrates quite at variance with those of Plato and Xenophon, sometimes Aristophanes' comic parody—so as to *be* parody—makes implicit contact with those accounts. Thus, it's worth observing that some of the cosmology attributed to Socrates in the *Clouds* is that of Diogenes of Apollonia (*Nu.* 227–265, 400–425, 626), whose account of the cosmos may well be Socrates' and/or Xenophon's source for some of the teleological cosmology we find in the *Memorabilia* (see Dover [1], xxxii–lvii).

(especially one that integrates as evidence observations concerning the arrangements of particular "things," such as eyelids). It is also probable that Socrates knew of Diogenes of Apollonia, who seems himself to have been influenced by Anaxagoras in his teleological outlook (Theophrastus *Phys. op.* fr. 2 *ap.* Simplicius *in Phys.* 25, 1). Diogenes is one step closer to the sort of teleology found in the *Memorabilia* than is Anaxagoras by emphasizing the idea that conscious purpose and forethought can be found *in nature* (Simplicius *in Phys.* 164, 24; 156, 13). Diogenes' position also shares a number of similarities with Xenophon's Socrates: both agree that all things are disposed "for the best" (κάλλιστα; DK 64 B3; *Mem.* 1.4.13) by divine dispensation, that this is exemplified by a variety of well-ordered phenomena (e.g., the seasons, night and day, the weather, and the human senses and intellect [DK 64 A19, B3–5; *Mem.* 1.4.8, 13, 17; 4.3.4–9, 11]), and that there is a close analogy between the human intelligence ruling the body and that Intelligence which guides the cosmos (a soul being but a small portion of all-embracing Air [Simplicius *in Phys.* 152, 22]).[126]

It is surely somewhat odd, then, that Diogenes is not mentioned along with Anaxagoras in the *Phaedo* as another source of teleological insight. Perhaps, as Norman Gulley has speculated, it is because Anaxagoras's dualism of Mind and matter—and not Diogenes' monism of Air—seemed a much more promising teleological route, and because Socrates did not much rely on Diogenes in formulating the teleological account of the cosmos we find in the *Memorabilia* (an account that far exceeds Diogenes' in its range, detail, moral import, and argumentative sophistication).[127] That, and the fact that there is simply no earlier explicit formulation of the kind of argument found in the *Memorabilia,* suggest that Socrates ought to be credited with making an original extension on previous teleological thought. He used the materials provided by his teleological predecessors to formulate new and challenging arguments for the existence of a Demiurge and then grafted onto them and related claims a forward-thinking, universalist moral theology and practical piety.[128]

Regardless of how we adjudicate the fine details of historical honor, however, Socrates' endorsement of the *Memorabilia*'s teleological argu-

126. Gulley, 186–187; Burkert (2), 319–320.
127. Gulley, 188. Theiler, 38; Adam (2), 349–350; and Gulley, 189, point out how Socrates borrows from (or lends to?) various poets some of his teleological pieces of "evidence" (e.g., note Euripides' enumerations of the blessings we owe the gods at *Suppl.* 201–213).
128. His teleological argument then is a natural complement to his philosophical mission, one we have seen to be both rational/philosophical and religious.

ment places him at the leading edge of fifth-century theological reform. Raised in a culture of passionate gods—gods hungry for honor, full of strife, morally distant, and confusedly and intermittently involved with the daily life of nature and humanity—Socrates managed to travel a very great conceptual distance indeed. For beginning there he appears to have arrived at an idea that was to dominate Western thought for many centuries to come: the existence of an immanent—albeit still anthropopsychic—cosmic Intelligence and loving Maker.

5.3 Apollonian Modesty and Platonic Hubris

The death of Socrates marked the death of Socratic religion. What little career it had as an independent phenomenon shows up only in the relatively conventional pieties of Xenophon and the slightly more thought-out theism found in some of Socrates' followers, notably Antisthenes and Aristippus.[129] The real measure of its importance is found instead in its varied contributions to the thought of Socrates' most talented pupil, Plato. There, preserved in his middle and late dialogues, many of the basic tenets of Socratic religion survived intact—e.g., the complete justice and goodness of the gods—while other elements were either rejected or transformed as Plato proceeded to elaborate his profoundly influential, mystical theology. For the time being I must leave it to others to tell the difficult, detailed story of this transformation and its results.[130] I close my account of Socratic piety, instead, with a brief sketch of the marked differences between the Socratic position Plato inherited and the mature Platonic piety of the middle and late dialogues.[131] Here I do not attempt to lay down any guidelines for future investigations of Platonic piety, but rather, merely offer a summary portrait of Socratic piety from the illuminating perspective of the later Plato.[132]

129. Possibly also Aeschines; see Guthrie (6), 169–178.
130. See, in particular, Morgan (2).
131. Thus, I neglect Euclides of Megara, who also appears to have reworked significantly the theism we may presume he inherited from Socrates (D.L. 2.106; Guthrie [6], 182).
132. Chapter 1 of Morgan's recent account of Platonic piety (2) discusses its Socratic precursor. For Plato's theology, see also, e.g., Cornford (3), F. Solmsen, M. Despland, P. E. More, and J. K. Feibleman.

5.3.1 Socratic and Platonic Piety

I see the basic issues dividing Socratic from Platonic religion as centering on their diametrically opposed assessment of the capacity of human beings to cross the traditional gap in knowledge, wisdom, and power separating the human from the divine: a gap that is, as we saw, *the* central category of Greek religion.[133] Socrates, on the one hand, ought to be seen as restoring and revivifying the principles of Apollonian religion by connecting (and reinterpreting) those traditional principles with the new and popularly suspect philosophical enterprise of elenctic inquiry. As Socrates saw it, his daily activity of fostering self-knowledge through elenctic inquiry had revealed the human capacity for achieving real wisdom to be exceedingly limited and, hence, as providing one more empirical reaffirmation of the established Apollonian dogma of human fragility and ignorance in the face of divine power and wisdom. Here Socrates, the strange street-philosopher, plants himself squarely within the poetic, moralizing tradition. His message is simple and antiromantic: although some partial measure of moral knowledge (and thus happiness) is made possible by maintaining a continual philosophical vigilance *via* elenctic examination of oneself and others, the prospects for human perfection—especially in comparison to divine perfection and happiness—are quite bleak. For all our efforts are insufficient to render us permanently free of incompatible beliefs about happiness and virtue and, worse, often fail to keep us from the most blameworthy ignorance of not recognizing our own confusion and lack of knowledge.[134] To "know thyself" is, finally—as it always was for Socrates' fellow Greeks—to know how ignorant and far from the divine one is.

Plato, however, proved much more philosophically ambitious and optimistic about our natural capacities for knowledge and wisdom. Influenced on the one hand by Socrates' theism and piety, and in particular, his insistence on an intellectualist, elenctic "caring of the soul," and on the other by the aim at human-initiated divine status (especially immortality) as expressed by some of the newer, post-Hesiodic religious forms that had entered into Greece, Plato's philosophical theology offered the quite unSocratic hope of an afterlife of intimate Form-contemplation in the realm of divinity (*Phd.* 79c–84b; *R.* 490a–b; *Phdr.* 247d–e). Self-knowledge here leads not to an appreciation of limits so much as the realization that

---

133. Sourvinou-Inwood, 303; Ostwald, 287.
134. Cf. Brickhouse and Smith (8), chap. 2.2.3.

we are ourselves divinities, δαίμωνες, immortal intellects that already have within them—if only we can but recollect it—all the knowledge there is to be had. The major elements of this difference between Socrates' Apollonian restraint and Plato's anti-Apollonian philosophy of divine ascent are as follows.

First, Socrates' philosophical and religious interests are focused primarily on the human, practical, moral domain of the here-and-now. He is concerned very little with epistemology and metaphysics, but is passionately interested in obtaining some measure of adequate response to his various and relentless "What is x?" questions, where x usually or always stands for some virtue or value directly connected to the issue of living a happy human life. In addition, it appears that x is assumed to refer to an immanent universal—form with a little "f"—that make instances of x what they are by being "in" them; e.g., the same piety "in every pious action" (Eu. 5d) and the courage "in all" the courageous ones (La. 191e). Socrates asks, "What is piety?" or "What is justice?" but not "What is knowledge of piety?" or "What is form?" He has forms, but no *theory* of them.[135] It is Plato's distinctive contribution, then, that he postulates over and above the properties "in" things—including *nonvalue* properties (e.g., tallness)—an entire metaphysics of separated Forms as objects of prenatal knowledge, populating a separate, divine realm of "greater being." These entities have a "separate existence" from their sensible images in this world by being "all by themselves," meaning that their existence is unconditioned by the dependent existence of their sensible manifestations. Destroy a beautiful thing (or them all) and Beauty remains untouched, but not the converse.[136] They are not apprehended by the senses (Phd. 65d–e), but rather, serve as the immaterial (Phd. 79a–d), invisible (79a), immutable (Phd. 78d–e), divine (Phd. 80b, 83e, 84a–b; R. 611e), and eternal (Phd. 79d) objects of knowledge for the soul.

Here Plato displays the anti-Apollonian strain in his thinking simply by confidently laying down a detailed metaphysics that maps out the structure of the divine realm. Of course, and as we have now seen, Socrates is at least epistemically adventurous enough to commit himself to the existence of this sort of realm, to populate it with deities, and to character-

---

135. Vlastos (14), 93.

136. As Vlastos has argued in (14), 256–262, the expression αὐτὰ καθ αὐτὰ εἶναι (Phd. 66a, 77d, 100b; Sym. 211b; Parm. 130b, 133a–c, 135a–b; Tim. 52c–d) makes the same claim as χωρὶς εἶναι (Parm. 130b–d); namely, that the Forms have existence that is unconditionally independent of every other entity (including god[s]).

ize it to some extent (in order, e.g., to justify and explain his having a divine, *god*-ordered mission to do philosophy). The teleological argument of the previous section also gives evidence that Socrates is willing to rely on conclusions concerning the divine that are the products of human reason. Nonetheless, Plato goes far beyond Socrates in his readiness to characterize that divine realm by reference to a detailed metaphysical and epistemological framework, one that includes a specification of the nature of the Demiurge and the gods (see esp. the *Timaeus*). Note in particular that while Socrates' conception of the gods appears relatively constrained by tradition, individual gods and their anthropopsychic properties all but disappear in Plato (e.g., his Demiurge does not feel love toward individual human beings).[137] And finally, whereas for Socrates the gods mark the limit of the transcendental, both gods and the Demiurge are made subordinate to the Forms by Plato.[138]

However, Plato's most definitive rejection of Socratic Apollonian modesty comes with the twofold hope contained within the theory of Forms: knowledge and immortality.[139] Socrates, as we saw, insists that even he lacks the moral knowledge he has long been seeking (see, e.g., *Ap.* 21b1–d7; *Eu.* 5a3–c7, 15c11–16a4; and *La.* 186b8–c5), and suggests with his distinction of "divine" from "human" wisdom (*Ap.* 23a–c) and the unteachability arguments of the *Protagoras* (319e–320b) and *Meno* (89d–96c) that no human can realistically hope to cross the epistemic gap that separates human from god. So it appears that for Socrates we are doomed to a lack of expert moral knowledge (and all other metaphysical knowledge for that matter) on naturalistic grounds. Because of the brute facts of our construction, because of our limited intellectual powers, it is impossible for a human being *qua* human being to achieve anything more than incomplete and fallible accounts of the virtues and, most important, the fragment of human wisdom insisted on by Delphi, that we are without divine wisdom (*Ap.* 23a–b). Socrates may have acknowledged the erotic longing for wisdom Plato speaks of in the *Symposium*, but it is a passion

137. Although note that in the *Symposium* (212a) Socrates thinks of himself as "god-loved"; see Vlastos (14), 95 n. 50, and Dover (4), 79.

138. This was, of course, a process initiated by Socrates with his rejection of the naive Divine Command Theory and his willingness to place even the gods under various moral constraints. Cf. Grube (2), 178.

139. On the place of both these in the context of Plato's natural theology, see, e.g., Gerson, chap. 2.

doomed to radically incomplete satisfaction at best; only the gods may have complete and certain knowledge of the good and the bad.[140]

For Plato, on the other hand, epistemic optimism rules the day. Although not everyone is capable of the exertions necessary for knowledge of the Forms, true philosophers are, and are thus able to apprehend Forms such as Beauty (*Sym.* 210a–211b), and even the superordinate Form the Good itself (*R.* 500d, 540a): "Mixing with real being, [the philosopher] will give birth to understanding and truth" (*R.* 490b6; cf. *Sym.* 211e–212a). This, perhaps, explains the odd elimination of the virtue of piety from the list of cardinal virtues in the *Republic*: piety—understood Socratically as a service of ignorant human servants to master knower-gods whose chief work is beyond our knowing—has no place in a system that puts expert knowledge within the grasp of humans.[141]

As for immortality, we saw in the last section that it was still a commonly accepted notion in Socrates' day that this was a prerogative of divinity,[142] and Socrates—if not *convinced* of this view—seems at least to have been restrained to a cautious agnosticism by his own reflections on the matter. A corollary of this is that Socrates was no mystic in the strict sense: he offered no hope of ecstatic visions of the divine or union with it[143] and positively rejected the aspiration to divine status as a form of the same dangerous hubris he observes in his interlocutors.[144] Gods may cross the gap between themselves and humans at will, entering our world on their various missions, but human beings cannot likewise raise themselves up by the bootstraps into the domain of the divine.

Plato, though, shares in his era's growing dissatisfaction with the Apollonian gap, as shown by the increasing influence of possession cults, ec-

---

140. Cf. Brickhouse and Smith (8), chap. 2.2.2; Kraut (2), 288–294; and McPherran (3). How Socrates is still able to maintain that he is a good person despite his ignorance and his view that "virtue is knowledge" is explained by Brickhouse and Smith (14) and (8), chap. 2.

141. Weiss (4), 281–282.

142. Again, see Guthrie (6), 174, who notes that immortality for humans was considered "strange and abnormal" by the Greeks of Socrates' time; cf. 176.

143. Cf. Burnet (4), xlvii; see Vlastos (12), 97 n. 51.

144. Cf. Morgan (2), chap. 1, who sees the *Apology* as showing a Socratic conviction that humans can attain divine status. Vlastos (12), 97 n. 52, claims that even the attempt to become like god (ὁμοίωσις θεῷ [*Tht.* 176b1–2]) is "alien to the thought of the early dialogues," but this seems to go too far in making the Socrates/Plato contrast. Imitation of god, on Vlastos's own view ([18], 234–235; [14], chap. 6, 173–174), is what Socrates does when he attempts to do what gods *cannot* do by improving human souls and by attempting to approximate them in virtue and wisdom.

static rites, and salvation-oriented rituals that all aimed in various ways at a human-initiated passage into the realm of the gods.[145] Socrates was no doubt well acquainted with this interest, since Plato is willing to portray him as an associate of Pythagoreans (*Phd.* 61d) and Diotima (*Sym.* 201c ff.) and seemingly knowledgeable about the views of the Pythagoreans, Orphics, and Corybantes (e.g., *Cr.* 54d; *Ion* 533e, 536c; *Eud.* 277d; *G.* 492e–493d, 523a–526d; *M.* 81a ff.; *Phd.* 70c; *Crat.* 399e–400c), Bendis-worshipers (*R.* 327a ff.), the followers of Asclepius (*Phd.* 118a), and the followers of the Thracian god-man, Zalmoxis (*Ch.* 155e ff.).[146] Some of these passages display a playful interest on Socrates' (and Plato's) part in using and recasting religious notions to emphasize the true piety of the elenctic enterprise.[147] These associations of philosophy with "new-wave" religion also suggest that Socrates may have at least attempted a conscious substitution of the latter's attempts at nonrational ascent to divinity by the rational means of elenctic inquiry, but again, a revisionary task restrained by his traditionalist insistence on the boundaries placed on such attempts by our own natural cognitive limitations.

Plato apparently follows Socrates in this rational revisioning. But with a new epistemic optimism reached by the time of the *Phaedo*'s composition, he abandons Socrates' Apollonian restraint and philosophizes convinced of the possibility of an ascent to a vision of the Forms that is both cognitive and mystical (e.g., *Phdr.* 249b6–d3).[148] And not just a momentary one either: as a corollary of *this* epistemic hope, Plato adds the stunning doctrine of recollection and its anti-Apollonian postulation of prenatal existence and immortality (*M.* 81c–d; *Phd.* 76c ff.).[149] Very like a mystic—but without the later mystical notion of the soul's union with the divine—Plato offers images of the soul's return to whence it came (*Phd.* 66e–67b) and its nourishment by its contact with the Forms (*Phdr.* 247d–e; cf. *R.* 490b6). However, and true to his allegiance to rationality, Plato does not

---

145. See Morgan (2), chaps. 3 and 4.

146. See references in G. J. de Vries; and in Morgan (2), 24, 30, 34, 38. Note also the epigraph for this book.

147. Note also, however, how Plato has Meno warn Socrates about the dangers of driving others into the same state of perplexity that he has been driven into by the *elenchos*: "You are wise not to have gone abroad, Socrates. For if you would do these things as a stranger in a foreign city, you would soon be expelled for being a magician [γόης]" (*M.* 80b4–7).

148. Vlastos (12), 94 n. 42.

149. Note too that whereas Plato often speaks of the soul's immortality in terms of its cycles of reincarnations (e.g., *R.* 618b–621d), the Socrates of the *Apology* (41c5–8) suggests that *if* death is a journey to another, better realm, that it is a one-way journey with permanent residence in Hades.

affirm these views with dogmatic assurance or rest them on sheer faith, religious authority, and/or divine revelation, but backs up his claims with multiple proofs (*Phd.* 64a ff.; *R.* 608d ff.; *Phdr.* 245c–e). These proofs direct us to an explanation for Plato's willingness to abandon the anti-hubristic Apollonian restraint of his teacher.

As we saw, Socrates' epistemic pessimism appears to derive from the continual failure of the *elenchos* to achieve the theoretical account of the virtues that Socrates posits as the necessary condition of the happy, thoroughly virtuous life. Not that all his elenctic searches end in *aporia*. Through the *elenchos* he is able to demonstrate a number of important and tradition-defying results (e.g., rejecting by elenctic argument, as we saw, the venerable principle of *lex talionis* and replacing it with the thesis that it is better to suffer injustice than to do it [*Cr.* 49a–b]).[150] But again, Socrates is no keen epistemologist: he is never portrayed, at any rate, as offering an analysis of how or why the *elenchos* succeeds or fails. Plato, however, consciously borrows from the mathematicians methods of philosophical investigation that he takes to overcome the limitations of the *elenchos*; especially the method of hypothesis (see, e.g., *R.* bks. 6–7).[151]

5.3.2 Plato and Philosophy's New "Face of Divinity"

The history of the development of Plato's dialectical methods has been the subject of much useful, detailed study.[152] Without getting into such details, let me make clear how the later Plato consciously distinguishes the methods and results of true philosophy—and thus, in addition, true piety—from that of his teacher by briefly considering his attempt in the *Sophist* to distinguish philosophy and the philosopher from sophistry and the Sophist. In a recent paper on this dimension of the *Sophist,* Michael Morgan shows how its dramatic setting and Plato's presumption that philosophy is a form of piety argue that we should pay close attention to affirmations of that presumption in the dialogue.[153] Morgan draws our attention to two places in the text that explicitly connect philosophy with divinity: first, 216a–d tells us that the philosopher is divine; second, 254a–b explains that divinity. Philosophers are divine (and thus pious) because

150. See Vlastos (14), chap. 7.
151. Vlastos (14), chap. 4.
152. See, e.g., R. Robinson (2); J. Moline; and esp. Vlastos (14), chap. 4.
153. Morgan (1).

their philosophical activity—unlike sophistry—brings them into intellectual contact with the nature of reality (into comprehension of divine objects, the Forms).[154] We can draw on these citations to further clarify the *Sophist*'s portrait of philosophy's religious dimension as Plato conceived it.

During the course of Plato's first introductory notice of the philosopher's divinity at 216a–d we are subtly reminded of Socrates' upcoming trial by Theodorus's reference to the previous day's appointment made just prior to Socrates's preliminary hearing (*Tht.* 210d)—and, thus, just before his fictionalized discussion of piety with Euthyphro—and this may fairly lead us to expect some defense of *Socratic* piety in what follows. But *instead* of that, Plato puts us on notice that he has moved well beyond his teacher's conception of the piety of philosophical activity. For observe that here it is *Socrates* who, after Theodorus's introduction of the Eleatic Stranger as a devotee of philosophy, suggests in response that the visitor may then well be a god, and in particular, a god of refutation (ἐλεγκτικός [216b6]) who will lay down the law of argument and expose their argumentative transgressions. This connection of divinity with the *elenchos* is just what we would expect of Socrates, who has been divinely commanded to inflict the *elenchos* on all and sundry and for whom elenctic care of the soul is a pious duty incumbent upon all. But when Theodorus denies Socrates' suggestions that the visitor is either a god or a specialist in *elenchos*, calling him instead a *philosopher* who, as such, is nonetheless divine, the implication is that one who simply engages in the *elenchos* is not *yet* a philosopher[155] *nor* is he or she *divine*. Plato thus signals here the demotion of Socratic elenctic purgation that is soon to follow. For as the discussion develops, we see that the *elenchos* no longer meets the new Platonic test of piety, but is only a procedure akin to sophistry that serves as a propaedeutic to the truly divine life of the Philosopher, who non-Socratically "surveys life from a height *far above it*" and who sometimes gives the non-Socratic impression of "simply being mad" (216c–d).[156] This, then, is why

154. Morgan (1), 108–110. Note also 265b–268d, which introduces a distinction between human and divine production (here both sophistry and philosophy are revealed to be forms of human productivity. The Sophist brings images of things into existence by means of speech and without knowledge whereas the philosopher—apparently—does so with a kind of knowledge). There is a fourth mention of divinity at 232b, but all we learn there and in the following discussion is that contrary to Theaetetus's initial claim, the Sophist's pupils do not gain a knowledge that extends "to divine things hidden from common eyes."

155. As Morgan (1), 96.

156. Some might worry that since Plato portrays Theodorus as being a philosophical lightweight (cf. *Tht.* 143d–146b, *St.* 257a–c) that he is unlikely to use him to signal something

immediately following this introduction Socrates is quickly moved offstage and the spotlight shifted to the new model of the Real Philosopher, the Eleatic Stranger. The complete philosopher must now be a master of those new, post-Socratic philosophical methods which serve as ladders into the high realm of the Forms once the ground had been cleared by the *elenchos,* and he will seem a madman of the sort outlined in the *Phaedrus* (249c–257b; cf. *Tht.* 173c–176e); that is, no mere, ever-so-sober elenctic physician of mental constipation (230c), but a crazed, drunken lover hot for the vision of Beauty-itself.[157]

The *Sophist,* then, reminds us that Platonic piety developed in conscious contrast to Socratic piety. Where Socrates advises the traditional, sober Apollonian virtue of "knowing that we are all worth nothing with respect to [divine] wisdom" (*Ap.* 23b; cf. 20d–e), Platonic piety might fairly be said to storm the heavens with an erotically passionate, epistemic optimism that Socrates would have found intolerably hubristic and unrealistic (and reminiscent of the previous day's encounter with the amazing Euthyphro). Beyond the mere announcement of this development in the *Sophist,* the text also carries that development forward in the sections on the soul's purification (226b–231b) and its intercourse with real being (248a–249d).

"Purification" (καθαρμός) is the topic of Plato's sixth definition of the Sophist (226b–231b, 231e). There he abruptly introduces the art of Separation and then turns to that part of it concerned with the separation of better from worse, namely, "purification." This can be of body or soul, and concerning the soul there are two kinds of evil and so two kinds of purification: of vice by punishment and of ignorance by instruction or education. The worst and most pervasive ignorance is believing that one knows what one does not, and here the best educational remedy is not rough reproof or gentle admonition (since ignorance is involuntary) but the *elenchos* as practiced by Socrates.[158] This purification cross-examines

---

correct as against Socrates. But in view of the later explicit demotion of the Socratic *elenchos* in the text we might read this worry in reverse; namely, that here we are being told that even an older, slower thinker of reasonable intelligence (Theodorus is, after all, a distinguished mathematician and is still able to spot budding talents like Theaetetus) can see that a full-blooded philosophical method must include more than mere elenctic removal of belief inconsistency.

157. Perhaps this is part of the point Plato has in mind when he emphasizes Socrates' resistence to wine in the *Symposium* (and hemlock in the *Phaedo*? [see C. Gill]): Socrates is more virtuous than his companions by virtue of his earthbound self-control (cf. *Mem.* 1.3.5–15, 4.5.1–12), but he is not yet ripe for the entire ascent up Diotima's ladder (*Sym.* 201d–212c).

158. Guthrie (3), 5:128.

the soul that falsely presumes to know something by eliciting relevant beliefs and then shows the inconsistencies between them. By parading these inconsistencies before the soul, that soul gains the modesty necessary for real learning to begin and comes to claim knowledge of only what is really known—the wisest and best state of mind. No one—not even the Great King of Persia—can be said to be truly happy without having been cleansed by this greatest sort of sophistical purgation (cf. G. 470e): a sophistry that if it must be called such is still "the Sophistry of noble lineage."

This section accurately recounts the primary philosophical method of Socrates and—as we should expect by now—implicitly connects it with Socratic piety.[159] It has been divinely mandated, after all, that Socrates should care for the souls of his fellow Athenians by wielding the purgative *elenchos* upon them. Such elenctic examination, as we've seen, is precisely what the Socratic virtue of piety demands of us all: to serve the gods by the elenctic purification of the soul. But here Plato once more signals the demotion of this form of piety to but a preparatory ablution by casually discarding the Socratic equation of ignorance with vice (e.g., G. 488a) and by conspicuously contrasting elenctic purging as a form of sophistry (!) with the *divine* activity of the pure, rightful lover of wisdom: the *dialectical* philosopher (cf. 253e–254b, *Tht.* 210b–d).[160] Thus, just as Socrates raised the religious stakes in Athens by making self-examination and not votive sacrifice the test of true piety, Plato now goes one step beyond his master by making the ascent of the soul into the realm of divinity the real measure of religious success (cf., e.g., R. 490b6, and *Sym.* 211e–212a). As we saw, close to the end of the *Sophist* (254a–b) Plato has moved on to characterizing philosophers as divine (and thus pious) because their activity brings them into the bright region of divinity, into communion with the divine Forms.

We also find in the *Sophist*'s discussion of the soul's intercourse with real being (246a–249d) a development of the Platonic doctrine of soul, one that takes Plato just all that much further from the lessons of his

159. Note, though, that while Plato accurately captures the primary, "anticonstructive" sense of the *elenchos,* he says nothing about the "constructive" sense I have been attaching to it (see chap. 1, n. 14). One way of understanding that silence is to view Plato as wishing to make an emphatic contrast between the weak epistemic results of the *elenchos* (inductive warrant for beliefs at best) and the impressive results of Platonic dialectic.

160. Note too the analysis of evil in terms reminiscent of the *Republic* (440b) as a matter of the soul's internal conflicts (228b; e.g., between opinions and desires) (Cornford [2], 179).

teacher. In this section, the friends of the Forms are led to see that their strict division of existence into the two realms of Becoming and changeless real Being is at odds with their view that the soul knows by "having intercourse with real being" (248a; cf. *Phd.* 78c–79a): if some knower *p* comes to know some Form F, then F must *change* in at least the sense that it gains the property known-by-*p*. The solution to this adopted here marks an important modification to both the theory of Forms and the theory of soul; namely, it will now be allowed that Forms may change in at least a "Cambridge" way, and soul—despite its motion and changes—is now acknowledged as having as real a being as the Forms.[161] Where before the philosopher's soul was characterized as only *akin* to the Forms, resembling them and at home in the same region (*Phd.* 79b–81a), it will now be acknowledged that the soul associates with them as a fully real, fully divine member of the Eternal Realm.[162] It might be said, then, that in this section of the *Sophist* the divinity of the philosopher is elevated one further notch: not only is he or she divine in a derivative fashion by consorting with the divine, but he or she *is* divine and "surveys life from a high region" (216c) equal in altitude and "brightness" (254a–b) to the perfect Forms.

No wonder, then, that when the true philosopher of this dialogue—the Eleatic Stranger—asks Theaetetus whether the natural world is the product of mindless forces or divine craftsmanship, Theaetetus—despite his youthful, shifting opinions—finds himself convinced of Nature's divine design simply by looking to the face of the Stranger (265d). We are not told in this passage what it is that Theaetetus sees there, but the dialogue has been preparing us all along in the epistemic optimism required to imagine the Stranger with a face that both exemplifies and radiates through flesh the bright, intelligible light of the soul's true home. It should be clear that on my account this optimism has its roots in the confidence Plato gained from Socrates in the teleological structure of the cosmos, in the divine sponsorship of the elenctic, philosophical life, and, fundamentally, in the ability of human reason to separate the true from the false. But it was then this same confidence that—thanks to the power of the new philosophical methods Plato discovered—finally outstripped the agnostic limitations at the heart of Socratic piety.

The preceding sketch of the important religious/philosophical differences

---

161. For a defense of this interpretation of 248a–249d, see McPherran (7).
162. Guthrie (3), 5:145.

between Socrates and Plato should not, then, be allowed to obscure the profound intellectual debt the latter owed to his teacher. It seems fairly obvious—though to an extent difficult to determine in detail—that Plato came to his notion of the Demiurge, his conception of and concern with the intellectual purification of the soul, his retention of the worth of religious ritual (*Laws* bks. 10–12), and perhaps—even—his basic religious sensibilities, as a result of the days he spent at the feet of his teacher. What he heard there, I believe, was something very much like what I have argued for in this book. Why not then—on a somewhat whimsical note—conclude with one of those things Plato might have heard, or is willing, anyway, to credit to the master?

> Dear Pan, and all you other divinities that dwell in this place, grant that I may become fair within, and that such outward things as I have will not war against the spirit within me. May I count him rich who is wise, and as for gold, may I possess only so much of it as a temperate man might carry. (*Phdr.* 279b–c)

Bibliography

Adam, J. (1) *Platonis Euthyphro*. Cambridge, 1902.

————. (2) *The Religious Teachers of Greece*. Clifton, 1965.

Adkins, A.W.H. (1) "Clouds, Mysteries, Socrates and Plato." *Antichthon, Journal of the Australian Society for Classical Studies* 4 (1970), 13–24.

————. (2) "Homeric Gods and the Values of Homeric Society." *Journal of Hellenic Studies* 92 (1972), 1–19.

————. (3) "Homeric Values and Homeric Society." *Journal of Hellenic Studies* 91 (1971), 1–13.

————. (4) *Merit and Responsibility: A Study in Greek Values*. Oxford, 1960.

Allen, R. E. (1) *Plato's "Euthyphro" and the Earlier Theory of Forms*. London, 1970.

————. (2) *Socrates and Legal Obligation*. Minneapolis, 1980.

————. (3) "The Trial of Socrates." In *Courts and Trials*, ed. M. L. Friedland. Toronto, 1975.

Alon, I. *Socrates in Mediaeval Literature*. Leiden, 1991.

Anastaplo, G. "Human Being and Citizen: A Beginning to the Study of Plato's *Apology of Socrates*." In Anastaplo, *Essays on Virtue, Freedom, and the Common Good*. Chicago, 1975.

Anderson, D. "Socrates' Concept of Piety." *Journal of the History of Philosophy* 5 (1967), 1–13.

Armleder, P. J. "Death in Plato's *Apology*." *Classical Bulletin* 42 (1966), 46.

Arnim, H. von. *Platons Jugenddialoge*. Leipzig and Berlin, 1914.

Arrowsmith, W., trans. *The Clouds*. New York, 1962.

Baker, W. W. "An Apologetic for Xenophon's *Memorabilia*." *Classical Journal* 12 (1916–17), 293–309.

Barker, A. "Why Did Socrates Refuse to Escape?" *Phronesis* 22 (1977), 13–28.

Barnes, J. (1) *The Presocratic Philosophers*. 2 vols. London, 1979. Reprint. London and New York, 1986.

————. (2) "Socrates and the Jury, Part II." *Proceedings of the Aristotelian Society*. Supp. 54 (1980), 193–206.

Baumann, E. D. "Het daimonion semeion van Sokrates." *Tijdschr. voor Wijsbegeerte* 31 (1938), 256–265.

Beck, F.A.G. *Greek Education, 450–350 B.C.* London, 1964.

Beckman, J. *The Religious Dimension of Socrates' Thought*. Waterloo, 1979.

Benson, H. (1) ed. *Essays on the Philosophy of Socrates*. Oxford, 1992.

————. (2) "Misunderstanding the 'What-is-F-ness?' Question." *Archiv für Geschichte der Philosophie* 72 (1990), 125–142. Reprinted in Benson (1).

————. (3) "A Note on Eristic and the Socratic Elenchus." *Journal of the History of Philosophy* 27 (1989), 591–599.

————. (4) "The Priority of Definition and the Socratic *Elenchos*." *Oxford Studies In Ancient Philosophy* 8 (1990), 19–65.

————. (5) "The Problem of the Elenchos Reconsidered." *Ancient Philosophy* 7 (1987), 67–85.

Berns, L. "Socratic and Non-Socratic Philosophy: A Note on Xenophon's *Memorabilia*, 1.1.13 and 14." *Review of Metaphysics* 28 (1974–75), 85–88.

Betty, L. "God and Modern Science: New Life for the Teleological Argument." *International Philosophical Quarterly* 27.4 (1987), 409–435.

Beversluis, J. (1) "Does Socrates Commit the Socratic Fallacy?" *American Philosophical Quarterly* 24 (1987), 211–223. Reprinted in Benson (1).

————. (2) "Socratic Definition." *American Philosophical Quarterly* 11 (1974), 331–336.

————. (3) "Vlastos' Quest for the Historical Socrates." *Ancient Philosophy* 13 (1993), 293–312.

Blits, J. "The Holy and the Human: An Interpretation of Plato's *Euthyphro*." *Apeiron* 14 (1980), 19–40.

Bluck, R. S. (1) "Logos and Forms in Plato: A Reply to Prof. Cross." *Mind* 65 (1956), 522–529.

————. (2) *Plato's Meno*. Cambridge, 1964.

Blumenthal, H. "Meletus the Accuser of Andocides and Meletus the Accuser of Socrates: One Man or Two?" *Philol.* 117 (1973), 169–78.

Blundell, M. W. *Helping Friends and Harming Enemies*. Cambridge, 1989.

Bolton, R. "Aristotle's Account of the Socratic Elenchus." *Oxford Studies in Ancient Philosophy* 11 (1993), 121–152.

Bond, G. W. *Euripides, Heracles*. Oxford, 1988.

Bonitz, H. *Platonische Studien*. Berlin, 1866.

Bonner, R. "The Legal Setting of Plato's *Apology*." *Classical Philology* (1908), 169–177.

Bonner, R., and G. Smith. *The Administration of Justice from Homer to Aristotle*. 2 vols. Chicago, 1938.

Bouche-LeClerq, A. *Histoire de la divination dans l'antiquité*. 4 vols. Paris, 1879–82. Reprint. New York, 1975.

Boudouris, K. *The Philosophy of Socrates*. Athens, 1991.

Bowra, C. M. (1) *Periclean Athens*. New York, 1971.

————. (2) *Tradition and Design*. Oxford, 1930.

Brandwood, L. *A Word Index to Plato*. Leeds, 1976.

Bremmer, J. *The Early Greek Concept of Soul*. Princeton, 1983.

Brickhouse, T., and N. Smith. (1) "'The Divine Sign Did Not Oppose Me': A Problem in Plato's *Apology*." *Canadian Journal of Philosophy* 16 (1986), 511–526.

————. (2) "The Formal Charges Against Socrates." *Journal of the History of Philosophy* 23 (1985), 457–481. Reprinted in Benson (1).

———. (3) "HE MANTIKE TECHNE: *Statesman* 260e1 and 290c4–6." *Polis* 12.1 (1993), 37–51.

———. (4) Letters to the *Times Literary Supplement,* January 5–11, 1990, 11 [L1], and January 26–February 1, 1990, 89 [L3].

———. (5) "A Matter of Life and Death in Socratic Philosophy." *Ancient Philosophy* 9.2 (1989), 155–165.

———. (6) "The Origin of Socrates' Mission." *Journal of the History of Ideas* 44 (1983), 657–666.

———. (7) "The Paradox of Socratic Ignorance in Plato's *Apology.*" *History of Philosophy Quarterly* 1.2 (1984), 125–131.

———. (8) *Plato's Socrates.* Oxford, 1994.

———. (9) Review of Vlastos (14). *Ancient Philosophy* 13 (1993), 395–410.

———. (10) "Socrates' Elenctic Mission." *Oxford Studies in Ancient Philosophy* 9 (1991), 131–159.

———. (11) "Socrates on Goods, Virtue, and Happiness." *Oxford Studies in Ancient Philosophy* 5 (1987), 1–27.

———. (12) *Socrates on Trial.* Oxford and Princeton, 1989.

———. (13) "Socratic Ignorance and Skepticism." *Skepsis* (forthcoming, 1995).

———. (14) "Vlastos on the Elenchus." *Oxford Studies in Ancient Philosophy* 2 (1984), 185–195.

———. (15) "What Makes Socrates a Good Man?" *Journal of the History of Philosophy* 28 (1990), 169–180.

Brown, H. "The Structure of Plato's *Crito.*" *Apeiron* 25 (1992), 67–82.

Bruell, C. "Xenophon and His Socrates." *Interpretation* 16.2 (1988–89), 295–306. Also revised as the Introduction to A. Bonnette, *Xenophon Memorabilia.* Ithaca, N.Y., 1994.

Burkert, W. (1) *Ancient Mystery Cults.* Cambridge, Mass., and London, 1987.

———. (2) *Greek Religion.* Cambridge, Mass., 1985.

———. (3) *Lore and Science in Ancient Pythagoreanism.* Cambridge, Mass., 1972.

Bultmann, R. "Zür Geschichte der Lichtsymbolik im Altertum." *Philologus* 97 (1948), 1–36.

Burnet, J. (1) *Greek Philosophy: Thales to Plato.* London, 1914. Reprint. 4th ed. Cleveland, 1967.

———. (2) *Platonism.* Berkeley, Calif., 1928.

———. (3) *Plato's Euthyphro, Apology of Socrates and Crito.* Oxford, 1924.

———. (4) *Plato's Phaedo.* Oxford, 1911.

———. (5) "Socrates." In *Encyclopedia of Religion and Ethics,* vol. 11. New York, 1908–26.

———. (6) "The Socratic Doctrine of the Soul." *Proceedings of the British Academy* 7 (1916), 235–259. Also in *Essays and Addresses.* New York, 1930.

Burns, S. "Doing Business with the Gods." *Canadian Journal of Philosophy* 15 (1985), 311–326.

Burnyeat, M. F. (1) "Socratic Midwifery, Platonic Inspiration." *Bulletin of the Institute of Classical Studies* 24 (1977), 7–16. Reprinted in Benson (1).

———. (2) Review of *The Trial of Socrates,* by I. F. Stone. *New York Review of Books* 35 (1988), 12–18.

————. (3) "Virtues in Action." In Vlastos (8).

Bury, J. (1) "The Life and Death of Socrates." In *Cambridge Ancient History,* 3d ed. (1940) 5:386–397.

————. (2) "The Trial of Socrates." *Rationalist Press Association Annual,* 1926.

Caird, E. *The Evolution of Theology in the Greek Philosophers.* Glasgow, 1904. Reprint: New York, 1968.

Caizzi, F. D. *Antisthenis fragmenta.* Milan, 1966.

Calef, S. (1) "Further Reflections on Socratic Piety: A Reply to Mark McPherran." *Oxford Studies in Ancient Philosophy* 13 (1995), 37–43.

————. (2) "Piety and the Unity of Virtue in *Euthyphro* 11e–14c." *Oxford Studies in Ancient Philosophy* 13 (1995), 1–26.

————. (3) "Why Is Annihilation a Great Gain for Socrates? The Argument of *Apology* 40c–e." *Ancient Philosophy* 17.2 (1992), 285–298.

Carpenter, T., and C. Faraone. *Masks of Dionysus.* Ithaca, N.Y., 1993.

Cartledge, P. "The Greek Religious Festivals." In Easterling and Muir.

Chamoux, F. *The Civilization of Greece.* Trans. B. Arthaud. London, 1965.

Chroust, A.-H. (1) "Socrates: A Source Problem." *New Scholasticism* 19 (1945), 48–72.

————. (2) "Socrates in the Light of Aristotle's Testimony." *New Scholasticism* 26 (1952), 327–366.

————. (3) *Socrates, Man and Myth: The Two Socratic Apologies of Xenophon.* London, 1957.

Ciholas, P. "Socrates, Maker of New Gods." *Classical Bulletin* 57 (1980), 17–20.

Clark, P. M. "The *Greater Alcibiades.*" *Classical Quarterly* 5 (1955), 231–240.

Claus, D. *Toward the Soul.* New Haven, 1981.

Clay, D. "The Origins of the Socratic Dialogue." In P. Vander Waerdt (3).

Cleary, J., ed. *Proceedings of the Boston Area Colloquium in Ancient Philosophy.* Vols. 1–6, 9. Lanham, Md., 1985–1990, 1993.

Cohen, D. (1) *Law, Sexuality, and Society.* Cambridge, 1991.

————. (2) "The Prosecution of Impiety in Athenian Law." *Zeitschrift der Savigny-Stiftung für Rechtsgeschichte* 118 (1980), 695–701.

Cohen, S. M. "Socrates on the Definition of Piety: *Euthyphro* 10a–11b." *Journal of the History of Philosophy* 9 (1971). Reprinted in Vlastos (8).

Cole, S. "Voices from beyond the Grave: Dionysus and the Dead." In Carpenter and Faraone.

Connor, W. R. "The Other 399: Religion and the Trial of Socrates." In *Georgica, Greek Studies in Honor of George Cawkwell.* Bulletin Supp. 58 (1991) of the Institute of Classical Studies, 49–56.

Cook, A. B. *Zeus.* Cambridge, 1914.

Cooper, J. G. *The Life of Socrates.* London, 1749.

Cornford, F. M. (1) "The Doctrine of Eros in Plato's *Symposium.*" In his *The Unwritten Philosophy, and Other Essays,* ed. W.K.C. Guthrie. 1950. Reprint. Cambridge, 1967.

————. (2) *Plato's Theory of Knowledge.* Indianapolis, 1957.

————. (3) *Principium Sapientiae.* Ed. W.K.C. Guthrie. 1952. Reprint. New York, 1965.

Coulter, C. "The Tragic Structure of Plato's *Apology*." *Philological Quarterly* 12 (1933), 137–143.

Coulter, J. A. "The Relation of the *Apology of Socrates* to Gorgias' *Defense of Palamades* and Plato's Critique of Gorgianic Rhetoric." *Harvard Studies in Classical Philology* 68 (1964), 269–303.

Croiset, M. *Platon, Oeuvres Complètes*. Vol. 1. Paris, 1920.

Crombie, I. M. *An Examination of Plato's Doctrines*. 2 vols. New York, 1962.

Cross, R. C. "Logos and Forms in Plato." *Mind* 63 (1954), 433–50.

Daniel, J., and R. Polansky. "The Tale of the Delphic Oracle in Plato's *Apology*." *Ancient World* 2 (1979), 83–85.

Davar, F. *Socrates and Christ*. Ahmedabad, India, 1972.

Decharme, P. *La Critique des traditions religieuses chez les Grecs des origines aux temps de Plutarque*. Paris, 1904.

DeFilippo, J. G., and P. T. Mitsis. "Socrates and Stoic Natural Law." In Vander Waerdt (3).

Delcourt, M. *L'oracle de Delphes*. Paris, 1955.

Deman, Th. (1) *Socrate et Jesus*. Paris, 1944.

———. (2) *Le témoignage d'Aristote sur Socrate*. Paris, 1942.

Derenne, E. *Les procès d'impiété intentés aux philosophes à Athènes au Vme et au IVme siècles avant J.-C.* Liège-Paris, 1930.

Despland, M. *The Education of Desire: Plato and the Philosophy of Religion*. Toronto, 1985.

Devereux, D. T. "Nature and Teaching in Plato's *Meno*." *Phronesis* 23 (1978), 118–126.

Dickerman, S. O. *De Argumentis Quibusdam apud Xenophontem, Platonem, Aristotelem*. Halle, 1909.

Diels, H., and W. Kranz. *Der Fragmente der Vorsokratiker*. 7th ed. Berlin, 1954.

Dietrich, B. C. *Death, Fate and the Gods*. London, 1965.

Dittmar, H. *Aischines von Sphettos*. 1912. Reprint. New York, 1976.

Dodds, E. R. (1) *The Ancient Concept of Progress*. Oxford, 1973.

———. (2) *Euripides Bacchae*. Oxford, 1960.

———. (3) "Euripides the Irrationalist." *The Classical Review* 43 (1929), 97–104.

———. (4) *The Greeks and the Irrational*. Berkeley, Calif., 1951.

———. (5) *Pagans and Christians in an Age of Anxiety*. Cambridge, 1956.

———. (6) Plato, *Gorgias*. Oxford, 1959.

———. (7) "The Religion of the Ordinary Man in Greece." In Dodds (1).

———. (8) "Supernormal Phenomena in Classical Antiquity." In Dodds (1).

Doering, A. *Die Lehre des Sokrates als sociales Reformsystem*. Munich, 1895.

Dorter, K. "Socrates on Life, Death and Suicide." *Laval Théologie et Philosophie* 32 (1976), 23–41.

Dover, K. J. (1) *Aristophanes: Clouds*. Oxford, 1968.

———. (2) "Freedom of the Intellectual in Greek Society." *Talanta* 7 (1975), 24–54.

———. (3) *Greek Popular Morality in the Time of Plato and Aristotle*. Berkeley and Los Angeles, 1974.

———. (4) "Socrates in the *Clouds*." In Vlastos (8).

Drachmann, A. B. *Atheism in Pagan Antiquity*. London, 1922.

Dupréel, E. *La légende socratique et les sources de Platon*. Brussels, 1922.

Easterling, P. E., and J. V. Muir, eds. *Greek Religion and Society*. Cambridge, 1985.

Edmunds, L. "Aristophanes' Socrates." In Cleary, 1:209–230.

Ehnmark, E. (1) *The Idea of God in Homer*. Diss. Uppsala. Uppsala, 1935.

———. (2) "Socrates and the Immortality of the Soul." *Eranos* 44 (1946), 105–122.

———. (3) "Some Remarks on the Idea of Immortality in Greek Religion." *Eranos* 46 (1948), 1–21.

Ehrenberg, V. (1) *From Solon to Socrates*. 2d ed. London, 1973.

———. (2) *The Greek State*. Oxford, 1960.

Elmore, J. "A Note on the Episode of the Delphic Oracle in Plato's *Apology*." *Transactions of the American Philological Association* 38 (1907), xxxiii–xxxiv.

Else, G. F. "God and Gods in Early Greek Thought." *Transactions of the American Philological Association* 80 (1949), 24–36.

Epp, R. H. "Katharsis and the Platonic Reconstruction of Mystical Terminology." *Philosophia* 4 (1974), 168–179.

Everson, S., ed. *Companions to Ancient Thought, 1: Epistemology*. Cambridge, 1990.

Fahr, W. *Theous Nomizein*. New York, 1969.

Faraone, C. *Hiera Magika: Ancient Greek Magic and Religion*. Oxford, 1989.

Feibleman, J. K. *Religious Platonism*. London, 1959.

Ferejohn, M. "Socratic Thought-Experiments and the Unity of Virtue Paradox." *Phronesis* 29 (1984), 105–122.

Ferguson, A. S. "The Impiety of Socrates." *Classical Quarterly* 7 (1913), 157–175.

Ferguson, J. (1) "On the Date of Socrates' Conversion." *Eranos* 62 (1964), 70–73.

———. (2) *Socrates*. London, 1970.

Ferrari, G.R.F. *Listening to the Cicadas: A Study of Plato's Phaedrus*. Cambridge, 1987.

Festugière, A.-J. (1) *Personal Religion Among the Greeks*. Berkeley, Calif., 1954.

———. (2) "La religion d'Euripide." In *L'Enfant d'Agrigente*. Paris, 1950.

Field, G. C. (1) *Plato and His Contemporaries*. London, 1930.

———. (2) "Socrates." In *The Oxford Classical Dictionary*. Oxford, 1953.

———. (3) *Socrates and Plato*. Oxford, 1913.

Finley, M. I. (1) "Socrates and Athens." In his *Aspects of Antiquity*. London and New York, 1972.

———. (2) *The World of Odysseus*. New York, 1954.

FitzPatrick, P. J. "The Legacy of Socrates." In Gower and Stokes.

Fontenrose, J. *The Delphic Oracle*. Berkeley, Los Angeles, and London, 1978.

Fox, M. "The Trials of Socrates." *Archiv für Philosophie* 6 (1956), 226–261.

Frank, E. "Begriff und Bedeutung des Dämonischen." In *Knowledge, Will and Belief*. Zurich and Stuttgart, 1955.

Friedländer, P. *Plato*. Trans. Hans Meyerhoff. Vol. 1, London, 1958. Rev. ed. Princeton, 1973. Vol. 2. Princeton, 1964.

Fritz, K. von. (1) "*Noos* and *noein* in the Homeric Poems." *Classical Philology* 38 (1943), 79–93.

———. (2) "*Nous, noein,* and Their Derivatives in Presocratic Philosophy." Part I, *Classical Philology* 40 (1945), 223–242. Part II, *Classical Philology* 41 (1946), 12–34.

Frost, F. *Greek Society.* Lexington, Mass., Toronto, and London, 1971.

Furley, D. J. "The Early History of the Concept of the Soul." *University of London Institute of Classical Studies Bulletin* 3 (1956), 1–18.

Furley, W. D. "The Figure of Euthyphro in Plato's Dialogue." *Phronesis* 30.2 (1985), 201–208.

Gadamer, H.-G. "Religion and Religiosity in Socrates." In J. Cleary, 1:53–75.

Gagarin, M. (1) *Early Greek Law.* Berkeley and Los Angeles, 1986.

———. (2) "Socrates' *Hybris* and Alcibiades' Failure." *Phoenix* 31 (1977), 22–37.

Gallop, D. *Plato, Phaedo.* Oxford, 1975.

Garland, R. (1) *The Greek Way of Death.* Ithaca, N.Y., 1985.

———. (2) *The Greek Way of Life.* Ithaca, N.Y., 1990.

———. (3) *Introducing New Gods.* Ithaca, N.Y.,1992.

———. (4) "Religious Authority in Archaic and Classical Athens." *ABSA* 79 (1984), 75–123.

Garnsey, P. "Religious Toleration in Classical Antiquity." *Proceedings of the Cambridge Philological Society* (1983).

Geach, P. T. "Plato's *Euthyphro:* An Analysis and Commentary." *Monist* 50.3 (1966), 369–82.

Gerson, L. P. *God and Greek Philosophy.* London, 1990.

Giannini, H. *Socrates o el oraculo de Delfos.* Santiago, 1971.

Gigon, O. *Sokrates: Sein Bild in Dichtung und Geschichte.* Berne, 1947.

Gill, C. "The Death of Socrates." *Classical Quarterly,* n.s. 23 (1973), 25–28.

Gómez-Lobo, A. *The Foundations of Socratic Ethics.* Indianapolis, 1994.

Gomperz, T. *Greek Thinkers.* 2 vols. New York, 1905.

Gosling, J.C.B., and C.C.W. Taylor. *The Greeks on Pleasure.* Oxford, 1982.

Gould, J. "On Making Sense of Greek Religion." In Easterling and Muir.

Gould, T. *Platonic Love.* New York, 1963.

Gower, B., and M. Stokes. *Socratic Questions.* London and New York, 1992.

Graf, F. "Dionysian and Orphic Eschatology: New Texts and Old Questions." In Carpenter and Faraone.

Graham, D. (1) "Socrates and Plato." *Phronesis* 37.2 (1992), 141–165.

———. (2) "Socrates, the Craft Analogy, and Science." *Apeiron* 23.4 (1990), 1–24.

Gray, J. G. *Hegel and Greek Thought.* 1941. Reprint. New York, 1968.

Greenberg, N. A. "Socrates' Choice in the *Crito.*" *Harvard Studies in Classical Philology* 70 (1965), 45–82.

Greene, W. C. *Moira: Fate, Good and Evil in Greek Thought.* 1944. Reprint. New York, 1963.

Griffin, J. *Homer on Life and Death.* Oxford, 1980.

Griswold, C. (1) *Platonic Writings, Platonic Readings.* New York and London, 1988.

———. (2) *Self-Knowledge in Plato's Phaedrus.* New Haven, 1986.

————. (3) "Unifying Plato: Charles Kahn on Platonic *Prolepsis.*" *Ancient Philosophy* 10 (1991), 243–262. See also its synopsis in *The Journal of Philosophy* 85.10 (1988), 550–551.

Grote, G. (1) *A History of Greece.* Vols. 1–10. London, 1888.

————. (2) *Plato and the Other Companions of Sokrates.* Vol. 1. London, 1865.

Grube, G.M.A. (1) "The Gods of Homer." In *Studies in Honour of Gilbert Norwood,* ed. M. E. White. Toronto, 1952.

————. (2) *Plato's Thought.* 1935. Reprint. Boston, 1958.

————. (3) *The Trial and Death of Socrates.* Indianapolis, 1975.

Guardini, R. *The Death of Socrates.* Trans. B. Wrighton. New York, 1948.

Gulley, N. *The Philosophy of Socrates.* New York, 1968.

Gundert, H. "Platon und das Daimonion des Sokrates." *Gymnasium* 61 (1954), 513–531.

Guthrie, W.K.C. (1) "Aristotle as a Historian." In *Studies in Presocratic Philosophy,* ed. D. J. Furley and R. E. Allen, vol. 3. London, 1970.

————. (2) *The Greeks and Their Gods.* Boston, 1950.

————. (3) *A History of Greek Philosophy.* Vols. 3, 4, and 5. Cambridge, 1969, 1975, and 1978.

————. (4) *Orpheus and Greek Religion.* London, 1952.

————. (5) "Plato's Views on the Nature of the Soul." *Recherches sur la tradition platonicienne.* Fondation Hardt, Entretiens sur l'antiquité classique, vol. 3. Vandoeuvres-Genève, 1955.

————. (6) *Socrates.* Cambridge, 1971.

————. (7) *The Sophists.* Cambridge, 1971.

Hack, R. K. *God in Greek Philosophy to the Time of Socrates.* 1931. Reprint. New York, 1970.

Hackforth, R. M. (1) "The *Apology* of Plato." *Journal of Hellenic Studies* 55 (1935), 83–84.

————. (2) *The Composition of Plato's Apology.* Cambridge, 1933.

————. (3) *Plato's Phaedo.* Indianapolis, 1955.

————. (4) "Socrates." *Philosophy* 11 (1933), 259–272.

Hall, J. C. "Plato: *Euthyphro* 10a1–11a10." *The Philosophical Quarterly* 18.70 (1968), 1–11.

Halliday, W. R. *Greek Divination.* London, 1913.

Halliwell, S. Review of Morgan (2). *Ancient Philosophy* 14 (1994), 391–397.

Halperin, D. (1) "Plato and Erotic Reciprocity." *Classical Antiquity* 5.1 (1986), 60–80.

————. (2) "Platonic *Erôs* and What Men Call Love." *Ancient Philosophy* 5 (1985), 161–204.

Hamilton, E., and H. Cairns, eds. *The Collected Dialogues of Plato.* New York, 1961.

Harrison, A.W.R. *The Law of Athens.* 2 vols. Oxford, 1971.

Harrison, E. L. "Notes on Homeric Psychology." *Phoenix* 14 (1960), 63–80.

Harrison, J. E. (1) *Epilegomena to the Study of Greek Religion* and *Themis.* Cambridge, 1921, 1927. Reprint. New York, 1962.

———. (2) *Prolegomena to the Study of Greek Religion.* Cambridge, 1903. Reprint. Princeton, 1991.

Hathaway, R. "Explaining the Unity of the Platonic Dialogue." *Philosophy and Literature* 8 (1984), 195–208.

Havelock, E. A. (1) "The Evidence for the Teaching of Socrates." In Patzer.

———. (2) *Preface to Plato.* Cambridge, Mass., 1963.

———. (3) "The Socratic Self as It Is Parodied in Aristophanes' *Clouds.*" *Yale Classical Studies* 22 (1972), 1–18.

———. (4) "Why Was Socrates Tried?" In *Studies in Honour of Gilbert Norwood,* ed. M. White. *Phoenix,* suppl. v. 1. Toronto, 1952.

Hawtrey, R.S.W. "Plato, Socrates, and the Mysteries: A Note." *Antichthon* 10 (1976), 22–24.

Hedrick, C. "The Temple and Cult of Apollo Patroos in Athens." *American Journal of Archaeology* 92 (1988), 185–210.

Heidel, W. A. "On Plato's *Euthyphro.*" *Transactions of the American Philological Society* 31 (1900), 164–181.

Heinimann, F. *Nomos und Physis.* Basel, 1945.

Heinricks, A. (1) "The Atheism of Prodicus." *Cronache Ercolanesi* 6 (1976), 15–21.

———. (2) "Two Doxographical Notes: Democritus and Prodicus on Religion." *HSCP* 79 (1975), 93–123.

Hegel, G.W.F. (1) *Lectures on the History of Philosophy.* Trans. E. S. Haldane. London, 1955.

———. (2) *The Philosophy of History.* Trans. J. Sibree. New York, 1956.

Helfer, J. S. *On Method in the History of Religions.* Middletown, Conn., 1968.

Henrichs, A. (1) "The Atheism of Prodicus." *Cronache Ercolanesi* 6 (1976), 15–21.

———. (2) "Two Doxographical Notes: Democritus and Prodicus on Religion." *HSCP* 79 (1975), 93–123.

Henry, M. "Socratic Piety and the Power of Reason." In *New Essays on Socrates,* ed. E. Kelley. Lanham, New York, and London, 1984.

Herrington, C. J. *Athena Parthenos and Athena Polias.* Manchester, 1955.

Hirsch, E. D. *The Aims of Interpretation.* Chicago, 1976.

Hoerber, R. G. (1) "Note on Plato's *Apologia* 42." *Classical Bulletin* 42 (1966), 92.

———. (2) "Plato's *Euthyphro.*" *Phronesis* 3 (1958), 95–107.

Holland, R. F. "Euthyphro." *Aristotelian Society Proceedings* 82 (1981–82), 1–15.

Hoopes, J. "Euthyphro's Case." *The Classical Bulletin* 47.1 (1970), 1–6.

Hume, D. *Dialogues Concerning Natural Religion.* 1779. Indianapolis, 1980.

Hyde, W. W. (1) "Atheism Among the Greeks." Abstract in *Transactions of the American Philological Society* 76 (1945), xxxiv–xxxv.

———. (2) *Greek Religion and Its Survivals.* Boston, 1923. Reprint. New York, 1963.

Hyland, D. A. "*Erôs, epithumia,* and *philia* in Plato." *Phronesis* 13 (1968), 32–46.

Irwin, T. H. (1) *Classical Thought.* Oxford, 1989.

————. (2) "Euripides and Socrates." *Classical Philology* 78 (1983), 183–197.

————. (3) trans. *Gorgias*. Oxford, 1979.

————. (4) *Plato's Moral Theory*. Oxford, 1977.

————. (5) "Reply to David L. Roochnik." In C. Griswold (1).

————. (6) " 'Say What You Believe.' " In *Virtue, Love and Form*, T. H. Irwin and M. Nussbaum. Edmonton, 1993.

————. (7) "Socrates and Athenian Democracy." *Philosophy and Public Affairs* 18.2 (1989), 184–205.

————. (8) "Socrates the Epicurean?" *Illinois Classical Studies* 11 (1986), 85–112. Reprinted in Benson (1).

Iwata, Y. "The Philosophical Implication of the Daimonion of Socrates." In Boudouris.

Jackson, B. D. "The Prayers of Socrates." *Phronesis* 16.1 (1971), 14–37.

Jackson, H. "The *Daimonion* of Socrates." *Journal of Philology* 5 (1874), 232–247.

Jacoby, F. *Diagoras ho atheos*. Abh. d. Deutschen Ak. d. Wiss. Berlin, Kl. f. Sprachen, Literatur und Kunst 3. Berlin, 1959.

Jaeger, W. (1) "The Greek Ideas of Immortality." *Harvard Theological Review* 52.3 (1959), 135–147.

————. (2) *Paideia: The Ideals of Greek Culture*. 3 vols. Trans. Gilbert Highet. Oxford, 1945–47.

————. (3) *The Theology of the Early Greek Philosophers*. 1947. Reprint. Oxford, 1967.

Joël, J. *Geschichte der antiken Philosophie*. Tübingen, 1921.

Joint Assoc. of Classical Teachers (JACT). *The World of Athens*. Cambridge, 1984.

Jordan, B. *Servants of the Gods: A Study in the Religion, History and Literature of Fifth-Century Athens*. Hypomnemata 55. Göttingen, 1979.

Jowett, B. *The Dialogues of Plato*. 4 vols. Oxford, 1953.

Juhl, P. *Interpretation: An Essay in the Philosophy of Literary Criticism*. Princeton, 1980.

Kahn, C. (1) "Did Plato Write Socratic Dialogues?" *Classical Quarterly*, n.s. 31 (1981), 305–320. Reprinted in Benson (1).

————. (2) "Drama and Dialectic in Plato's *Gorgias*." *Oxford Studies in Ancient Philosophy* 1 (1983), 75–121.

————. (3) "In Response to Mark McPherran." *Oxford Studies in Ancient Philosophy* 9 (1991), 161–168.

————. (4) "On the Relative Date of the *Gorgias* and the *Protagoras*." *Oxford Studies in Ancient Philosophy* 6 (1988), 69–102.

————. (5) "Plato and Socrates in the *Protagoras*." *Méthexis*, Revista Argentina de Filosofia Antigua 1 (1988), 33–52.

————. (6) "Plato's *Charmides* and the Proleptic Reading of Socratic Dialogues." *The Journal of Philosophy* 85.10 (1988), 541–549.

————. (7) "Plato's Methodology in the *Laches*." *Revue Internationale de Philosophie* 40 (1986), 7–21.

————. (8) "Vlastos' Socrates." *Phronesis* 37.2 (1992), 233–258.

Karavites, P. "Socrates in the *Clouds*." *Classical Bulletin* 50 (1973–74), 65–69.

Kaufmann, W. "Socrates and Christ." *Harvard Studies in Classical Philology* (1951).

Kerferd, G. B. *The Sophistic Movement.* Cambridge, 1981.

Kidd, I. G. (1) "The Case of Homicide in Plato's *Euthyphro.*" In *"Owls to Athens"; Essays on Classical Subjects Presented to Sir Kenneth Dover,* ed. E. M. Clark. Oxford, 1990.

———. (2) "Socrates." *The Encyclopedia of Philosophy.* Vol. 7. Ed. P. Edwards et al. London and New York, 1967.

Kierkegaard, S. *The Concept of Irony.* Trans. L. M. Capel. 1965. Reprint. Bloomington, 1968.

Kirk, G. S., J. E. Raven, and M. Schofield. *The Presocratic Philosophers.* 2d ed. Cambridge, 1983.

Kitto, H.D.F. *Greek Tragedy.* 1939. Reprint. New York, 1986.

Klonoski, R. "Setting and Characterization in Plato's *Euthyphro.*" *Diálogos* 44 (1984), 123–139.

Kraut, R. (1) "Comments on Gregory Vlastos, 'The Socratic Elenchus.'" *Oxford Studies in Ancient Philosophy* 1 (1983), 59–70.

———. (2) Review of Brickhouse and Smith (8). *Ancient Philosophy* 15 (1995), 619–625.

———. (3) *Socrates and the State.* Princeton, 1983.

Krentz, A. "Dramatic Form and Philosophical Content in Plato's Dialogues." *Philosophy and Literature* 7 (1983), 32–47.

Lacey, A. R. "Our Knowledge of Socrates." In Vlastos (8).

Lacey, W. K. *The Family in Classical Greece.* Ithaca, N.Y., 1968.

Laguna, T. de. "The Interpretation of the *Apology.*" *Philosophical Review* 18 (1909), 23–37.

Lefkowitz, M. (1) "Commentary on Vlastos." In Cleary, 5:239–246.

———. (2) "'Impiety' and 'Atheism' in Euripides' Dramas." *Classical Quarterly* 39 (1989), 70–82.

Lesher, J. H. "Socrates' Disavowal of Knowledge." *Journal of the History of Philosophy* 25 (1987), 275–288.

Lesses, G. "Is Socrates an Instrumentalist?" *Philosophical Topics* 13 (1985), 165–174.

Lewis, M. "An Interpretation of Plato's *Euthyphro.*" *Interpretation* (March 1985), 33–65.

Linforth, I. (1) "The Corybantic Rites in Plato." *University of California Publications in Classical Philology* 13.5 (1946), 121–162.

———. (2) "Soul and Sieve in Plato's Gorgias." *University of California Publications in Classical Phiiology* 12.17 (1944), 295–313.

Lipsius, J. H. *Das attische Recht und Rechnerfahren.* Leipzig, 1905–15.

Lloyd-Jones, H. *The Justice of Zeus.* Berkeley, Calif., 1971.

Lofberg, J. O. "The Trial of Socrates." *Classical Journal* 23 (1928), 601–609.

Long, A. A. "Socrates in Hellenistic Philosophy." *Classical Quarterly* 38 (1988), 150–171.

Luck, G. *Arcana Mundi.* Baltimore and London, 1985.

MacDowell, D. M. (1) *Andokides on the Mysteries.* Oxford, 1962.

————. (2) *The Law in Classical Athens*. Ithaca, N.Y., 1978.

MacNaghten, R. E. "Socrates and the *Daimonion*." *Classical Review* 28 (1914), 185–189.

Magalhaes-Vilhena, V. de. *Le Problème de Socrate: Le Socrate historique et le Socrate de Platon*. Paris, 1952.

Maier, H. *Sokrates: Sein Werk und seine geschichtliche Stellung*. Tübingen, 1913.

Mansfeld, J. "The Chronology of Anaxagoras' Athenian Period and the Date of His Trial." Part 2. *Mnemosyne* 4.33 (1980), 17–95.

Marrou, Irene. "A History of Education in Antiquity." Trans. G. Lamb. New York, 1956.

McKim, R. "Shame and Truth in Plato's *Gorgias*." In Griswold (1).

MacNaghten, R. E. "Socrates and the *Daimonion*." *Classical Review* 28 (1914): 185–189.

McPherran, M. (1) "Aristotle's Socrates." Unpublished.

————. (2) "Commentary on Morgan." In Cleary, 9:112–129.

————. (3) "Commentary on Woodruff." In Cleary, 3:116–130.

————. (4) "Kahn on the Pre-Middle Platonic Dialogues." *Oxford Studies in Ancient Philosophy* 8 (1990), 211–236.

————. (5) "Plato's Reply to the 'Worst Difficulty' Argument of the *Parmenides: Sophist* 248a–249d." *Archiv für Geschichte der Philosophie* 68.3 (1986), 233–252. Reprinted in *Essays in Ancient Greek Philosophy*, vol. 3, ed. J. Anton and A. Preus. Albany, 1988.

————. (6) Review of C.D.C. Reeve, *Socrates in the Apology*. *The Philosophical Review* 101.4 (1992), 827–830.

————. (7) Review of I. Alon, *Socrates in Mediaeval Literature* (Leiden, 1991). *Ancient Philosophy* 13.2 (1993), 472–475.

————. (8) Review of T. Brickhouse and N. Smith, *Socrates on Trial*. *Ancient Philosophy* 11 (1991), 161–169.

————. (9) "Socrates and the Duty to Philosophize." *Southern Journal of Philosophy* 24 (1986), 541–560.

————. (10) "Socrates on Teleological and Moral Theology." *Ancient Philosophy* 14 (1994), 245–262.

————. (11) "Socrates on the Immortality of the Soul." *Journal of the History of Philosophy* 32.1 (1994), 1–22.

————. (12) "Socrates on Trial," letter to the *Times Literary Supplement*, February 16–22, 1990, 171 [L4].

————. (13) "Socratic Piety: In Response to Scott Calef." *Oxford Studies in Ancient Philosophy* 13 (1995), 27–35.

————. (14) "Socratic Piety in the *Euthyphro*." *Journal of the History of Philosophy* 23.3 (1985), 283–309. Reprinted in Benson (1).

————. (15) "Socratic Reason and Socratic Revelation." *Journal of the History of Philosophy* 29.3 (1991), 345–373.

Meijer, P. A. "Philosophers, Intellectuals, and Religion in Hellas." In Versnel (2).

Mikalson, J. D. (1) *Athenian Popular Religion*. Chapel Hill, N.C., 1983.

————. (2) *Honor Thy Gods*. Chapel Hill, N.C., 1991.

——. (3) "Religion and the Plague in Athens, 431–423 B.C." *Greek, Roman and Byzantine Monographs* 10 (1984) (Festschrift Dow), 217–225.

——. (4) "Unanswered Prayers in Greek Tragedy." *JHS* 109 (1989), 81–98.

Miller, J. "The Socratic Meaning of Piety." *Southern Journal of Philosophy* 9 (1971), 141–149.

Miller, M. (1) " 'The Arguments I Seem to Hear': Argument and Irony in the *Crito.*" Presented to the 1994 Annual SAGP/SSIPS Conference, Binghamton University.

——. (2) *Plato's Parmenides.* Princeton, 1986.

Moline, J. *Plato's Theory of Understanding.* Madison, Wis., 1981.

Momigliano, A. (1) *The Development of Greek Biography.* Cambridge, Mass., 1971.

——. (2) "Impiety in the Classical World." In *Dictionary of the History of Ideas,* vol. 2, ed. P. Wiener. New York, 1973.

Montuori, M. (1) "Nota sull'oracolo a Cherefonte." *Quaderni Urbinati di Cultura Classica* 39 (1982), 113–118.

——. (2) *Socrates, Physiology of a Myth.* Trans. J.M.P. Langdale and M. Langdale. Amsterdam, 1981.

Moravcsik, J.M.E. "Reason and Eros in the 'Ascent'-Passage of the *Symposium.*" In *Essays in Ancient Greek Philosophy,* ed. J. P. Anton with G. L. Kustas. Albany, 1971.

More, P. E. *The Religion of Plato.* Princeton, 1921.

Morgan, M. (1) "Philosophy in Plato's *Sophist.*" In Cleary, 9:83–111.

——. (2) *Platonic Piety.* New Haven, Conn., 1990.

Morris, T. "Plato's *Euthyphro.*" *The Heythrop Journal* 31 (1990), 309–323.

Morrison, D. "On Professor Vlastos' Xenophon." *Ancient Philosophy* 7 (1987), 9–22.

Morrow, G. R. *Plato's Cretan City: A Historical Interpretation of the Laws.* Princeton, N.J., 1960.

More, P. E. *Platonism.* Princeton, N.J., 1926.

Mourelatos, A. *The Route of Parmenides: A Study of Word, Image, and Argument in the Fragments.* New Haven, Conn., 1970.

Mueller, C. W. "Protagoras über die Götter." *Hermes* 96 (1967), 140–159.

Muir, J. V. "Religion and the New Education: The Challenge of the Sophists." In Easterling and Muir.

Murdoch, I. *Acastos: Two Platonic Dialogues.* London, 1986.

Murray, G. *Five Stages of Greek Religion.* Oxford, 1930.

Mylonas, G. E. *Eleusis and the Eleusinian Mysteries.* Princeton, N.J., 1961.

Nails, D. (1) *Agora and Academy: An Alternative Approach to the Socratic Problem.* Dissertation, University of Witwatersrand, Johannesburg, 1993.

——. (2) "Problems with Vlastos' Platonic Developmentalism." *Ancient Philosophy* 13 (1993), 273–291.

Natorp, P. "Über Socrates." *Philosophische Monatshefte* 30 (1894), 337–370.

Navia, L. E. (1) "A Reappraisal of Xenophon's *Apology.*" In *New Essays on Socrates,* ed. E. Kelley. Lanham, New York, and London, 1984.

————. (2) *Socrates: The Man and His Philosophy*. Lanham, New York, and London, 1985.

Nehamas, A. (1) "Confusing Universals and Particulars in Plato's Early Dialogues." *Review of Metaphysics* 29 (1975), 287–306.

————. (2) "Socratic Intellectualism." In Cleary, 2:275–316.

————. (3) "Voices of Silence: On Gregory Vlastos' Socrates." *Arion* 1.4 (1991), 157–186.

Nestle, W. *Griechische Religiosität vom Zeitalter des Perikles bis auf Aristoteles*. Berlin and Leipzig, 1933.

Neumann, H. "Socrates in Plato and Aristophanes." *American Journal of Philology* 90 (1969), 201–214.

Newmann, H. "The Problem of Piety in Plato's *Euthyphro*." *The Modern Schoolman* 43 (1966), 265–272.

Nilsson, M. P. (1) *Cult, Myths, Oracles, and Politics in Ancient Greece*. Lund, 1951.

————. (2) "Götter und Psychologie bei Homer." *Archiv für Religionswissenschaft* 22 (1923–24), 363–390.

————. (3) *Greek Folk Religion*. New York, 1940. Reprint. Philadelphia, 1972.

————. (4) *Greek Piety*. 1948. Trans. H. J. Rose. Reprint. New York, 1969.

————. (5) *A History of Greek Religion*. 2d ed. Reprint. New York, 1964.

————. (6) "The Immortality of the Soul." *Eranos* 39 (1941), 1–16.

Nock, A. D. *Essays on Religion and the Ancient World*. Vols. 1 and 2. Oxford, 1972.

Norvin, W. *Sokrates*. Copenhagen, 1933.

Nussbaum, M. (1) "Aristophanes and Socrates on Learning Practical Wisdom." In *Yale Classical Studies* 26: *Aristophanes: Essays in Interpretations*, ed. J. Henderson. Cambridge, 1980.

————. (2) "Commentary on Edmunds." In Cleary, 1:231–240.

O'Brien, M. J. *The Socratic Paradoxes and the Greek Mind*. Chapel Hill, N.C., 1967.

Oldfather, W. A. "Socrates in Court." *Classical Weekly* 31 (1938), 203–211.

Onians, R. B. *The Origins of European Thought*. Cambridge, 1954.

Ostwald, M. *From Popular Sovereignty to the Sovereignty of Law*. Berkeley, Calif., 1986.

Otto, W. *The Homeric Gods*. 1954. Trans. M. Hadas. Reprint. Boston, 1964.

Panagiotou, S. "Plato's *Euthyphro* and the Attic Code on Homicide." *Hermes* 102 (1974), 419–437.

Parke, H. W. (1) "Chaerephon's Inquiry about Socrates." *Classical Philology* 56 (1961), 249–250.

————. (2) *Festivals of the Athenians*. London, 1977.

————. (3) *Greek Oracles*. London, 1967.

————. (4) *A History of the Delphic Oracle*. Oxford, 1939.

Parke, H. W., and D.E.W. Wormell. *The Delphic Oracle*. 2 vols. Oxford, 1956.

Parker, R. (1) "Greek Religion." In *Greece and the Hellenistic World*, ed. J. Boardman, J. Griffin, and O. Murray. Oxford, 1986.

————. (2) *Miasma: Pollution and Purification in Early Greek Religion*. Oxford, 1983.

Patzer, A., ed. *Der historische Sokrates*. Darmstadt, 1987.

Paxson, T. D., Jr. "Plato's *Euthyphro* 10a to 11b." *Phronesis* (1972), 171–190.

Penner, T. M. "The Unity of Virtue." *Philosophical Review* 82 (1973), 35–68. Reprinted in Benson (1).

Phillipson, C. *The Trial of Socrates*. London, 1928.

Plantinga, A. *God and Other Minds*. Ithaca, N.Y., 1967.

Plekert, H. W. "Religious History as the History of Mentality: The 'Believer' as Servant of the Deity in the Greek World." In Versnel (2).

Powell, C. A. "Religion and the Sicilian Expedition." *Historia* 28 (1979), 15–31.

Rabinowitz, W. G. "Platonic Piety: An Essay Toward the Solution of an Enigma." *Phronesis* 3 (1958), 108–120.

Rachels, J. *The Elements of Moral Philosophy*. New York, 1993.

Randall, J. H., Jr. *Plato: Dramatist of the Life of Reason*. New York, 1970.

Rankin, H. D. *Sophists, Socratics and Cynics*. London, 1983.

Raven, J. E. *Plato's Thought in the Making*. Cambridge, 1965.

Reale, G. *From the Origins to Socrates*. Ed. and trans. J. Catan. Albany, 1987.

Reeve, C.D.C. *Socrates in the Apology*. Indianapolis, 1989.

Reverdin, O. *La religion de la cité platonicienne*. Paris, 1945.

Rhodes, P. J. *The Athenian Boule*. Oxford, 1972.

Rice, D., and J. Stambaugh. *Sources for the Study of Greek Religion*. Ann Arbor, Mich., 1979.

Richardson, N. J. "Early Greek Views about Life after Death." In Easterling and Muir.

Rist, J. M. *Eros and Psyche*. Toronto, 1964.

Ritter, C. *Sokrates*. Tübingen, 1931.

Robertson, M. "Greek Art and Religion." In Easterling and Muir.

Robin, L. (1) "Les 'Mémorables' de Xenophon et notre connaissance de la philosophie de Socrate." *L'Année Philosophique* (1910), 1–47.

———. (2) "Sur une hypothèse récent relative à Socrate." *Revue des Études Greques* 29 (1916), 129–165.

Robinson, R. (1) *Essays in Greek Philosophy*. Oxford, 1969.

———. (2) *Plato's Earlier Dialectic*. Oxford, 1953.

———. (3) "Socratic Definition." In Vlastos (8).

Robinson, T. M. *Plato's Psychology*. Toronto, 1970.

Rogers, A. K. *The Socratic Problem*. New Haven, Conn., 1933.

Rohatyn, D. "The *Euthyphro* as Tragedy: A Brief Sketch." *Dialogos* 9 (1973), 147–151.

Rohde, E. *Psyche: The Cult of Souls and Belief in Immortality among the Greeks*. 2 vols. Eng. trans. 1925. Reprint. New York, 1966.

Roochnik, D. L. "*Apology* 40c4–41e7: Is Death Really a Gain?" *Classical Journal* 80 (1985), 212–220.

Rosen, F. "Piety and Justice: Plato's *Euthyphro*." *Philosophy* 43 (1968), 105–116.

Ross, W. D. (1) *Aristotle's Metaphysics*. Oxford, 1924.

———. (2) *Plato's Theory of Ideas*. Oxford, 1951.

———. (3) "The Problem of Socrates." *Proceedings of the Classical Association* 30 (1933), 7–24. Reprinted in A. Patzer.

318   Bibliography

Rostovtzeff, M. *Greece.* 1926. Reprint. Oxford, 1963.
Rudberg, G. *Platonica Selecta.* Stockholm, 1956.
Rudebusch, G. "Death Is One of Two Things." *Ancient Philosophy* 11.1 (1991), 35–45.
Rudhardt, J. (1) "La définition du délit d'impiété d'après la législation attique." *MH* 17 (1960), 87–105.
———. (2) *Notions fondamentales de la pensée religieuse et actes constitutifs du culte dans la Grèce classique.* Geneva, 1958.
Ryle, G. *Plato's Progress.* Cambridge, 1966.
Santas, G. (1) *Socrates, Philosophy in Plato's Early Dialogues.* London and Boston, 1979.
———. (2) "The Socratic Fallacy." *Journal of the History of Philosophy* 10 (1972), 127–141.
Saunders, T. J. *Plato's Penal Code.* Oxford, 1991.
Sayre, K. "Plato's Dialogues in Light of the *Seventh Letter.*" In Griswold (1).
Schaerer, R. *La Question platonicienne.* Neuchâtel, 1969.
Schleiermacher, F. *Introductions to the Dialogues of Plato.* Trans. W. Dobson. London, 1836. Reprint. New York, 1973.
Seeskin, K. R. (1) "Courage and Knowledge: A Perspective on the Socratic Paradox." *Southern Journal of Philosophy* 14 (1976), 511–521.
———. (2) *Dialogue and Discovery: A Study in Socratic Method.* Albany, 1987.
———. (3) "Is the *Apology of Socrates* a Parody?" *Philosophy and Literature* 6 (1982), 94–105.
———. (4) "Socratic Philosophy and the Dialogue Form." *Philosophy and Literature* 8 (1984), 181–194.
Segal, C. "Aristophanes' Cloud-Chorus." *Arethusa* 2 (1969), 143–161.
Sharvy, R. "*Euthyphro* 9d–11b: Analysis and Definition in Plato and Others." *Nous* 6 (1972), 119–137.
Shero, L. R. (1) "*Apology* 26D–E and the Writings of Anaxagoras." *Classical Weekly* 35 (1941–42), 219–220.
———. (2) "Plato's *Apology* and Xenophon's *Apology.*" *Classical Weekly* 20 (1927), 107–111.
Shorey, P. *What Plato Said.* Chicago, 1933.
Sider, D. "Did Socrates Call Himself a Midwife? The Evidence of the *Clouds.*" In Boudouris.
Skemp, J. B. "Plato's Account of Divinity." *Durham University Journal* 29 (1967–68), 26–33.
Skorpen, E. "Socrates on Piety." *Humanist* 22 (1962), 184–185.
Smith, N. D. (1) "Diviners and Divination in Aristophantic Comedy." *Classical Antiquity* 8.1 (1989), 138–158.
———. (2) Review of Reeve. *Ancient Philosophy* 11.2 (1991), 399–407.
Snell, B. *The Discovery of the Mind.* Trans. T. G. Rosenmeyer. 1953. Reprint. New York, 1960.
Snider, E. "The Conclusion of the *Meno:* Socrates on the Genesis of *Aretê.*" *Ancient Philosophy* 12 (1992), 73–86.
Solmsen, F. *Plato's Theology.* Ithaca, N.Y., 1942.

Sourvinou-Inwood, C. "What is Polis Religion?" In *The Greek City*, ed. O. Murray and S. Price. Oxford, 1990.

Sparshott, F. E. "Socrates and Thrasymachus." *Monist* 50 (1966), 421–459.

Stalley, R. F. "Punishment in Plato's *Protagoras*." *Phronesis* 40.1 (1995), 1–19.

Stokes, M. C. (1) *Plato's Socratic Conversations: Drama and Dialectic in Three Dialogues*. Baltimore, 1986.

———. (2) "Socrates' Mission." In Gower and Stokes.

Stone, I. F. *The Trial of Socrates*. Boston, 1987.

Straten, F. T. van. "Gifts for the Gods." In Versnel (2).

Strauss, B. S. *Athens After the Peloponnesian War: Class Faction, and Policy, 403–386 B.C.* Ithaca, N.Y., 1987.

Strauss, L. (1) *The City and the Man*. Chicago, 1964.

———. (2) "On the *Euthyphron*." In *The Rebirth of Classical Political Rationalism: An Introduction to the Thought of Leo Strauss*, ed. T. Pangle. Chicago, 1989.

———. (3) *Xenophon's Socrates*. 1972. Reprint. Ithaca, N.Y., 1973.

———. (4) *Xenophon's Socratic Discourse: An Interpretation of the Oeconomicus*. Ithaca, N.Y., 1970.

Striker, G. "Origins of the Concept of Natural Law." In Cleary, 2:79–94.

Strycker, E. de. (1) "Le *Criton* de Platon." *Les Etudes Classiques* 39 (1971), 417–436.

———. (2) "The Oracle Given to Chaerephon About Socrates (Plato *Apology* 20e–21a)." In *Kephalaion: Studies in Greek Philosophy and Its Continuation Offered to Professor C. J. DeVogel*, ed. J. Mansfeld and L. M. de Rijk. Assen, 1975.

———. (3) "Socrate et l'au-déla d'après l'*Apologie* platonicienne." *Les Études Classiques* 18 (1950), 269–284.

———. (4) "The Unity of Knowledge and Love in Socrates' Conception of Virtue." *International Philosophical Quarterly* 6 (1966), 428–444.

Strycker, E. de., and S. R. Slings. *Plato's Apology of Socrates. A Literary and Philosophical Study with a Running Commentary. Mnemosyne Supplement* 137. Leiden, 1994.

Swinburne, R. *The Existence of God*. Oxford, 1979.

Tate, J. (1) "Greek for 'Atheism.'" *Classical Review* 50 (1936), 3–5.

———. (2) "More Greek for 'Atheism.'" *Classical Review* 51 (1937), 3–6.

———. (3) "Plato, Socrates, and the Myths." *Classical Quarterly* 30 (1936), 142–145.

———. (4) "Reply to Professor A. E. Taylor." *Classical Quarterly* 27 (1933), 159–161.

———. (5) "Socrates and the Myths." *Classical Quarterly* 27 (1933), 74–80.

Taylor, A. E. (1) *Plato: The Man and His Work*. 1926. Reprint. London, 1960.

———. (2) *Socrates*. 1933. Reprint. Garden City, N.Y., 1953.

———. (3) "Socrates and the Myths." *Classical Quarterly* 27 (1933), 158–159.

———. (4) *Varia Socratica*. Oxford, 1911.

Taylor, C.C.W. "The End of the *Euthyphro*." *Phronesis* 27 (1982), 109–118.

Teloh, H. (1) "The Importance of Interlocutor's Characters in Plato's Early Dialogues." In Cleary, 2:25–38.

————. (2) *Socratic Education in Plato's Early Dialogues.* Notre Dame, Ind., 1986.

Theiler, W. *Zur Geschichte der teleologischen Naturbetrachtung bis auf Aristoteles.* Zürich, 1925.

Thesleff, H. "Platonic Chronology." *Phronesis* 34.1 (1989), 20–26.

Toole, H. "Socrates: Was He a Mystical and Superstitious Person?" (in Greek). *Athena* 75 (1974–75), 318–334.

Toynbee, A. "The Search for a Prophet: Socrates and Jesus." In *The State Versus Socrates: A Case Study in Civic Freedom,* ed. J. D. Montgomery. Boston, 1954.

Turner, F. M. *The Greek Heritage in Victorian Britain.* New Haven, Conn., 1981.

Van Camp, J., and P. Canart. *Le Sens du mot chez Platon.* Louvain, 1956.

Vander Waerdt, P. (1) "Socrates in the *Clouds.*" In Vander Waerdt (3).

————. (2) "Socratic Justice and Self-Sufficiency." *Oxford Studies in Ancient Philosophy* 11 (1993), 1–48.

————. (3) ed. *The Socratic Movement.* Ithaca, N.Y., 1994.

Vermule, E. *Aspects of Death in Early Greek Art and Poetry.* Berkeley, Calif., 1979.

Vernant, J.-P. (1) *Mortals and Immortals.* Princeton, N.J., 1991.

————. (2) *Myth and Society in Ancient Greece.* Hassocks, 1980.

Versenyi, L. (1) *Holiness and Justice: An Interpretation of Plato's Euthyphro.* Lanham, New York, and London, 1982.

————. (2) *Socratic Humanism.* New Haven, Conn., 1963.

Versnel, H. S. (1) "Heis Dionysos." In *Ter Unus.* Leiden, 1990.

————. (2) "Religious Mentality in Ancient Prayer." In *Faith, Hope and Worship: Aspects of Religious Mentality in the Ancient World.* Leiden, 1981.

Veyne, P. *Did the Greeks Believe Their Myths?: An Essay on the Constitutive Imagination.* Chicago, 1988.

Vlastos, G. (1) "Editor's Introduction to Plato's *Protagoras.*" In *Protagoras,* trans. M. Ostwald. Indianapolis, 1976.

————. (2) "Elenchus and Mathematics." As revised in Vlastos (14), chap. 4.

————. (3) "Happiness and Virtue in Socrates' Moral Theory." As revised in Vlastos (14), chap. 8.

————. (4) "The Historical Socrates and Athenian Democracy." As revised in Vlastos (19), chap. 4.

————. (5) "Introduction, The Paradox of Socrates." In Vlastos (8).

————. (6) Letters to *Times Literary Supplement,* January 19–25 (1990) [L2], 63; February 23–March 1 (1990) [L5].

————. (7) "On the Socrates Story." *Political Theory* 7 (1979), 253–254.

————. (8) ed. *The Philosophy of Socrates.* Garden City, N.Y., 1971.

————. (9) *Platonic Studies.* Princeton, 1981.

————. (10) "The *Protagoras* and the *Laches.*" In Vlastos (19), chap. 5.

————. (11) Review of *Socrates on Trial* by T. Brickhouse and N. Smith. *Times Literary Supplement,* December 15–21, 1989, 1393.

————. (12) "Socrates." *Proceedings of the British Academy* 74 (1988), 87–111.

————. (13) "Socrates' Disavowal of Knowledge." As revised in Vlastos (19), chap. 2.

———. (14) *Socrates: Ironist and Moral Philosopher.* Ithaca, N.Y., 1991.

———. (15) "Socrates On 'the Parts of Virtue.'" In Vlastos (9).

———. (16) "The Socratic Elenchus: Method Is All." As revised in Vlastos (19), chap. 1.

———. (17) "Socratic Irony." As revised in Vlastos (14), chap. 1.

———. (18) "Socratic Piety." In Cleary, 5:213–238.

———. (19) *Socratic Studies.* Ed. M. Burnyeat. Cambridge, 1994.

———. (20) "Theology and Philosophy in Early Greek Thought." *The Philosophical Quarterly* 2.7 (1952), 97–123.

———. (21) "The Unity of the Virtues in the *Protagoras.*" In Vlastos (9).

Voegelin, E. *Order and History.* Vol. 3. Baton Rouge, 1956.

Vogel, C. J. de. (1) "The Present State of the Socratic Problem." *Phronesis* 1 (1955), 26–35.

———. (2) "Who Was Socrates?" *Journal of the History of Philosophy* 1 (1963), 143–161.

Voltaire, F.-M. *Charlatan, Socrate, Dictionnaire Philosophique, Oeuvres Complètes.* Vol. 24. Paris, 1817.

Vries, G. J. de. "Mystery Terminology in Aristophanes and Plato." *Mnemosyne* 26 (1973), 1–8.

Wakefield, J. "Why Justice and Holiness Are Similar: *Protagoras* 330–331." *Phronesis* 32 (1987), 267–276.

Ward-Scaltsas, P. "Virtue Without Gender in Socrates." *Hypatia* 7.3 (1992), 126–137. Also in Boudouris.

Watson, L. *Arae.* Leeds, 1991.

Weiss, R. (1) "'Especially an Orator': Rhetoric and Principle in Plato's *Crito.*" Presented to the 1994 Eastern Division Meeting of the American Philosophical Association.

———. (2) "Euthyphro's Failure." *Journal of the History of Philosophy* 24.4 (1986), 437–452.

———. (3) "Ignorance, Involuntariness and Innocence: A Reply to McTighe." *Phronesis* 30.3 (1985), 314–322.

———. (4) "Virtue Without Knowledge: Socratic Piety in Plato's *Euthyphro.*" *Ancient Philosophy* 14 (1994), 263–282.

Wellman, R. R. "Socratic Method in Xenophon." *Journal of the History of Ideas* 37 (1976), 307–318.

Wenley, R. M. *Socrates and Christ: A Study in the Philosophy of Religion.* Edinburgh and London, 1889.

West, M. L. *Early Greek Philosophy and the Orient.* Oxford, 1971.

West, T. G. *Plato's Apology of Socrates.* Ithaca and London, 1979.

West, T. G., and G. S. West. *Four Texts on Socrates.* Ithaca and London, 1984.

Weston, A. H. "The Question of Plato's *Euthyphro.*" *Classical Bulletin* 27 (1951), 57–58.

Wilamowitz-Moellendorff, U. von. *Der Glaube der Hellenen.* Vol. 1. Darmstadt, 1959.

Willink, C. W. "Prodikos, 'Meteorosophists' and the 'Tantalus' Paradigm." *Classical Quarterly,* n.s., 33 (1983), 25–33.

Winspear, A. D., and T. Silverberg. *Who Was Socrates?* New York, 1960.

Wood, E. M., and N. Wood. *Class Ideology and Ancient Political Theory: Socrates, Plato, and Aristotle in Social Context.* New York, 1978.

Woodbury, L. (1) "The Date and Atheism of Diagoras of Melos." *Phoenix* 19 (1965), 178–211.

———. (2) "Socrates and Archelaus." *Phoenix* 25 (1971), 299–309.

Woodhead, M. D. "The Daimonion of Socrates." *Classical Philology* 35 (1940), 425–426.

Woodruff, P. (1) "Expert Knowledge in the *Apology* and *Laches:* What a General Needs to Know." In Cleary, 3:79–115.

———. (2) "Plato's Early Theory of Knowledge." In Everson. Reprinted in Benson (1).

———. (3) *Plato, The Hippias Major.* Indianapolis, 1982.

———. (4) "Socrates on the Parts of Virtue." *Canadian Journal of Philosophy,* supp. vol. 2 (1976), 101–116.

Woozley, A. D. (1) *Law and Obedience: The Argument of Plato's Crito.* Chapel Hill, N.C., 1979.

———. (2) "Socrates on Disobeying the Law." In Vlastos (8).

Xenophon. *Memorabilia, Oeconomicus, Symposium, and Apology.* Trans. E. C. Marchant and O. J. Todd. Loeb edition. Cambridge and London, 1923.

Yonezawa, S. "Socrateses in the *Crito* and *Apology*—One Possibility." Unpublished.

Young, G. "Socrates and Obedience." *Phronesis* 19 (1974), 1–29.

Yunis, H. *A New Creed: Fundamental Religious Belief in the Athenian Polis and Euripidean Drama. Hypomnemata* 91 (Göttingen, 1988).

Zaidman, L. B., and P. S. Pantel. *Religion in the Ancient Greek City.* Trans. P. Cartledge. Cambridge, 1992.

Zeller, E. *Socrates and the Socratic Schools.* Trans. O. J. Reichel. New York, 1962.

Zeyl, D. J. "Socrates and Hedonism: *Protagoras* 351b–358d." *Phronesis* 25 (1980), 250–269.

General Index

Index of Passages

Titles of spurious or doubtful works are bracketed

PLATO